I0022660

Swedish Social Democracy
and the Vietnam War

SWEDISH
SOCIAL
DEMOCRACY
AND THE
VIETNAM WAR

CARL-GUSTAF SCOTT

Södertörns högskola
(Södertörn University)
Library
SE-141 89 Huddinge

www.sh.se/publications

© Carl-Gustaf Scott
Cover: Jonathan Robson
Graphic form: Per Lindblom & Jonathan Robson

Printed by Elanders, Stockholm 2017

Södertörn Academic Studies 64
ISSN 1650-433X

ISBN 978-91-87843-35-8 (print)
ISBN 978-91-87843-36-5 (digital)

*This book is dedicated to Frank and "Farmor" and to
the two fellowships that made all of this possible*

Contents

Abbreviations
9

Preface
11

CHAPTER 1
Swedish Social Democracy and the Vietnam War: Domestic Foreign Policy?
17

CHAPTER 2
The Emergence of the Vietnam Issue in Swedish Politics, 1964–1967
49

CHAPTER 3
The Social Democrats Seize the Initiative:
The Swedish Committee for Vietnam and Palme at Sergels torg, 1968
91

CHAPTER 4
The Deserter Question 1967–1973:
A Case Study in Domestic Foreign Policy
133

CHAPTER 5
Swedish Diplomatic Recognition and Humanitarian Aid to the Democratic
Republic of Vietnam 1969–1970: A Case Study in Domestic Foreign Policy
171

CHAPTER 6
Dénouement 1970–1974: Conflict and Stalemate on Both Fronts
217

CHAPTER 7
Swedish Vietnam Policy Reconsidered
261

Bibliography
287

Abbreviations

ADC	American Deserters Committee
CUF	Centerpartiets ungdomsförbund = the Center Party Youth organisation
DFFG	De förenade FNL-Grupperna = the United NLF Groups (was an umbrella group for the Maoist oriented FNL-groups)
DRV	Democratic Republic of Vietnam
FPU	Folkpartiets ungdomsförbund = the Liberal Youth of Sweden
GVN	Government of [South] Vietnam
KFML	Kommunistiska Förbundet Marxist-Leninisterna = the Communist League of Marxist-Leninists (Maoist defectors from SKP broke away from the party and established the KFML in 1967)
KFML(r)	Kommunistiska Förbundet Marxist-Leninisterna Revolutionärerna = the Communist League of Revolutionary Marxist-Leninists (in 1970, the KFML(r) split away from the KFML on the grounds that the latter party was not revolutionary)
KMA	Kampanjen mot Atomvapen (the Campaign against Nuclear Weapons)
LO	Landsorganisationen = Swedish Trade Union Confederation (the central organization for all Social Democratic-oriented trade unions)
NLF	National Liberation Front
PRR	Provisional Revolutionary Government of South Vietnam (the political wing of the Communist-controlled NLF)
SAP	Sveriges Socialdemokratiska Arbetareparti = Social Democratic Labor Party of Sweden
SPD	Sozialdemokratische Partei Deutschlands = Social Democratic Labor Party of [West] Germany
SFIF	Solidaritetsfronten för Indokinas folk = the Solidarity Front for the People of Indochina (the KFML(r)'s Vietnam group)

SKfV	Svenska Kommittén för Vietnam = the Swedish Committee for Vietnam (was the main organization of the pacifist and parliamentary oriented anti-war movement)
SKP	Sveriges Kommunistiska Parti (SKP) = the Swedish Communist Party (In 1967, the SKP changed its name to VPK)
SKSF	Sveriges Kristna Socialdemokraters Förbund (SKSF) = the Swedish Association of Christian Social Democrats
SSKF	Sveriges Socialdemokratiska Kvinnoförbund = the Association of Social Democratic Women
SSSF	Sveriges Socialdemokratiska Studentförbund = the Association of Social Democratic Students
SSU	Sveriges Socialdemokratiska Ungdomsförbund = the Association of Social Democratic Youth
SVK	Svenska Vietnamkommittén = the Swedish Vietnam Committee (was the principal organization of the parliamentary oriented anti-war movement until it was replaced by the SKfV in late 1967)
VPK	Vänsterpartiet Kommunisterna (VPK) = the Left Communist Party (In 1967 the SKP changed its name to VPK)

Preface

This book analyzes the Vietnam War's gravely destabilizing impact on trans-Atlantic relations. West European leaders had good reason to oppose U.S. Vietnam policy, as it threatened to alter fundamentally the global balance of power, while simultaneously igniting social unrest at home. Such turbulence was heightened by the emerging détente, which undermined the earlier Cold War consensus, leading to a radicalized political atmosphere domestically. In this new environment the "New Left" was able to establish a powerful foothold among the so-called "68-generation;" and in many West European countries the latter rejected the older Socialist and Communist parties in favor of more radical political alternatives. All of this created a difficult situation for Social Democratic governments who struggled to maintain a workable relationship with Washington, while at the same time placating domestic anti-war opinion – lest this issue be hijacked by the far left. This study explores how the Swedish Social Democrats tried to resolve this dilemma by adopting a vocal stance against the war as a means to divert radical energies away from the domestic status quo. This is not to suggest that the Swedish Social Democrats' outspoken opposition to the war was completely insincere, but only that the party leadership's handling of this question was consistently informed by domestic political calculations. This is the first work on this topic to assert the *primacy* of domestic politics.

In light of the tensions that this policy caused with Washington, it is perhaps not surprising that this is the most written about episode in Swedish postwar diplomacy. The vast majority of these studies have, however, been produced either by political scientists, journalists, politicians, or retired diplomats; this is thus the first major scholarly historical work on the topic. It is also one of the only studies based on archival research on both sides of the Atlantic. In addition, very little on this subject has so far been written in English – this despite the fact that Sweden is widely recognized to have been

the principal West European critic of the American war effort. Consequently, a major function of this work is also to introduce this topic to non-
Swedish speakers.

Another important way that this book distinguishes itself from its fore-
runners lies in the desire to look beyond Sweden, and to locate the Swedish
Social Democrats' vocal opposition to the American war effort in the broader
framework of West European discontent about U.S. policy. Previous studies
have generally examined the Swedish position in isolation, and by so doing
have in effect made it appear unique, and by extension also independent from
larger pan-European trends. This study, in contrast, insists that the Swedish
Social Democrats' approach to this issue can only be understood in the context of widespread West European dissatisfaction about the war.

Chapter 1 is chiefly intended to introduce the reader to the historiographical debate, and political controversy that has surrounded the Swedish
Social Democratic government's handling of the Vietnam issue. Above all,
this chapter outlines the various party tactical considerations that informed
the Social Democratic hierarchy's approach to this question; and it finds
that these calculations were far more complex than the party's international
and domestic critics claimed at the time. Rather than being mostly directed
at the radical youth vote, this policy was primarily meant for internal Social
Democratic consumption. In hindsight, the government's approach to the
Vietnam War appears to have been a success in the short term, in that it
held the party together in the face of radicalized political atmosphere of the
1960s – and this without fatally damaging either the party's immediate
electoral prospects, or the country's core national interests.

Chapter 2 analyzes the gradual emergence of the Vietnam War as a
major issue in Swedish politics, starting in 1964–1965. It shows that the
advent of this question was very much tied to the growing importance of
the youth vote, which by 1968 was expected to count for as much as 20 % of
the entire electorate. However, the emergence of this issue was also very
much tied to the political revitalization of the Swedish Communist Party.
As the latter party de-Stalinized itself in early 1960s, it came to pose a real
threat to the Swedish Social Democrats for the first time since the late
1940s. From the point of view of the Social Democratic establishment, the
domestic political situation was further complicated by the sudden appearance of the Maoist anti-war movement which, like the Communists, sought
to use the Vietnam question not only to attract younger radical voters, but
also to drive wedge into the Social Democratic Party in an attempt to
dislodge its left-wing. By late 1967 the threat from these two groups was

growing, and for this reason Social Democratic anti-war activists became more and more concerned that the party risked being outflanked on this issue, with the result that it might lose the loyalty of the entire "68-generation." These anxieties, in turn, led to heightened internal pressure for the government to take a stronger public stance against the war.

Chapter 3 demonstrates that after having originally lagged behind their far left rivals on this question, the Social Democrats finally seized the initiative in 1968; and once they did so the party hierarchy was determined not to relinquish it again. Accordingly, from 1968 on, the Social Democratic administration became increasingly vocal in its opposition to the war. The most visible sign of this new militancy was Olof Palme's joint appearance with a North Vietnamese dignitary at a huge anti-war rally in Stockholm on 21 February 1968. This demonstration had been organized by the Swedish Committee for Vietnam, which the government and the SAP hierarchy would subsequently come to rely on as a firewall against the more radical elements of the Swedish anti-war movement. While this strategy was largely successful, the cabinet had now effectively opened itself up to intensified internal agitation in favor of an ever more radical stance on the war, which also followed.

The first concrete manifestation of this was the government's decision to allow American deserters sanctuary in Sweden, which is also the subject of Chapter 4. The government had granted the deserters asylum following a plea from the Swedish Committee for Vietnam. Both the committee and the cabinet, however, would quickly come to regret this decision. For not only did the deserters' behavior generate a lot of negative attention, but the deserters' main political organization, the American Deserter Committee, soon turned its back on both the government and the Swedish Committee for Vietnam, opting instead to ally itself with the Maoist wing of the anti-war movement. This episode underscores that in several crucial instances the government's Vietnam policy had a reactive character to it that did not show evidence of much careful planning or forethought. That having been said, the government did firmly withstand the anti-war movement's calls to confer political refugee status on the deserters. It realized that to do so would be far too provocative in Washington's eyes; and thus to the disappointment of radical anti-war activists the deserters were only given "humanitarian asylum," a classification that at the time was considered far less politically explosive.

The limits of how far the Social Democratic cabinet was willing to challenge the U.S. in its efforts to accommodate internal anti-war opinion was also made quite evident in the early fall of 1969, in conjunction with its public promise to provide humanitarian assistance to the Democratic Republic of Vietnam. The Swedish decision to diplomatically recognize the D.R.V earlier that same year had already irritated the Americans, and when faced with the threat of U.S. economic sanctions following its aid announcement to North Vietnam, the Social Democratic government quickly retreated, in effect withdrawing its offer of humanitarian assistance. Not surprisingly, such backpedaling angered many within the Swedish anti-war movement, but the cabinet was not about to endanger the country's economic well-being in order to help the D.R.V. Chapter 5 illustrates how the government always needed to balance its desire to appease internal anti-war opinion against the necessity of protecting Sweden's core national interests. Indeed, when "push came to shove" the government consistently prioritized *realpolitik* over its self-stated ideals of promoting international solidarity with the people of North Vietnam.

Chapter 6 reaches a similar conclusion, emphasizing the fundamental continuity of Swedish-American relations in this era, this despite the two countries' diplomatic conflict over Vietnam. This chapter studies the domestic and international fallout following Olof Palme's strident condemnation of the American bombing of Hanoi in December 1972, at which time Palme had compared the so-called "Christmas bombings" to the Holocaust. This analogy infuriated the Nixon administration, which retaliated by freezing diplomatic relations with Sweden. Though the Social Democratic hierarchy was of course alarmed by this unexpected turn of events, in the end the Americans' attempt to punish Sweden proved to be an asset to the Social Democrats during the 1973 election campaign. For it energized the base of the party heading into the elections, as the party closed ranks in the face of Conservative criticism, and the American diplomatic sanctions. This chapter additionally stresses the fact the diplomatic freeze did not negatively affect other, more important, areas of Swedish-American cooperation, such as trade, scientific exchanges, and military intelligence sharing. In fact, if anything, military cooperation and coordination between the two countries actually intensified during the Vietnam era, and the freeze did little to disrupt this.

The seventh and final chapter explores Swedish Vietnam War policy in a broader West European context, and explains why most of European governments opted to adopt a more low-key approach to the Vietnamese conflict, even though they too privately opposed the war. It concludes that the answer to this question can principally be located in domestic politics, for in no other European country did the Vietnam War become such a major political issue as did in Sweden. This chapter, furthermore, seeks to reevaluate the relative merits of the government's Vietnam policy. On the one hand, the Social Democratic hierarchy's handling of this question allowed the party to cling to power during the radicalized political climate of the 1960s; but, on the other hand, by giving into these same radical energies the party was ill equipped to adjust to the more conservative mood of the late 1970s. Hence while other more moderate Social Democratic parties in Europe managed to remain in (or to reenter) office in these years, the Swedish Social Democrats were ousted in 1976 following nearly five decades in power. Finally, this chapter suggests that while the Social Democratic government's high profile stance on the war brought it considerable attention, this did not necessarily translate into more influence on the world stage. In relation to Vietnam, the Swedish Social Democratic leadership notably claimed that it had played a key role in turning world opinion against the war, but in truth none of Sweden's West European neighbors choose to adopt an equally militant approach to this question. In retrospect, the so-called "activist phase" in Swedish foreign policy probably had a detrimental impact on the country's international standing, in that it turned the country's focus towards the Third World, and away from Europe where its attention arguably should have been all along. Indeed, in the long run the Swedish Social Democrats' new visible profile in global affairs brought the country few tangible awards; and looking back, the former's self-appointed role as the moral consciousness of the international community appears to have been mostly a self-aggrandizing illusion.

This monograph is a revised and truncated version of my unpublished dissertation entitled: "A good offensive is the best defense: Swedish Social Democracy, Europe and the Vietnam War" (Dept of History, University of Wisconsin-Madison, 2005.) I would like to thank Karl Molin, Hans Weinberger, Kent Zetterberg, Dag Blanck, Rudy Koshar, Jeremi Suri, Marilyn Young, Laird Boswell and Pekka Hamalainen for their help and advice both in relation to the original dissertation, and the current manuscript. Above all, I would like to express my appreciation to Kjell Östberg, Stanley Payne and Steven Koblik for their insight and consistent support over the years.

Swedish Social Democracy and the Vietnam War: Domestic Foreign Policy?

This study follows in the footsteps of Fritz Fischer's groundbreaking book, *Griff nach der Weltmacht*, which was one of the first historical works to highlight the often intimate relationship between foreign and domestic policy.[1] While Fischer looked at how conservative elites in pre-World War I Germany had gone to war as a means to preserve the status quo, this book will instead examine how a democratically elected Social Democratic government in postwar Sweden adopted an anti-war platform in order to remain in power.

Between 1965 and 1973, Sweden's Social Democratic government, led by Olof Palme, emerged as the most strident and persistent non-Communist critic of the American war effort in South East Asia. During this nine-year period, the Swedes' criticism of the US not only grew progressively belligerent, but Swedish policy also came to favor the Vietnamese Communists more and more, leading to a rift in Swedish-American relations. It did not take long before Washington came to regard Sweden as the most caustic Western opponent of the Vietnam War.[2]

Clashing with the Americans: Olof Palme, the Social Democratic Party, and the "Activization" of Swedish Foreign Policy

The Swedish-American clash began in mid-1965 and steadily escalated over the next two years as Social Democratic leaders became increasingly boisterous in their attacks against US policy. In addition, the Swedes' allowed the Bertrand Russell War Crimes Tribunal to convene in Stockholm. In early 1968, the simmering trans-Atlantic quarrel sharply accelerated when Sweden offered sanctuary to American deserters and Palme appeared side by side with a visiting North Vietnamese dignitary at an anti-war rally in Stockholm. The following year, the dispute was further exacerbated as Sweden became the first Western nation to diplomatically recognize the Democratic Republic of Vietnam (DRV), and soon thereafter

Sweden also extended significant financial aid to North Vietnam. Then, after a two-year relative lull, the conflict climaxed in December 1972 when Palme compared the US bombing of North Vietnam to the Nazis' atrocities at Treblinka. Palme's strongly worded analogy caused Washington to withdraw its *chargé d'affairs* from Sweden, while at the same time informing Stockholm that it would not accept a new Swedish ambassador. The ensuing diplomatic freeze would last until May 1974.

In hindsight, West European opposition to the Vietnam War has become internationally identified with the Swedish Social Democrats,[3] and with Olof Palme in particular. This association with Palme personally is not totally unwarranted, for he had developed a strong profile on this issue well prior to becoming Prime Minister in 1969. From 1965 on, Palme's vocal protests against the war elicited significant foreign media interest,[4] not least in the US press.[5] In America, the Swedish Vietnam position was usually attributed almost exclusively to Palme,[6] and this tendency was also evident among American policy-makers and politicians.[7] In the eyes of US officials, Palme soon supplanted Charles de Gaulle as the most vocal West European critic of the American war effort.[8]

In Sweden, too, this policy remains primarily associated with Palme, and it continues to be regarded as key to his political legacy.[9] Palme, for his part, evidently shared this view, and he considered his stance against the war to have been one of his proudest achievements.[10] This positive assessment has subsequently been upheld in both Kjell Östberg's and Henrik Berggren's biographies,[11] as well as in Kristina Lindström and Maud Nycander's 2012 documentary about Palme.[12]

At the time, Palme's boisterous opposition to the war certainly elevated him to an internationally recognized statesman, while also helping him to consolidate his position within *Sveriges Socialdemokratiska Arbetareparti* (SAP, Social Democratic Labor Party of Sweden). To be sure – Vietnam or no Vietnam – Palme would have been the favorite candidate to succeed his mentor, Tage Erlander;[13] but still this issue's importance to his political assent can hardly be overstated. Palme's outspoken criticism of the war helped him to create an independent political identity for himself, as well as a broader base within the SAP.[14]

It would be a grave mistake, however, to interpret Palme's high-profile position on this question solely in terms of his own political ambitions. Rather, his conduct can only be understood within the broader framework of the SAP's domestic and international objectives. By the time Olof Palme took over the reins of the party in 1969, the Social Democrats had been in power for three and a half decades, and they had been the dominant partner in every Swedish government since 1932. A large part of the SAP's success can be attributed to the party's ability to continually reinvent itself and to adjust to shifts in the domestic political climate. In the 1960s – in the context of growing youth rebellion and a more generally radicalized atmosphere – this meant tilting leftward (a point to which we will return).[15] Among the party's leaders, it was Palme's designated role to corral younger militants and leftist intellectuals into the Social Democratic camp,[16] and more than anyone else Palme helped the SAP to negotiate this new political environment.[17]

After the fact, Palme has also been strongly linked to the so-called "activization" of Swedish foreign policy.[18] This "activization" represented a more assertive approach to international affairs that distinguished it from the cautious demeanor that had previously characterized the country's postwar diplomacy. With Palme at the helm, a moralistic (and on occasion even combative) tone soon became the signature traits of the "activist" era in Swedish foreign affairs.[19] Perhaps it should come as no surprise, then, that the government's vociferous objections to the Vietnam War became the main outward symbol of this new phase in the country's international relations.[20]

Above all, this policy shift signaled the SAP's desire to play a more visible role on the world stage.[21] This was especially evident in relation to North–South issues, where the Swedish Social Democrats had more leeway to act independently than they did in the East–West standoff. Accordingly, Sweden's deepening involvement with the developing world was both a rewarding, and fairly harmless, outlet for the party's growing international ambitions.[22] The Swedish Social Democrats promptly took advantage of the new international opportunities (and greater autonomy) that the emerging détente and the accelerated pace of decolonization had combined to create.[23]

The government's new "activist" foreign policy was launched just as the country reached one of the highest standards of living in the world. Following the end of the Second World War, Swedish industrial exports skyrocketed, producing an unprecedented level of prosperity. This trend was exceptionally marked in the first half of the 1960s when the nation's GNP climbed 5 per cent annually, which by extension laid the foundation for one of the world's most comprehensive welfare systems. Between 1960 and 1970, social expenditures in Sweden doubled, creating a social security network that provided for each citizen from cradle to grave. The vast expansion of the welfare state not only proved to be crucial to the SAP's hegemonic hold over postwar Swedish politics,[24] but it also led to a surge of international interest in Sweden.[25]

For their part, Social Democratic spokesmen began to speak of a "Swedish model," which they touted as an attractive (and even implicitly superior) alternative to both the Soviet and US systems.[26] Social Democratic propaganda specifically elevated the rectitude of the country's neutrality along with its progressive social legislation, which, in turn, was favorably compared to the supposedly egotistical and aggressive conduct of the two superpowers. Pronouncements to this effect pointed to a rising national self-confidence that, on occasion, bordered on outright arrogance.[27]

The alleged virtue of Swedish neutrality, coupled with the nation's recent domestic achievements, became a source of national pride that went far beyond the Social Democratic rank and file, making a deep impression on the Swedish public as a whole. The country's new "activist" foreign policy was unmistakably spurred on by a growing national hubris, and, in this period, the idea that Sweden should serve as the international community's moral consciousness enjoyed widespread domestic support.[28] In retrospect, it is plain to see that the SAP's tactical considerations were of paramount importance to the "activization" of Swedish foreign policy.[29]

As already implied, the government's outspoken opposition to the Vietnam War rapidly became the chief avenue for Social Democratic self-promotion internationally.[30] Most strikingly, the SAP leadership employed its criticism of the American war effort to boost its influence in the Third World.[31] An additional advantage of this policy was that it also helped to place Swedish–Soviet relations on a better footing. This was unquestionably a welcome development at a time when many West European leaders worried that the global balance of power was beginning to tilt in favor of the USSR.[32]

The Social Democratic administration's stance on the war, on the other hand, tested the country's historically amicable relationship with the United States, although it never fatally ruptured this bond. This study consequently emphasizes the overall continuity in Swedish–American relations during these years, arguing that, in the long run, this dispute amounted to little more than diplomatic shadow boxing. First of all, it never disrupted Swedish–American cultural or scientific exchanges, and secondly, trade between the two countries actually increased in this period.[33] Similarly, the two countries' disagreement about the war did not negatively affect their collaboration in security-related matters in Europe.[34]

Research has revealed that Sweden's military ties to NATO were far more extensive than the country's officially declared policy of neutrality ever suggested. We now know that during the Cold War Sweden made extensive preparations to receive Western military assistance in the event of a Soviet invasion – an arrangement to which neither the Swedish public nor parliament were ever privy to. While a full account of the country's defensive arrangements with the Western alliance is beyond the scope of this study, it is sufficient to note that these preparations went far beyond just idle talk and found a number of concrete expressions. Swedish airfields were, for instance, extended in order to accommodate American bombers.[35]

Sweden had first been clandestinely included within NATO's defensive perimeter in northern Europe in the early 1950s, and then a decade later the country was brought under the American nuclear umbrella as well. Subsequently, the Swedes were also integrated into the West's intelligence network against the East. At the end of the day, both sides were eager to keep this arena separate from their disagreement about the war, and Swedish–American cooperation in the military realm actually intensified during the Vietnam era.[36]

It is clear that their differences over the situation in South East Asia did not change the reality that the two countries' security interests in northern Europe, though not identical, in many respects overlapped. Their disagreement about Vietnam was basically irrelevant to the Americans' strategic calculations in the Nordic region, where the Swedish Armed Forces were seen as a vital complement to NATO's defenses.[37] Thus it remained in the United States' best interests to continue to buttress Sweden's military capacity, particularly at a time when many of America's formal European allies were curtailing their defense spending at much sharper rates than the Swedes.[38] If anything, for the US, the importance of the Swedish Armed Forces grew in these years as Washington desperately sought to reduce its own military expenditures in Europe.[39]

Strategic realities consequently outweighed the Americans' displeasure with the Social Democratic administration's Vietnam criticism, which was tolerable to Washington so long as Stockholm remained firmly anchored in the Western camp in Europe.[40] The détente had done much to loosen the American grip over Western Europe, and as a result Washington was forced to accept a level of dissent that would have been unthinkable only a decade earlier.

Conversely, from the Social Democrats' point of view, this dispute allowed the government to cast itself in the morally gratifying role of David versus Goliath,[41] and its criticism of the US clearly played to Swedish nationalist sentiments, which were only further fueled by the two countries' conflict over the war. Hence, Sweden's new assertive profile in world affairs must additionally be understood in the broader context of intensified European nationalism. Like other West Europeans,[42] the Swedish Social

21

Democrats wanted to mark their independence vis-à-vis the United States, and West European nationalism in the postwar period was almost by definition anti-American. The Swedish challenge to the US was therefore in many ways analogous to its French equivalent, as they were both largely symbolic in nature.[43] In the end, the Social Democratic administration's outspoken opposition to the war was a relatively low-risk policy – one that was worth pursing in view of its potential domestic dividends. During this period in time, standing up to the United States was often good politics in Western Europe, and this was irrefutably the case in Sweden.

In the Balance: Swedish Foreign Policy and National Interests

American diplomats recognized that this new "activist" phase in Swedish foreign policy was mainly intended for domestic consumption.[44] In the minds of US officials, nowhere was this tendency as pronounced as in relation to the Swedish government's handling of the Vietnam issue, which they always suspected of being rooted in Social Democratic party tactical considerations.[45] On numerous occasions, the apparent validity of this interpretation was privately confirmed by Swedish businessmen,[46] diplomats,[47] and military officers.[48]

Not unexpectedly, conservatives on Capitol Hill time and again voiced similar suspicions,[49] as did many conservative-leaning papers in the United States.[50] However, this assessment was also shared by liberal dailies, such as the New York Times and the Washington Post, that otherwise took a generally positive view of Swedish Vietnam policy.[51] Indeed, regardless of political affiliation, most American commentators (sympathizers of the Swedish position included) believed that the SAP leadership's approach to the war was rooted in Swedish domestic politics,[52] and other international observers generally reached the same conclusion.[53]

American officials nonetheless appreciated that the Social Democratic hierarchy was faced with a delicate balancing act, because accommodating internal anti-war opinion could not be done at the expense of Swedish national interests.[54] These interests would be badly harmed if the government's attempt to mollify domestic opinion caused irreparable damage to Swedish–American relations. US diplomats, then, were well aware that the Social Democratic administration was walking a tightrope on the Vietnam issue, which was not always an easy task in light of the growing internal pressure that it was under in relation to this question.[55]

Leading Social Democrats would later acknowledge that each element of the government's Vietnam policy had to be weighed against possible "negative consequences."[56] What these exact consequences were was left unsaid, but this undoubtedly referred to the necessity of shielding Swedish trade and military security. When push came to shove, Swedish Vietnam policy was consistently subordinated to the dictates of *Realpolitik* – and especially to the necessity of keeping the country's trade out of harm's way. With this in mind, there is little merit to the Social Democratic claim that the government never backed down in the face of US pressure or economic threats,[57] an assertion that has also gone unchallenged by many scholars of this topic.[58] The bottom line for Social Democratic Vietnam policy was that the attempt to placate domestic anti-war sentiments always had to be balanced against the imperative of protecting Swedish exports as well as national security, and accordingly there were real limits to how far the government dared to challenge Washington. (This topic will be examined at length in Chapters 4, 5, and 6.)

Consequently one is left with the impression that the Social Democratic administration was engaging in an act of brinkmanship, seeing exactly how far it could defy Washington without seriously harming Swedish national interests. In the end, the Social Democratic establishment must be said to have successfully achieved this balance of largely appeasing anti-war opinion without causing grave harm to the country's basic interests.[59] This was certainly the conclusion the SAP hierarchy itself reached, as it determined that the government's support for the Vietnamese Communists had not had any significant detrimental consequences for Sweden.[60]

Still, at the time, this did not stop Swedish industrialists from worrying that the Social Democrats' protests against the war would hurt Swedish exports in the United States,[61] and they continued to regard the government's criticism of Washington as imprudent.[62] Representatives of the Swedish business community were as a rule pro-American, and they would have preferred a less "adventurous" approach to international affairs.[63] In their opinion, the SAP leadership was putting its own needs ahead of the nation's best interests, and they resented the Social Democratic administration for playing politics with Swedish foreign policy in order to accommodate radical groups at home.[64]

In these years, likeminded grievances could be heard from parts of the Swedish military establishment[65] and the diplomatic corps.[66] In their memoirs, a number of top diplomats complain that that the government's Vietnam policy was all too often governed by short-term party tactical calculations,[67] and it probably did not help that this policy was repeatedly formulated without their input. Here it should simultaneously be added that the government's stance on the war was not without supporters within the Swedish Foreign Ministry, and many younger diplomats openly sympathized with the cabinet's position.[68]

Among the general public, opinions were also often sharply divided about the government's high-profile stance against the war, but even those who, on the whole, backed the government's Vietnam posture did not fail to register its domestic origins.[69] These types of complaints were routinely leveled by radical anti-war activists[70] – although identical protests were also heard from members of the non-socialist opposition.[71] Detractors from both sides of the political spectrum were therefore quick to rebuke the Social Democratic government for using the Vietnamese conflict to its own ends.

This critique was famously articulated by the future leader of the Conservative Party, Gösta Bohman, in his book, *Inrikes utrikespolitik. Det handlar om Vietnam* (*Domestic Foreign Policy: It is About Vietnam*). Published in 1970, Bohman's book attacked the Social Democratic administration for cynically employing its opposition to the war for short-term electoral gains at the expense of Swedish national interests.[72] Many other Conservative politicians seconded Bohman's interpretation of the government's Vietnam policy,[73] and accusations to this effect were likewise put forth by the non-socialist press.[74] This was even true of Sweden's two largest Liberal dailies, *Expressen* and *Dagens Nyheter*, that generally approved of the Social Democrats' Vietnam stance[75], but they, too, deduced that this policy was chiefly the byproduct of the Social Democrats' electoral ambitions.[76]

The Conservatives were never able to capitalize fully on these accusations. In part this was due to the party's heightened isolation in the radical political and cultural climate of the late 1960s and early 1970s. Although the party did its best to accommodate itself to the new *zeitgeist* of the times by switching its name to the Moderate Party in 1969, it still remained deeply out of step with the general electorate, and for this reason the Social Democratic administration could usually afford to ignore the Conservatives.[77]

In no other area was the Conservative Party's isolation as conspicuous as it was in relation to Vietnam.[78] If anything, Conservative protests were an asset to the government because they provided the Social Democrats with political cover when the party was attacked by its Marxist adversaries for being too timid on this issue.[79] The Social Democratic hierarchy was fully cognizant of the Conservatives' utter isolation with regard to this subject,[80] and only in the wake of the American decision to freeze diplomatic relations in early 1973 did the SAP leadership momentarily worry that the Conservatives would be able to capitalize on this question,[81] though these fears soon proved to be unfounded.

The Conservative leadership later felt that its criticism of the government's Vietnam policy had helped to distinguish their party from the Liberals,[82] but during the war such criticism rarely enabled the Conservatives to score any significant political points against the Social Democratic administration. Initially the Conservatives had defended the American war effort,[83] but after the Tet Offensive of early 1968 they too began to dissociate themselves from the war.[84] Still, even after this, the Conservatives continued to view the United States in a basically positive light, regarding the American war effort as well intentioned, if somewhat misdirected. More to the point, the Conservative Party never really warmed up to the Social Democratic government's Vietnam stance.[85]

The problem for the Conservatives, however, was that there was only so far that they could vocalize such criticism against the government without putting themselves into conflict with the other two non-socialist parties, the Center Party and the Liberal Party. This is because following the 1968 election these two parties more or less fell in line behind the Social Democratic administration's approach to the war, and they eventually also began to assert their own anti-war credentials.[86] Originally some older members of both the Center Party and the Liberal Party had opposed the government's handling of this issue,[87] but both parties gradually abandoned these reservations in the face of increased anti-war agitation from their own youth organizations.[88] In the case of the Liberal Party, this shift was also very much attributable to the big urban Liberal papers' mounting support for the cabinet's Vietnam policy.[89]

This left the Conservatives as the sole party in parliament standing outside the domestic consensus in favor of the government's Vietnam stance. This internal fissure within the non-socialist camp was naturally seized upon by the Social Democrats who sought to make the most out of this disagreement.[90] The SAP hierarchy tried to utilize the Vietnam issue to drive a wedge between the three non-socialist parties in an attempt to weaken the credibility of a future non-socialist coalition government.[91]

Another important inhibiting factor for the Conservatives was the fear of being branded as traitors. Sweden had a strong tradition of consensus-oriented politics, and this impulse was strengthened in the 1960s as both the Center Party and Liberals shifted leftwards and the Communist Party moved towards the political center, which acted to minimize party differences and to contract the political spectrum even further. This tradition was exceptionally strong with regard to international matters, where the opposition was expected to loyally back the government.[92] This consensus-oriented approach to world affairs therefore sharply curtailed the Conservatives' freedom of maneuver in relation to the Vietnam question, and on the occasions when they did challenge the Social Democrats about Vietnam, the latter skillfully played the nationalism card, implying that the Conservatives were running Washington's errands.[93]

These various factors combined to discourage the Conservative Party from taking a more resolute stand against the Social Democratic administration's approach to the war. From 1969 onwards, the Conservatives by and large sought to avoid this question because it placed them in a no-win situation. Hereafter, Conservative criticism grew quite circumscribed, content to attack the style, rather than the substance, of the government's position on Vietnam.[94]

Farther Left? Anti-War Sentiment and Radicalization in the Social Democratic Party

In the wake of the Tet Offensive of January 1968, the war had virtually no apologists left in Sweden, and henceforward public opinion remained solidly against it. As early as September 1965, a poll revealed that most Swedes had already turned against US policy in Indochina, with only a meager 12 per cent backing the American war effort.[95] From this point on, popular support for the war continued to erode in Sweden, and by March 1967 the public disapproval rating had reached 83 per cent.[96] In the fall of 1968, another American poll showed that the Swedes were far more critical of US policy in Indochina than the Italians, French, British, or West Germans.[97] Subsequent American diplomatic reports reaffirmed this conclusion, noting that the Swedish public's strong antipathy toward the war was unrivaled in the West.[98]

The composition of the Swedish anti-war movement was also exceptional in its heterogeneity. Its appeal extended far beyond the New Left and well into the political mainstream, and the movement eventually came to encompass everyone from temperance groups and scouts to the trade unions.[99] One major reason that the anti-war movement grew into such a broad-based popular cause in Sweden was because four out of the five established parliamentary parties legitimized anti-war opinion by actively wooing it. The Swedish press, led by the country's leading Social Democratic and Liberal dailies, also actively fostered popular opposition to the war by assuming a critical stance against US policy at a very early stage.[100]

Without the sanction of the major parliamentary parties and the country's most influential newspapers, it is very unlikely that the anti-war movement would have had such a profound impact on Swedish politics. Deprived of such backing, agitation against the war would likely have remained a far more marginal cause with limited appeal outside of radical intellectual circles. That said, opposition to the American war effort (and sympathy for the Vietnamese Communist cause) was most keenly felt among young radicals and the urban intelligentsia,[101] and for this reason the government's Vietnam policy was also chiefly directed at these two audiences.[102] While the general electorate was typically less interested in questions concerning the plight of the developing world,[103] in relation to this specific issue the opinion of social elites made a significant impression upon the mass of ordinary citizens, and anti-war sentiments eventually pervaded virtually all segments of Swedish society.[104]

This also does much to explain why the Swedish anti-war movement was proportionally far larger than any of its Western counterparts. An estimated 2 million people, that is, approximately every fourth Swede, was at least nominally affiliated with the anti-war movement, and at the zenith of its strength in early 1973 some 2.6 million Swedes signed a petition calling for an immediate end to the conflict.[105] Last but not least, the Swedish anti-war movement also distinguished itself from the majority of its international equivalents by the sheer length of its duration. Unlike, for example, its American counterpart, which disintegrated in the fall of 1970, the anti-war movement in Sweden remained a vibrant political force until the Paris Peace Treaty in March 1973, and only thereafter did it finally begin to fall apart.

Under these conditions, it is easy to see why the Social Democratic establishment did not need to be overly concerned about the Conservatives' objections to the government's Vietnam policy. Instead, the SAP's energies were wholly preoccupied with hindering the party's Marxist rivals from capitalizing upon the public's (and especially the youth's) strong opposition to the war.[106] This situation was all the more serious from a Social Democratic point of view because the far left sought to use this question to poach Social Democratic voters and cadre away from the party. Early on, the SAP did lose some party members and voters to its left over Vietnam,[107] which needless to say was unsettling to the party hierarchy.[108]

In this era, Social Democratic anxieties were additionally heightened by events in Norway and Denmark where both the Communist and Social Democratic parties had been hurt by the electoral advances of newly founded socialist parties. Special attention was paid to Norway where the electoral success of the new Socialist Peoples Party had significantly contributed to the Norwegian Labour Party's fall from power in 1965 following two decades of continuous rule.[109] Nor did the Swedish Social Democrats fail to register how the Socialist Peoples' Party had adroitly employed the Vietnam issue against their Norwegian colleagues.[110]

All of these developments taken together were thus a source of real concern to the SAP hierarchy,[111] and Social Democratic leaders privately let it be known to American officials that they could not allow this question to be hijacked by the far left.[112] Publicly, however, Social Democratic spokesmen categorically denied that the government's approach the war was informed by such domestic political considerations.[113] Moreover, they countered that, if anyone, it was their political opponents (both left and right) who were trying to exploit the Vietnam issue[114] – an accusation that was frequently repeated in the Social Democratic press as well.[115]

These assertions have been reiterated again and again by various Social Democratic champions of the government's Vietnam stance[116], who have likewise insisted that this policy was principally based on a sense of international solidarity with the Vietnamese people.[117] According to Social Democratic spokesmen, the main intent of Swedish Vietnam policy was always to bolster international opinion against the war while simultaneously serving as a source of moral support for American anti-war activists.[118] For a long time these claims went mostly unchallenged by scholars.[119]

Recent scholarship has, however, taken a more measured approach to this subject, concluding that domestic calculations related to the party's rivalry with the far left played at least a secondary role in the formulation of Social Democratic Vietnam policy.[120] In hindsight, a handful of Social Democratic officials have likewise conceded that the government's approach to the war was partially shaped by party tactical considerations.[121] These officials typically emphasize that it was vital to prevent this question from being monopolized by groups to the party's left,[122] and candid admissions to this effect have become more and more common in the past decade or so.[123]

These disclosures, in conjunction with new archival research, warrant a fundamental re-evaluation of this topic, and taken together these new sources of evidence strongly support this book's assertion that the government's approach to the Vietnam War was primarily rooted in party tactical calculations. Simply put, this study argues that a sense of moral indignation cannot alone explain the Swedish Social Democrats' handling of this question. The war was never very popular in Europe, yet no other Social Democratic Party or Western European government was ever as strident in its critique of the United States – or ever went to the same lengths to assist the Vietnamese Communists – as the Swedes did. Indeed, the Social Democratic administration's political and economic support for the National Liberation Front (NLF) and the DRV was without parallel in the West – and the Social Democrats' conduct in this instance only becomes comprehensible when examined in the context of internal Swedish politics.

This study therefore confirms Bohman's allegation concerning the domestic origins of the government's Vietnam policy, though it also suggests that his definition of "domestic foreign policy" was too narrowly defined, for this policy was not simply designed to appeal to younger voters. In the final analysis, the government's Vietnam stance was directed just as much, if not more, at pacifying internal Social Democratic agitation against the war.

At first, many older Social Democrats were reluctant to publicly criticize the United States, and this was definitely the case for the heads of the Social Democratically affiliated Swedish Trade Union Confederation (*Landsorganisationen*, LO.)[124] This hesitancy, however, was not universally shared within the SAP, and many of the party's auxiliary organizations were increasingly opposed to the American war effort.[125] At least initially, such sentiments were most likely to be found among the party's younger and more intellectual members,[126] though these ideas eventually spread to the rest of the SAP as well. The Social Democratic cadre's interest in the developing world generally surged in these years,[127] yet with regard to the Vietnam issue, it was above all the party's youth organization, *Sveriges Socialdemokratiska Ungdomsförbund* (SSU), that prodded the party in a more radical direction.[128] While the SSU served as a crucial bulwark against the far left,[129] it simultaneously saw it as its duty to push the party leftward overall.[130]

On the international front, this caused the SSU, and other groups on the party's left wing, such as *Sveriges Socialdemokratiska Studentförbund* (SSSF, the Association of Social Democratic Students), to call for the implementation of a "socialist" foreign policy. In concrete terms, this meant intensified Swedish support for a variety of Marxist groups and states throughout the Third World. By extension, this translated into strong internal support for the Vietnamese Communist cause,[131] and in some instances also into open sympathy for the far left's accusation that the government's approach to the war was far too cautious and reverential towards Washington.[132]

On the whole, the party cadre became less and less deferential towards the Social Democratic leadership,[133] and nowhere was this tendency as manifest as within the SAP district in Stockholm, *Stockholms arbetare-kommun,* which during these years became a hotbed of militant anti-war activism. Consequently, Torsten Nilsson, the Social Democratic Foreign Minister from 1962 to 1971 and the district's chairman, was repeatedly forced to defend the government's handling of the Vietnam question to the district.[134] By virtue of its preeminent size and status, *Stockholms arbetare-kommun* exercised considerable authority over Social Democratic policy,[135] and the district certainly made its influence felt in relation to the war. In retrospect, it is apparent that every major government decision on the Vietnam question was preceded and shaped by internal Social Democratic mobilization. Sometimes this lobbying came about through extra-parliamentary agitation, but at other times it took the form of motions to the SAP Congress or bills in the parliament.

Although the Social Democratic leadership by and large welcomed this heightened level of participation in regard to both Vietnam and other issues,[136] the problem was that this internal democratization process concomitantly radicalized the party cadre even further and made it more difficult to control.[137] This observation applied to the party press as well, and in particular to *Aftonbladet,* the country's largest Social Democratic daily.[138] The SAP leadership was intermittently troubled by the paper's defense of radical anti-war activists,[139] and worse yet *Aftonbladet* occasionally also seconded the revolutionary left's criticism of the cabinet's handling of the Vietnam issue.[140] In addition to providing a vital forum for internal Social Democratic dissent concerning this question,[141] *Aftonbladet* likewise opened up its editorial pages to the government's Marxist detractors.[142]

In this period, the paper acted as a mouthpiece for the party's left wing – not least with regard to Vietnam.[143] Internal Social Democratic opposition to the war was first expressed in the editorial pages of *Stockholms-Tidningen,*[144] but when that paper folded in early 1966, this left *Aftonbladet* as the undisputed Social Democratic press critic of the American war effort. In the beginning, *Aftonbladet's* Vietnam stance was far more radical than the rest of the Social Democratic press, but by late 1967/early 1968 this distinction had begun to blur as the party's smaller regional papers also came to assume a more and more militant posture on the war.[145]

According to Gunnar Fredriksson, the paper's editor between 1966 and 1982, *Aftonbladet* consciously saw it as its mission to build both public and internal Social Democratic opinion against the war. Hence, it wanted to strengthen the government's and the party's opposition to US Vietnam policy,[146] and there is little disagreement about the fact that the paper was ultimately quite successful at this.[147] As a direct result of *Aftonbladet's* efforts, and rising internal anti-war agitation more generally, the party's stance on the war grew increasingly militant especially from 1968 on – and hereafter the party was pretty much united behind this policy, including the trade unions.[148]

Initially the government's escalating militancy on the war was mostly meant to ensure that the Social Democrats would not be outflanked by the newly de-Stalinized Communist Party, which was aggressively courting the youth vote.[149] So long as *Sveriges Kommunistiska Parti* (SKP, the Swedish Communist Party) remained dogmatic and fiercely sectarian, the SAP hierarchy had not needed to worry about any real competition from the Communists. But this all began to change in the mid-1960s as the SKP shed its traditional loyalty to Moscow and commenced to move in an increasingly independent and Euro-Communist direction. Once the SKP started to inch closer towards the political mainstream, it immediately posed a much greater a threat to the Social Democrats. This process of internal reform would culminate in May 1967, when the party changed its name from the SKP to *Vänsterpartiet Kommunisterna* (VPK, the Left Communist Party.)[150] The SKP's (and later VPK's) threat to the SAP was, in turn, greatly boosted by the reality that the former's positions on the Vietnam question closely corresponded to the views held by many Social Democratic anti-war activists, thereby raising the specter of leftward defections to Communists for the first time in a generation.[151]

Spurred on by its rivalry against the Communists, the SAP steadily drifted in a more radical direction during the later part of the 1960s, and this also had the effect of strengthening the internal position of the party's left wing.[152] This expressed itself not only in heightened demands for a more "activist" foreign policy, but also in calls for greater social leveling at home.[153] Overall, there was a rebirth of ideology in Social Democratic discourse, and Marxist terminology also made a return to the party's outward propaganda. At the time, this was a remarkable departure from moderate and non-ideological approach to politics that had come to characterize Swedish Social Democracy ever since the early 1930s.[154]

Unlike most of their West European counterparts, the Swedish Social Democrats sought to neutralize these new radical energies by politically absorbing them and diverting them outward and away from the domestic status quo. The SAP hierarchy quickly concluded that the Vietnam issue provided a comparatively safe outlet for these energies – though by giving into them, the party's own position on the war also moved in an ever more militant direction. It is no coincidence that the government's backing of the Vietnamese Communists is widely regarded as the principal manifestation of the party's leftward shift during the second half of the 1960s.[155]

This radicalization became more and more marked following the SKP's gains at the SAP's expense in the 1966 municipal elections. In the wake of this electoral setback, the Social Democratic establishment was alarmed by the party's poor showing among young first-time voters, and the fear was that if the SAP did not adopt a more radical outward image then it would risk growing out of sync with its own cadre as well as with younger voters.[156]

The Social Democratic hierarchy had good reason to fret about this. First of all, the party's election machine was anchored by the trade union movement, and while the LO was an extremely effective vehicle for mobilizing working-class voters,[157] it was not in a strong position to capture radical and educated elements among the 68-generation. A related worry had to do with the sheer size of the baby-boom generation, which drastically enhanced the electoral significance of voters under 30 years old. (Between 1964 and 1973, this age bracket's share of the total electorate jumped from 15.2 per cent to 20.5 per cent.) This sharp demographic rise in young people, in conjunction with the lowering of the voting age down to 18, made it absolutely imperative for the SAP to establish a strong foothold within this specific segment of the general electorate.[158]

Finally, these Social Democratic concerns must also be understood within the framework of the extraordinary stability of the Swedish electorate. In this period there was still very limited movement of voters between the socialist and non-socialist blocs, and most electoral shifts occurred within each respective camp.[159] Given that the 68-generation was discernibly gravitating leftwards politically, this meant that the contest for this group's loyalty was principally going to be fought between the Social Democrats and their Marxist rivals.[160]

Beyond these electoral concerns, during this era the Social Democratic leadership also grew progressively alarmed about the escalating militancy of the country's youth, fearing that the 68-generation might forsake the party in favor of more radical political alternatives.[161] Similarly to their West German counterparts,[162] the Swedish Social Democrats were anxious that the youth might be seduced by revolutionary rhetoric and lured outside the confines of the parliamentary system. The government was fully committed to protecting the democratic status quo from any revolutionary challenge,[163] and its Vietnam policy was, therefore, also partially designed to keep the 68-generation within the parliamentary system.[164]

More specifically, Social Democratic leaders worried about the Maoists' influence within the anti-war movement, and they rightly viewed the Maoist-oriented United NLF-groups (*De förenade FNL-grupperna*, DFFG) as formidable competitors for the youth's loyalty.[165] The SAP hierarchy was keenly aware of the fact that the Vietnam question was at the heart of the party's contest against the Maoists[166] and that both sides were trying to use popular opposition to the war to their own advantage.[167] This rivalry was further heightened when a number of young Maoists broke away from the Communists in SKP in 1967 and established their own political organiza-tion, *Kommunistiska Förbundet Marxist-Leninisterna* (KFML, the Communist League of Marxist-Leninists), and sought to make inroads among the SAP's core constituency, the Swedish working class.[168]

Following the 1970 elections, however, it became clear that neither the KFML nor the SKP would pose much of an electoral threat to the SAP – though this could not have been immediately foreseen. While the final electoral impact of the government's Vietnam stance remains unclear, this policy was probably more important to keeping the SAP together than it was in purely electoral terms to the party. What we do know is that the SAP leadership retroactively valued the Vietnam issue's contribution to ener-gizing the party's own cadre – and core voters – leading up to both the 1968 and 1973 elections.[169]

Consequently, the government's Vietnam stance might best be categorized as a forward policy that was essentially defensive in nature – mainly aimed at holding on to the SAP's share of first-time voters, while at the same time fending off Communist and Maoist encroachment against its left wing. Originally, the SAP had lagged behind both the Communists and the Maoists on the Vietnam question. In the early years between 1965 and 1967, the Social Democratic leadership was not only increasingly out of step with young radical opinion outside of the SAP, but also – and more seriously – with the intensifying anti-war sentiments among the party's own rank and file.[170] This led to escalating internal agitation for the cabinet to take a stronger stand against the war,[171] which in time it did. Once the Social Democratic establish-ment finally seized the initiative on this issue in early 1968, it was determined to not relinquish it again;[172] and from this moment onwards, the party leader-ship took pains to appease internal anti-war opinion.

All in all, the government's Vietnam policy must be considered to have been a success because it enabled the Social Democrats to hold off the Communist/Maoist advance. Looking back, the SAP hierarchy demonstrated considerable skill in its ability to contain, usurp, and channel radical anti-war opinion to its own ends, while at the same time fending off attempts at revolutionary subversion.

***

There is nothing objectionable about the SAP's commitment to keeping the anti-war generation within the parliamentary fold. Nor can the Social Democratic establishment be faulted for seeking to distinguish itself on an issue that it deemed to be so critical to the party's own cadre, and to a lesser extent also to the general electorate. In light of the public's overwhelming opposition to the war, it would have been odd indeed had the party ignored this question. Similarly, the Social Democrats cannot really be criticized for having exploited this issue given that all of the other parties (the Conservatives included) were just as guilty of trying to do this. If anything, the SAP should perhaps be credited with having played the Vietnam card more effectively than its competitors. So, while a bit disingenuous, the Social Democrats' use of the war to their own ends is neither terribly surprising nor especially objectionable.

This argument about the primacy of domestic politics is not meant to suggest that the government's anti-war stance was born entirely out of political expediency. Instead, as the party's domestic detractors have repeatedly pointed out, the SAP leadership's approach to this question should not be interpreted as an either-or proposition. The government's opposition to the war was unquestionably genuine – but, all the same, this policy conveniently dovetailed with the party's overarching political ambitions.[173] The line between opportunism and genuine conviction was admittedly often quite fluid, but the party tactical element was never absent. Here it should additionally be stressed that the Social Democratic rank and file's heartfelt protests against the war were undoubtedly devoid of the kind of political calculations that consistently informed the SAP hierarchy's handling of this issue. It was exactly because of the former's passionate engagement against the war that this matter became so crucial to the party leadership.[174]

In short, there is no need to doubt the sincerity of the party's anti-war beliefs. After all, even American officials did not necessarily question the authenticity of the Social Democrats' opposition to the war.[175] Yet, it is equally transparent that the government's Vietnam stance served many other purposes than its publicly declared intent because it also facilitated a number of other Social Democratic domestic and international aspirations that were far removed from any altruistic notions of solidarity with the Vietnamese people.

Chapter 1: Notes

[1] In retrospect, most scholars agree that Fischer overstated his case, but he is nevertheless still accredited with opening a new and important avenue of historical inquiry. Originally published in 1961, *Griff nach der Weltmacht: die Kriegszielpolitik des Kaiserlichen Deutschland 1914–18*, was subsequently translated into English under the title, *Germany's War Aims in the First World War* (London, W.W. Norton & Co, 1967).

[2] Undated (ca. April 1970). European Section Dept. of State. Unsigned. Memo. Briefing Material Ambassador Holland's Arrival in Stockholm – April 1970. Subject Numeric Files 1970–1973. Political and Defense. Sweden. RG 59; 4 Dec 1970. Scandinavian Desk Dept. of State. George Mason Ingram. Letter to an unidentified American scholar. Subject Numeric Files 1970–1973. Political and Defense. Sweden. RG 59.

[3] B. Vivekanandan, *International Concerns of European Social Democrats* (New York: St. Martins Press, 1997) 11; Donald Sassoon, *One Hundred Years of Socialism* (London: IB Touris Press, 1996) 320, 327–328, 347.

[4] For specific examples, see interviews with Olof Palme in the *London Daily Telegraph* 7 April 1970, *Politiken* 3 Jan. 1971, and *Le Monde* 19 July 1972.

[5] For example, in the days immediately following Palme's public appearance with a North Vietnamese dignitary at an anti-war rally in Stockholm on 21 February 1968, Palme's portrait graced the front pages of no less than 367 American dailies. Olof Palme, *Med egna ord* (Uppsala: Bromberg, 1977) 36.

[6] Lars Göran Stenelo, *The International Critic* (Lund: Studentlitteratur, 1984) 166.

[7] Magnus Jerneck, "Olof Palme – internationell propagandist" in Bo Huldt and Klaus Misgeld (eds.), *Socialdemokratin och svensk utrikespolitik* (Göteborg: M H Publishing, 1990) 133.

[8] 27 Feb. 1969. Scandinavian Desk Dept. of State. Paul Hughes. Memo. Briefing Paper – Sweden. Central Foreign Policy File 1967–1969. Political and Defense. Sweden. RG 59.

[9] Hans Haste, *Boken om Olof Palme* (Stockholm: Tiden, 1986) 58; Ann-Marie Ekengren, *Olof Palme och utrikespolitiken* (Umeå: Boréa, 2005) 10–11, 40–41, 220.

[10] Thage G. Peterson, *Olof Palme som jag minns honom* (Stockholm: Bonnier, 2002) 390–391.

[11] Kjell Östberg, *När vinden vände* (Stockholm: Leopard, 2009) 14, 108–147; Henrik Berggren, *Underbara dagar framför oss* (Stockholm: Norstedt, 2010) 354–357, 390, 464–467, 510–511.

[12] "Palme." (2012) Directed by Kristina Lindström and Maud Nycander. www.imdb.com/title/tt2070768/ accessed 01/02/2013.

[13] Åke Ortmark, *Maktspelet i Sverige* (Stockholm: Wahlström & Widstrand, 1969) 59–63.

[14] Carl-Gustaf Scott, "Olof Palme, the Swedish Far Left, and the Vietnam War" *Arbetarhistoria* 2005 11(3): 49–54.

[15] Per Ohlsson, *Svensk politik* (Lund: Historiska Media, 2014) 403–404.

[16] Kjell Östberg, *1968* (Stockholm: Prisma, 2002) 71.

[17] Björn Elmbrant, *Palme* (Stockholm: Författarförlaget, 1989) 42; Bertil Östergren, *Vem är Olof Palme?* (Stockholm: Timbro, 1984) 368.

[18] Kent Zetterberg, "Det strategiska spelet" in Lars Wedin and Gunnar Åselius (eds.), *Mellan byråkrati och stridskonst* (Stockholm: Försvarshögskolan, 1999) 55–56; Kjell Östberg, "Inledning" in *Olof Palme i sin tid* (Stockholm: Södertörns Högskola, 2001) 15–27.

[19] Alf W. Johansson and Torbjörn Norman, "Sweden's Security and World Peace" in Klaus Misgeld, *et al.* (eds.), *Creating Social Democracy* (University Park, PA: The Pennsylvania State University Press, 1988) 364–365; Ulf Bjereld, Alf W. Johansson and Karl Molin, *Sveriges säkerhet och världens fred* (Stockholm: Santérus, 2008) 224-226, 233–251, 273–274.

[20] Ulf Bjereld and Marie Demker, *Utrikespolitiken som slagfält* (Stockholm: Nerenius & Santérus, 1995) 186; Nils Andrén and Yngve Möller, *Från Undén till Palme* (Stockholm: Norstedt, 1990) 80.

[21] Olof Kleberg, "De stora och de små" in Bertil Dunér, *et al.* (eds.), *Är svensk neutralitet möjlig?* (Stockholm: Liber, 1977) 63; Ole Elgström, *Aktiv utrikespolitik* (Lund: Studentlitteratur, 1982) 186.

[22] Ann-Marie Ekengren, *Av hänsyn till folkrätten?* (Stockholm: Nerenius & Santérus, 1999) 311; Bo Huldt, *Sweden, the United Nations, and Decolonization* (Lund: Esselte Stadium, 1974) 33–36.

[23] Kaj Björk, *Vägen till* Indokina (Stockholm: Atlas, 2003) 104.

[24] Nils Elvander, *Skandinavisk arbetarrörelse* (Stockholm: Liber, 1980) 225, 332; Olof Ruin, *I välfärdstatens tjänst* (Stockholm: Tiden, 1986) 11–21.

[25] Stephen Padget and William Patterson, *A History of Social Democracy in Postwar Europe* (New York: Longman, 1991) 58.

[26] Hans Lödén, *För säkerhetens skull* (Stockholm: Nerenius & Santérus, 1999) 201; Sten Ottoson, *Sverige mellan öst och väst* (Stockholm: Utrikespolitiska Institutet, 2003) 42–47.

[27] Alf W. Johansson, "Vill du se monument, se dig omkring!" in Kurt Almqvist and Kaj Glans (eds.), *Den svenska framgångsagan?* (Stocholm: Fischer & Co, 2001) 202–203.

[28] Ann-Sofie Nilsson, *Den moraliska stormakten* (Stockholm: Timbro, 1991) 7–11, 114–119; Andrén and Möller, *Från Undén till Palme*, 79.

[29] Barbara Haskel, "Det moraliserande Sverige" *Internationella Studier* 1976 (1): 30; Krister Wahlbäck, "Från medlare till kritiker" *Internationella Studier* 1973 (3): 95–96; Nils Andrén, *Den totala säkerhetspolitiken* (Stockholm: Rabén & Sjögren, 1972) 69–70.

[30] Yngve Möller, *Sverige och Vietnamkriget* (Stockholm: Tiden, 1992) 302; Jerneck, "Olof Palme – en internationell propagandist," 124, 130, 135.

[31] Nils Andrén, "Istället för syntes" in Huldt and Misgeld (eds.), *Socialdemokratin och svensk utrikespolitik*, 220–221. See also Yngve Möller, *Mina tre liv* (Stockholm: Tiden, 1983) 311.

[32] Carl-Gustaf Scott, "Swedish Vietnam Criticism Reconsidered" *Cold War History* 2009 9(2): 243–266.

[33] Leif Leifland, *Frostens år* (Stockholm: Nerenius & Santérus, 1997) 96–108. Between 1965 and 1974, American exports to Sweden increased from 2,147 to 4,594 million

Swedish crowns; Swedish exports to the US meanwhile rose from 1,232 to 3,742 million crowns. *Statistisk Årsbok för Sverige 1965–1975.*

[34] SOU, *Fred och säkerhet* (Stockholm: SOU 2002: 108) 221–242.

[35] Wilhelm Agrell, *Fred och fruktan* (Lund: Historiska Media, 2000) 140–155; Mikael af Malmborg, *Neutrality and State Building in Sweden* (New York: Palgrave, 2001) 148–157. See also Robert Dalsjö, *Life-Line Lost* (Stockholm: Santérus Academic Press, 2006).

[36] SOU, *Om Kriget kommit* (SOU 1994: 11) 301–308; SOU, *Fred och säkerhet*, 268, 283–288, 692. See also Mikael Holmström, *Den dolda alliansen* (Stockholm: Atlantis, 2011).

[37] 3 March 1965. US Ambassador to Sweden 1961–1967. J. Graham Parsons. Telegram to State. Subject Numeric Files 1964–1966. Political and Defense. Sweden. RG 59; Undated (ca. Jan.- March 1967.) Scandinavian Desk Dept. of State. Paul Hughes. Memo. Central Foreign Policy File 1967–1969. Political and Defense. Sweden. RG 59; 3 June 1969. David McKillop. Memo. Re: Munitions Control Policy Book. Central Foreign Policy File 1967–1969. Political and Defense. Sweden. RG 59; 4 Jan. 1971. Acting Secretary of State. Alexis U. Johnson. Telegram to the US Embassy Stockholm. Subject Numeric Files 1970–1973. Political and Defense. Sweden. RG 59; 23 Aug. 1972. Jerome Holland. Telegram to State. Re: US Policy Assessment – Sweden 1972. Subject Numeric Files 1970–1973. Political and Defense. Sweden. RG 59.

[38] 20 Jan. 1967. J. Graham Parsons. Telegram to State. Central Foreign Policy File 1967–1969. Political and Defense. Sweden. RG 59; Undated (ca. April 1970). European Section Dept. of State. Unsigned. Memo. Re: Briefing Material for Ambassador Holland's Arrival in Sweden – April 1970. Subject Numeric Files 1970–1973. Political and Defense. Sweden. RG 59.; 31 July 1972. Executive Secretary Dept. of State. Memo to Brig. General John M. Dunn, Office of the Vice-President. Nixon Project. White House Special Files. 1969–1974. Country File: Sweden. Box 9.

[39] SOU, *Fred och säkerhet*, 240–242, 246–291; Leifland, *Frostens år*, 105-107.

[40] 11 June 1968. US Ambassador to Sweden 1968–1969. William W. Heath. Memo. US Policy Assessment – Sweden 1968. Central Foreign Policy File 1967–1969. Political and Defense. Sweden. RG 59; 23 Aug. 1972. US Ambassador to Sweden 1970–1972. Jerome Holland. Telegram to State. US Policy Assessment – Sweden 1972. Subject Numeric Files 1970–1973. Political and Defense. Sweden. RG 59.

[41] Haskel, "Det moraliserande Sverige," 31; Björk, *Vägen till Indokina*, 229.

[42] Richard Barnett, *The Alliance* (New York: Simon & Schuster, 1983) 283–299, 314.

[43] Caroline Page, *US Official Propaganda during the Vietnam War* (London: Leicester University Press, 1996) 179.

[44] 17 Sept. 1965. Second Secretary US Embassy Stockholm. George R. Andrews. Telegram to State. Subject Numeric Files 1964–1966. Political and Defense. Sweden. RG 59; Undated (ca. April 1970.) Unsigned. European Section Dept. of State. Memo. Briefing Material for Ambassador Holland's Arrival in Stockholm – April 1970. Subject Numeric Files 1970–1973. Political and Defense. Sweden. RG 59.

[45] Magnus Jerneck, *Kritik som utrikespolitiskt medel* (Lund: Dialogus, 1983) 114; Stenelo, *The International Critic*, 145–146. See also interview with U.S Ambassador to Sweden

1967–1969. William W. Heath. 25 May 1970. Oral History Collection. L.B.J. Library. Tape # 2, 18–19.

[46] 2 Feb. 1966. J. Graham Parsons. Telegram to State. Re: Lunch with Marcus Wallenberg on 1 Feb. 1966. Subject Numeric Files 1964–1966. Political and Defense. Sweden. RG 59; 14 March 1967. J. Graham Parsons. Memo to State. Re: Lunch with Marcus Wallenberg on 14 March 1967. Central Foreign Policy File 1967–1969. Political and Defense. Sweden. RG 59.

[47] 17 April 1967. *Chargé d'affairs* US Embassy Stockholm. Turner C. Cameron, Jr. Telegram to State. Re: Parsons' meeting with Richard Hichens-Bergström, Director of Political Affairs Division Swedish Foreign Ministry on 16 April 1967. Central Foreign Policy File 1967–1969. Political and Defense. Sweden. RG 59; 21 June 1968. William W. Heath. Telegram to State. Re: Private conversation with Per Anger, Director of the Dept. of International Assistance on 18 June. 1968. Central Foreign Policy File 1967–1969. Political and Defense. Sweden. RG 59; 20 Jan. 1970. US Ambassador to Austria. John Humes. Memo. Re: Recent undated conversation with the new Swedish Ambassador to Austria, Lennart Petri. US Dept. of State. Bureau of European Affairs. Office of Northern Affairs. Records relating to Sweden 1957–1975. RG 59.

[48] For a specific illustration, see Admiral Bengt Lundvall's remarks to the US Chief of Naval Operations, Elmo Zumwalt as cited in SOU, *Fred och säkerhet*, 285–286.

[49] Senator Hugh Scott as cited in the Congr. Rec. 93rd Congr., 1st Sess., 11 January 1973: 736; Representative Robert Price as cited in the Congr. Rec. 93rd Congr., 1st Sess., 3 Aug. 1973: 28265.

[50] *US World & News Report* 18 March 1968; *Washington Evening Star* 1 March 1973.

[51] *Washington Post* 10 March 1968; *The New York Times* 28 Nov. 1969.

[52] Senator Claiborne Pell as cited by Stenelo, *The International Critic*, 146. Senator Pell repeatedly defended Sweden's right to criticize the American war effort, though he also recognized the domestic dimension of this policy.

[53] See, for instance, *London Times* 10 April 1968, *Frankfurter Allemeine Zeitung* 11 Jan. 1969, *Hindustan Times* 24 Jan. 1969 and *Ontario Star* 19 Aug. 1972.

[54] 11 June. 1969. Turner Cameron Jr. Memo. US Policy Assessment – Sweden 1969. Political and Defense. Sweden. Central Foreign Policy File 1967–1969. Political and Defense. Sweden. RG 59; 3 Dec. 1970. Jerome Holland. Memo. US Policy Assessment – Sweden 1970. Subject Numeric Files 1970–1973. Political and Defense. Sweden. RG 59; 29 June 1972. Jerome Holland. Telegram to State. Subject Numeric Files 1970–1973. Political and Defense. Sweden. RG 59.

[55] 13 Aug. 1965. J. Graham Parsons. Telegram to State. Subject Numeric Files 1964–1966. Political and Defense. Sweden. RG 59; 26 April 1966. J. Graham Parsons. Telegram to State. Subject Numeric Files 1964–1966. Political and Defense. Sweden. RG 59; 15 Nov. 1967. Director of Intelligence and Research Dept. of State. Thomas L. Hughes. Memo. Re: Scheduled upcoming meeting between US State Department officials and Torsten Nilsson on 16 Nov. 1967. Central Foreign Policy File 1967–1969. Political and Defense. Sweden. RG 59.

[56] Olof Palme, Tage Erlander and Krister Wickman as cited by Jerneck, *Kritik som utrikespolitiskt medel*, 65; Olof Palme as cited by Elgström, *Aktiv utrikespolitik*, 132.

[57] Olof Palme as cited in *Aftonbladet* 17 May 1967; Tage Erlander as cited in *Dagens Nyheter* 17 March 1968; Torsten Nilsson as cited in *Aftonbladet* 6 Jan 1973. See also Pierre Schori, *Dokument inifrån* (Stockholm: Tiden, 1992) 142.

[58] Jussi Hanhimäki, *Scandinavia and the United States* (New York: Twayne Publishers, 1997) 142; Fredrik Logevall, "The Swedish–American Conflict over Vietnam" *Diplomatic History* 1993 17(3): 444. Logevall, for instance, states that Sweden "did not hesitate to tell the US what it saw as the truth, regardless of the consequences." Otherwise, Logevall's article provides an excellent introduction to the topic.

[59] Andrén, *Den totala säkerhetspolitiken*, 80.

[60] Olof Palme as cited in *SAP PS-protokoll* 17 March 1970. A group specifically set up by the Swedish Foreign Ministry to study this question came to the same conclusion. 9 Jan. 1974. USA-gruppens rapport. "Relationerna Sverige-USA." Avd HP. Grupp 1. Mål Ua. Politik Allmänt. Förenta Staterna. # 269.

[61] Axel Iveroth, Chairman of the Association of Swedish Industrialists, as cited in *Dagens Nyheter* 14 May 1966; Lars Åkerman, spokesman for the Swedish Export Association, as cited in *Kvällsposten* 15 May 1969.

[62] Erik Braunerheilm, Chairman of the Association of Swedish Industrialists, as cited by James Waite, "Sweden and the Vietnam Criticism" *Southeast Asia* 1973 2 (4): 464; Stig Ramel, *Pojken i dörren* (Stockholm: Atlantis, 1994) 157, 190.

[63] Stig Ramel, Chairman of the Swedish Export Association, as cited in *Värmlands Folkblad* 31 July 1970. See also editorial in *Svensk Export* # 14 1969, 2.

[64] Tore Browaldh as cited by Nordal Åkerman, *Apparaten Sverige* (Stockholm: Wahlström & Widstrand, 1970) 149–150; Axel Iveroth as cited in *Sydsvenska Dagbladet* 8 May 1969.

[65] Unidentified Swedish general as cited by Åke Ortmark, *De okända makthavarna* (Stockholm: Wahlström & Widstrand, 1969) 250; Torsten Rapp, the former Commander-in-Chief, as cited in *Aftonbladet* 4 Nov. 1973.

[66] Bo Siegbahn, *Den svenska säkerheten* (Stockholm: Bonnier, 1971) 16–25; Åke Sjölin, "Vietnamdramat i Skandinavien" *Svensk Tidskrift* 1981 (1): 510–514; Gunnar Jarring, *Utan glasnost och perestrojka* (Stockholm: Bonnier, 1989) 122.

[67] Lennart Petri, *Sverige i stora världen* (Stockholm: Atlantis, 1996) 406; Wilhelm Wachtmeister, *Som jag såg det* (Stockholm: Norstedt, 1996) 173–174; Richard Hichens-Bergström, *Spillror från en sällskapsresa* (Stockholm: Norstedt, 1989) 167–171, 201–203.

[68] Christer Isaksson, *Palme privat* (Stocholm: Ekerlids, 1995) 164–165. For a specific illustration, see Jean-Christophe Öberg as cited in *Expressen* 27 Nov. 1969.

[69] See, for example, Sven Svensson, *I maktens labyrinter* (Stockholm: Bonnier, 1968) 168. This was even true of some of the SAP's own constituents. In a letter from a Social Democratic voter to Olof Palme dated 31 March 1968, the author affirms his support for Palme's anti-war stance, despite the fact that it (in the author's view) was obviously partially being driven by domestic motives. The letter's author adds that the party's outspoken

opposition to the war should be an asset heading into the upcoming September election. Olof Palme. Brevsamling. Vol 31–33. "Brev angående Vietnamtalet 1968."

[70] Unidentified NLF-activist as cited in *Dagens Nyheter* 22 Feb. 1968; DFFG, "Solidaritet Sverige-Vietnam. Vietnamarbetet i Sverige Januari–Februari 1973" *DFFG:s Skiftserie # 15* 1973, 22-24.

[71] Erik Boheman, *Tankar i en talmansstol* (Stockholm: Norstedt, 1970) 144, 215; Erik von Heland, *Välfärdssamhällets förfall* (Stockholm: Lundqvists, 1970) 99–105. See also Center Party representative Johannes Antonsson as cited in *Dagens Nyheter* 17 March 1968.

[72] Gösta Bohman, *Inrikes utrikespolitik* (Stockholm: Geber, 1970).

[73] Conservative leader Yngve Holmberg as cited in *Dagens Nyheter* 9 March 1968; Conservative representative Bo Turesson as cited in *Riksdagsprotokollet # 13*, 21 March 1968, 110.

[74] See editorials in *Svenska Dagbladet* 23 Feb 1968, *Västerviks-Tidningen* 2 March 1968, and *Vestmanlands Länstidning* 12 March 1968.

[75] Eva Queckfeldt, *"Vietnam"* (Lund: Gleerup, 1981) 32.

[76] See editorials in *Expressen* March 10 1968 and *Dagens Nyheter* 19 Oct. 1969.

[77] Ortmark, *Maktspelet i Sverige*, 116–119, 123–127. For simplicity's sake, this book will continue to refer to the party as the Conservatives.

[78] Olof Petersson, *Väljarna och världspolitiken* (Stockholm: Norstedt, 1982) 79, 91–92; Bjereld and Demker, *Utrikespolitiken som slagfält*, 293–294. Conservative spokesmen were well aware of this fact. See, for instance, Anders Björk as cited in *Dagens Nyheter* 23 April 1972.

[79] Andrén and Möller, *Från Undén till Palme*, 82.

[80] For a specific illustration, see Olof Palme and Krister Wickman as cited in *Riksdagsprotokollet # 48*, 21 March 1973, 44–46, 55–56, 60.

[81] This issue was discussed internally amongst the SAP leadership. Olof Palme as cited in *SAP PS-protokoll* 26 April 1973.

[82] Bohman, *Så var det*, 160, 165. See also Conservative Party functionary Lars Tobisson as cited in *Dagens Nyheter* 16 June 1994.

[83] For a specific illustration, see Conservative representative Bo Turesson as cited in *Riksdagsprotokollet # 12*, 8 March 1967, 62.

[84] For a specific example, see Leif Cassel, *Så vitt jag minns* (Stocholm: Askild & Kärnekull, 1973) 195.

[85] Ove Nordenmark, *Aktiv utrikespolitik* (Stockholm: Almqvist & Wiksell, 1991) 161–165. For a specific example, see Anders Arfwedson, *et al., Moderat Samhällssyn* (Stockholm: Almqvist & Wiksell, 1970) 16.

[86] Peter Wallensten, "Aktiv utrikespolitik" in Dunér, *et al.* (eds.), *Är svensk neutralitet möjlig?*, 89–94.

[87] For a specific illustrations, see Liberal leader Bertil Ohlin as cited in *Riksdagsprotokollet # 12*, 8 March 1967, 15–16; and Center Party representative Torsten Bengtsson as cited in *Riksdagsprotokollet # 13*, 21 March 1968, 37–40.

[88] Bjereld and Demker, *Utrikespolitiken som slagfält*, 148–173, 297–300. For specific examples, see Center Party representatives Lars Eliasson and Göran Johansson, as well as Liberal representative David Wirmark, as cited by James Waite, *Contemporary Swedish Foreign Policy* (Dissertation. Southern Illinois University, 1971) 378.

[89] Ortmark, *Maktspelet i Sverige*, 108, 116–119. See also Olof Lagercrantz, *Ett år på sextiotalet* (Stockholm: Wahlström & Widstrand, 1990) 230–236.

[90] See, for example, Olof Palme and Evert Svensson as cited in *Riksdagsprotokollet* # 13, 21 March 1968, 88, 140, and Krister Wickman as cited in *SAP Kongressprotokoll*. 25:e Kongressen. 1–7 Oct. 1972, 842.

[91] Wahlbäck, "Från medlare till kritiker," 95–96. For a specific illustration, see Olof Palme as cited in *Aftonbladet* 18 Aug. 1973.

[92] Ruin, *I välfärdsstatens tjänst*, 308–309; Bjereld and Demker, *Utrikespolitiken som slagfält*, 14–17, 182–198, 365–366.

[93] Jerneck, "Olof Palme – en internationell propagandist," 138–139. This tactical advantage was repeatedly acknowledged by the SAP leadership. Lars Henriksson, for example, declared that even though foreign policy issues generally should not be used for domestic purposes, in this instance the party should try to play the nationalism card even harder against the Conservatives. Henriksson as cited in *SAP PS-protokoll* 21 May 1970.

[94] Bjereld and Demker, *Utrikespolitiken som slagfält*, 293–294. See also Bo Carlsson as cited by Waite, *Contemporary Swedish Foreign Policy*, 378–378. and Bohman, *Så var det*, 163.

[95] 12 Oct. 1965. U.S.I.A. Report. Office Files of Frederick Panzer. Box 218. L.B.J. Library.

[96] Martin Schiff, "The United States and Sweden: A Troubled Relationship" *American Scandinavian Review* 1973 61 (4): 369.

[97] Kurt Törnqvist, *Svenskarna och omvärlden* (Stockholm: Beredskapsnämnden för psykologiskt försvar, 1969) 22–23.

[98] 23 March 1970. U.S.I.A. Office of Research and Assessment. Swedish Public Opinion on the US Special Reports 1964–1982. Box 8. S # 50; 20 Sept. 1972. U.S.I.A. Office of Research and Assessment. US Standing in Sweden between the President's China and USSR Visits. Special Reports 1964–1982. Box 8. S # 50.

[99] By the war's end, the only significant group that really stood outside of this consensus were Evangelical Christians. Although the latter were also ambivalent toward the war, they nevertheless felt reluctant about openly criticizing the United States. Harald Lundberg, *Broderskapsrörelsen(s) i svensk politik och kristenhet 1930–1980* (Stockholm: Broderskaps Förlag, 2004) 233–234.

[100] Eva Block, *Amerikabilden i svensk dagspress 1964–1968* (Lund: Gleerup, 1976); Queckfeldt, "*Vietnam*." See also Bengt Ulfner, "Inställningen till Vietnamkriget i AB, DN och Svd" (University of Uppsala, 1969.)

[101] Ludwig Rasmusson, *Fyrtiotalisterna* (Stockholm: Norstedt, 1985) 90–100; Olof Petersson, *Väljarna och världspolitiken* (Stockholm: Norstedt, 1982) 109–114.

[102] Bjereld and Demker, *Utrikespolitiken som slagfält*, 39.

[103] Stig Lindholm, *U-Landsbilden* (Stocholm; Almqvist & Wiksell, 1970) 263; Petersson, *Väljarna och världspolitiken*, 117.

[104] Östberg, *1968*, 165.

[105] Möller, *Sverige och Vietnamkriget*, 291. Being "nominally affiliated" meant that a person belonged to either a political party or trade union that officially backed the Swedish Committee for Vietnam.

[106] Enn Kokk, "Vart tog den där elden vägen" in Enn Kokk (ed.), *Var blev ni av ljuva drömmar?* (Stockholm: Ordfront, 2002) 40–43; Möller, *Sverige och Vietnamkriget*, 141–143.

[107] For specific illustration, see Göran Therborn's open letter "Avsked till Socialdemokratin" in *Tidssignal* # 47 1967, 12. See also Hans Sjöström, "Han rör ju på sig" in Kokk (ed.), *Var blev ni av ljuva drömmar?*, 205–219.

[108] Ortmark, *Maktspelet i Sverige*, 144–146; Enn Kokk, *Vitbok* (Stockhlm: Hjalmarson och Högberg, 2001) 41.

[109] Elvander, *Skandinavisk arbetarrörelse*, 123–125. See also Björk, *Vägen till Indokina*, 133.

[110] This topic was specifically discussed by the SAP leadership. *SAP PS-protokoll* 17 Sept. 1965. See also *Tiden* # 6 1965, 321–324. and *Tiden* # 7 1965, 447–448.

[111] The SAP leadership repeatedly discussed this issue internally. *SAP VU-protokoll* 10 Feb. 1968; *SAP Riksdagsgruppens protokoll* 21 April 1970.

[112] Behind closed doors, Social Democratic leaders were on occasion quite candid about the fact that it was crucial for the SAP to seize the initiative on the Vietnam issue, lest it be exploited by the far left. 11 March 1968. Head of Political Division FM. Wilhelm Wachtmeister. Memo. Re: Meeting between Prime Minister Tage Erlander and US Ambassador William W. Heath on 6 March 1968. Avd HP. Grupp 1. Mål Ua. Politik Allmänt. Förenta Staterna. # 222; 11 March 1968. William W. Heath. Memo. Re: Private meeting with Foreign Minister Torsten Nilsson. Central Foreign Policy File 1967–1969. Political and Defense. Sweden. RG 59. According to Kaj Björk, Krister Wickman (the Social Democratic Foreign Minister 1971–1973) conceded that Swedish Vietnam policy was indeed being driven by domestic calculations during a private discussion with the American Secretary of State William Rogers. Björk, *Vägen till Indokina*, 209.

[113] Evert Svensson's op-ed in *Aftonbladet* 14 Nov. 1965; Sten Andersson as cited in *Riksdagsprotokollet* # 21, 29 April 1970, 102–103. See also Torsten Nilsson, *Åter Vietnam* (Stockholm: Tiden, 1986) 164–168.

[114] Olof Palme as cited in *Aftonbladet* 17 Sept. 1970; Bosse Ringholm, *Efter 1970 års val* (Stockholm: Frihets Förlag, 1970) 14; Enn Kokk, *VPK och SKP* (Stockholm: Tiden, 1974) 80–88.

[115] See editorials in *Stockholms-Tidningen* 12 Oct. 1965, *Arbetet* 2 March 1968 and *Aftonbladet* 9 June 1972.

[116] See, for instance, Harry Schein as cited in Tom Alandh and Birgitta Zachrisson, *Berättelser om Palme* (Stockholm: Norstedt, 1999) 217–224. and Anders Ferm, *Caleb J. Andersson. Palmes okände rådgivare* (Stockholm: Bokförlaget DN, 1997) 16, 105.

[117] Elmbrant, *Palme*, 152; Haste, *Boken om Palme*, 37; Schori, *Dokument inifrån*, 141–142.

[118] Olof Palme, Krister Wickman, Tage Erlander, and Sven Andersson as cited by Jerneck, *Kritik som utrikespolitiskt medel*, 58–65.

[119] For specific illustrations, see Ulf Bjereld, *Kritiker eller medlare?* (Stockholm: Nerenius & Santérus, 1992) 122–131; Kleberg "De stora och de små," 61–87; Wallensten, "Aktiv utrikespolitik," 88–103.

[120] Nilsson, Den moraliska stormakten, 32, 73; Lödén, För säkerhetens skull, 366–370; Elgström, Aktiv utrikespolitik, 186–188; Ekengren, Av hänsyn till folkrätten?, 141–144, 238–240.

[121] Möller, *Mina tre liv*, 310–311. See also Carl Lidbom as cited in Alandh and Zachrisson, *Berättelser om Palme*, 60–61. Lidbom, a former Social Democratic cabinet member, while rejecting the charge of "domestic foreign policy," allows that Palme was well aware of the Vietnam issue's domestic political significance to the SAP.

[122] In a 1982 interview, Tage Erlander, for instance, affirmed that the government had actively sought to steer the public's anti-war feelings in a "constructive direction." Erlander as cited in Jerneck, *Kritik som utrikespolitiskt medel*, 4.

[123] For two recent examples, see Björk, *Vägen till Indokina*, 156, 159, 169, 190, 194, 212 and the former Commander-in-Chief, Stig Synnergren, as cited in *Svenska Dagbladet* 14 March 1998. According to Synnergren, Palme privately indicated that his handling of the Vietnam issue was domestically motivated. This was also confirmed by Anders Thunborg, the former International Secretary of the SAP. Thunborg interview with the author on 4 May 2003.

[124] Charles Kassman, *Arne Geijer och hans tid 1957–1979* (Stockholm: Tiden, 1991) 373–376.

[125] See, for instance, SSKF Årsberättelse 1968, 25–27. See also Lundberg, Broderskapsrörelsen(s) i svensk politik och kristenhet 1930–1980, 52–54, 216–246.

[126] Sten Anderson, *I de lugnaste vatten...* (Stockholm: Tiden, 1993) 151; Anna-Greta Leijon, *Alla Rosor ska inte tuktas!* (Stockholm: Tiden, 1991) 71–72.

[127] Peter Esaiasson and Sören Holmberg, *De folkvalda* (Stockholm: Bonnier, 1988) 93–99, 212–213, 271; Bjereld and Demker, *Utrikespolitiken som slagfält*, 89–112, 267–268.

[128] Birgitta Dahl, "Solidaritetsarbetet för Vietnam" in Kokk (ed.), *Var blev ni av ljuva drömmar?*, 177–178; Björk, *Vägen till Indokina*, 108–115, 139, 146.

[129] Thage G. Peterson, *Resan mot mars* (Stockholm: Bonnier, 1999) 80–87; Hans Sjöström, *Klassens ljus* (Stockholm: Norstedt, 1987) 130–134, 232, 253.

[130] Kaj Axelsson, *Ungdom i en föränderlig värld* (Stockholm: SAP, 1967) 25–31, 72. See also SSU Chairman, Bosse Ringholm, as cited in Lars Svedgård, *Palme* (Stockholm: Rabén & Sjögren, 1970) 129.

[131] Carl-Gunnar Petersson, *Ungdom och politik* (Stockholm: Frihets Förlag, 1975) 123, 147–157, 211, 216–217; Axelsson, *Ungdom i en föränderlig värld*, 27, 87–107.

[132] Enn Kokk, "Laboremus 1902–1987" in Tuula Eriksson, *et al.* (eds.), *Framtidens utmaningar* (Uppsala: Laboremus, 1987) 39–44. See also Torsten Nilsson as cited in *Vi #* 37 1970, 12.

[133] Leif Andersson, *Beslut(s)fattarna* (Stockholm: PM Bäckström, 1996) 172–178; Ruin, *I välfärdsstatens tjänst*, 165–166.

[134] See, for instance, *Stockholms arbetarekommun. Årsmötesprotokoll.* 16–17 April 1967, 13–14. and *Stockholms arbetarekommun. Årsmötesprotokoll.* 17–18 April 1970, 13–15, 21–23.

[135] Bengt Owe Birgersson, *et al.*, *Socialdemokratin i Stockholms Län 1907–1982* (Stockholm: SAP, 1982) 157–174.

[136] Elmbrant, *Palme*, 131–132. See also Andersson, *I de lugnaste vatten...*, 181, 190–194.

[137] Yvonne Hirdman, *Vi bygger landet* (Stockholm: Tiden, 1988) 305, 311–312, 358–360; Kokk, "Vart tog den där elden vägen?," 10–11, 49–51.

[138] This issue was repeatedly discussed by the SAP leadership. Arne Geijer as cited in *SAP PS-protokoll* 13 Dec. 1968; Lars Henriksson as cited in *SAP PS-protokoll* 25 Jan. 1969.

[139] Björk, *Vägen till Indokina*, 192. This problem was repeatedly subject to internal discussion among the Social Democratic parliamentary group. Tage Erlander as cited in *SAP Riksdagsgruppens protokoll* 7 May 1968; Anna Lisa Lewén-Eliasson as cited in *SAP Riksdagsgruppens protokoll* 21 April 1970.

[140] See, for example, editorials in *Aftonbladet* 9 Oct. 1969; 22 Oct. 1969 and 18 April 1970.

[141] For specific examples, see Allan Björk's op-ed in *Aftonbladet* 23 May 1966 and Leif Dahlberg's open letter to Torsten Nilsson in *Aftonbladet* 3 Jan. 1970.

[142] For specific illustrations, see Jan Myrdal's op-eds in *Aftonbladet* 31 Dec. 1967 and 11 Feb. 1968, as well as Sara Lidman's op-eds in *Aftonbladet* 18 Oct. 1969 and 30 May 1970.

[143] Gunnar Fredriksson, *Farvatten* (Stockholm: Norstedt, 1989) 220–235, 245–246.

[144] See, for instance, *Stockholms-Tidningen* 10 Oct 1965.

[145] Gunnar Fredriksson, the Chief Editor of *Aftonbladet* 1966–1980, interview with the author 27 April 2003. For a specific example, see the editorial in *Arbetet* 29 Oct. 1967. This shift was signficant because *Arbetet* was the country's second largest Social Democratic daily, and at the time it was also considered to be official voice of the the party.

[146] Fredriksson interview with the author 27 April 2003. According to Fredrikson, this had also been *Stockholms-Tidningen's* aim. See, for instance, the editorial in *Stockholms-Tidningen* 26 Feb. 1966. Fredriksson had previously served as the editor of *Stockholms-Tidningen* between 1965 and 1966, which undoubtedly explains the similarity between the two papers' positions on Vietnam.

[147] Birgitta Dahl interview with the author 27 May 2004; Sten Andersson interview with the author 27 May 2004.

[148] Rune Nordin, *Fackföreningsrörelsen i Sverige* (Stockholm: Prisma, 1981) 348–349. For a specific illustration, see the editorial in *Fackföreningsrörelsen* # 7 1968, 186–187.

[149] See *Tiden* # 6 1965, 321–325. and *Tiden* # 5 1968, 310–312.

[150] Åke Sparring, "The Communist Party of Sweden" in A.F. Upton (ed.), *The Communist Parties of Scandinavia and Finland* (London: Weidenfeld & Nicholson, 1973) 83–96.

[151] André Rouge, *Sådan är oppositionen* (Stockholm: SAP, 1970) 23–26; Kokk, *SKP och VPK*, 88–96.

[152] Both Birgitta Dahl and Sten Andersson confirmed that the left wing's internal clout grew in this period. Dahl, interview with the author, 27 May 2004. Andersson, interview with the author, 27 May 2004.

45

[153] Bengt Lundberg, Jämlighet? Socialdemokratin och jämlikhetsbegreppet (Lund: Dialog, 1979) 146–165.

[154] Kokk, "Vart tog den där elden vägen?," 18–31; Ruin, I välfärdsstatens tjänst, 224, 250–253.

[155] Möller, Sverige och Vietnamkriget, 46.

[156] Ruin, I välfärdsstatens tjänst, 21–22, 98. See also Tage Erlander, 60-talet (Stocholm: Tiden, 1982) 209–213.

[157] Erik Anners, Den socialdemokratiska maktapparaten (Stockholm: Askild och Kärnekull, 1976) 206–207.

[158] Petersson, Ungdom och politik, 11.

[159] Magnus Isberg, et al., Partierna inför väljarna (Stocholm: Allmäna Förlaget, 1974) 75–77.

[160] Mikael Gilljam and Sören Holmberg, Väljare och val i Sverige (Stockholm: Bonnier, 1987) 313–316.

[161] Dahl, "Solidaritetsarbetet för Vietnam," 184–185; Torsten Nilsson as cited in Arbetet 24 Oct. 1967.

[162] Padget and Patterson, A History of Social Democracy in Postwar Europe, 79–80; Willy Brandt, My Life in Politics (London: Penguin, 1992) 364.

[163] See, for instance, Tage Erlander as cited in Dagens Nyheter 9 May 1968 and Olof Palme as cited in Riksdagsprotokollet # 13, 21 March 1968, 83–84.

[164] Ruin, I välfärdsstatens tjänst, 307–308.

[165] Although not all of the NLF-groups' members were Maoists, the Maoists nevertheless excerised considerable authority within the DFFG, and they also used the organization as a recruiting ground. Kim Salomon, Rebeller i takt med tiden (Stockholm: Rabén Prisma 1996) 110–114, 157; Lars-Åke Augustsson and Stig Hansén, De svenska maoisterna (Göteborg: Lindelöws Bokförlag, 2001) 74–75, 134. See also Åke Kilander, Vietnam var nära (Stockholm: Leopard, 2007) 307–314.

[166] Kokk, VPK och SKP, 24–28, 80–88. This issue was repeatedly discussed among the SAP leadership. SAP VU-protokoll 24 Nov 1970; SAP Riksdagsgruppens protokoll 16 May 1972.

[167] SAP Secretary Sten Andersson as cited in SAP VU-protokoll 24 Nov 1970.

[168] Bosse Ringholm and Hjalmar Mehr as cited in SAP PS-protokoll 30 Sept. 1970; SAP, "Fakta och argument i valrörelsen" # 17 (SAP, 1970). Originally the KFML was not engaged in electoral politics, but in 1970 it also became a political party running against the SAP and the VPK.

[169] Andersson, I det lungnaste vatten..., 254, 314–337.

[170] Social Democratic officials repeatedly discussed this issue. Tage Erlander as cited in SAP Riksdagsgruppens protokoll 29 June 1966; Evert Svensson as cited in SAP Riksdagsgruppens protokoll 7 May 1968.

[171] Kurt Wald and Ulla Lidström as cited in SAP PS-protokoll 1 Oct. 1966. See also Tiden # 5 1965, 270–275.

[172] Olof Palme, Birgitta Dahl and Mats Hellström as cited in SAP Riksdagsgruppens protokoll 21 April 1970; Birgitta Dahl as cited in SAP Riksdagsgruppens protokoll 16 May 1972.

[173] Wachtmeister, *Som jag såg det*, 173–174; Östergren, *Vem är Olof Palme*, 125–126. See also the editorial in *Expressen* 8 Nov. 1965 and C-H Hermansson, *C-H Minnen* (Stockholm: Arena, 1993) 223.

[174] For specific illustrations, see Yngve Persson as cited in *SAP Riksdagsgruppens protokoll* 12 March 1968 and Daniel Fleming as cited in *SAP Kongressprotokoll. 23:e Kongressen. 9–15 June 1968*, 268.

[175] Stenelo, *The International Critic*, 145–147.

The Emergence of the Vietnam Issue
in Swedish Politics, 1964–1967

The first sporadic public manifestations against the US's Vietnam policy surfaced during the early fall of 1964, but it was not until February/March 1965 that they became regularly organized events in Sweden. Over the next couple of months, these protests evolved into small weekly vigils outside of the American Embassy in Stockholm.[1] The initial trajectory of the Swedish anti-war movement thus largely followed the same pattern as its American counterpart, and neither one gained any substantial momentum prior to President Johnson's decision to unleash a bombing campaign against North Vietnam in mid-February 1965.[2]

The Swedish anti-war movement was, of course, greatly influenced by its American equivalent, though it was also shaped by the broader political currents that swept through Western Europe in the late 1950s and early 1960s. Like elsewhere in Europe, the genesis of the Swedish anti-war movement was intimately linked to the emergence of the New Left.[3] This development was, in turn, spurred on by a deepening interest in the plight of the Third World, and the advent of the New Left was likewise nourished by demands for educational reform and greater domestic socio-economic equality. In these years, many young intellectuals in Sweden came to embrace the anti-capitalist, anti-bureaucratic, and anti-imperialist tenets of the New Left, organizing themselves in a wide variety of new extra-parliamentary groupings. These groups rejected both Soviet-style communism and the reformist ideas espoused by the liberal and parliamentary left as societal blueprints. Instead, they envisioned the establishment of an innovative anti-authoritarian socialist society. The advance of the New Left in Sweden conformed to a broader pan-European trend[4] in that its rise was originally facilitated by the growth of the anti-Apartheid and anti-nuclear protest movements, and then it was subsequently sustained by a common opposition the American war effort in Vietnam.[5]

Anti-War Protest and Factions in the Swedish Political Landscape

In a similar manner to most of its Western counterparts, the Swedish New Left was never politically homogeneous, and internal tensions were present from the very start.[6] Almost immediately, the New Left was divided into two separate discernable camps: the first was composed of a small group of Maoist dissidents within the SKP, and the other was a loose mix of left-leaning Social Democrats and Communist peace activists. Before long this schism was duplicated within the Swedish anti-war movement, thereby shattering the early collaborative efforts between pacifist anti-nuclear opponents and the more militant Maoists. A dispute over China's acquisition of nuclear weapons consequently developed into a larger disagreement about whether Swedish anti-war activists should support an international settlement to the war or if they should unequivocally back the Vietnamese Communists' armed struggle as was advocated by Peking. The Maoists predictably endorsed the second alternative, pitting them against the pacifists.[7]

The Maoists' militant approach to the Vietnamese conflict quickly set them on a collision course with the SKP and the SAP, both of which had informal ties to the pacifist-oriented peace movement. The Maoists similarly ran into conflict with those parts of the New Left that were inspired by the Norwegian and Danish Socialist Parties, and which remained close to the modernizing elements within SKP.[8] This clash precluded any unified opposition against the war, and in mid-1965 the nascent anti-war movement split apart, creating two distinct and mutually antagonistic branches of the Swedish anti-war movement. In the long run, this rivalry was instrumental to nourishing popular agitation against the war, but initially it was the Maoist faction that gained the upper hand.

Beginning in the summer of 1965, the Maoists seized the initiative by successfully pushing their anti-war message into the domestic political limelight. In order to bring more attention to their cause, in late May the Maoists moved their weekly vigils away from the somewhat isolated location of the US Embassy in Stockholm down to Hötorget in the heart of the city. Even there, their activities at first went largely unnoticed, and it was not until the police forcefully prevented them from demonstrating that their protests received substantial media coverage. On 14 June 1965, several protesters were manhandled by the police, which instantly generated an enormous amount of attention in the press. This coverage was surprisingly sympathetic towards the demonstrators, and Maoist leaders would later state that this publicity had been a public relations boon to their cause, resulting in vast numbers of new recruits.[9]

The protesters received particularly friendly treatment in the two Stockholm-based Social Democratic papers, *Aftonbladet* and *Stockholms-Tidningen*,[10] and ensuing protests would likewise elicit a benevolent response from the country's largest Liberal daily, *Dagens Nyheter*.[11] The publicity surrounding the Hötorget protests was made all the more important because it dovetailed with the beginnings of an extensive debate about the war in the three above-mentioned papers.

The Swedish media had only shown limited interest in the brewing conflict in South East Asia prior the summer of 1965, and as a result a critical examination of the war had not yet really gotten under way in Sweden. These sorts of discussions initially appeared in the cultural pages of *Dagens Nyheter*, and they were soon followed by similar ones in the editorial pages of *Stockholms-Tidningen*. Although an occasional voice in support of the American war effort was expressed during this debate, the general tenor of this discussion was quite negative toward US policy in South East Asia.[12]

It is noteworthy that *Stockholms-Tidningen* was not content to just upbraid Washington, but it additionally assailed the Social Democratic administration's passivity on the Vietnam issue. *Stockholms-Tidningen* specifically demanded that the latter assume a more forceful stance against the war,[13] and at this point sentiments to this effect could be heard in other quarters as well.[14]

The paper's viewpoint reflected growing anti-war agitation within the SAP's own ranks. The Hötorget demonstrators were themselves not infrequently affiliated with the party, and especially members from SSSF, the party's student organization, had played a highly visible role in these early protests.[15] Nor were the latter the sole Social Democratic opponents of US policy, and by the late spring of 1965 anti-war sentiments were rapidly spreading throughout the entire left wing of the party.[16] Social Democratic critics of the war stressed that it was essential for the government to lead public opinion and to not fall behind on the Vietnam issue[17] – which was precisely what was occurring at the time.

While the government's official approach to the Vietnamese conflict had so far been quite timid, SKP, in contrast, had already assumed a very aggressive posture on this question.[18] As early as March 1965, the SKP leadership had condemned American policy in South East Asia,[19] and its opposition to the war had continued to grow more vocal thereafter.[20] The SKP had, moreover, sought to court militant anti-war opinion by siding with the Hötorget protesters against the police.[21] Most of all, Communist spokesmen complained about the government's failure to publicly repudiate the American war effort.[22]

That the SAP was lagging behind on this question was understandably a cause for concern to more and more Social Democrats. In June 1965, the Social Democratic monthly *Tiden* warned in an editorial that if the government did not take a more forceful stance against the war, then this question risked being appropriated by the Communists and the Liberals – or maybe in the near future even by a brand new left-socialist party along the lines of the ones that had recently sprung up in Norway and Denmark. The editorial concluded that the party could only avert this turn of events by taking a high-profile stand against the US war effort, which many younger Social Democrats were already calling for.[23]

Such anxieties, in conjunction with mounting internal Social Democratic opposition to the war,[24] created the context in which Olof Palme for the first time publicly questioned the wisdom of American military intervention in Indochina. On 30 July 1965, during the annual gathering of the Brotherhood of Christian Social Democrats, Palme (then still only a Minister without Portfolio) declared, "It is an illusion to believe that demands for social justice can be put down by military force."[25] After the fact, this address has become known as "the Gävle speech" (named after the town where it was delivered), and scholars have often viewed this address as a watershed event that represented a new and more assertive epoch in Swedish foreign policy.[26]

Although Palme's Gävle address refrained from explicitly condemning the United States, it indirectly went much further in its criticism of the American war effort than any previous Social Democratic commentaries on this topic. It certainly ushered in a new era of unprecedented tensions between the two countries, in effect serving as the opening salvo in the high-profile dispute over the Vietnamese conflict that would come to dominate Swedish–American diplomatic relations for the next decade. Up until this point the cabinet had taken a very cautious approach to the war, and the Social Democratic Foreign Minister Torsten Nilsson's earlier comments on this topic had done little more than express hope for a speedy resolution to the conflict.[27]

Unlike Palme's Gävle speech, Nilsson's prior remarks had not elicited much attention either domestically or internationally.[28] Nor had the situation in Indochina yet seriously entered into Swedish–American relations. To be sure, off the record, Swedish officials had articulated their apprehensions about the widening conflict in South East Asia, but they had never openly challenged America's escalating military involvement in the region.[29]

Such prudence would again make itself heard in Torsten Nilsson and the Social Democratic Prime Minister Tage Erlander's statements in the immediate aftermath of Palme's Gävle address, and both men were noticeably careful not to cause any additional offense to Washington.[30] Despite ostensibly defending Palme's right to speak out against US policy, their remarks were widely interpreted as a partial retreat from the more confrontational point of view that had been put forth by Palme.[31]

This renewed moderation notwithstanding, it is indisputable that the Gävle speech obliquely signaled a more forceful Social Democratic posture in relation to Vietnam, especially in view of the fact that both Nilsson and Erlander had approved of Palme's address.[32] Such prior authorization clearly suggests that the SAP leadership had recognized the heightening domestic clamor for a more assertive Swedish profile in foreign affairs, and with regard to the Vietnam issue in particular.[33] (In fact, on the very same day that Palme appeared in Gävle, the former Social Democratic Foreign Minister, Östen Undén, had urged the government to voice its reservations about the current direction of American policy in South East Asia.)[34]

This shift in tone did not escape the attention of US officials, who had already noted that the Social Democratic administration was under intensifying pressure to speak out against the war. American diplomats, moreover, observed that the ire of Swedish anti-war activists, including those within the Social Democratic fold, was increasingly being redirected away from Washington toward Stockholm, and that the SAP hierarchy was now becoming more and more of a target of criticism, not least from the Social Democratic-affiliated press. Up until this point the government had been able to stave off internal demands to denounce the war, but American officials realized it could not be expected to do so indefinitely.[35]

Still, when this critique finally came in the form of Palme's Gävle Speech, the Americans were nevertheless taken somewhat off guard, and this was also true of the Swedish Foreign Ministry, which had previously reassured US Embassy officers in Stockholm that the Social Democratic administration had no intention of giving in to this pressure.[36] As it turns out, they too had been kept in the dark about the Social Democratic leadership's intent to denounce the American war effort. Apparently the cabinet had not informed anyone in the Foreign Ministry about the contents of Palme's Gävle address, and as a consequence the speech took the Swedish diplomatic corps by surprise as well.[37] During subsequent private discussions,

Swedish diplomats intimated that they personally disapproved of Palme's conduct, which, in their judgment, had been driven by Social Democratic party tactical considerations.[38] (Reportedly, Palme privately admitted as much to the Swedish Ambassador to China, Lennart Petri, saying that his address had chiefly been directed at the far left.)[39]

Such feedback naturally only validated the Americans' assessment concerning the domestic impetus behind Palme's critique. To them, the Gävle Speech indicated that the Social Democratic establishment had capitulated to domestic agitation on this question. In their estimation, the SAP's new stance on Indochina had a two-fold purpose, to mollify internal unrest and to insure that the Communists were not allowed to monopolize this issue. If anything, US diplomats anticipated that the Socialist People's Party's recent gains in Norway were likely to give additional momentum to the Swedish Social Democrats' increasingly vocal opposition to the war.[40] American diplomats would in hindsight consider Palme's Gävle address to have been a decisive turning point in Swedish foreign policy, for it was at this juncture that the latter became subordinated to domestic political calculations.[41]

Likeminded suspicions were also harbored by many members of the non-socialist opposition, which complained that the Social Democrats' quest for short-term electoral advantages risked undermining the credibility of the country's neutrality. These kinds of objections to Palme's Gävle Speech were most likely to be heard from leading Liberal and Conservative politicians,[42] and they were of course seconded by many Conservative newspapers, as well as by some parts of the Liberal press.[43]

In the face of these attacks, the party rallied around Palme, and whatever reservations that might have existed about his speech among the Social Democratic faithful were by and large kept private in the name of maintaining a united outward front.[44] In the aftermath of Palme's Gävle appearance, the SAP leadership (while sidestepping any additional direct criticism of the United States) vehemently defended Palme against his non-socialist detractors,[45] as did the Social Democratic press.[46] This was especially true of *Aftonbladet* and *Stockholms-Tidningen*, which both expressed full confidence in Palme, while simultaneously hailing the government's new approach to the war.[47] Taken as a whole, Palme's speech was well received in moderate left-liberal anti-war circles,[48] and it definitely struck a cord among Social Democratic opponents of the war.[49]

Sveriges Kristna Socialdemokraters Förbund (SKSF, the Association of Christian Social Democrats) was already deeply engaged with the Vietnam issue prior to Palme's speech, and the SKSF was quite pleased by his implicit critique of American policy.[50] His anti-war message resonated equally positively throughout the party's left wing, which celebrated that the SAP had at last begun to move forward its positions on this question. Social Democratic anti-war activists reiterated that it was absolutely critical for the party to keep pace with the cadre and the general public's rising antipathy towards the war.[51] Henceforth, internal Social Democratic opinion against the war continued to gather force, progressively gaining strength throughout the fall and into the winter of 1965–1966.[52]

The party's revised stance on Indochina materialized in the shadow of stepped up Communist attacks against the American war effort – a reality that was not lost upon the non-socialist opposition.[53] Even though the Communists nominally supported Palme's position on the war, they still dismissed the government's record on this issue as being far too passive.[54] At this time, the SKP was sharpening its own profile in foreign affairs, mostly by strengthening its support for Marxist national liberation movements in the Third World. The party's new international posture, including its heightened agitation in favor of the Vietnamese Communists,[55] was clearly aimed at harnessing radical anti-war opinion to its own ends.

The SKP's efforts to bring Maoist anti-war activists under its own wing were, however, ultimately in vain, and the relationship between the two groups actually continued to worsen.[56] This conflict was largely ignited by the Maoist allegation that the SKP/SAP-oriented pacifists were betraying the Vietnamese people by virtue of their support for an internationally sponsored peace settlement. The Maoists insisted that the Vietnamese people had to be backed on their own terms by actively assisting the National Liberation Front's armed struggle. The Maoists proposed that instead of working for peace per se, the primary focus of Swedish political activism should be to unconditionally back the DRV and NLF's efforts to achieve national self-determination. In their view, the pacifist approach heralded by the Swedish parliamentary left served the interests of Washington and Moscow – not the Vietnamese people.[57]

The pacifists, however, conversely accused the Maoists of revolutionary romanticism, disparaging the latter's unadulterated admiration of "Red China." The pacifists' opposition to the war was not originally rooted in an anti-imperialist outlook, but rather it was born out of the fear that tensions in South East Asia could endanger the détente. In a worst-case scenario, this localized proxy war might even provoke a global nuclear conflict. Most pacifists had strong ties to the parliamentary left, and hence they felt that it was vital that the traditional Swedish peace movement involve itself with the

Vietnam issue so that this cause would not be commandeered by the Maoists.[58]

To this end, peace activists affiliated with the SKP and SAP established the *Svenska Vietnamkommittén* (SVK, Swedish Vietnam Committee) in August 1965. A majority of its founders had previously been involved with the Swedish anti-nuclear movement *Kampanjen mot Atomvapen* (KMA, the Campaign against Nuclear Weapons).[59] The stated purpose of SVK was to support the government's new and more proactive stance against the war. First and foremost, the SVK called upon the Social Democratic administration to work for a peaceful resolution to the conflict, as well as to mitigate the suffering of the Vietnamese people by providing state-financed humanitarian aid.[60] The Committee's guiding principle was "Peace in Vietnam" – a slogan that some of its more militant members found hard to accept, and for this reason they soon also defected from the SVK.[61]

These two rivaling factions of the burgeoning Swedish anti-war movement definitively went in separate directions in September 1965 when the Maoists broke away from the pacifist-dominated SVK and set up their own organization, *Arbetsgruppen för stöd åt FNL* (the Working Group for Support to the NLF) – better known as "the NLF-groups." The membership of this new organization was mostly composed of young politically unaffiliated activists, with a handful of older radical Social Democrats and Communists sprinkled in. This split was the logical outcome of several years of simmering tensions between the Maoists and those peace activists who still remained loyal to the SKP and SAP. *Arbetsgruppen för stöd åt FNL* immediately cast the SVK's "Peace in Vietnam" slogan aside in favor of the more bellicose motto "US out of Vietnam!" It perhaps goes without saying that the NLF-groups were not overly impressed with Palme's Gävle speech, and from the outset they were harsh critics of the government's Vietnam policy.[62]

Arbetsgruppen för stöd åt FNL's clash with the Social Democratic administration – and with the parliamentary and pacifist-oriented branch of the anti-war movement – first came to public light in the early spring of 1966 in conjunction with the SVK's initiative to solicit humanitarian aid for the Vietnamese people. The collection drive, entitled *Nationalinsamlingen* (the National Collection for Vietnam), was backed by all five parliamentary parties, the trade unions, and leading representatives of the Swedish church and the business community. This scheme was a reaction to rising popular concern about the suffering that was being caused by the war, and it promoted an allegedly neutral approach to the Vietnamese conflict by promising an equal amount of assistance to the DRV, the NLF, and the Government of [South] Vietnam (GVN).[63]

From the NLF-groups' perspective, this tripartite allocation of funds was an act of treachery against the Vietnamese people because it failed to make a sufficient distinction between the conflict's "aggressors" and "victims." To the Maoists, any endeavor that would lend assistance to the Saigon regime was totally unacceptable, and accordingly they assailed *Nationalinsamlingen* as "a pacifist fraud." The NLF-groups additionally opposed this project on the grounds that it was a ploy by the political establishment to derail its own collection drive for the NLF. This latter collection (which had gotten underway in the early fall of 1965) did not place any stipulations on how the funds should be used, and so these monies could therefore also be utilized by the Communist insurgents to buy weapons.[64]

The NLF-groups' belligerent opposition to *Nationalinsamlingen* was subject to intense media scrutiny, and the dispute between the two branches of the anti-war movement was soon publicly vented in the editorial pages of *Aftonbladet*.[65] This situation presented the Communist leadership with a serious dilemma; on the one hand, the SKP wanted to appeal to militant anti-war opinion, but on the other hand the party had endorsed the pacifist position in order to shore up its new and more centrist image. While its support for *Nationalinsamlingen* might well have helped the SKP to bolster its moderate credentials, the downside was that it simultaneously opened the party up to heightened criticism from the Maoists.[66] The SKP tried to resolve this dilemma by starting its own separate collection for the NLF as an autonomous supplement to *Nationalinsamlingen*. This move, however, did little to improve the party's standing in Maoist-oriented anti-war circles, and in truth it only discredited the SKP even further in the eyes of the new revolutionary left.[67]

Nationalinsamlingen likewise created trouble for the Social Democratic establishment. The cabinet and the SAP hierarchy's official endorsement of this campaign was not welcomed by everyone in the party,[68] and the Social Democratic militants led by the SSSF were vehemently opposed to the national collection. *Sveriges Socialdemokratiska Studentförbund* (SSSF) openly sided with the Maoists and demanded that the SAP shift all of its financial support to the National Liberation Front.[69] Although *Sveriges Socialdemokratiska Ungdomsförbund* (SSU) was basically of the same opinion, it did not openly criticize the government's backing of *National-insamlingen* outright. However, the SSU implicitly disassociated itself from this effort by launching its own independent collection for the Vietnamese Communists.[70]

The Social Democratic Party and Anti-War Sentiment

This deepening fissure within the anti-war movement meant that Social Democratic activists had ended up on both sides of this divide, and by the spring of 1966 it became more and more evident that many younger party activists overtly sympathized with the Maoists' Vietnam agenda.[71] Members of both the SSU and SSSF were, for instance, regularly seen marching in the NLF-groups' demonstrations. This chain of events put the SAP leadership in an awkward position because these protests also routinely attacked the government's unwillingness to challenge the American war effort.[72]

In the spring and into the summer of 1966, young Social Democrats were a conspicuous presence in the general upsurge of anti-war activities, and in addition they did a lot to cultivate internal Social Democratic opposition to the war.[73] They did so, most notably, by turning the Vietnam issue into a major theme during the party's 1 May celebrations.[74] In many places, the 1 May demonstrations in 1966 took on a decidedly anti-American slant – especially in Stockholm where an American flag was set on fire.[75] This was the first time the Vietnamese conflict was centrally featured in the party's 1 May rallies, but it would not be the last.

The outburst of such protests on 1 May was the culmination of a progressive mobilization against the war that had taken place over the course of the winter of 1965–1966. In these months the Maoists had begun to establish a foothold outside of the capital, with new NFL-groups sprouting up in at least six other communities across the country.[76] The spread of the NFL-groups, in turn, gave birth to the first so-called "Vietnam Week." This would become a bi-annual event consisting of a weeklong series of anti-war teach-ins, photo exhibits, theater productions, etc., that were then always capped off with a big rally. The first one was held in the third week of March 1966, and it concluded with 26 separate anti-war demonstrations in 12 different locations – an estimated 1,600 protesters attended the one in Stockholm, making it, at that time, the largest anti-war rally in Swedish postwar history.[77]

Thereafter the anti-war movement continued to gain momentum as antipathy towards the American war effort slowly began to disseminate well beyond radical student groups into more moderate left-liberal political circles.[78] This broadening of the anti-war movement was concomitantly accompanied by increased Maoist attacks against the government, which the Maoists derided for not taking an even stronger public stand against the United States.[79]

The cabinet, however, was still reluctant to anger the Johnson administration, as was evidenced by its quick apology following the flag burning incident on 1 May.[80] In recognition of mounting popular opposition to the war, Social Democratic officials did certainly address the situation in South East Asia on several different occasions during the spring of 1966, but their remarks returned to their modest pre-Gävle form, that is, to mere expressions of hope that the conflict would soon find a peaceful resolution. In this period, Social Democratic spokesmen did admittedly call for a cessation of US bombings against North Vietnam and they also criticized the Saigon regime, but they stopped well short of directly attacking American policy.[81] According to Nilsson, this was mainly because the government did not want to risk dividing domestic anti-war opinion, though he also conceded that it did not wish to aggravate Swedish–American relations.[82]

The basic trouble with this timid approach was that it was more and more out of step with anti-war opinion both inside and outside of the party. For this reason, the SAP hierarchy was increasingly called upon to justify its cautious handling of this question.[83] More than anything else, the government's critics drew attention to its refusal to diplomatically recognize the DRV as well as to its support for *Nationalinsamlingen*.[84] This caused the Social Democratic press to come to the government's defense, proclaiming that the government had gone much further in its opposition to the war than any of its European counterparts.[85] While this was unquestionably a welcome source of moral support for the SAP leadership, it could not hide the fact that the party was starting to fall more and more behind on the Vietnam issue – and not just to the Maoists, but also to the Communists.

Leading up to the 1966 municipal elections, the SKP intensified its attacks against the American war effort. Communist leaders asserted that solidarity with their Vietnamese comrades was crucial to the party's new electoral profile.[86] SKP spokesmen specifically demanded greater financial assistance for the NLF/DRV and further assailed the Social Democratic administration's unwillingness to extend full diplomatic relations to North Vietnam.[87] The Communists even went so far as to advocate that Sweden should actively consider selling weapons to the National Liberation Front.[88]

In virtue of its role as the ruling party – the Social Democrats were required to show significantly more restraint in their foreign policy pronouncements, and consequently the party could not always match the radicalness of the Communists' proposals concerning the war. In spite of this disadvantage, the SAP still sought to showcase its own credentials on the Vietnam issue during the 1966 election campaign,[89] and heading into the election the party leadership apparently felt that it had done enough to distinguish itself on this question.[90]

In the campaign's final months, American officials privately remarked that the SAP hierarchy's ability to retain a moderate stance on Vietnam was being severely tested by rising internal agitation. In addition, they observed that the cabinet's situation was being made even more difficult as a result of the SKP's efforts to woo radical anti-war opinion. US diplomats predicted that the combination of these factors would continue to push the SAP leftward on the Vietnam issue. They also anticipated that, regardless of the 1966 election result, the negative political climate in Sweden toward American policy in South East Asia was unlikely to change.[91]

The American analysis of this situation was essentially correct, though at the same time it should be emphasized that the war did not play a major role in the election campaign itself, nor can this question be said to have influenced the election's final outcome. The 1966 municipal election was a huge disappointment for the Social Democrats. The party posted its worst electoral results since 1934, whereas both the non-socialist opposition and the Communists advanced. This setback was primarily caused by the government's ineffectual response to the housing shortage crisis, and the party's dismal electoral showing was mostly a consequence of its inability to mobilize its own voters – all too many of whom had stayed at home on election day.[92]

This, however, did not prevent the Communists from attributing a large part of their success to the party's militancy on the Vietnam issue. This was the second consecutive election that the SKP's share of the popular vote had risen, and the Communists themselves felt that they had found a winning formula to poach young voters away from the SAP.[93] Although the Social Democrats would in retrospect acknowledge that the SKP had benefited from its outspoken opposition to the American war effort,[94] in the immediate aftermath of the 1966 election the SAP leadership was more preoccupied with the party's own poor showing among first-time voters than with the SKP's gains.

Indeed, the SAP hierarchy's post-election analysis largely focused on the party's paltry support among the baby boomers. Various interpretations were offered to explain the SAP's weakened standing within this slice of the electorate, including the party's failure to respond to the youth's deepening engagement against the war. After some discussion, it was agreed that a new and more radical image was the best antidote to the party's flagging appeal among younger voters. The party leadership surmised that after three and half decades in power the SAP had – in the minds of the youth – become associated with the "establishment." Therefore, in order to bring the 68-generation into the Social Democratic camp, the party needed to return to its socialist roots and to encourage a rejuvenated ideological debate. A general radicalization of the party's profile was thus seen as critical to mobilizing both the party's cadre and voters in preparation for the next election. The party hierarchy determined that if it could not energize the party's own base, then the SAP was likely to suffer an even worse fate in 1968.[95]

A radicalization of the party's outward image would gradually become more and more visible in the aftermath of the 1966 election.[96] Directly following the election, a stronger anti-war posture had been proposed as one possible avenue to help the party to attract – or at least to hold on to its customary share of – the youth vote, though it was not until late 1967/early 1968 that the SAP leadership specifically identified a more radical stance on the war as a remedy for the party's dwindling support among first-time voters.[97] In the intervening period, the Social Democratic hierarchy would continue to fret about the youth's escalating radicalness.[98]

Due to the sheer demographic size of the baby boom generation, the youth vote was expected to have a substantial impact on the 1968 election because this was anticipated to be a very tight race. The SAP needed to retain its share of first-time voters if it hoped to stave off the challenge from the non-socialist opposition, which for the first time in many years was believed to have a reasonable chance of unseating the Social Democrats. Internal Social Democratic critics warned that if the party did not accommodate itself to the radical youth vote, then it was sure to lose in 1968. Although the SKP – and after 1967 the VPK – was not the SAP's principal rival going into this election, the Communists were nonetheless believed to be the SAP's main competitors for this particular segment of the electorate, and they were expected to make additional gains at the Social Democrats' expense.[99]

For their part, Communist leaders had good reason to feel confident about their future electoral prospects;[100] and in order to build on the party's momentum, they made sure to not ease up on their attacks against the American war effort in wake of the 1966 election.[101] Solidarity with the NLF/DRV was embraced as a mainstay in the SKP's revamped platform,[102] and the Vietnamese conflict was accordingly expected to figure heavily in the party's election strategy in 1968.[103]

This appeared to be a sound tactic given that Swedish public opposition to the war showed no signs of dissipating, and more to the point, domestic criticism of the government's Vietnam policy also seemed to be on the rise over the next several months.[104] Although Social Democratic officials defended themselves and lashed out against the far left,[105] policy-wise the cabinet more or less stood pat in relation to Vietnam.[106] The government's continued disinclination to upset the Americans was illuminated by Tage Erlander's reaction to the news that anti-war protesters had vandalized the American Embassy in January 1967. Erlander responded by stating: "I am embarrassed that such a thing could have happened, and I am sure that the whole Swedish nation is ashamed about this incident."[107]

Erlander's expression of contrition was subsequently mocked by the Social Democrats' Marxist adversaries. The latter argued that, if anything, it was the government that should be embarrassed about its failure to speak out more resolutely against the war.[108] The winter of 1966–1967 represented a crossroads in the anti-war activities of the far left, for henceforth its criticism would be principally directed against the Social Democratic establishment. Erlander and LO Chairman Arne Geijer were usually the targets of the worst attacks and were denounced as lackeys of American imperialism.[109]

Not unexpectedly, the Maoists were at the forefront of these attacks.[110] In general, the NLF-groups underwent a perceptible radicalization during this period, as was highlighted by their bombastic offer to send volunteers to fight side by side with the Viet Cong.[111] The Maoists turned their previous singular focus away from the war, and instead took aim against the domestic minions of American imperialism, which in their eyes were Swedish big capital and the Social Democratic administration.[112]

This heightened militancy coincided with a vast expansion of the NLF-groups. In contrast to *Svenska Vietnamkommittén* (SVK), which had never gained much traction politically (and whose project *Nationalinsamlingen* had faded into oblivion by late 1966),[113] the Maoists had continued to pick up steam in the winter of 1966–1967. In less than 12 months, the number of local NLF-chapters had more than doubled.[114] Equally importantly, the movement had also become more efficiently organized. In the early fall of 1966 all of the groups came together for the first time, and this laid the foundation for the establishment of *De förenade FNL-grupperna* (DFFG) a year later. The creation of the DFFG, in turn, brought all of the local NLF-chapters under a common charter and subjected them to a centralized leadership structure.[115] These changes considerably strengthened the political muscle of DFFG and spurred continued growth.[116] The conclusion of the NLF-movement's Vietnam Week in April 1967, for example, drew over 2,000 participants in Stockholm, thereby surpassing the previous attendance record that had been set only six months earlier. Many of these newcomers, moreover, were drawn from the country's cultural, media, and artistic elites, which only acted to raise the NLF-groups' visibility even further.[117]

The rapid ascendancy of the Maoist branch of the anti-war movement came at a time when popular opposition to the war was growing by leaps and bounds. A poll taken in March 1967 revealed that 83 per cent of the Swedish public thought that the Americans should withdraw from Vietnam.[118] By this time, dissent against the war had begun to make itself felt across the entire political spectrum, as was perhaps best illustrated by the state church's increasingly outspoken objections to US policy in Indochina.[119]

At this juncture, anti-war opinion had also spread to the trade unions. While scattered protests against the war had taken place on the local level as early as 1965,[120] officially the Social Democratically-affiliated trade unions led by LO had originally kept a low profile on the Vietnam issue to the point of declining to support *Nationalinsamlingen*.[121] As was noted in the previous chapter, the LO leadership was at first quite ambivalent about challenging Washington,[122] but the hierarchy had not been able to completely stamp out internal anti-war agitation, which had first emerged out into the open in conjunction with the Seventeenth LO Congress in September 1966.[123] In the long run, all efforts to discourage such activities proved to be of no avail because by early 1967 it was plain to see that antagonism toward the American war effort had managed to gain a strong foothold among the rank and file of the Swedish trade union movement.[124] (At this point some local union chapters were already petitioning the government to take a more resolute stand against the war.)[125] This shift had consequently come about against the LO hierarchy's wishes.[126]

That ill will towards US policy in Vietnam had now overtaken the entire Social Democratic movement was also confirmed by American officials in Stockholm. In an April interview in the *Washington Post*, the US Ambassador to Sweden J. Graham Parsons revealed that 90 per cent of the protest letters against the war that arrived at the Embassy came from either Social Democratic auxiliary organizations, local party chapters, or affiliated unions.[127] That this antipathy towards the war was no longer exclusively limited to more radical elements within the SAP was also revealed by the progressively negative treatment that American Vietnam policy received in the more centrist Social Democratic press, such as the Malmö daily *Arbetet* and the official party magazine *Aktuellt*.[128]

This transformation can largely be attributed to heightened internal agitation as Social Democratic anti-war activists continued to prod the SAP in an ever more radical direction on the Vietnam issue. These activists remained deeply critical of the government's timid opposition to US policy and ceaselessly called upon the cabinet to take an ever more resolute stance against the war.[129] Such criticism frequently echoed that of the far left, and the non-socialist press was quick to note that the Social Democratic administration's resolve was beginning to falter in the face of continuous internal pressure.[130]

Pressure on the Swedish Government:
The Bertrand Russell War Crimes Tribunal

That the government's ability to withstand such anti-war agitation had started to erode became quite apparent during the annual meeting of *Stockholms arbetarekommun* in mid-April 1967. At this gathering, Torsten Nilsson was excoriated and made to account for the government's cautious handling of this question;[131] and it was also in this setting that he announced the cabinet's decision to downgrade diplomatic relations with South Vietnam. Although this move did not formally break off relations with the Saigon regime, the decision to no longer accredit a Swedish Ambassador to the GVN effectively spelled the end to any official relations between Stockholm and Saigon.[132] This pronouncement was subsequently followed by a refusal to accredit a new South Vietnamese ambassador to Sweden.[133] (Internal Foreign Ministry documents make clear that the government had already previously discouraged the GVN from presenting a new envoy to Sweden because it feared that the acceptance of a South Vietnamese representative was sure to provoke a negative reaction from domestic anti-war activists.)[134]

The intent behind this announcement was unmistakably to counteract, and thereby neutralize, internal demands calling for the diplomatic recognition of North Vietnam (a subject to which we will return in Chapter 5).[135] Nilsson later denied that this initiative had been informed by domestic political calculations, but he did admit that it was a demonstrative act designed to underscore the government's disapproval of the GVN.[136] Nilsson's explanation was accepted at face value by the Social Democratic press, which commended the cabinet's decision.[137] Most other contemporary observers, however, reacted more skeptically to Nilsson's version of events.

This skepticism included some Swedish Foreign Ministry officials, to whom the party tactical aspects of this decision were patently obvious.[138] Nor did this measure's domestic origins escape the attention of the non-socialist press.[139] Needless to say, this dimension was also recognized by American diplomats, who regarded this as yet another example of "domestic foreign policy." Even though the latter understood the underlying logic of the government's decision, the Americans still did not like it. US officials, furthermore, predicted that giving in to such pressure would only lead to additional, and more far-reaching, demands in this area.[140] At the time, they were specifically concerned about a new campaign in favor of allowing the Bertrand Russell War Crimes Tribunal to convene in Sweden.[141]

The Bertrand Russell War Crimes Tribunal was supposedly an impartial international body set up to investigate American atrocities in Vietnam. It was named after the world-renowned British philosopher Bertrand Russell. The tribunal itself was a rather colorful affair, and its proceedings were led by international celebrities such as Jean-Paul Sartre and Stokely Carmichael. These "hearings" were originally supposed to convene in London in the fall of 1966, but when the British Labour government denied entry visas to the Vietnamese witnesses, Russell was forced to move the tribunal. He first tried to relocate it to Paris, but De Gaulle thwarted this. Only at this point did Russell become interested in Stockholm, requesting that the tribunal be permitted to use the city as a last-minute alternative.[142]

As early as December 1966, Erlander had privately pleaded with Russell to not bring the tribunal to Sweden on the grounds that hosting such an (anti-American) event would undermine the country's credibility as a future mediator in the Vietnamese conflict.[143] Over the next couple of months, Erlander and other government spokesmen repeatedly reiterated their opposition to holding these proceedings in Sweden.[144]

Erlander's negative response was instantly assailed by the far left, which lambasted the government's reluctance to welcome the tribunal, citing this as evidence of its complicit support for the American war effort.[145] In particular, VPK (formerly SKP) effectively capitalized on this issue, asserting its unconditional backing of the tribunal.[146] Prominent Communists, such as Sara Lidman and John Takman, would later also serve on the Swedish host committee.[147]

Some Social Democratic politicians likewise endorsed hosting the hearings.[148] In the months immediately leading up to the tribunal, internal left wing support for it had been building within the SAP, compelling the government to justify its opposition to Russell's initiative.[149] Lobbying in favor of the tribunal had been intense during the previously mentioned meeting of *Stockholms arbetarekommun* in mid-April, during which time the government's position on this issue had been berated by Social Democratic radicals.[150] In light of this escalating criticism, it came as no real surprise when at the end of April the government suddenly reversed course, permitting the tribunal to convene in Stockholm. That the cabinet's position on this matter was likely to soften had already been made clear a month earlier when Erlander had informed a group of university students that the government could not legally prohibit the tribunal from gathering in Sweden.[151]

On April 25, Erlander officially relented, declaring that although the cabinet was still against hosting the tribunal, it had no legal means of stopping it and consequently the government had little choice but to allow the hearings to proceed in Stockholm.[152] This explanation, however, is not very credible because Sweden presumably could have followed the British example and denied entry visas to many, if not all, of the tribunal's foreign participants. Owing to the political situation in Sweden at the time, however, this was not really much of an option for the cabinet. By all accounts, Social Democratic officials privately remained very ill at ease about hosting these proceedings,[153] and when asked about the tribunal they answered that their reservations against it continued to be based on fears of jeopardizing Sweden's future ability to act as a credible mediator in the Vietnamese conflict.[154] Yet this response was disingenuous as well. In spite of their protests to the contrary,[155] Social Democratic leaders mainly appear to have been worried about the Americans' reaction to the tribunal, which the Swedes quite correctly anticipated to be quite negative.[156]

As expected, the Johnson administration strongly disapproved of the Swedish decision because it was gravely concerned about the tribunal's potential propaganda value to the Vietnamese Communists. This subject was discussed in person between Erlander and Johnson in conjunction with Konrad Adenauer's funeral in Bonn at the end of April.[157] The Americans were not at all persuaded by the Social Democratic administration's claim that it could not legally block Russell's associates from assembling in Stockholm. Washington had, in fact, briefly considered implementing diplomatic sanctions against Sweden in protest against its hosting of these proceedings, but instead the Americans simply opted to ignore the Russell hearings altogether.[158]

With the notable exception of *Aftonbladet*,[159] most Swedish papers[160] (including most Social Democratic ones) originally rejected the tribunal as a Communist show trial.[161] While a few non-socialist papers defended the government's right to host these hearings, they were certainly not blind to the party tactical motives behind the cabinet's abrupt reversal on the tribunal issue. From their point view, it was obvious that this backpedaling had been caused by the SAP hierarchy's desire to appease internal party agitation in favor of the tribunal.[162]

American officials made a similar judgment, and they regarded the SAP leadership's sudden change of heart as evidence of the fact that it was trying to avert defections to the far left.[163] Yet by the same token, this interpretation simultaneously seems to have muted Washington's adverse reaction, for American officials were not entirely unsympathetic towards the Social Democratic administration's predicament. This is because they appreciated that Erlander's government was facing substantial pressure in relation to the tribunal, and for this reason it could not afford to appear to have caved in to American protests.[164]

That the cabinet had flip-flopped on this errand was equally apparent to Social Democratic champions of this decision, though they obviously did not object to this policy reversal.[165] Once the hearings finally got under way in Sweden, the Social Democratic cadre and press alike generally threw their support behind both the tribunal and the government's decision to allow it.[166] (Rather disingenuously, the party leadership would later credit the proceedings with having helped to educate the public about the Vietnamese conflict.)[167] Some Social Democratic radicals, however, had not forgotten the government's original opposition to the tribunal, griping that the cabinet had cowered in the face of American disapproval.[168]

These complaints mirrored those of the far left, which was not pacified by the cabinet's about-face on this matter. From the DFFG's perspective, this sudden turnaround only validated its overarching suspicions concerning Social Democratic opportunism in relation to Vietnam. During the late spring of 1967, the NLF-groups intensified their anti-government agitation, and this made itself felt during the Swedish labor movement's traditional 1 May celebrations. The SAP's 1 May rallies were disrupted in Stockholm, Gothenburg, and Malmö, as Social Democratic orators were repeatedly heckled by Maoist counter-demonstrators. In Stockholm, where the worst disturbances took place, the party had even invited a representative from the Russell War Crimes Tribunal to address the crowd, but this did little to silence the government's far left critics.[169]

Growing Party Militancy and the SAP Extra Congress

These events kept the Social Democratic establishment on the defensive,[170] and while a majority of the party faithful undoubtedly still stood behind the government, it was nevertheless clear that internal agitation in favor of a more assertive Vietnam stance was also continuing to mount.[171] Over the next several months and into the fall of 1967, the party's left wing kept up its crusade to nudge the government in an ever more radical direction in relation to the war.[172]

Such efforts were prompted by an upsurge of domestic anti-war protests, which the Communists still stood the best poised to take electoral advantage of. Throughout 1967 the Communists were very active on the Vietnam issue, both outside and inside of the parliament, and they presented several motions in support of the NLF/DRV.[173] As SKP transformed itself into VPK, the party redoubled its efforts to court radical opinion.[174] Among other things, it directly participated in some of the DFFG's anti-war activities.[175] The Communists' persistent militancy in this area caused Social Democratic anti-war activists to urge their own party to move forward its positions in relation to Vietnam, lest it lose the entire 68-generation to VPK.[176] Identical concerns also existed with regard to the Maoists.[177]

The Maoists' ranks had exploded over the past year, and by the late fall of 1967 the number of NLF-chapters had once again jumped more than two fold, now reaching approximately 50 groups. In this same time span, the bi-annual Vietnam Week had nearly tripled in size, and in October 1967 it drew an estimated 12,000 participants in over 35 different locations.[178]

This was the political climate leading up to the SAP Extra Congress that opened in late October 1967, which coincided with the finale of the DFFG-sponsored Vietnam Week.[179] The overlap between these two events made certain that anti-war sentiments were running high as the Congress opened,[180] and on its second day representatives from the SSU, SSSF, SKSF, SSKF, and Verdandi (the Social Democratic Temperance organization) held their own separate anti-war rally to rival the one hosted by the Maoists.[181] This en-sured that the Vietnam issue would be prominently featured during the Congress. The Extra Congress was originally supposed to focus mainly on economic matters, but the immediate events surrounding its opening dictated that Vietnam receive a much higher billing than had at first been planned.[182]

Although a tougher Social Democratic posture against the American war effort was already discernable in Erlander's opening address to the Congress,[183] it was not until Torsten Nilsson's foreign policy speech that it became fully transparent that the party leadership had finally settled on a more militant approach to the Vietnam question.[184] Most strikingly, it formally endorsed the political platform of the NLF. The Congress subsequently adopted a resolution expressing solidarity with the Vietnamese peoples' struggle for national emancipation and social justice. This resolution additionally demanded that all "foreign" (read American) troops to be withdrawn from Vietnam and that the National Liberation Front be recognized as an independent and equal partner in the peace talks. Lastly, the Congress decided that the party would officially take over the SSU's solidarity fund for the NLF and that the SAP should vastly expand its contacts with the Vietnamese Communists as well as provide the latter with greater amounts of humanitarian assistance.[185]

The party's endorsement of the National Liberation Front now de facto became official government policy as well because after this the distinction between the two began to blur more and more.[186] Privately, Social Democratic officials had few illusions about the totalitarian nature of Communist rule in Vietnam,[187] but this did not prevent them from consistently assuming a pro-NLF/DRV position hereafter.[188] This discrepancy points to the cynicism that occasionally informed the SAP leadership's approach to the Vietnamese conflict.

When pressed to provide a frank evaluation of the Vietnamese Communists, Social Democratic leaders carefully added the proviso that they did not necessarily approve of the kind of system that the former sought to impose – though they at the same time claimed to be absolutely confident that the NLF and the DRV (as opposed to the Saigon regime) represented the true will of the Vietnamese people.[189] Such disclaimers aside, this does not change the reality that the Social Democratic administration's actions greatly assisted the Communists' propaganda efforts in Europe.[190]

Representatives of the NLF and the DRV were, for example, over and over again invited by the Swedish Social Democrats to speak at their official functions. From 1967 on, the government also lent considerable economic and political assistance to the NLF/DRV – and all of this was greatly appreciated by the Vietnamese Communists.[191]

In fact, no other Western country offered as much assistance to the Vietnamese Communist cause as Sweden did.[192] On occasion, Swedish Democratic leaders admitted as much (even boasting about their unparalleled support to the NLF/DRV),[193] though at other times they denied that their approach to the Vietnamese conflict fundamentally differed from that of other European and American critics of the war.[194] What narrative was selected simply depended upon what audience was being addressed at the time; and during the later half of 1967 it appears that the SAP hierarchy prioritized appeasing domestic anti-war opinion above all else. This also accounts for the party's newfound militancy on the Vietnam issue.

In retrospect, the Extra Congress has been regarded as a decisive turning point in Social Democratic Vietnam policy, and thereafter it would continue to drift in a progressively NLF/DRV-friendly direction.[195] At the time, this radicalization did not go undetected by outside observers,[196] with the non-socialist press generally interpreting this as an attempt by Social Democratic leaders to placate internal agitation.[197] In the latter's eyes, it was one thing to oppose the American war effort, but it was quite another to champion the Vietnamese Communist cause.[198] This change was likewise noted in Washington, and the State Department predicted that the Social Democrats' new course in relation to the war was bound to last up through end of the 1968 election campaign.[199]

Interestingly, the second largest Social Democratic paper, *Arbetet* (which was commonly considered to be the party's unofficial voice) came to an analogous conclusion, anticipating that a resolute anti-war stance would be an enormous electoral asset for the party in 1968.[200] *Aftonbladet* was equally pleased by the Congress' declaration of solidarity with the Vietnamese Communists,[201] as was the rest of the party's left wing,[202] which had long urged the government to throw its full backing behind the NLF.[203] This was, therefore, a significant victory for Social Democratic anti-war activists.[204]

This new course on Vietnam seems to have had the desired effect, as it energized the party faithful heading into the next election, which was also the Congress' primary purpose to begin with. A firmer stand against US policy, moreover, helped to unify the SAP by bringing the party platform in line with the growing anti-war sentiments of its cadre. This shift further indicated that the party hierarchy had at last begun to identify the Vietnam issue as a central component in its upcoming election strategy. Perhaps most importantly, it denoted that the party leadership was no longer just reacting to radical anti-war agitation, but that it was now actively seeking to seize the initiative on this issue.[205]

Prior to this point, the Social Democratic administration's ability to aggressively oppose American policy had purportedly been hamstrung by its clandestine attempt to mediate an end to the Vietnamese conflict. This effort had necessitated a low-key approach to the current situation in Indochina because an overly critical stance against the US would have hurt Sweden's credibility as an impartial negotiator.[206] This is at least what the

Social Democrats themselves said, though one might surmise that this explanation was mostly a way to justify the government's initial timidity vis-à-vis Washington. The Swedish mediation attempt, which the Americans codenamed ASPEN, was launched in early 1966 and theoretically it remained in play all the way up until March 1968.[207]

Officially the Swedes never characterized ASPEN as a mediation attempt, but only as "an endeavor to facilitate contacts between Hanoi and Washington." Even though its apologists concede that ASPEN did not produce any tangible results, they have nevertheless continued to defend this as a worthy undertaking.[208]

In contrast, many former Swedish diplomats who were personally familiar with this effort have since given it a failing grade.[209] Even those who are willing to give the Social Democratic administration the benefit of the doubt see ASPEN as misdirected and essentially doomed to fail.[210] Its detractors highlight the fundamental contradiction in Swedish policy, pointing out that the government's covert mediation attempt was ultimately irreconcilable with its public attacks against the American war effort.[211] That such criticism undermined the credibility of Sweden's mediator role is obvious even to apologists of the government's Vietnam policy such as Yngve Möller, the former Swedish Ambassador-Designate to the United States.[212]

Some Swedish diplomats, like Lennart Petri, have offered an even less generous interpretation of ASPEN, dismissing it basically as a sham chiefly born out of Social Democratic party tactical considerations.[213] Between 1963 and 1964, Petri had on several occasions approached the cabinet with proposals for Sweden to spearhead a peaceful end to the Vietnamese conflict, but the government had not shown much interest. As late as February 1965, Torsten Nilsson and Olof Palme had rebuffed a renewed mediation scheme by Petri, saying that it was inappropriate for Sweden as a small neutral country to insert itself into an international dispute that did not directly affect its own interests. It was not until the summer of 1965 – in reaction to escalating anti-war protests at home – that the government at last had begun to exhibit any real curiosity about Petri's ideas, soon ordering him to establish direct contact with the North Vietnamese. By March 1966, however, Petri felt that any mediation attempt was bound to fail because the window of opportunity for Sweden to act had already closed. At this stage, neither Washington nor Hanoi was still genuinely committed to negotiations, and both sides now mainly hoped to make additional gains on the battlefield. That the Social Democratic administration wanted to go forward with this initiative, in spite of the necessary prerequisites for success, underscored to Petri that the cabinet's handling of this errand was being driven by domestic political calculations and not by a sincere desire to achieve any concrete results.[214] Åke Sjölin, who that time was the Swedish Ambassador to Thailand, additionally calls attention to the fact that if the government had truly wanted to promote a peaceful settlement, then it would have directed Swedish diplomats to approach the Saigon regime as well, which it did not.[215]

The suspicion that the Social Democratic administration was acting in bad faith was certainly also shared by Washington. Despite Torsten Nilsson's claims to the contrary,[216] the Americans never showed any genuine enthusiasm about ASPEN, mostly because they deemed that it was principally rooted in Social Democratic party tactical considerations. Similarly to the mediation attempts made by many other European governments, the Johnson administration believed that the Swedish one was born out of a need to satisfy domestic opinion, noting that a Nobel Peace Prize would be a highly desirable political prize for anyone who managed to capture it. As for the specifics surrounding ASPEN, Washington apparently never had much confidence in this undertaking, but because the White House – for public relations reasons – could not openly reject any peace proposal it was politely forced to play along with this charade. In the end, the Americans actually held the Swedish endeavor in lower esteem than most comparable efforts.[217]

In hindsight, it is of course difficult to evaluate the sincerity of the Social Democrats' intentions, but at a minimum it is obvious that ASPEN was in no small part a response to domestic pressure for the cabinet to take some tangible action to promote a peaceful resolution to the conflict. Demands to this effect had first been raised in the early spring of 1965, and they had only grown louder thereafter.[218] Once ASPEN finally came to light publicly, the government's labors were rewarded with high praise in the Social Democratic press,[219] especially in *Aftonbladet*, which incidentally was also the first paper to break this story in late March 1968.[220]

News of the government's secret mediation effort had been leaked to the *Aftonbladet* in the aftermath of Olof Palme's participation in an anti-war rally in Stockholm on 21 February 1968 (a subject to which we will return in the next chapter.) Palme's presence at the rally had spelled the definitive death knell for ASPEN because at this point even the North Vietnamese recognized that the United States would no longer have any confidence in Sweden's ability to serve as an impartial mediator. As far as the Americans were concerned, Sweden's credibility had in all likelihood been destroyed at a much earlier date – at the very latest in conjunction with Erlander and Nilsson's attacks against US policy during the SAP Extra Congress.[221]

Nilsson denied any knowledge of the leak,[222] but in view of the fact that this story turned up in *Aftonbladet* it does not seem very far-fetched that the paper had been fed this information by someone with close proximity to the SAP hierarchy. The timing of this leak is highly noteworthy given that it happened right on the heels of ASPEN's disintegration. To American officials, the timing of this revelation was too convenient to be a coincidence, and it was transparent that the Social Democrats were now trying to milk ASPEN for all that it was worth.[223]

It is hard to disagree with this assessment because even before ASPEN's existence had been officially confirmed, Social Democratic leaders had continually intimated that the government was interested in serving in some kind of mediating function,[224] and once this scheme was revealed the SAP hierarchy made the most of this disclosure.[225] Nilsson, for one, gloated that this effort proved that the country's neutrality did not require it to remain passive in world affairs,[226] which was a veiled jab against the non-socialist opposition. In the following few months, Social Democratic spokesmen touted ASPEN's virtues on the campaign trail.[227] Its meager results, however, were obscured by the alleged need for continued secrecy. Hence the public was only informed that the government had clandestinely been working to bring about a peaceful solution to the Vietnamese conflict, but it was not provided with enough specifics to be able to objectively assess the project's merits (or more precisely the lack thereof).[228]

Regardless of the SAP hierarchy's initial motives, by late 1967 and early 1968 ASPEN was worth more dead than alive to the Social Democrats. After its final demise, this initiative continued to provide the party with substantial public relations benefits. Heading in to the 1968 election, it was cited as proof of the Social Democrats' long-standing concern about the situation in Indochina.[229] In all fairness, it should be added that the Social Democratic administration's conduct was by no means unique, for virtually all West European attempts to mediate the conflict were also driven by domestic politics. Over and over again this specific tactic was used to silence public dissent against the war.[230]

Originally the prospect of Sweden playing a mediating role had been employed mainly as an alibi for why the government could not take a more aggressive stance against the United States. Although this pretext that did not always persuade its detractors,[231] the cabinet had frequently relied on this justification to explain its handling of this issue.[232] In the short term, this had been a rather effective strategy because it had somewhat placated anti-war agitation within the party without seriously straining Swedish–American relations. Moreover, it had bought the Social Democratic establishment some valuable time. By the spring of 1967, however, this argument was beginning to lose all plausibility, and it was therefore less and less capable of pacifying internal unrest. By the time of the Extra Party Congress in October, a timid approach to the Vietnam issue – one that was realistically required to play a credible mediating role – had become an albatross around the SAP hierarchy's neck and hence it was cast aside in favor of a more radical approach to the war. In sum, ASPEN was never really a failure, but at a certain point it had outlived its political value to the SAP. Consequently, from the very start this undertaking had presented the government with a win-win situation. If this effort succeeded it would pay great dividends both domestically and internationally, and even if it failed the mere attempt to mediate was good politics because this was at least bound to satisfy many Social Democratic opponents of the war.

From this point on, Social Democratic criticism of the US steadily escalated. While this unquestionably pleased the party faithful, it was still insufficient to appease the revolutionary left. The latter recognized that the SAP had moved forward its position on the war, yet from the Maoists' point of view the Social Democratic administration had not gone nearly far enough.[233] In the fall of 1967, the DFFG's attitude toward the government had continued to harden, and it now considered itself to be essentially at war with the Swedish state. At this juncture, the NLF-groups explicitly invited conflict in hopes that it would induce a "revolutionary situation" in Sweden.[234]

Outwardly this meant that militant anti-war activities accelerated – a trend that at the time was discernable elsewhere in Europe as well.[235] In Sweden this tendency was illustrated by the events of 20 December 1967 when Maoist demonstrators fought with police outside the US Trade Center in downtown Stockholm. This clash was sparked by the marchers' attempt to reach the American Embassy. The authorities had denied permission for this particular demonstration route, and violence broke out when NLF activists defied this prohibition and the police tried to stop them. After the demonstration, spokesmen for the demonstrators complained of police brutality, and ominously warned that the next time they would not come unarmed.[236]

In the days immediately following the December 20th showdown outside the US Trade Center, the Maoists accused the government of using force to silence them, which to them proved that the Social Democratic establishment was indeed running the errands of American imperialism.[237] The protesters' case was at once championed by the Communists, who called for an investigation of the police's heavy-handed conduct.[238] Government representatives, in turn, rejected these allegations, condemning the demonstrators' acts of violence.[239]

The melee outside the US Trade Center was almost immediately followed by an attack on Philippe Trezise, the American Ambassador to the OCED, who was pelted with eggs and snowballs by NLF activists on 4 January. (Trezise was in Stockholm for the day to discuss Swedish backing of the dollar, which he received.) The Swedish government, for its part, at once issued a formal apology to Washington and further castigated the protesters' actions.[240]

This pattern of behavior among the NLF-groups was also roundly condemned in the Swedish press,[241] including *Aftonbladet*, which previously had portrayed the NLF-groups in a mostly positive light.[242] The rest of the Social Democratic press was equally keen to defend the party leadership and government against the Maoist threat.[243]

Emboldened by the press' negative reaction to these incidents, the SAP hierarchy forcefully moved against the NLF-groups in the aftermath of Trezise incident. Its main line of attack was to try to discredit the DFFG by characterizing the latter's tactics as profoundly undemocratic and counterproductive.[244] This effort was buttressed by the party press, which unleashed its own campaign against the Maoists.[245] Over the next couple of months, the party kept up the counter-offensive,[246] and this tougher stance against the Maoists appeared to have been heartedly welcomed within the Social Democratic camp.[247]

* * *

The SAP leadership was deeply concerned about losing the youth to the far left,[248] and therefore all precautionary measures were taken. On occasion this did not rule out engaging in unconstitutional activities, most notably the use of agent provocateurs. The Maoist threat was met by expanding both IB and SÄPO's clandestine surveillance of the far left to also encompass the DFFG. This campaign – of which only a select few Social Democratic leaders were kept closely informed – had first gotten underway in the spring of 1966, but it was vastly intensified in the fall of 1967 in response to the NLF-groups' escalating radicalism. During the next couple of years, IB and SÄPO alike focused their attention on the DFFG, which at the time was regarded as the principal threat to the nation's security.[249] The Maoists were aware that they were being monitored,[250] but they would not know the full scope of the security apparatus' operations against them until the war was over.[251]

The Social Democrats' desire to ensure that public anti-war sentiment was not monopolized by the far left could not rely solely on covert action, rather the Communist/Maoist challenge also had be countered by overt political means. By late 1967 and early 1968, after having lagged behind for several years, the Social Democratic establishment was thus now fully committed to preventing their Marxist adversaries from capitalizing upon the Vietnam issue.[252] At this point, it was clear that the SAP had little choice but to drastically overhaul its approach to the war, for it could no longer afford to passively wait for this issue to magically disappear. One of its top priorities was to establish a viable alternative to the Maoist anti-war movement because public antipathy towards the war had to be channeled back into the Social Democratic fold. Specifically, it was imperative for the SAP to keep up with its Marxist competitors if it hoped to both preserve internal party harmony and to gain the allegiance of a new generation of voters.

Chapter 2: Notes

[1] Erik Tängerstad, "Att organisera ett engagemang" (University of Stockholm, 1988) 19, 30.

[2] Erik Svanfeldt, "Svenska kommittén för Vietnam" (Uppsala University, 1990) 11; Marilyn Young, *The Vietnam Wars 1945-1990* (New York: Harper Collins, 1991) 194-202.

[3] Kjell Östberg, *1968* (Stockholm: Prisma, 2002) 66-67, 99-103.

[4] Carole Fink, *et al.*, "Introduction" in Carole Fink, *et al.* (eds.), *1968: The World Transformed* (New York: Cambridge University Press, 1998) 17-27.

[5] Sven Olof Josefsson, *Året var 1968* (Dissertation. University of Göteborg, 1996) 234-258; 278-280; Janerik Gidlund, *Aktionsgrupper och lokala partier* (Lund: C. W. Gleerup, 1978) 56-61.

[6] Tängerstad, "Att organisera ett engagemang," 7-8.

[7] Christopher Sundgren, "Splittrad Solidaritet" in Maj-Lis Erikson, *et al.* (eds.), *Med eller mot strömmen?* (Stockholm: Sober, 1980) 138-142.

[8] Lars Åke Augustsson and Stig Hansén, *De svenska maoisterna* (Göteborg, Lindelöws, 2001) 22-23; Tängerstad, "Att organisera ett engagemang," 27-35, 59-60.

[9] Kim Salomon, *Rebeller i takt med tiden* (Stockholm: Rabén Prisma, 1996) 95; Tommy Hammarström, *FNL i Sverige* (Stockholm: AB Solidaritet, 1975) 8-16. See also NLF-spokesman, Sköld Peter Matthis, as cited in Micke Leijnegard, *Var blev ni av ljuva drömmar. 68:orna* (Stockholm: Norstedt, 2013) 20-22.

[10] Eva Block, *Amerikabilden i svensk dagspress 1964-1968* (Lund: Gleerup, 1976) 89. For specific examples, see *Stockholms-Tidningen* 16 June 1965 and *Aftonbladet* 17 June 1965.

[11] See, for example, *Dagens Nyheter* 21 July 1965 and 29 Jan. 1966.

[12] Eva Queckfeldt, *"Vietnam"* (Lund: Glenstrup, 1981) 29. For a complete overview of this debate, see *Verdandi debatt. Vietnam i svensk pressdebatt sommaren 1965* (Stockholm: Prisma, 1965).

[13] Editorials in *Stockholms-Tidningen* 13 June 1965 and 27 June 1965. Lars Forsell and Folke Isaksson gave voice to similar opinions in their op-eds in *Dagens Nyheter* on 1 June 1965 and 10 June 1965.

[14] A petition signed by 90 well-known intellectuals, for example, called upon the Social Democratic administration to speak out resolutely against US policy in Vietnam. *Norrskensflamman* 22 June 1965.

[15] *Dagens Nyheter* 30 March 1965; *Stockholms-Tidningen* 16 June 1965; *Aftonbladet* 17 June 1965. See also *Libertas* # 2 1965, 32. and *Libertas* # 3 1965, 3-4.

[16] Yngve Möller, *Sverige och Vietnamkriget* (Stockholm: Tiden, 1992) 37. For a specific illustration, see *Frihet* # 6-7 1965, 5. Social Democratic dissent against the war was, for example, in evidence during the party's 1 May celebrations in Stockholm. In response to building internal opposition to US policy, *Stockholms arbetarekommun* passed its first resolution against the war on June 18 1965. *Stockholms arbetarekommun Verksamhetsberättelse 1965*, 5-9, 28.

[17] For a specific example, see *Tiden* # 4 1965, 249–253. See also Birgitta Dahl, "Solidaritetsarbetet för Vietnam" in Enn Kokk (ed.), *Var blev ni av ljuva drömmar?* (Stockholm: Ordfront, 2002) 176–177.

[18] Tängerstad, "Att organisera ett engagemang," 19–20. See, for example, Demokratisk Ungdom, *Dagens Ungdom- politisk ungdomsrevy* # 3 1965, 6.

[19] Communist leader C-H Hermansson as cited in *Riksdagsprotokollet* # 13, 24 March 1965, 68–69.

[20] For a specific example, see John Takman, *Vietnam – ockupanterna och folket* (Malmö: Bo Cavefors, 1965).

[21] See, for example, *Norrskensflamman* 16 June 1965 and *Ny Dag* 25 June 1965.

[22] C-H Hermansson cited in *Norrskensflamman* 9 July 1965.

[23] *Tiden* # 6 1965, 321–324.

[24] For a specific illustration, see Östen Undén's op-ed in *Stockholms-Tidningen* 9 July 1965.

[25] Palme as cited in UD, *Utrikesfrågor 1965* (Stockholm: UD, 1965) 42–47.

[26] See, for example, Fredrik Logevall, "The Swedish–American Conflict over Vietnam" *Diplomatic History* 1993 17 (3): 427: and Ann-Sofie Nilsson, *Den moraliska stormakten* (Stockholm: Timbro, 1991) 61.

[27] See, for example, Torsten Nilsson as cited in UD, *Utrikesfrågor 1964* (Stockholm: UD, 1964) 40; and Torsten Nilsson as cited in UD, *Utrikesfrågor 1965*, 40.

[28] Torsten Nilsson, *Åter Vietnam* (Stockholm: Tiden, 1981) 46–47.

[29] 26 Feb. 1965. US Ambassador to Sweden 1961–1967. J. Graham Parsons. Telegram to State. Subject Numeric Files 1964–1966. Political and Defense. Sweden. RG 59; 26 March 1965. J. Graham Parsons. Telegram to State. Subject Numeric Files 1964–1966. Political and Defense. Sweden. RG 59.

[30] Kaj Björk, *Vägen till Indokina* (Stockholm: Atlas, 2003) 114. For a comparison between Palme, Nilsson, and Erlander's respective comments, see *Utrikesfrågor 1965*, 42–53.

[31] For a specific example, see Gösta Bohman, Sven Wedén, Bertil Ohlin, Torsten Nilsson and Olof Palme as cited in *Rikdagsprotokollet* # 33, 2 Nov. 1965, 69–81. See also editorials in *Svenska Dagbladet* 19 Aug. 1965, *Östgöta Correspondenten* 20 Aug. 1965 and *Göteborgs handels- och sjöfartstidning* 25 Aug. 1965.

[32] Tage Erlander, *60-talet* (Stockholm: Tiden, 1982) 203–204; Nilsson. *Åter Vietnam*, 48.

[33] Torsten Nilsson as cited in UD, *Utrikesfrågor 1965*, 47–52. See also *Tiden* # 5 1965, 385–388.

[34] Undén radio interview on 30 July 1965 as cited in *Svenska Dagbladet* 2 Aug. 1965. Just a few days prior to Palme's Gävle speech, another Social Democrat, Hjalmar Mehr, had similarly called upon the government to take a more vocal stance on the war. Mehr as cited in *Aftonbladet* 29 July 1965.

[35] 18 June 1965. *Chargé d'affairs* ad interim US Embassy. Alfred S. Jenkins. Telegram to State. Subject Numeric Files 1964–1966. Political and Defense. Sweden. RG 59; 24 June 1965. J. Graham Parsons. Telegram to State. Subject Numeric Files 1964–1966. Political and Defense. Sweden. RG 59.

[36] 24 June 1965. J. Graham Parsons. Telegram to State. Subject Numeric Files 1964–1966. Political and Defense. Sweden. RG 59; 30 July 1965. J. Graham Parsons. Telegram to State. Subject Numeric Files 1964–1966. Political and Defense. Sweden. RG 59.

[37] 4 Aug 1965. Political Division FM. Axel Lewenhaupt. Telegram to Swedish Embassy Washington. Avd HP. Grupp 1. Mål Ua. Politik Allmänt. USA. # 210.

[38] 6 Aug. 1965. J. Graham Parsons. Telegram to State. Re: Undated conversation with Axel Lewenhaupt. Subject Numeric Files 1964–1966. Political and Defense. Sweden. RG 59; 13 Aug. 1965. J. Graham Parsons. Telegram to State. Re: Conversation with Richard Hitchens-Bergström, Head of Political Division Swedish Foreign Ministry on 11 Aug. 1965. Subject Numeric Files 1964–1966. Political and Defense. Sweden. RG 59.

[39] Lennart Petri, *Sverige i stora världen* (Stockholm: Atlantis, 1996) 398.

[40] 7 Sept. 1965. Counselor for Political Affairs US Embassy Stockholm. Jerome Holloway. Telegram to State. Subject Numeric Files 1964–1966. Political and Defense. Sweden. RG 59; 17 Sept. 1965. *Chargé d'affairs ad interim* US Embassy Stockholm. Turner Cameron Jr. Telegram to State. Subject Numeric Files 1964–1966. Political and Defense. Sweden. RG 59.

[41] 25 April 1967. J. Graham Parsons. Memo. Reflections on Swedish–American relations 1961–1967. Central Foreign Policy File 1967–1969. Political and Defense. Sweden. RG 59.

[42] For specific illustrations, see Liberal leader Bertil Ohlin cited in *Dagens Nyheter* 13 Aug. 1965 and Sven Wedén's op-ed in *Sydsvenska Dagbladet* 2 Oct 1965. See also Conservative representative Gösta Bohman as cited in *Riksdagsprotokollet* # 33, 2 Nov. 1965, 20–21, 72–73, 76.

[43] For specific examples, see editorials in *Expressen* 5 Aug 1965, *Örnsköldviks Allehanda* 19 Aug. 1965, *Kvällsposten* 24 Aug. 1965 and *Gotlands Allehanda* 30 Aug. 1965.

[44] The only real exception was Kaj Björk's op-ed in *Aftonbladet* 12 Aug. 1965, which implied that Palme's speech had been too biased against the United States.

[45] See, for example, Torsten Nilsson and Tage Erlander as cited in UD, *Utrikesfrågor* 1965, 47–53. See also *Aktuellt* # 11 1965, 8–9.

[46] See, for instance, editorials in *Arbetet* 13 Aug. 1965, *Dala-Demokraten* 19 Aug. 1965 and *Norrländska Socialdemokraten* 28 Aug. 1965.

[47] Gun Rehnberg, "Efter Gävle och Sergels torg" in Lars Svedgård, *Palme* (Stockholm: Rabén & Sjögren, 1970) 132–133. For specific examples, see editorials in *Aftonbladet* 31 July 1965 and *Stockholms-Tidningen* 31 July 1965.

[48] For specific illustration, see Sven Lindqvist's op-ed in *Dagens Nyheter* 10 Aug. 1965.

[49] See, for instance, Ulla Lindström, *Och regeringen satt kvar* (Stockholm: Bonnier, 1970) 264. See also *Libertas* # 4 1965. 3–4.

[50] For specific illustration, see SKSF Chairman Evert Svensson's op-ed in *Aftonbladet* 14 Nov. 1965.

[51] For specific examples, see "Stuvre" by-line in *Stockholms-Tidningen* 1 Aug. 1965 and *Tiden* # 7 1965, 385–388. Among left-leaning Social Democrats, Palme's Gävle speech would in retrospect be regarded as a crucial turning point in the SAP's approach to the Vietnam issue, and it was seen as the first step in bringing government policy into line

with the public's growing opposition to the war. See *Tiden* # 2 1966, 79–85. and *Libertas* # 2 1968, 2.

[52] See, for example, Social Democratic representative Ingemund Bengtsson as cited in *Riksdagsprotokollet* # 40, 9 Dec. 1965, 47–48. See also Dahl, "Solidaritetsarbetet för Vietnam," 177. and Enn Kokk, "Laboremus 1902–1987" in Tuula Eriksson, *et al.* (eds.), *Framtidens utmaningar* (Uppsala, Laboremus, 1987) 31.

[53] See, for instance, Gösta Bohman, Sven Wedén, and Bertil Ohlin as cited in *Riksdagsprotokollet* # 33, 2 Nov. 1965, 20–21, 72–76, 78.

[54] For specific illustrations, see John Takman and Kjell E. Johansson's op-ed in *Ny Dag* 24 Sept. 1965 and C-H Hermansson as cited in *Riksdagsprotokollet* # 33, 2 Nov. 1965, 58–62.

[55] For specific illustration, see CH Hermansson's op-ed in *Norrskensflamman* 6 Aug. 1965. See also C-H Hermansson, *För Socialismen* (Stockholm: Arbetarkultur, 1974) 69–84.

[56] Sören Wibbe, "Från pacifism till marxism-leninism" in Jan Engberg, *et al.* (eds.), *Utanför systemet* (Stockholm: Rabén & Sjögren, 1978) 41.

[57] Tängerstad, "Att organisera ett engagemang," 42–45.

[58] Svanfeldt, "Svenska Kommittén för Vietnam," 13; Sundgren, "Splittrad solidaritet," 140–145.

[59] Östberg, *1968*, 94.

[60] *Ny Dag* 8 Oct. 1965.

[61] Bengt Liljenroth, "Vietnamrörelsen i Sverige" in Lars Torbiörnsson (ed.), *Tålamodets triumf* (Stockholm: Prisma, 1973) 233.

[62] Salomon, *Rebeller i takt med tiden*, 97–98, 169–170; Sundgren, "Splittrad solidaritet," 140–145.

[63] *Dagens Nyheter* 25 Feb. 1966.

[64] Henry Bäck, *Den utrikespolitiska dagsordningen* (Stockholm: Gotab, 1979) 37–38; Tängerstad, "Att organisera ett engagemang," 35–37. See also *Clarté* # 4 1966, 27.

[65] See exchange between NLF-spokesman Evert Kumm and SVK Chairman Bertil Svanström as cited in *Aftonbladet* 25 March 1966, 29 March 1966, and 4 April 1966.

[66] Wibbe, "Från pacifism till marxism-leninism," 41.

[67] Tängerstad, "Att organisera ett engagemang," 35–37.

[68] See, for example, Olof Palme, *Politik är att vilja* (Stockholm: Prisma, 1968) 184–194.

[69] 17 April 1966. SSSF Förbundsmedelande. SSSF. B:2 "Handlingsprogram med förslag och uttalanden." 1964–1967.

[70] SSU, *Ungdomsinsamlingen* (Stockholm: SAP, 1966).

[71] Liljenroth, "Vietnamrörelesen i Sverige," 234–237.

[72] Tängerstad, "Att organisera ett engagemang," 39. See also Hans Sjöström, *Klassens ljus* (Stockholm: Norstedt, 1988) 34–35.

[73] Dahl, "Solidaritetsarbetet för Vietnam," 178. For a specific example, see *Skövde Nyheter* 10 Aug. 1966.

[74] Bäck, *Den utrikespolitiska dagsordningen*, 37–38.

[75] *Aftonbladet* 2 May 1966; *Ny Dag* 6 May 1966. See also *Stockholms arbetarekommun Verksamhetsberättelse* 1966, 4–7.

[76] Åke Kilander, *Vietnam var nära* (Stockholm: Leopard, 2007) 75–79; Hammarström, *FNL i Sverige*, 8–9.

[77] Salomon, *Rebeller i takt med tiden*, 203. See also *Aftonbladet* 27 March 1966.

[78] US Embassy officials in Stockholm closely traced the rise in Swedish anti-war opinion. By the late spring of 1966 the Embassy was already being inundated by anti-war petitions sent from a whole host of different Swedish sources, ranging from local SSU and SKP groups to individual priests and cultural workers. WHCF. Country File. Sweden. Box 68. L.B.J. Library. See also the article about anti-war agitation among cultural workers in *Dagens Nyheter* on 16 May 1966.

[79] *Ny Dag* 13 May 1966.

[80] *Dagens Nyheter* 2 May 1966.

[81] See, for example, Torsten Nilsson and Tage Erlander as cited in UD, *Sverige och Vietnamfrågan* (Stockholm: UD, 1968) 21–27.

[82] Nilsson as cited in *Stockholms arbetarekommun. Årsmötesprotokoll.* 24 April 1966, 1–4.

[83] Björk, *Vägen till Indokina*, 131–132.

[84] Tängerstad, "Att organisera ett engagemang," 39. For a specific examples, see Folke Isaksson's op-ed in *Dagens Nyheter* 17 April 1966 and Allan Björk's op-ed in *Aftonbladet* 23 May 1966.

[85] See, for example, editorials in *Örebro-Kuriren* 2 May 1966 and *Aftonbladet* 27 May 1966.

[86] C-H Hermansson as cited in *Ny Dag* 12 Aug. 1966. See also editorials in *Ny Dag* 30 Aug. 1966 and *Norrskensflamman* 15 Sept. 1966.

[87] C-H Hermansson, *C-H Minnen* (Stockholm: Arena, 1993) 268–269. See also *Dagens Nyheter* 21 May 1966.

[88] C-H Hermansson as cited in *Dagens Nyheter* 23 Aug. 1966. See also Kent Lidman, "Vietnamdebatten i Sverige" (University of Umeå, 1973) 8.

[89] SAP, *Valboken 66* (Stockholm: SAP, 1966) 104–105. See also Torsten Nilsson as cited in UD, *Utrikesfrågor 1966* (Stockholm: UD, 1966) 30–32. and Tage Erlander as cited in *Dagens Nyheter* 23 Aug. 1966.

[90] In response to a question from Nancy Eriksson, Anders Thunborg assured her that the SAP's Vietnam position was popular among young voters and that the party did not need to be concerned about losing young voters on this issue. Thunborg as cited in *SAP Riksdagsgruppens protokoll* 29 June 1966.

[91] 26 July 1966. Jerome K. Holloway. Telegram to State. Subject Numeric Files 1964–1966. Political and Defense. Sweden. RG 59; 27 Aug. 1966. J. Graham Parsons. Telegram to State. Subject Numeric Files 1964–1966. Political and Defense. Sweden. RG 59.

[92] Nils Elvander, *Skandinavisk arbetarrörelse* (Stockholm: Liber, 1980) 314, 332; Gustaf Olivencrona, *Hur väljarna vanns* (Stockholm: Wahlström & Widstrand, 1968) 17–18.

[93] C-H Hermansson as cited in *Ny Dag* 23 Sept. 1966. See also editorial in *Norrskensflamman* 19 Sept. 1966 and Kjell-Olof Bornemark's op-ed in *Ny Dag* 30 Sept. 1966.

[94] *Tiden* # 7 1968, 388–389.

[95] *SAP PS-protokoll* 1 Oct. 1966; *SAP Riksdagsgruppens protokoll* 11 Oct. 1966. See also Sten Andersson, *I de lugnaste vatten...* (Stockholm: Tiden, 1993) 240–241 and Lindström, *Och regeringen satt kvar*, 306–311.

[96] Elvander, *Skandinavisk arbetarrörelse*, 225–228. See also Erlander, *60-talet*, 218.

[97] *SAP VU-protokoll* 20 Dec. 1966; *SAP VU-protokoll* 28 June 1967; *SAP VU-protokoll* 18 Oct. 1967.

[98] Sven Svensson, *I maktens labyrinter* (Stocholm: Bonnier, 1968) 39. See also Tage Erlander as cited in Alvar Alsterdahl, *Samtal med Tage Erlander mellan två val* (Stockholm: Tiden, 1967) 67–68.

[99] Åke Ortmark, *Maktspelet i Sverige* (Stockholm: Wahlström & Widstrand, 1968) 144–146. See also Tage Erlander, *Sjuttiotal* (Stockholm: Tiden, 1979) 22–33.

[100] See, for instance, Bo Hammar, *Ett långt farväl till kommunismen* (Stockholm: Bromberg, 1992) 87–88.

[101] For specific illustrations, see C-H Hermansson as cited in *Riksdagsprotokollet # 30*, 1 Nov. 1966, 49–50). See also Hermansson, *För Socialismen*, 108–113.

[102] See, for example, editorials in *Ny Dag* 22 Sept. 1966 and *Norrskensflamman* 20 Nov. 1966.

[103] Olivencrona, *Hur väljarna vanns*, 77.

[104] See, for instance, Olof Kleberg's editorial in *Liberal Debatt # 7* 1966, 17–23. For an illustration of continued Communist criticism, see Sara Lidman's op-ed in *Aftonbladet* 13 Dec. 1966.

[105] For a specific example, see Kaj Björk's op-ed in *Aftonbladet* 16 Dec. 1966. See also Kaj Björk and the Social Democratic Minster of Justice, Herman Kling, as cited in *Riksdagsprotokollet # 37*, 8 Dec. 1966, 9–10.

[106] For an overview of Social Democratic declarations about the Vietnamese conflict during the winter of 1966–1967, see UD, *Sverige och Vietnamfrågan*, 33–41. In this period the government's statements continued to be quite cautious, averting any explicit criticism of the United States. The closest that any Social Democratic leader came to criticizing Washington was Palme's comment that the American war effort risked to discredit Western democracy in the eyes of the Third World.

[107] Erlander as cited in *Svenska Dagbladet* 29 Jan. 1967.

[108] See, for example, Sara Lidman's op-ed in *Aftonbladet* 11 Feb. 1967. See also *Vietnambulletinen # 1-2* 1967, 6–13, 40–43.

[109] Hammarström, *FNL i Sverige*, 42–43, 61. For a specific illustration, see Socialistiska Förbundet, *Program för socialism* (Stockholm: Bonnier, 1967) 45–49.

[110] *Ny Dag* 23 March 1967; *Clarté # 2* 1967, 5.

[111] Salomon, *Rebeller i takt med tiden*, 262.

[112] Tängerstad, "Att organisera ett engagemang," 52.

[113] Svanfeldt, "Svenska Kommittén för Vietnam," 14–16.

[114] Bäck, Den utrikespolitiska dagsordningen, 38–39; Hammarström, FNL i Sverige, 43.

[115] Kilander, *Vietnam var nära*, 121–122.

[116] Salomon, *Rebeller i takt med tiden*, 12–13, 100; Tängerstad, "Att organisera ett engagemang," 38, 62–64.

[117] *Aftonbladet* 10 April 1967; *Ny Dag* 14 April 1967.

[118] Martin Schiff, "The United States and Sweden" *American Scandinavian Review* 1973 61 (4): 369. Another poll taken that spring showed that the Swedes, along with the French, had the lowest regard for Lyndon Johnson in all of Western Europe. *Aftonbladet* 19 May 1967.

[119] *Expressen* 27 Feb. 1967; *Vår Kyrka* Feb. 1967.

[120] *Ny Dag* 22 Oct. 1965; *Ny Dag* 10 Dec 1965; *Ny Dag* 23 Dec. 1965.

[121] *Fackföreningsrörelsen* # 7 1966, 237.

[122] For a specific illustration, see *Fackföreningsrörelsen* # 18 1966, 97.

[123] *LO Kongressprotokoll.* 17:e Kongressen. 3–9 Sept. 1966, 549–556. Bill # 118 condemned LO's cautious approach to the Vietnam issue, demanding that it speak out against the war and endorse *Nationalinsamlingen*.

[124] *Aftonbladet* 17 Feb 1967; *Ny Dag* 6 1967; *Dagens Nyheter* 12 March 1967. See also *Metallarbetaren* # 10 1967, 2.

[125] Anti-war resolutions sent to the government by Sv. Transportarbetarförbundet, Avd. # 40 (4 March 1967) Sv. Byggarbetarförbundet, Avd. # 13 (20 April 1967). Avd HP. Grupp 1. Mål O. Opinionsyttringar Vietnam. # 110.

[126] Geijer's reservations about Vietnam issue were evident during discussions among the SAP leadership in early 1967. *SAP PS-protokoll* 3 Jan. 1967.

[127] Parsons as cited in the *Washington Post* 3 April 1967.

[128] For specific illustrations, see "Vietnam supplement" in *Arbetet* 7 Feb. 1967 and *Aktuellt* # 7 1967, 8–9.

[129] For a specific example, see editorial in *Aftonbladet* 4 March 1967. See also *Frihet* # 2 1967, 24.

[130] See, for example, editorials in *Expressen* 25 April 1967, *Västernorrlands Allehanda* 26 April 1967 and *Barometern* 9 May 1967.

[131] *Stockholms arbetarekommun. Årsmötesprotokoll.* 15–17 April 1967, 13–16.

[132] Möller, *Sverige och Vietnamkriget*, 82. See also UD, *Utrikesfrågor 1967* (Stockholm: UD, 1967) 118.

[133] *Aftonbladet* 30 July 1968.

[134] 17 May 1966. Political Division FM. Jean-Christophe Öberg. Memo. Avd HP. Grupp 12. Mål Xv. Erkännande av stater och regeringar. Vietnam # 63; 10 March 1967. Unsigned. Telegram from FM to the Swedish Embassy in Bangkok. Avd HP. Grupp 12. Mål Xv. Erkännande av stater och regeringar. Vietnam # 63.

[135] Ann-Marie Ekengren, *Av hänsyn till folkrätten?* (Stockholm: Nerenius & Santérus, 1999) 187. This topic was also dicussed by Swedish and American diplomats. 18 April 1967. Unsigned. Telegram from FM to the Swedish Embassy in Washington. Re: Meeting between Richard Hichens-Bergström and the US *Chargé d'affairs* Turner Cameron Jr. on 17 April 1967. Avd HP. Grupp 1. Mål Ua. Politik Allmänt. USA # 218. Hichens-Bergström apparently told Cameron that Nilsson's decision to downgrade relations with the GVN was motivated by the cabinet's desire to defuse radical anti-war agitation.

[136] Nilsson as cited in *Dagens Nyheter* 18 April 1967.

[137] See editorials in *Aftonbladet* 17 April 1967, *Arbetet* 18 April 1967 and *Värmlands Folkblad* 21 April 1967.

[138] 21 April 1967. Swedish Ambassador to the US 1963–1972. Hubert de Besche. Telegram to Stockholm. Avd HP. Grupp 1. Mål Ua. Politik Allmänt. USA # 218. See also Petri, *Sverige i stora världen*, 417.

[139] See, for example, editorials in *Svenska Dagbladet* 18 April 1967, *Nya Upsala Tidning* 26 April 1967 and *Vestmalands Läns Tidning* 9 May 1967.

[140] 20 April 1967. Political Division FM. Marc Giron. Memo. Re: Today's conversation with the US *Chargé d'affairs* Turner Cameron Jr. Avd HP. Grupp 1. Mål Ua. Politik Allmänt. USA # 218. Cameron stated that Washington appreciated the amount of pressure that the Social Democratic administration was currently facing with regard to the Vietnam issue, but the US government still questioned the wisdom of giving in to such agitation.

[141] 19 April 1967. Secretary of State. Dean Rusk. Telegram to the US Embassy Stockholm. Central Foreign Policy File 1967–1969. Political and Defense. Sweden. RG 59; 22 April 1967. Turner Cameron Jr. Telegram to State. Central Foreign Policy File 1967–1969. Political and Defense. Sweden. RG 59.

[142] John Duffett (ed.), *Against the Crime of Silence* (New York: O'Hare Books, 1968) 17–51.

[143] *Göteborgs handels- och sjöfartstidning* 6 Dec. 1966; *Dagens Nyheter* 4 Feb. 1967.

[144] Tage Erlander *Dagens Eko*. P1. 25 April 1967. Radio. See also Torsten Nilsson as cited in *Riksdagsprotokollet* # 12, 8 March 1967, 47–48, 50.

[145] For specific examples, see Sara Lidman's op-ed in *Aftonbladet* 11 Feb. 1967 and *Clarté* # 2 1967, 5.

[146] For a specific illustration, see VPK, *Samling vänster i svensk politik* (Göteborg: VPK, 1967) 13, 97, 103–105, 133–135. See also Hammar, *Ett långt farväl till kommunismen*, 69–70.

[147] Duffet, *Against the Crime of Silence*. 17–51. See also *Dagens Nyheter* 4 Feb. 1967.

[148] See, for instance, Social Democratic representative, Stellan Arvidsson as cited in *Riksdagsprotokollet* # 12, 8 March 1967, 80–81. See also Björk, *Vägen till Indokina*, 140–141.

[149] Sjöström, *Klassens ljus*, 138. See also *Aktuellt* # 6 1967, 8–10.

[150] Bengt Owe Birgersson, *et al*, *Socialdemokratin i Stockholms län 1907–1982* (Stockholm: SAP, 1982) 160. The tribunal was subject to intense discussion within the SAP district in Stockholm. *Stockholms arbetarekommun. Årsmötesprotokoll*. 15–17 April 1967, 13–16. The district ultimately defeated a motion endorsing the tribunal.

[151] Erlander as cited in *Dagens Nyheter* 18 March 1967.

[152] Erlander as cited in UD, *Utrikesfrågor 1967*, 118–119.

[153] Svensson, *I maktens labyrinter*, 35–36.

[154] See, for example, Tage Erlander as cited in *Dagens Nyheter* 9 May 1967.

[155] See, for instance, Olof Palme's op-ed in *Aftonbladet* 17 May 1967.

[156] Tage Erlander. *Lunchekot*. P 1. 12 Dec. 1966. Radio. In this interview, Erlander conceded that his reluctance to host the tribunal was largely due to the expected adverse American response.

[157] 25 April 1967. President's Daily Diary Entry. Box 4. L.B.J. Library. See also Erlander, *60-talet*, 110.

[158] 29 April 1967. Scandinavian Desk Dept. of State. Paul R. Hughes. Memo to the Assistant Secretary of State for European Affairs John Leddy. Central Foreign Policy File 1967–1969. Political and Defense. Sweden. RG 59; 8 May 1967. Dean Rusk. Telegram to US Embassy Stockholm. Central Foreign Policy File 1967–1969. Political and Defense. Sweden. RG 59.

[159] Editorials in *Aftonbladet* 25 April, 27 April, 4 May; 5 May, 10 May, 11 May and 19 May 1967.

[160] See, for examples, editorials in *Borås Tidning* 27 April 1967, *Sundsvalls Tidning* 11 May 1967 and *Smålandsposten* 16 May 1967.

[161] See, for instance, editorials in *Arbetarbladet* 28 April 1967 and *Dala-Demokraten* 11 May 1967.

[162] See editorials in *Helsingborgs Dagblad* 27 April 1967, *Göteborgs-Posten* 28 April 1967, *Eskilstuna-Kuriren* 29 April 1967 and *Expressen* 17 May 1967.

[163] 7 May 1967. Turner Cameron Jr. Telegram to State. Central Foreign Policy File 1967–1969. Political and Defense. Sweden. RG 59; 16 June 1967. William W. Heath. Telegram to State. Central Foreign Policy File 1967–1969. Political and Defense. Sweden. RG 59.

[164] Erlander had apparently told Walt Rostow that his administration was actively trying to moderate the Vietnam debate in Sweden. Rostow, in turn, expressed sympathy for the Social Democratic administration's domestic political dilemma with regard to the war. 27 April 1967. Swedish Ambassador to West Germany. Ole Jödahl. Telegram to FM. Re: Erlander's private conversation with Walt Rostow on 25 April 1967. Avd HP. Grupp 1. Mål Ua. Politik Allmänt. USA # 218.

[165] *SSSF Förbundsmedelande # 4 1967*. SSSF. B:2 "Handlingsprogram med förslag och uttalanden." 1964–1967. See also Svedgård, *Palme*, 84–85.

[166] See, for instance, SKSF, *Årsberättelse 1967–1968*, 23–24. and Stig Carlsson's op-ed in *Arbetarbladet* 13 May 1967.

[167] For specific illustrations, see Olof Palme as cited in *Arbetet* 11 July 1967 and Östen Undén as cited in *Tiden* # 6 1967, 327, 342.

[168] See, for example, the exchange between Leif Dahlberg and Olof Palme in the op-ed pages of *Aftonbladet* 11 May, 17 May, 24 May and 26 May 1967. See also Bernt Jansson's op-ed in *Aftonbladet* 16 May 1967.

[169] Hammarström, *FNL i Sverige*, 42; 61. See also *Arbetet* May 2 1967, *Aftonbladet* May 2 1967, *Norrskensflamman* May 2 1967 and *Sydsvenska Dagbladet* May 2 1967.

[170] *Stockholms arbetarekommun. Verksamhetsberättelse 1967*, 4–8. See also Aktuellt # 7 1967, 7–9.

[171] See, for example, *Tiden* # 7, 435–436., *Frihet* # 8 1967, 22–23. and *Aktuellt* # 14 1967, 6–7. See also Social Democratic representative, Nancy Eriksson's bill to the Second Chamber of parliament. Motion # 180. *Riksdagsprotokollet. Motioner 1967*.

[172] For a specific example, see *SSU Kongressprotokoll*. SSU 18:e Kongressen, 11–17 June 1967, 7, 82–108. See also Leif Dahlberg, *Över folkets huvud* (Stockholm: Bonnier, 1967) 9–31.

[173] Lidman, "Vietnamdebatten i Sverige," 15–17; Tängerstad, "Att organisera ett engagemang," 62. See for instance, Bill # 51 and Bill # 185 in the First Chamber of parliament. *Riksdagsprotokollet. Motioner 1967.*

[174] Hermansson, *C-H Minnen*, 259–260. See also VPK, *Samling vänster i svensk politik*, 3, 13, 59–69, 96–98, 103–105, 133–135.

[175] *Ny Dag* 13 Oct. 1967; *Ny Dag* 27 Oct. 1967.

[176] Dahlberg, *Över folkets huvud*, 29–31, 113. See also open letter by Göran Therborn, "Avsked till Socialdemokratin" *Tidsignal* # 42 1967, 12.

[177] See, for example, Ingemar Färm, Alf Karlsson and Jan Mild as cited in *SSU Kongressprotokoll*. 18:e Kongressen. 11–17 June 1967, 101–105. See also Arne Färdigh's letter to the editor in *Aktuellt* # 18 1967, 2.

[178] Bäck, *Den utrikespolitiska dagsordningen*, 38–39. See also Hammarström, *FNL i Sverige*, 43.

[179] *Aftonbladet* 23 Oct. 1967.

[180] On the same day that the SAP Congress began, several Social Democratic organizations in Stockholm, as well as a number of different trade union locals, signed an open letter in support of the National Liberation Front. It was printed in both *Aftonbladet* and *Dagens Nyheter*, and several prominent Communists and Maoists also signed the letter. *Dagens Nyheter* 20 Oct. 1967; *Aftonbladet* 20 Oct. 1967.

[181] *Dagens Nyheter* 22 Oct. 1967.

[182] *SAP VU-protokoll* 30 June 1967; *SAP VU-protokoll* 10 Oct. 1967.

[183] Erlander cited in *Arbetet* 22 Oct. 1967.

[184] Nilsson as cited in *SAP Kongressprotokoll*. Extra Kongress. 20–23 Oct. 1967, 451–454.

[185] *SAP Kongressprotokoll*. Extra Kongress. 20–23 Oct. 1967, 6, 451–458. See also Björk, *Vägen till Indokina*, 139, 145–146.

[186] Although Erlander insisted that the party and the government's stances on the war were not identical to each other, he simultaneously admitted that there was not really much of a difference between the two. According to Erlander, the government had in theory not gone as far as in its endorsement of the NLF as the party had. This was because the cabinet still needed to maintain a neutral position with regard to the Vietnamese conflict. Erlander as cited in *Expressen* 26 Oct. 1967.

[187] See, for instance, Torsten Nilsson as cited in *SAP Riksdagsgruppens protokoll* 12 March 1968 and SAP Party Secretary, Sten Andersson, as cited in *SAP PS-protokoll* 17 March 1970.

[188] For specific illustrations, see Birgitta Dahl cited in *Arbetet* 5 Oct 1971 and Torsten Nilsson as cited in *Dagens Nyheter* 9 Nov. 1971.

[189] Social Democratic representative Ingemund Bengtsson and Olof Palme as cited in *Riksdagsprotokollet* # 13, 21 March 1968, 75, 91, 112; Torsten Nilsson. *Aktuellt*. TV 1. 17 April 1967. Television.

[190] Robert Brigham, *Guerilla Diplomacy* (Ithaca: Cornell University Press, 1995) 80.

[191] 16 June 1967. SSU International Secretary. Pierre Schori. Memo. Re: Recent meeting between SSU leaders and visiting NLF representatives. Avd HP. Grupp 1. Mål Xv. Politik Allmänt. Vietnam. # 1196; 30 June 1969. Political Division FM. Jean-Christophe Öberg. Memo. Re: Today's meeting between Tage Erlander and the North Vietnamese Ambassador to Sweden, Nygen Tho Chan. Avd HP. Grupp 1. Mål Xv. Politik Allmänt. Vietnam. # 1204; 26 June 1973. Political Division FM. Jan Lundvik. Memo: Re: Krister Wickman's visit to the DRV 8–11 June 1973. Avd HP. Grupp 1. Mål Xv. Politik Allmänt. Vietnam. # 1209. See also North Vietnamese Ambassador to Sweden, Nguyen Tho Chan as cited in Hammarström, *FNL i Sverige*, 209–210.

[192] Donald Sassoon, *One Hundred Years of Socialism* (London: IB Touris Press, 1996) 327–328; Alastair Parker, "International Aspects of the Vietnam War" in Peter Lowe (ed.), *The Vietnam War* (New York: St Martin's Press, 1998) 211–212.

[193] See, for instance, Tage Erlander as cited in *SAP Riksdagsgruppens protokoll* 15 Aug. 1967 and Torsten Nilsson as cited in *SAP Kongressprotokoll*. 23:e Kongressen. 9–15 June 1968, 270. See also Anders Ferm, *Caleb Andersson* (Stockholm: Bokförlaget DN, 1997) 104–105.

[194] For a specific example, see Social Democratic representative Evert Svensson as cited in *Riksdagsprotokollet* # 13, 21 March 1968, 141–142. See also Olof Palme as cited in *Expressen* 31 Dec. 1969.

[195] Lidman, "Vietnamdebatten i Sverige," 12, 24. See also Möller, *Sverige och Vietnamkriget*, 84–85. and Björk, *Vägen till Indokina*, 145–146.

[196] See, for example, Jan Myrdal as cited in *Dagens Nyheter* 22 Oct. 1967.

[197] See editorials in *Dagens Nyheter* 24 Oct. 1967 and *Expressen* 24 Oct. 1967.

[198] See, for example, editorials in *Göteborgs handels- och sjöfartstidning* 24 Oct 1967, *Expressen* 26 Oct. 1967 and *Upsala Nya Tidning* 25 Oct. 1967.

[199] 25 Oct. 1967. Director of Intelligence and Research. Dept. of State. Thomas L. Hughes. Memo to the Secretary of State. Central Foreign Policy File 1967–1969. Political and Defense. Sweden. RG 59.

[200] See editorials in *Arbetet* 24 Oct 1967 and 28 Oct. 1967.

[201] See editorials in *Aftonbladet* 24 Oct. 1967 and 27 Oct 1967.

[202] For specific illustrations, see *Frihet* # 11–12 1967, 26–67. and *SKSF Årsberättelse 1967–1968*, 38–42.

[203] SSSF, *Verksamhetsberättelse 1966*, 11. See also Motioner # 4–7. *Stockholms arbetarekommun. Årsmötesprotokoll.* 23–24 April 1966.

[204] For a specific example, see *Aktuellt* # 16 1967, 19.

[205] During an address to ABF in Stockholm on November 29, Olof Palme, for instance, declared that the time had now come to sharpen the Swedish tone against the American war effort even further. Palme as cited in *Svenska Dagbladet* 30 Nov. 1967.

[206] Logevall, "The Swedish–American Conflict over Vietnam," 428–429.

[207] US Dept. of State, *Foreign Relations of the United States 1964–1968. Vol IV*. Vietnam 1966, 829–835, 856–859.

[208] Jean-Christophe Öberg, *Varför Vietnam?* (Stockholm: Rabén & Sjögren, 1985) 121–122; Nilsson, *Åter Vietnam*, 66–125. See also Ulf Bjereld, *Kritiker eller medlare?* (Stockholm: Nerenius & Santérus, 1992) 110–122, 128–131.

[209] For specific illustrations, see Gunnar Jarring, *Utan glasnost och perestrojka* (Stockholm: Bonnier, 1989) 117–133. and Åke Sjölin "Torsten Nilsson om Vietnam" *Svensk Tidskrift* 1985 (1): 45–46.

[210] Leif Leifland, *Frostens år* (Stockholm: Nerenius & Santérus, 1997) 22, 191. See also Sverker Åström, *Ögonblick* (Stockholm: Bonnier Alba, 1992) 128.

[211] For a specific example, see Wilhelm Wachtmeister, *Som jag såg det* (Stockholm: Norstedt, 1996) 166, 174–175.

[212] Möller, *Sverige och Vietnamkriget*, 91.

[213] Petri is not alone in this assessment. Gunnar Jarring, the Swedish Ambassador to the Soviet Union, likewise deems the government's mediation attempt to have been primarily driven by the Social Democrats' domestic political needs. Jarring, *Utan glasnost och perestrojka*, 121–124.

[214] Petri, *Sverige i stora världen*, 388–398. Petri's version of events is corroborated by Kaj Björk, who similarly maintains that the government appeared to have virtually no interest in the Vietnamese conflict prior to it becoming a topic of domestic dispute in the summer of 1965. Björk, *Vägen till Indokina*, 101–103.

[215] Sjölin, "Torsten Nilsson om Vietnam," 45–46.

[216] See, for example, Nilsson as cited in *Aftonbladet* 5 July 1972. Kaj Björk dismisses Nilsson's statements to this effect as complete nonsense. Björk, *Vägen till Indokina*, 159.

[217] George C. Herring, *The Secret Diplomacy of the Vietnam War* (Austin: University of Texas Press, 1983) 211., 374–378, 519–521, 667, 690; Thomas Schwartz, *Lyndon Johnson and Europe* (Cambridge: Harvard University Press, 2003) 85, 232.

[218] See, for example, editorials in *Stockholms-Tidningen* 27 June 1965; *Frihet #* 5 1966, 16–19. and *Frihet #* 4 1967, 4–5. See also Birgersson, *et al.*, *Socialdemokratin i Stockholms län 1907–1982*, 157.

[219] See editorials in *Dala-Demokraten* 25 July 1968, *Arbetet* 26 July 1968 and *Norrländska Socialdemokraten* 26 July 1968.

[220] *Aftonbladet* 22 March 1968, 24 March 1968 and 25 July 1968.

[221] Möller, *Sverige och Vietnamkriget*, 87; Björk, *Vägen till Indokina*, 146–147.

[222] See, for instance, Nilsson as cited in *Dagens Nyheter* 26 March 1968.

[223] 28 March 1968. Turner Cameron Jr. Letter to the US Ambassador to Sweden 1967–1969. William W. Heath. Central Foreign Policy File 1967–1969. Political and Defense. Sweden. RG 59.

[224] See, for instance, Torsten Nilsson as cited in *Riksdagsprotokollet #* 12, 8 March 1967, 10.

[225] According to Kaj Björk, Torsten Nilsson used this revelation about ASPEN's existence to score political points at home. Björk, *Vägen till Indokina*, 159.

[226] See, for example, Nilsson as cited in *Dagens Nyheter* 26 March 1968.

[227] For specific examples, see Olof Palme as cited in UD, *Utrikesfrågor 1968*, 28–33. and Social Democratic representative Oskar Lindkvist as cited in *Riksdagsprotokollet* # 21, 3 May 1968, 54.

[228] See, for instance, Torsten Nilsson as cited in *SAP Kongressprotokoll*. 23:e Kongressen. 9–15 June 1968, 244, 270. See also UD, *Sverige och Vietnamfrågan*, 3–6.

[229] The publication of the government white book, *Sverige och Vietnamfrågan*, in late July 1968 was presumably intended to serve a similar purpose.

[230] Eugenie Blang, *To Urge Common Sense on the Americans* (Dissertation. College of William and Mary, 2000) 34–35, 45–55, 63–71; Herring, *The Secret Diplomacy of the Vietnam War*, 211, 374–378, 519–526.

[231] 21 March 1967. Letter to the government from the leadership of Svenska Clarté-förbundet. Avd. HP. Grupp 1. Mål O. Opinionsyttringar Vietnam # 110. In a recently adopted resolution Clarté condemned the government for hiding behind its potential mediating role as a way to justify its cautious approach to the war. See also Allan Björk's op-ed in *Aftonbladet* 23 May 1966.

[232] See, for instance, Tage Erlander as cited in *Dagens Nyheter* 4 Feb 1967 and Torsten Nilsson as cited in *Stockholms arbetarekommun. Årsmötesprotokoll*. 15–16 April 1967, 13–15.

[233] For a specific illustration, see Jan Myrdal as cited in *Dagens Nyheter* 22 Oct 1967.

[234] Salomon, *Rebeller i takt med tiden*, 100–101, 128–131, 304–307; Hammarström, *FNL i Sverige*, 180–181.

[235] Parker, "International Aspects of the Vietnam War," 209–210.

[236] *Aftonbladet* 20 Dec. 1967; *Expressen* 21 Dec. 1967; *Svenska Dagbladet* 21 Dec. 1967. See also Östberg, *1968*, 101. and Kilander, *Vietnam var nära, 126–133*.

[237] *Expressen* 22 Dec. 1967; *Ny Dag* 22 Dec. 1967; *Aftonbladet* 28 Dec. 1967.

[238] See, for example, CH Hermansson as cited in *Aftonbladet* 22 Dec. 1967.

[239] Erlander as cited in *Svenska Dagbladet* 22 Dec. 1967.

[240] *The New York Times* 5 Jan. 1968; *Dagens Nyheter* 5 Jan. 1968; *Svenska Dagbladet* 6 Jan. 1968. See also Hammarström, *FNL i Sverige*, 58–63.

[241] See, for example, editorials in *Svenska Dagbladet* 7 Jan. 1968, *Expressen* 8 Jan. 1968, *Göteborgs-Posten* 9 Jan. 1968 and *Dagens Nyheter* 12 Jan. 1968.

[242] For specific illustrations, see *Aftonbladet* 17 June 1965, 18 March 1966 and 7 March 1967.

[243] Editorials in *Arbetarbladet* 5 Jan. 1968 and *Dala-Demokraten* 5 Jan. 1968.

[244] See, for example, the exchange between Tage Erlander and spokesmen for the NLF-groups in the editorial pages of *Dagens Nyheter* 8 Jan. 1968, 10 Jan. 1968 and 11 Jan. 1968.

[245] See editorials in *Örebro-Kuriren* 8 Jan. 1968, *Folket* 8 Jan. 1968, *Västgöta-Demokraten* 8 Jan. 1968, *Arbetarbladet* 9 Jan. 1968 and *Arbetet* 12 Jan. 1968.

[246] For specific illustrations, see Gunnar Myrdal's op-ed in *Dagens Nyheter* 25 Jan. 1968 and Social Democratic representative Elisabeth Sjövall's op-ed in *Göteborgs handels- och sjöfartstidning* 14 May 1968.

[247] *Aftonbladet* 31 March 1968. See also editorials in *Aftonbladet* 24 Feb. 1968, *Piteå-Tidningen* 27 Feb. 1968 and *Västerbottens Folkblad* 28 Feb. 1968.

[248] See, for instance, Torsten Nilsson as cited in *SAP Riksdagsgruppens protokoll* 12 March 1968.

[249] While SÄPO was the official state security service, IB might best be described as the SAP's own clandestine intelligence organization. Magnus Hjort, *Den farliga fredsrörelsen* (SOU 2002: 90) 187–262; Lars Olof Lampers, *Det grå brödraskapet* (SOU 2002: 92) 490–510.

[250] Salomon, *Rebeller i takt med tiden*, 214–215; Hammarström, *FNL i Sverige*, 79–80.

[251] *FIB/Kulturfront* # 9 1973, 2–11; *Vietnambulletinen* # 4 1973, 16.

[252] Dahl, "Solidaritetsarbetet för Vietnam," 184–185; Björk, *Vägen till Indokina*, 150–151.

The Social Democrats Seize the Initiative: The Swedish Committee for Vietnam and Palme at Sergels torg, 1968

At the turn of 1967–1968, the Social Democratic leadership had finally grasped that it could no longer afford to take a wait-and-see approach to the Vietnam issue. In all likelihood, this conclusion was partially informed by the wave of violent anti-war protests that at the time was sweeping across much of Western Europe,[1] though above all it was rooted in recent domestic events.

Popular opposition to the war was in Sweden to stay, and consequently the Maoist and Communist attempt to capitalize on public anti-war opinion had to be thwarted by a proactive response. Social Democratic concerns were at this point split; on one hand, the party hierarchy worried about the NLF-groups' rising influence among the baby boomers and, on the other hand, it was anxious that the VPK was the best poised to capture the anti-war vote in the upcoming September election.

When the Social Democrats' top decision-making body (*Verkställande utskottet*, VU) convened on 10 February 1968, it drew up a strategy to counteract the dual Communist/Maoist threat. In particular, the VU's members agreed that the SAP needed to assume a more assertive posture on the Vietnam issue lest the party relinquish the youth to its Marxist adversaries. During the meeting, Hjalmar Mehr observed that many young people were simply bypassing the Social Democrats on route to the far left. The leftward trajectory of the 68-generation was undeniable, and therefore it was imperative that the party try to harness young peoples' antipathy toward the war or it would risk losing this group of voters – maybe indefinitely. To this end, the party hierarchy reiterated the Extra Congress' decision to establish a Social Democratic collection fund specifically earmarked for the National Liberation Front. The VU additionally decided to give a generous grant to the newly reformulated *Svenska Kommittén för Vietnam* (SKfV),[2] which had previously been known as the *Svenska Vietnamkommittén* (SVK).

Having existed in name only for over a year or so, the SVK had begun to show signs of life again in the late fall of 1967, organizing its own rally at the conclusion of the Vietnam Week in Stockholm on 21 October.[3] A handful of Social Democratic and Communist anti-war activists had joined forces to establish the Stockholm Conference on Vietnam, which was intended to act as an alternative to Maoist-sponsored anti-war agitation. At the beginning of October, the founders of the Stockholm Conference on Vietnam subsequently decided that SVK should be revamped. On 4 October 1967, the SVK was formally supplanted by SKfV, and Evert Svensson, the chairman of the SKSF (the Association of Christian Social Democrats), became its new leader.[4]

In order to give the new committee more clout, Gunnar Myrdal, the internationally renowned Nobel Laureate economist, replaced Svensson as the committee's chairman on 24 January 1968. While politically independent, the SKfV's pro-Social Democratic leanings were indisputable. This was underscored by the fact that Gunnar's wife Alva was presently sitting in the cabinet.[5] When Myrdal eventually resigned in 1971, Social Democratic parliamentary representative Birgitta Dahl succeeded him as the chairperson. Dahl, a vocal anti-war activist in her own right, was persuaded by SAP Party Secretary Sten Andersson to accept this very important assignment. According to Andersson, the committee had the dual purpose of leading public opinion on the Vietnam question and preventing the anti-war movement from being overtaken by extremists. He stressed that it was absolutely crucial that the youth's dissent against the war not be hijacked by the far left.[6]

Consequently there were strong personal ties between the new committee and the SAP hierarchy.[7] In addition, SKfV was principally funded by Social Democratic organizations and unions,[8] which were also the committee's target audience.[9] The SKfV thus, in effect, became the SAP's main political weapon against the Maoist-oriented anti-war movement, and it played a central role in the party's efforts to neutralize this threat. Indeed, a formal endorsement of the government's Vietnam policy was also directly spelled out in the SKfV's founding charter.[10]

Challenges to the US Policy on Vietnam: The Swedish Committee for Vietnam and Palme's Sergels torg Speech

That it was the committee's mission to defend the Social Democratic administration's Vietnam policy was plain from the very start.[11] As soon as

Gunnar Myrdal took over the chairmanship from Evert Svensson, he launched an all-out attack against the NLF-groups,[12] which instantly led to heated polemics between Myrdal and various spokesmen for the revolutionary branch of the anti-war movement.[13] This initial acrimony would shape the SKfV's subsequent relationship to the DFFG, and henceforward there was no love lost between the two organizations.[14]

The NLF-groups rightly saw the SKfV as a Social Democratic vehicle to usurp and contain radical anti-war opinion.[15] First of all, the SKfV's approach to the war was considerably more militant than the one that been pursued by its predecessor, the SVK. Although SKfV stopped short of adopting the DFFG's imperialist interpretation of US Vietnam policy, it enthusiastically backed the latter's call for an immediate withdrawal of all American troops from South East Asia. The committee likewise seconded the Maoists' unconditional support for the NLF/DRV. The earlier slogan of "Peace in Vietnam" was no longer heard, and the original pacifist position that had guided the SKV's activities had now de facto also been abandoned. The only ideological distinctions that still really remained between the two groups had more to do with their differing domestic outlooks than with their views about the Vietnamese conflict itself. Equally significantly, SKfV appropriated many of the DFFG's agitation techniques by setting up their own rivaling petition and collection drives, etc.[16]

While the Maoists' suspicion that the SKfV was trying to outmaneuver them was essentially correct, the committee's relationship to the SAP was nonetheless far more autonomous than the NLF-groups claimed. The SKfV was not simply a servile tool in the hands of the Social Democratic establishment; rather, it was a semi-independent lobbying group whose demands grew more radical as time wore on.[17] Even though the committee consistently defended the government against Maoist attacks, this loyalty was contingent upon the Social Democratic administration's persistent responsiveness to the SKfV's agenda.

Here it is also important to stress that the committee's members were not all drawn from the SAP. To be sure, Social Democrats dominated the top leadership posts, but Communists also exercised considerable influence within the SKfV, at times promoting policies that defied the government's wishes.[18] The SAP hierarchy, moreover, deeply distrusted some of the committee's leading personalities, especially Bertil Svanström,[19] whose pro-Soviet sympathies were unmistakable.[20] Nor was it any secret that the USSR would have liked to use the committee for its own propaganda purposes.[21] From the SAP hierarchy's point of view, it was also quite disconcerting that many of the committee's younger members identified with the DFFG's basic analysis of the war.[22]

These apprehensions notwithstanding, the SAP leadership proved to be very sensitive to the SKfV's wishes, and the committee would indisputably have a substantial impact on the government's Vietnam policy.[23] This relationship worked both ways, however, and the SKfV's influence was always implicitly subject to its continued willingness to back the Social Democratic administration. The committee's first major undertaking was to host an anti-war demonstration in Stockholm that was jointly organized by the SAP district in Stockholm.[24] The impetus behind this manifestation could be found in the December 20th disturbances outside the US Trade Center and the NLF-groups' attack on American envoy Philippe Trezise in early January, and the intent behind this rally was to channel popular opposition to the war back into the parliamentary fold. The rally enjoyed the support of the trade union movement, as well as the parliamentary left and center. The demonstration, which took place on 21 February 1968, drew around 6,000 people, making it at that time the largest anti-war protest in Sweden.[25]

Because Palme had been designated as the SAP's front man on the Vietnam issue, it was no coincidence that he was the rally's top-billed speaker. Palme's address, which later became known as the Sergels torg Speech (after the plaza in Stockholm where it took place), was notable for its strong endorsement of the Vietnamese Communist cause. It further offered the most strident Social Democratic critique of US Vietnam policy so far.[26] The fact that both Torsten Nilsson and Tage Erlander had approved the speech's contents signifies that the Social Democratic establishment had now fully committed itself to a new and more aggressive posture against the American war effort.[27]

Palme's participation in the demonstration elicited an enormous amount of interest worldwide, at once elevating Palme to an internationally recognized statesman.[28] Most of the attention did not focus on what he had said, but on the fact that he had appeared side by side with visiting North Vietnamese dignitary Nguyen Tho Chan. Some of the government's Conservative detractors felt that this was inappropriate decorum for an official representative of the Swedish state in light of the country's official policy of neutrality.[29] Social Democratic spokesmen would later claim that Chan's participation in the rally came as a last minute surprise to them, at which point it was too late for Palme to withdraw.[30] This version of events, however, is a fabrication that was created after the fact.[31] For earlier on that same day, Nilsson had already given Chan the green light to partake in the demonstration, even inviting him to address the marchers – an offer that Chan naturally accepted.[32] Social Democratic officials presumably denied any prior knowledge of Chan's plans because to admit this publicly would have been seen as too provocative towards the Americans.[33] This approach allowed the government to avoid responsibility without undermining the rally's propaganda value to the party. Chan's presence was undoubtedly an enormous asset for the SAP leadership by providing the party with an alibi against the Maoist' complaint that the cabinet was afraid to offend Washington.

The DFFG had at first not intended to take part in the demonstration, and it had tried to persuade Chan to pull out as well. When this effort failed, the Maoists felt that they too had to participate in the rally, though they brought their own banners and heckled Palme and Gunnar Myrdal.[34] In their eyes, Palme's Sergels torg appearance was the consummate act of Social Democratic treachery because they fully appreciated that the demonstration's overarching objective was to wrestle the Vietnam issue away from them.[35]

The government's non-socialist opponents likewise interpreted Palme's conduct as politically motivated – specifically as a disguised attempt to court the anti-war vote.[36] This assessment was echoed by virtually the entire non-socialist press,[37] and even in *Dagens Nyheter*, which otherwise ordinarily sympathized with the government's stance on the war.[38] These claims were predictably dismissed by the SAP leadership,[39] which in concert with the Social Democratic press leveled identical counter-allegations against the non-socialist opposition.[40]

Off the record, Social Democratic officials did not always refute that domestic considerations had informed the cabinet's recent handling of the Vietnam question. For instance, when Tage Erlander discussed this matter with the American Ambassador William W. Heath on 6 March, he conceded that it was essential for his administration to take a resolute stand against the war in order to ensure that the Communists did not appropriate popular anti-war sentiment to their own ends. (However, Erlander simultaneously denied that Palme's conduct had been driven by electoral considerations.)[41] Torsten Nilsson made the exact same refutation during his personal audience with Heath on 11 March, though he too stated that it was critical that the Communists not be permitted to monopolize this issue.[42]

American officials obviously appreciated the necessity of keeping the Communists in check, but they were still quite upset by Palme's appearance at Sergels torg,[43] and Ambassador Heath was immediately recalled to Washington for consultations. This was an unprecedented move in the history of Swedish–American relations. While there is no evidence that this action was intended to influence the outcome of the upcoming Swedish elections, it was certainly a ploy by the Johnson administration to quiet Swedish criticism. Heath's recall was meant to publicly denote Washington's rising dissatisfaction with Stockholm, and it was an implicit warning that Sweden could not endlessly abuse the United States with impunity.[44]

This was a big story internationally,[45] particularly in the US where the press by and large interpreted the decision to recall Heath as a protest against the Social Democratic administration's eagerness to woo the anti-war vote.[46] In Sweden this action was similarly regarded as a tactic to silence Swedish criticism of the Vietnam war.[47] American diplomats would never confirm this publicly (because it would be poor form to admit that Washington was directly trying to influence Swedish policy), but in private they made known their desire to mute Social Democratic criticism.[48]

At the same time, US Embassy officials in Stockholm also recognized that this present irritation with Sweden had to be balanced against America's long-term interests. Accordingly, they cautioned Washington not to overreact to Social Democratic Vietnam protests because this issue more or less was an aberration in the totality of the Swedish–American relations, which otherwise were quite good.[49] So although the SAP leadership's uncooperative attitude in relation to the war was a real irritant, this was tolerable to the US so long as the Swedes could continue to be relied upon in the areas where it really mattered, that is, in economics and security issues in northern Europe. Throughout the entire war, this was also always the Americans' top priority in their dealings with Sweden, and even the Social Democrats' support for the Vietnamese Communists did not change this reality.[50]

By late 1967 the Social Democratic administration's stance on Vietnam had started to seriously grate on the Americans,[51] and Heath's recall signaled that Washington's patience was being seriously tested. From the outset, Stockholm had showed precious little enthusiasm for Washington's designs to aid and pacify South Vietnam. Swedish diplomats had almost immediately deemed the conflict to be unwinnable,[52] and the Social Democratic administration had never given a lot of credence to any of the justifications that the Americans had offered for the war, including the so-called "domino theory." If anything, the Swedes deemed US military intervention to be misconceived from the very start and their confidence in this endeavor never really subsequently improved. Thus the Tet Offensive in early 1968 only confirmed the validity of the Swedes' initial pessimism.[53]

Washington originally appears to have anticipated a more positive Swedish response to the American war effort, believing that Sweden might at least provide some material assistance to the GVN. However, by September 1964 the Americans had abandoned any such hopes, though they still felt that Stockholm appreciated the necessity of US military intervention in Indochina.[54] It did not take long, however, for it to become plain to the Americans that this assessment had been overly optimistic. Already in August 1965, the American Ambassador to Sweden, J. Graham Parsons, advised the State Department that "Sweden should be removed from the category of countries whose leaders have privately expressed support for the US Vietnam effort, and should be shifted to the category of countries whose governments have taken an ambivalent position."[55]

Any lingering ambiguity about the Swedish position was definitively answered by Palme's Gävle speech in July 1965. Hereafter, US diplomats in Stockholm were increasingly compelled to try to defend American policy in South East Asia to an ever more skeptical government and public. Indeed, by the fall of 1967 American diplomats warily concluded that Swedes' aversion toward the US war effort was unmatched in all of Western Europe.[56] From this point forward, the Americans pretty much accepted that they had lost the public relations battle in Sweden, conceding that a majority of the Swedish public was irreversibly set against the war.[57] A 1970 United States Information Agency (USIA) report later determined that the Vietnamese conflict had severely undermined the Swedes' faith in America's global leadership more generally. This report also observed that this lack of confidence was especially evident among members of the Swedish intellectual elite, and the USIA further highlighted the pivotal role that journalists had played in Sweden in fostering popular opposition to the war.[58]

"Anti-American" Sentiment and Diplomatic Maneuvers

American officials' incessantly griped about the one-sided nature of the Vietnam debate in Sweden, expressing their frustration about the seeming pro-Communist bias of the Swedish media.[59] These objections were mainly directed at the Social Democratic press, and at *Aftonbladet* specifically,[60] and at the time analogous complaints were also raised by a handful of Swedish commentators.[61]

Scholars who have studied this topic agree that Swedish news accounts about the war normally favored the Vietnamese Communists[62] and that this tendency was most pronounced in the Social Democratic and Liberal press.[63] (On occasion some Social Democratic and Liberal papers arguably even allowed themselves to become a direct conduit for North Vietnamese propaganda.)[64] The pro-NLF/DRV position adopted by vast parts of the Swedish press set it apart from most of its West European equivalents. In other West European countries, non-Communist papers were often equally critical of the American war effort, but they rarely, if ever, expressed any sympathy for the Vietnamese Communist cause.[65]

The Swedish media's increasingly negative perception of the US was not just limited to the war, but also touched upon the American domestic scene, and poverty, violence, and racial discrimination started to dominate its coverage of the United States.[66] The earlier postwar view of America as a role model and protector of the free world was now rapidly evaporating. This shift had first become visible in the early 1960s and grew more discernible as the decade wore on – and to a great extent it was a direct result of the war.[67] All of this combined to negatively affect popular attitudes towards the United States, even among older Swedes.[68]

Such antipathy towards to US was of course most keenly felt by radical anti-war activists,[69] though it had likewise spread to large parts of the parliamentary liberal-left,[70] including much of the Social Democratic rank and file.[71] Anti-American sentiments were by no means entirely new to the Swedish Social Democrats, as many older party activists had in the past nursed their own misgivings about select aspects of American society.[72] However, their reservations about the Unites States had never reached anything near the level of hostility that was now regularly being articulated by many younger Social Democrats.[73]

That anti-American opinion was on the rise in Sweden certainly did not escape the notice of US officials.[74] While the latter suspected that this phenomenon was being aided by Chinese and Soviet propaganda, they still laid most of the blame for this development at the feet of the Social Democratic administration. The Americans felt that the SAP leadership had indirectly facilitated the spread of such attitudes, first by its vocal critique of the war and second by its reluctance to take a stronger stance against the surging tide of political radicalism.[75]

The effloresce of anti-American sentiments was very tangible to US Embassy officials in Stockholm, whose daily work was often directly impeded by it. From 1967 onwards, American emissaries were regularly prevented from making public appearances by demonstrators, and they were often subject to verbal abuse as well as other forms of harassment when they tried to perform their official functions.[76] This behavior also extended to the destruction of US government property, resulting in extensive police measures to protect the Embassy.[77] All of this made for a hostile work environment, and American diplomats complained about their political and social isolation in Sweden.[78] In the words of Jerome Holland (the American Ambassador to Sweden 1970–1972): "as far as I know I am the only [US] Ambassador in Europe (including the USSR) that has to have a bodyguard at all times...the next US Ambassador [to Sweden] should receive hardship pay."[79]

Although the situation in Sweden, by any standard, was quite bad, the reality was that American officials experienced comparable problems in many other European countries during this period.[80] At the root of this problem was Washington's failure to convince the West European public about the rightness of its Vietnam policy.[81] Hence it was not just in Sweden that the Americans' efforts to generate goodwill for the war effort fell on deaf ears, but the bankruptcy of this undertaking was perhaps noticeable there earlier than it was in some other European countries.

In relation to Sweden, the Americans' problems were compounded by the reality that the United States' ability to pressure the Social Democratic administration to revise its stance on Vietnam was severely circumscribed. First of all, it must be recalled that the Swedish–American diplomatic conflict over the war took place at a time when the US saw its economic and strategic position in the world erode. This not only changed the power dynamics between the United States and Western Europe,[82] but it also greatly enhanced the relative importance of continued Swedish–American cooperation in several key areas. The end result was that Washington was in less of a position to dictate the terms of the two countries' relationship than it might previously have been.

American officials quickly determined that despite the vast disparity in power between the two nations, they did not have much leverage to use against Sweden. This was because in most areas of Swedish–American interaction, either the US government had no direct control, or to enact sanctions was only going to be detrimental to Washington's own interests.[83] Sweden notably did not owe any significant debts to the US, nor was it dependent on American economic assistance to pay for its defense expenditures. Deprived of these types of leverage, American policy-makers were left holding few trump cards in their dealings with Stockholm.

The nature of the predicament that the Americans found themselves in was aptly illustrated when Washington briefly considered cutting research grants to Sweden in retaliation against the Social Democratic government's Vietnam policy, but these plans were promptly dropped when it became clear that such a move would be counter-productive. Upon reviewing this issue, the State Department determined that Swedish–American scientific exchanges represented a net gain for the United States, and consequently any planned sanctions in this area should be shelved.[84] At one point Washington also contemplated denying Sweden continued access to American missile components, but it soon concluded that this too would not be in its own interests.[85]

The rationale for not implementing military sanctions against Sweden was rather straightforward in light of the reality that the two countries' security interests in northern Europe largely overlapped with each other. The reasons for not pursuing economic retribution appear to have been equally self-evident. (To a certain degree these two areas were directly inter-linked because an embargo of military equipment against Sweden would have further aggravated the United States' balance-of-payments problem.)[86] The specter of American economic sanctions had first been raised in conjunction with the Bertrand Russell War Crimes Tribunal in the late spring of 1967, and it resurfaced again in the aftermath of Palme's Sergels torg appearance.[87] While the possible ramifications of Heath's recall were enough to worry Swedish business interests,[88] there is no evidence that either the State Department or the Johnson administration ever contem-plated taking such punitive measures in this specific instance (or on any earlier occasion for that matter).[89]

There was a twofold explanation for this. First, economic sanctions were likely to be extremely unpopular among American businessmen who engaged in trade with Sweden, and they would be very difficult to enforce.[90] Second, the US enjoyed a positive trade balance with Sweden.[91] Accordingly, any such sanctions would inevitably hurt American economic interests as much as they would hurt Swedish interests, and this reality was not lost on some American politicians.[92] Nor were economic reprisals probably a very realistic course of action at a time when the US economy was already in grave trouble due to rising "stagflation." This latter phenomenon was, in turn, very much fueled by mounting trade deficits.[93] With this in mind, sanctions against one of the few Western European nations with which the United States enjoyed a favorable trade balance would have been ill advised. A possible final reason for avoiding punitive trade measures was because they would almost certainly have attracted further international attention to the Swedish Social Democrats' criticism of the war, which was something that the US stood little to gain from. (One might also speculate that this course of action was shunned because it was bound to estrange America's friends within the Swedish business community.)[94] All of this thus discouraged Washington from implementing any type of economic sanctions against Stockholm.

In retrospect, one is left with the distinct impression that the Johnson administration simply sought to ignore the Swedes as much as possible, which is also how it dealt with the French.[95] In the end, the White House rejected a more confrontational stance vis-à-vis its European detractors because such a course of action risked igniting isolationist sentiments at home, and additionally because it would undercut a unified Western front against the Soviet Union.[96]

This does not mean, however, that the Americans were overly concerned about the Swedes' protests against the war, and while President Johnson was not unaware of the Swedish position,[97] the Swedes had absolutely no influence on the White House's thinking about Vietnam.[98] Generally speaking, Johnson exhibited little interest in Scandinavia, or in Europe overall. His attention was directed elsewhere, mostly on domestic policy, and in the realm of foreign affairs the President's overriding concern was on the conduct of the war itself.[99]

Perhaps not surprisingly, Johnson's policy towards Europe has received mostly negative reviews from historians.[100] In no small part, this policy faltered due to the President's dogged pursuit of a military solution to the crisis in Indochina – an approach that did not win him many admirers in Europe. The Europeans' antipathy was underscored by their staunch refusal to participate directly in the Vietnamese conflict. Having failed to obtain such support, the President strove to ensure that America's allies would at least refrain from openly condemning the US war effort.[101]

With the exception of Sweden and France,[102] Johnson largely managed to secure this secondary objective. To the White House, it was crucial to get tacit West German and British approval for the American war effort, which it more or less received. The Johnson administration, in contrast, was willing to live with France's hostile attitude, so long as this did not spread to the rest of the Western alliance.[103] It goes without saying that this observation was also applicable to Sweden, whose insolence was bearable exactly because of the country's relative insignificance to Washington.[104]

Fredrik Logevall points out that Washington was fairly successful at keeping its conflict with Stockholm localized and preventing it from spreading to Sweden's Nordic neighbors.[105] That having been said, the US was at the same time never able to totally silence the Swedish Social Democrats' criticism of the war, which was one of its chief aims towards Sweden in these years.[106] Taken as a whole, the Johnson administration's policy towards Sweden in this specific area must be said to have been static and unimaginative, and at times even wholly counter-productive. Rather than taking the initiative, the Johnson administration was seemingly always on the defensive vis-à-vis the Swedes, and it never developed an effective antidote to this challenge. Nor was President Richard Nixon's record any better in this regard. In fact, as we shall see, both presidential administrations inadvertently bolstered both Palme and the Social Democrats' political standing at home by trying to punish them for their stance on the war.

Like his predecessor, Nixon cared little about Sweden, or about any of the small Western European nations, except in those few occasions when their problems were directly related to NATO.[107] Aside from this, the President did not pay much attention to Western Europe, as he was mostly preoccupied with China and the Soviet Union, as well as with the American exit from Vietnam. Initially Nixon had set out to repair the United States' rapport with Europe, but this effort quickly collapsed, and by the time he left office, trans-Atlantic relations were worse than ever.[108]

This development occurred because the late 1960s and early 1970s had ushered in an era of exceptionally tense relations between America and its European allies, and while these tensions did not exclusively arise out of their disagreements about the war, the Vietnamese conflict was nonetheless critical to stirring up European discontent about Washington's leadership in world affairs.[109] The growing détente had loosened America's grip over its European allies, providing the latter with a newfound autonomy in international matters.[110] In the Swedish case, this meant that US officials had to be far more patient with the Social Democrats' behavior than they had to be even a decade earlier under the harsher political environment that had dominated the first decade and a half of the Cold War.

In this new international climate, a too heavy-handed American response to Social Democratic criticism of the Vietnam war was only bound to generate sympathy for Sweden among other West Europeans, even among those who did not necessarily approve of the Swedes' belligerency.[111] US decision-makers were not unaware of this problem, realizing that they could not afford to appear to bully Sweden because this surely would be negatively received elsewhere.[112] In particular, American officials were concerned about how the Swedish–American dispute might adversely affect Washington's relationship to the rest of Scandinavia.[113] In view of the hostile reception that Heath's recall had received in Denmark, Norway, and Finland, this was a legitimate worry.[114] The gravity of this situation was undoubtedly made worse by the fact that, at this time, the Nordic NATO members were all experiencing various degrees of rising domestic opposition to any continued affiliation with the alliance.[115]

A final consideration influencing American decision-making was the inherent risk of antagonizing the entire Swedish public if Washington reacted too harshly to the Social Democratic administration's protests against the American war effort. This issue received a lot of attention when it became known that Olof Palme was planning a private visit to the US in the summer of 1970. The White House, led by Nixon, was inclined to completely ignore Palme during his visit,[116] but the State Department cautioned against such an approach. The latter argued that this course of action was guaranteed to provoke the whole population and cause the Swedes to rally around Palme regardless of their individual opinions of him, for Palme would surely turn an overt US snub to his political advantage.[117] (In the end, these considerations won out, and Palme was granted a private audience with the new Secretary of State, William Rogers.)

All of these various considerations consequently had an inhibiting effect on American policy towards Sweden. In the aftermath of Palme's Sergels torg appearance, when American officials examined what possible options were open to them, they soon discovered that they really did not have many viable forms of punishment at their disposal, that is, beyond temporarily restricting a few official high-level trips to Sweden and canceling naval visits.[118] (This last measure was not a bad idea at any rate considering the number of American deserters that had already made their way to Sweden.) Aside from these two restrictions, US diplomats determined that they should concentrate on those areas where the two countries' cooperation continued to be most fruitful. It was furthermore decided that Washington would only ask for Stockholm's support when it absolutely needed it in various international forums; otherwise, America should adopt "a cool and correct," though not overtly hostile, attitude toward Sweden.[119] Over the next few years, this would remain the basic American approach, with Washington mostly relying on petty diplomatic snubs when it wanted to express its displeasure with Stockholm.[120]

Uniting the Party: Palme and Domestic Opinion

While not ideal, the Swedes could survive being spurned by the Americans in various official settings. This was bearable as long as this dispute did not escalate beyond diplomatic measures into realms that directly affected the country's overall well being. It was, however, just as important to the SAP hierarchy that its disagreement with Washington not harm the party domestically, though in the spring of 1968 this did not prove to be much of a concern. This was largely because Heath's recall was met with widespread resentment in Sweden, and it did not take long for American diplomats to see that this move had done considerable harm to the United States' standing in Sweden.[121]

As soon as this dawned upon the Americans, they made a quick about-face and attempted to tone down the seriousness of this episode. Upon his return to Stockholm in mid-April, Ambassador Heath immediately set out to reassure the Swedes about the United States' eagerness to resume normal relations. He now emphatically denied that his return to Washington had ever been intended as a protest against Social Democratic Vietnam policy, characterizing it instead as "a routine visit."[122]

As might be expected, the Social Democratic administration was equally keen to minimize this conflict. Its spokesmen insisted that the media had blown this whole matter out of proportion, adding that it was not at all certain that Heath's recall was intended to signal American disapproval with Sweden.[123] Palme further rejected the notion that his appearance at Sergels torg had been detrimental to the two countries' relationship.[124] Social Democratic leaders additionally affirmed that Sweden wanted good relations with the United States.[125]

These assurances indicated that the SAP hierarchy was anxious that the cabinet's dispute with the Americans was on the verge of spinning out of control. The above-mentioned Social Democratic disclaimers were therefore unmistakably motivated by a desire to protect Swedish national interests and were clearly likewise designed to deescalate the conflict. However, Social Democratic declarations to this effect were always also made with an eye toward domestic opinion.

Following Heath's recall, Social Democratic officials vehemently denied that their opposition to the war was driven by anti-Americanism.[126] This claim would be reiterated again and again through the rest of the war, usually at times when US–Swedish tensions were at their worst.[127] The timing of these statements underscores how the Social Democrats employed these sorts of pronouncements as a crisis management tool. This is not to imply that these disclaimers were totally insincere or that the SAP hierarchy was inherently anti-American. However, as its domestic and American detractors both correctly observed, the Social Democratic administration's strident critique of US policy in Vietnam indisputably played to anti-American opinion, and by so doing it also indirectly bolstered the growth of such sentiments in Sweden.[128]

Still, even in the face of rising anti-Americanism there existed a substantial reservoir of goodwill towards the United States in Sweden, which American diplomats were well aware of.[129] They also realized that the Social Democratic establishment had to walk a delicate balance on this issue, for the government could not afford to satisfy radical anti-war opinion if it came at the expense of offending the pro-American sympathies of many Swedish voters.[130] As soon as the American decision to recall Heath had been announced, the US Embassy received a huge number of letters, telegrams, and flower bouquets from Swedish well-wishers, which all expressed regret about the deteriorating state of Swedish–American relations.[131] Such declarations of support for the United States were by no means unique during these years,[132] though these tended to receive less attention.[133]

At this juncture, it is also imperative to point out that the Swedish public was not entirely unreserved in its support for the government's approach to the war. This was revealed in a poll conducted by the country's second largest Liberal daily, *Expressen*, which indicated that 49 per cent of the respondents disapproved of Palme's participation in the Sergels torg rally and only 33 per cent felt that he had acted appropriately.[134] In other words, the public's deep antipathy towards the American war effort did not automatically translate into an unqualified embrace of the cabinet's stance on Vietnam.

Palme's actions, then, could potentially have been a huge liability for the SAP had it not been for the opposition's clumsy response to Heath's recall. While the Center Party avoided any direct criticism of the Social Democratic administration,[135] members of both the Conservative and Liberal parties strongly castigated the government once the news broke that Heath was being called back to Washington. At this stage, the domestic debate about the war was not about the relative merits of US policy (since by now virtually everyone agreed that it was deeply flawed), but rather it focused on the question of whether or not the conduct of the Social Democratic administration had damaged the credibility of Swedish neutrality.[136] Had the non-socialist opposition stopped there, its objections probably would not have sparked much controversy. However, a handful of its leading representatives professed to "understand" the American reaction and called upon the government to issue a formal apology.[137] The Conservative leader Yngve Holmberg went so far as to suggest that Palme should resign.[138]

This last demand proved to be a terrible blunder on Holmberg's part because it cast Palme into the role of martyr, and even worse it opened the Conservatives up to the charge that they were running Washington's errands.[139] Some within the Conservative Party at once recognized the inherent risk in calling for such a drastic step, and they would later concede that this had been a major tactical mistake.[140] Most other non-socialist politicians, meanwhile, distanced themselves from Holmberg's position.[141] For this reason Holmberg was forced to retreat, and this was also gleefully noted in the Social Democratic press.[142] All in all, Holmberg's call for Palme to resign was not well received in the non-socialist press, which for the most part disapproved as much of the American action as they did Palme's decision to appear by Chan's side at the rally.[143]

The SAP leadership adeptly made the most of the circumstances, accusing both the Conservatives and Liberals of caving in to American pressure.[144] Social Democratic spokesmen moreover insinuated that the opposition's response to Heath's recall proved that the non-socialist bloc was not a trustworthy guardian of the country's neutrality.[145] These allegations were naturally echoed by the Social Democratic press, which launched a fierce counterattack against the opposition, implying that the Conservatives and Liberals were essentially American pawns.[146]

Interestingly, the Social Democrats reserved their sharpest barbs for the Liberals[147] despite the fact that it had been the Conservatives who had attacked Palme the hardest. Presumably this was because the SAP viewed the Liberal Party as its primary non-socialist adversary heading into the election.[148] Even though the VPK remained the Social Democrats' chief competitor for the anti-war vote, the Social Democrats skillfully converted the domestic fallout from Heath's recall into an opportunity to discredit the non-socialist opposition as well.[149]

The SAP would subsequently play the nationalism card throughout the rest of the election campaign, portraying itself as the only reliable guarantor of an independent Swedish posture in world affairs. To great effect, party spokesmen stressed that only under a Social Democratic government would Sweden be the sole arbitrator of its own foreign policy.[150]

To their credit, American officials grasped that Heath's recall had been a dismal failure from both a political and public relations standpoint. Not only had it provoked a very adverse reaction, but it had also allowed the Social Democrats to cast themselves in the role of David versus Goliath. This being the case, US interests would be best served by Heath returning to Stockholm as quickly as possible, and the Embassy in Stockholm should just seek to lay low for a while. Although the Americans resented being a Social Democratic punching bag, they recognized that, at the moment, any further US initiatives on this front would only help the SAP in the upcoming election. They likewise realized that in the future the non-socialist opposition would probably not be able to effectively challenge the Social Democratic administration's policy on Vietnam because to do so would once again make them vulnerable to allegations of disloyalty.[151] Sure enough, hereafter the opposition's criticism of the government's approach to the war grew considerably more muted.

That the non-socialist parties had failed to capitalize on Palme's Sergels torg appearance did not change the reality that some parts of the electorate continued to have serious qualms about the whole affair. This caused *Expressen* to conclude that this incident would harm Palme politically and undermine his chances of succeeding Erlander.[152] The paper also reiterated this argument once the results of the (previously mentioned) poll were released in late March. *Expressen* cited the fact that 49 per cent of those polled expressed reservations about Palme's participation in the rally as proof that his actions did not enjoy broad popular backing.[153] The fundamental weakness of this argument, however, was that this poll did not break down the results by the respondents' respective political affiliations. If it had, it is highly probable that it would have shown that most Social Democrats condoned his behavior.

This is not to say that there were not any dissenting voices within the SAP as well,[154] but if one examines the Social Democratic reaction overall, one finds overwhelming support for Palme.[155] In the wake of Heath's recall, resolutions backing Palme – and his stance on Vietnam – poured in from the SAP districts as well as from the party's auxiliary organizations.[156] The SSSF even proposed that Sweden should return in kind and retrieve the Swedish Ambassador from Washington.[157] Though few other Social Democrats were willing to go quite that far, there can be little doubt that the party was now united behind the government's new assertive approach to the situation in Indochina.[158]

To the SAP leadership, this was undoubtedly also its main concern. If one examines the letters that Palme received from private individuals after the Sergels torg rally, favorable responses outnumbered the negative ones by almost a 5 to 1 ratio (95 to 20.) In the 39 instances in which the author explicitly identified themselves as either a Social Democratic voter or party member, only 3 complained about Palme's participation in the demonstration. These messages otherwise typically thanked Palme for his courage, pleading with him to stand his ground. Many of these Social Democratic letter writers further professed that Palme was a source of personal inspiration and praised him for ideologically reinvigorating the party.[159]

Such approval was by no means limited to the Social Democratic faithful, as was demonstrated by the great number of favorable letters that Palme also received from assorted local VPK chapters and peace groups.[160] Yet, generally speaking, it should simultaneously be stressed that Palme's conduct in this instance seems to have been more popular among younger voters than among older ones.[161] So although this episode cannot be said to have been an entirely unqualified success for the SAP, in the end it still probably greatly boosted the party's chances of capturing the youth anti-war vote.

Beyond its likely electoral impact, Palme's mere presence at the Sergels torg rally helped to establish a closer rapport between the government and the SKfV.[162] In reaction to Heath's recall, SKfV issued a press release declaring its unconditional support for Palme.[163] The committee specifically urged the cabinet to not let itself be intimidated by the Americans.[164] This sort of appeal, in turn, made it virtually impossible for the Social Democratic leadership to disavow Palme's conduct, even if it had wanted to do so. Palme himself certainly did not express any regrets about his appearance at the rally.[165]

If anything, the party hierarchy circled the wagons around Palme, fending off outside criticism.[166] Internally, SAP leaders stressed the Sergels torg rally's importance to the party's counter-offensive against the far left by emphasizing that it would have been totally irresponsible to have let the NLF-groups hijack popular anti-war opinion.[167] The Social Democratic press took the same tack, energetically defending Palme's (as well as the government's) right to speak out against the war.[168] At this point, some of the smaller rural Social Democratic papers' earlier cautiousness with regard to the Vietnam issue also gave way to a resounding endorsement of Palme's more confrontational approach to US policy.[169]

In response to these events, *Arbetet* (the second largest and most influential Social Democratic daily after *Aftonbladet*) sponsored a write-in campaign in support of Palme. *Arbetet* subsequently claimed that it had gotten an overwhelmingly positive reaction from its readers, who with few exceptions had expressed their complete faith in Palme.[170] *Aftonbladet* similarly boasted that Palme's anti-war stance was widely championed by the party's rank and file,[171] and this outpouring of support for Palme continued well into the summer of 1968.[172]

In retrospect, it is plain to see that the events surrounding the Sergels torg rally considerably strengthened Palme's standing within the SAP. Consequently, Washington and the non-socialist opposition had inadvertently helped Palme a great deal. This was widely recognized by his supporters and detractors alike, and at the time many people were additionally convinced that this entire ordeal had secured his status as Erlander's successor.[173]

On the heels of Heath's recall, Erlander speculated that if the election for his replacement was to be held right now, there was little doubt that Palme would have been appointed as the new SAP leader because his status within the party had never been higher.[174] This observation was seemingly validated by a lot of the letters that Palme received in the months immediately following the Sergels torg demonstration. Indeed, some Social Democratic well-wishers congratulated Palme on surpassing his competitors on route to the prime ministership, while many others expressed a desire for him to inherit the top post once Erlander retired.[175] Prior to this, many people had likewise regarded Krister Wickman and/or Gunnar Sträng as strong candidates to take over the reigns from Erlander. While it is difficult to definitively establish what exact role Palme's Sergels torg appearance had in catapulting him to the frontrunner position, all who have studied this matter agree that this episode indisputably bolstered his position in the party.[176] In this context, it is of some interest that a phone poll conducted by *Aftonbladet* in mid-March indicated that Palme (at least according to the paper's readers) was currently the most admired politician in Sweden and that his popularity easily surpassed that of both Wickman and Sträng.[177] These findings were subsequently confirmed by another poll in late fall of 1968, which revealed that Palme's stock had risen drastically among Social Democratic voters over the course of the past year. At this juncture, he had then seemingly established himself as the uncontested favorite to succeed Erlander.[178]

This it not to suggest that Palme's rising political star was wholly tied to his outspoken opposition to the American war effort. Irrespective of Indochina, by early 1968 Palme was already the most probable candidate to replace Erlander.[179] Hence it would be an oversimplification to accredit this question exclusively for Palme's promotion to prime minister, but at the same time it is undeniable that his vocal critique of the American war effort appreciably facilitated his political assent.

It is also quite apparent that the fallout from the Sergels torg rally energized the Social Democratic faithful. The events surrounding Heath's recall had caused the political climate to heat up and propelled the Social Democratic cadre into action.[180] This development was welcomed by the party hierarchy because the latter had made mobilizing the cadre and the party's voters a key priority in its election strategy,[181] and the reality that the election campaign had partially been transformed into a referendum for or against Palme did much to advance this objective.[182] The attacks that were directed at him ultimately served to unify the party, and many Social Democrats would later credit him with orchestrating the SAP's dramatic "comeback" victory in 1968.[183]

Needless to say, Social Democratic anti-war activists were especially pleased by Palme's actions, and they celebrated that the party and the government had substantially moved forward their respective positions on Vietnam.[184] Above all, they were glad that the SAP hierarchy had once and for all resolved to wrest this question away from the Communists and the Maoists. The party no longer lagged behind its Marxist rivals – and no less significantly – it had also caught up with the deeply felt anti-war sentiments of its own party activists.[185] Looking back, this question was probably far more important to the party cadre than it ever was to the average Social Democratic voter.

Right and Left Opposition Loses Ground

The next several months witnessed a spike in Social Democratic protests against the war,[186] and Vietnam was prominently featured in the party's 1 May celebrations[187] as well as during the SAP Congress in June.[188] Buoyed by this renewed sense of purpose, the party stepped up its counter-attacks against the revolutionary left, and against the DFFG in particular.[189]

In no small part, this was a reaction to the NLF-groups' heightened agitation against the Social Democrats, which showed no signs of lessening. Quite the contrary actually, for the end of April was marked by a spate of bellicose protests against the government's Vietnam policy.[190] The Maoist advance, however, was soon seriously hampered by two separate events in May. The first was a violent standoff in Bålstad between radical demonstrators and police during a protest against the Ian Smith regime in Rhodesia, and the second was the occupation of the student union at Stockholm University. Both episodes were very unfavorably looked upon by most older Swedes, and taken together they amounted to a public relations disaster for the far left[191] because these incidents appear to have angered, and by extension also mobilized, many older Social Democratic voters who came out in defense of the status quo.[192]

Around this same time, the revolutionary branch of the anti-war movement was also destabilized by the sudden appearance of a new splinter group. Although the so-called "rebel" faction quickly self-imploded, it survived just long enough to wreak significant havoc among the NLF-groups and briefly slow their forward momentum.[193] The rebels' bizarre sect-like behavior also generally damaged the far left's image. So while not fatally wounded, the DFFG was nevertheless suddenly plunged into a state of internal turmoil, and as a result the organization was temporarily forced to concentrate its energies on rebuilding. *De förenade FNL-grupperna* (DFFG) did not subsequently participate in the 1968 election campaign; instead, they indirectly advocated a boycott by refusing to endorse either the SAP or the VPK.[194]

The upshot of this entire situation was that the Maoists did not noticeably affect the Social Democrats' election strategy, thereby allowing the SAP to focus on VPK as its chief competitor for the anti-war vote. Stressing the party's own Vietnam credentials,[195] the Social Democratic leadership cited Sweden's earlier role in trying to facilitate a peaceful solution to the Vietnamese conflict, and it additionally promised to increase Swedish humanitarian assistance to the NLF/DRV.[196] Nor did the government seek to hide that its posture against the American war effort had hardened in recent months.[197] By this time there existed internal consensus that this question must play a key role in the election campaign and that the party should highlight its policy of solidarity with the Third World in a bid to appeal to younger voters.[198]

That the Social Democrats were seeking to distinguish themselves on the Vietnam question against the Communists on the campaign trail did not go unnoticed by either the non-socialist opposition[199] or the Americans. US Embassy officials believed that this move was mostly designed to hold on to the party's traditional share of first-time voters.[200]

For their part, the Communists were very optimistic about making further gains at the SAP's expense,[201] and to that end the VPK had kept up an aggressive stance on the war leading up to the 1968 election.[202] On one hand, the Communists had defended Palme's participation in the Sergels torg rally vis-à-vis the non-socialist opposition; but on the other, they had concomitantly rebuked the government for not taking an even stronger stand in favor of the NLF/DRV.[203] At the moment, this clearly appeared to be a promising electoral strategy given that popular sentiments against the American war effort remained exceedingly high. A poll taken just prior to the election indicated that 80 per cent of the Swedish public felt that the US should withdraw from Indochina.[204]

The Communists' militancy on Vietnam ultimately did not provide them with the electoral dividends they had anticipated. There were several reasons for this. First of all, by the late summer of 1968 popular passions about the war had begun to die down somewhat owing to the partial halt to the bombing and the commencement of the Paris peace talks.[205] American officials in Stockholm were naturally encouraged by this development, noting that during the last two months of the Swedish election campaign the Vietnamese conflict had lost some of its previous importance.[206] Instead, the electorate's attention was mainly preoccupied with domestic issues, and in the final weeks leading up to the election the war retreated more and more into the background.[207]

Secondly, and even worse for the Communists, was that the culmination of the election campaign unfolded in the shadow of the Soviet invasion of Czechoslovakia. The SAP leadership reacted swiftly to the Red Army's march into Prague, condemning Soviet aggression in no uncertain terms.[208] Though the VPK also vigorously protested the Soviet action, this was to no avail, because the invasion tarnished the Swedish Communists by association. As a result, the VPK was punished at the polls, spelling a disaster for the Communists who registered their lowest level of support in 20 years. In contrast, the election was an unparalleled triumph for the SAP, which captured 50.1 per cent of the total vote giving it a majority in the parliament.[209] While it is hard to measure precisely the electoral impact of the events in Czechoslovakia, Communist and Social Democratic leaders alike deemed it to have been a decisive factor in the election result.[210]

Social Democratic criticism of the Soviet invasion not only helped the SAP to nab voters from the Communists, but it was also a useful alibi against accusations of anti-Americanism. Hereafter the Social Democratic leadership would frequently cite the government's boisterous opposition to the crushing of the Prague Spring as proof that it did not favor the Soviets over the United States.[211] This was a key point for the SAP to impress upon the party's more moderate voters. By the same token, the SAP's outspoken protests against Soviet aggression in no way hurt the party in its efforts the court the 68-generation because the latter was also extremely hostile to the USSR.[212] Hence, it seems almost certain that the invasion of Czechoslovakia likewise harmed the VPK's standing among young radical voters.

An additional reason for the Communist losses stemmed from their zealous support of the student left, which appears to have discredited the party in the eyes of many older blue-collar voters who felt little sympathy for the youth revolt.[213] (This was another situation that the SAP hierarchy was quick to exploit.)[214] However, the two main reasons that are usually cited to explain the Social Democrats' landslide victory in 1968 are the party's effective mobilization of its own cadre and voters and the SAP's successful retention of its customary share of first-time voters.[215] The Vietnam issue undeniably played a crucial, albeit indirect, part in both of these accomplishments.

While the government's new posture on the war clearly seems to have invigorated Social Democratic campaign workers,[216] its overall electoral benefit for the party remains more uncertain. Still, this policy probably did help to lure at least some new younger voters to the party.[217] This seems like a safe bet considering that the Social Democrats did very well among first-time voters in 1968. The SAP recovered its losses within this segment of the electorate from the previous election, and it further reestablished its historically robust standing among university students and voters under 30.[218]

What we do know for certain is that the Social Democratic establishment itself attributed these gains in no small part to the party's increasingly assertive posture in world affairs. This was especially so of its newfound approach to the war, which the party hierarchy was convinced had brought the SAP a new generation of voters.[219] All in all, Social Democratic leaders determined that the party's more radical and overtly ideological profile had been a significant electoral asset and that the SAP should stay true to this path during the next election as well.[220]

American officials similarly concluded that in view of this impressive election victory, the SAP hierarchy was sure to think it had stumbled upon a very successful political formula that could deliver large numbers of first-time voters, while at the same time keeping the Communists in check. For this reason, US diplomats did not expect Swedish Vietnam policy to undergo any major revisions,[221] and they anticipated that the SAP would stick to this strategy up through the 1970 election.[222] That the Social Democrats' strident anti-war position was not likely to change seemed like a reasonable assumption given that a poll conducted immediately after the election showed that the Swedes (and the younger ones in particular) were far more antagonistic towards the American war effort than any other West Europeans.[223]

For the Social Democrats, then, the election result vindicated the party's new forward strategy with regard to this question. Following the election, the SAP at last seemed to have gained the upper hand over both the Communists and the Maoists, and the party was determined not to relinquish its improved standing among younger voters. In relation to the Vietnam issue, however, this required continual vigilance, and special attention still had to be paid to the lingering Maoist threat (a point to which we will return in Chapter 6.)

***

Indeed, from the 1968 election onward, the Social Democratic establishment was fully committed to leading public opinion against the war, and to this end it would rely heavily on the revamped SKfV. To a great extent, the SKfV managed to contain the DFFG's attempt to commandeer popular opposition to the war, but the Social Democratic administration would simultaneously pay a steep price for this arrangement, unwittingly becoming hostage to the committee in the process.

The future leader of the Conservative Party, Gösta Bohman, had anticipated this problem, and after the Sergels torg rally he had warned Torsten Nilsson about the potential dangers of becoming captive to the anti-war movement. Nilsson apparently conceded that such a risk existed, but stated that under the current circumstances the cabinet did not feel it had much choice but to heed rising public opposition to the war lest this question be usurped by the far left.[224] American officials had already previously cautioned Social Democratic officials not to give in to radical anti-war agitation.[225] If it did so, this would only make the Social Democratic administration more susceptible to this type of pressure in the future[226] and this is exactly what occurred.

This tendency was very discernable in the government's relationship to the SKfV, which upon its reestablishment at once set out to push Swedish Vietnam policy in a more NLF/DRV-friendly direction.[227] With good reason, the committee would later claim to have had considerable influence over the cabinet's handling of the Vietnam issue,[228] which is something that few Social Democrats would dispute after the fact.[229] For the remainder of the war, the government was usually willing to accommodate the SKfV, de facto giving the latter a significant say in the formulation of the administration's approach to the war.

The committee's political clout was perhaps best illustrated by the fact that the Social Democratic administration permitted it to maintain its own contacts with the Vietnamese Communists that ran parallel the government's diplomatic relations with the NLF/DRV. The SKfV rapidly established a warm rapport with the Vietnamese Communists, and this relationship was sustained through regular visits.[230] For instance, following one such trip to Hanoi, the Swedish Ambassador to the DRV, Jean-Christophe Öberg, reported that the SKfV's Chairperson, Birgitta Dahl, had received the "royal treatment" during her stay. According to Öberg, she had been welcomed in this manner because the North Vietnamese "fully appreciated the committee's political influence in Sweden."[231]

Somewhat astonishingly, the SKfV had on its own initiative invited the National Liberation Front to set up an information bureau in Stockholm.[232] Originally the government had apparently expressed reservations about this prospect, but at the same time it had been wary of offending domestic anti-war opinion. The cabinet had sought to avoid this question altogether, hoping that the Vietnamese would not ask for permission to open such an office.[233] However, once the SKfV had formally extended this invitation, the Social Democratic administration accepted it *a fait accompli*, welcoming the NLF delegation to Stockholm.[234] The SAP actually even provided the necessary funds to set up the bureau,[235] and the government would later also give in to the SKfV's demand that Sweden establish an Embassy in Hanoi.[236]

This last initiative had followed Sweden's diplomatic recognition of the DRV in January 1969, which the committee had likewise had a big hand in. It would later take credit for this decision, along with the one to open Sweden up to American deserters. As we shall see in the next chapter, SKfV successfully put pressure on the Social Democratic administration to grant asylum to US military fugitives. Thus by complying with the committee's wishes, the government secured the latter's goodwill but at the expense of its own freedom of maneuver.

Chapter 3: Notes

[1] Geoff Eley, *Forging Democracy* (New York: Oxford University Press, 2002) 341–342.

[2] *SAP VU-protokoll* 10 Feb. 1968. According to Kaj Björk, it was predominantly those Social Democratic leaders who represented urban and university areas (such as Hjalmar Mehr, Sten Andersson, and Torsten Nilsson) that pushed for the party to take a more aggressive stance on this issue, whereas those people who represented more conservative rural areas were less concerned about the Vietnam question. Kaj Björk, *Vägen till Indokina* (Stockholm: Atlas, 2003) 151.

[3] *Dagens Nyheter* 22 Oct. 1967.

[4] Erik Svanfeldt, "Svenska kommittén för Vietnam" (University of Uppsala, 1990) 14–17.

[5] Gunnar himself had earlier been a Minister in a Social Democratic government.

[6] Birgitta Dahl, "Solidaritetsarbetet för Vietnam" in Enn Kokk (ed.), *Var blev ni av ljuva drömmar?* (Stocholm: Ordfront, 2002) 192. Palme was apparently quite up front about this point in his discussions with US officials, commending Dahl for containing Communist subversion both inside and outside of the SKfV. 12 Dec. 1972. *Chargé d'affairs* US Embassy Stockholm. John Guthrie. Telegram to State. Re: Yesterday's conversation with Olof Palme. Subject Numeric Files 1970–73. Political and Defense. Sweden. RG 59.

[7] A majority of the SKfV's original board members were either directly or indirectly affiliated with the SAP. In addition to Gunnar Myrdal and Evert Svensson, Bengt Liljenroth, Yngve Persson, Erik Eriksson, Folke Isaksson, Arne Eriksson, Ann-Marie Sundbom and Hans-Göran Franck all also served on the committee. There was a particularly strong tie between the SKfV and *Stockholms arbetarekommun*, which, like the SSU, became an official member of the committee. Kaj Björk states that *Stockholms arbetarekommun's* decision to join the SKfV was in no small part informed by Torsten Nilsson's need to quell internal criticism of the government's Vietnam policy. Björk, *Vägen till Indokina*, 150.

[8] Rune Nordin, *Fackföreningsrörelsen i Sverige* (Stockholm: Prisma, 1981) 345–349, 367–379; Svanfeldt, "Svenska Kommittén för Vietnam," 36–38.

[9] Birgitta Dahl, SKfV Chairperson 1971–1977, interview with author 27 May 2004.

[10] SKfV, "Appell för Vietnams folk." Svenska kommittén för Vietnam, Laos och Kambodja. 1568/B/1/1 Utgående handlingar. Vol 1967–1989. 3077. See also Yngve Möller, *Sverige och Vietnamkriget* (Stockholm: Tiden, 1992) 109.

[11] *Aftonbladet* 7 Jan. 1968. See also Evert Svensson as cited by Svanfeldt, "Svenska Kommittén för Vietnam," 21.

[12] See, op-eds by Gunnar Myrdal in *Dagens Nyheter* 25 Jan. 1968 and 29 Feb. 1968

[13] For specific illustrations, see Peter Weiss and Jan Myrdal's op-eds in *Aftonbladet* 6 Feb 1969 and 11 Feb. 1968. See also *Tidsignal* # 12 1968, 13.

[14] Christopher Sundgren, "Splittrad Solidaritet" in Maj-Lis Erikson, *et al.* (eds.), *Med eller mot strömmen?* (Stockholm: Sober, 1980) 146–147.

[15] Tommy Hammarström, *FNL i Sverige* (Stockholm: AB Solidaritet, 1975) 104–107.

[16] Bengt Liljenroth, "Vietnamrörelsen i Sverige" in Lars Torbiörnsson (ed.), *Tålamodets triumf* (Stockholm: Prisma, 1973) 241–242; Sundgren, "Splittrad Solidaritet," 140–145.

[17] Möller, *Sverige och Vietnamkriget*, 109.

[18] Svanfeldt, "Svenska Kommittén för Vietnam," 30.

[19] Torsten Nilsson as cited in *SAP PS-protokoll* 17 March 1970. See also Björk, *Vägen till Indokina*, 167, 200.

[20] Incidentally, in 1970 Moscow awarded Svanström the Lenin Peace Prize for his work against the war. *Svenska Dagbladet* 18 April 1970.

[21] Dahl interview with the author 27 April 2004. In this context, it is also worth noting that the Stockholm Conference on Vietnam had strong ties to the Soviet-controlled World Peace Council.

[22] Svanfeldt, "Svenska Kommittén för Vietnam," 22–23.

[23] Möller, *Sverige och Vietnamkriget*, 360–361; Björk, *Vägen till Indokina*, 200–204.

[24] *Stockholms arbetarekommun. Verksamhetsberättelse 1968*, 16.

[25] Svanfeldt, "Svenska Kommittén för Vietnam," 20.

[26] Palme as cited in UD, *Utrikesfrågor 1968* (Stockholm: UD, 1968) 115–121. Among other things, Palme stated that the American war in Vietnam "is a threat to the ideals of democracy not only in Vietnam, but in the whole world."

[27] Björn Elmbrant, *Palme* (Stockholm: Författarförlaget, 1989) 71–79; Sven Svensson, *I maktens labyrinter* (Stockholm: Bonnier, 1968) 168–169.

[28] Bertil Östergren, *Vem är Olof Palme?* (Stockholm: Timbro, 1984) 134; Hans Haste, *Boken om Palme* (Stockholm: Tiden, 1986) 38, 42.

[29] See, for example, Gösta Bohman as cited in *Riksdagsprotokollet* # 13, 21 March 1968, 41–42; and Bo Turesson as cited in *Expressen* 29 Feb. 1968. See also Gustaf von Platen's column in *Veckojournalen* # 11 1968, 2–3.

[30] See, for instance, Tage Erlander as cited in *Dagens Nyheter* 10 March 1968.

[31] Möller, Sverige och Vietnamkriget, 114–120; Björk, Vägen till Indokina, 157.

[32] 12 March 1968. Letter to Tage Erlander from Bertil Svanström. Svenska kommittén för Vietnam, Laos och Kambodja. 1568/E/1/2 Korrespondens. Vol 1967–1968. 3077.

[33] According to Kaj Björk, both Nilsson and Erlander were actually quite worried about how Washington might react to Palme's joint appearance with Chan, to the point that Erlander had tried to get *Stockholms arbetarekommun* to find a last minute replacement for Palme. Yet in the end, Erlander and Nilsson did not prevent him from participating because they both feared that, if they did, they would be attacked by Social Democratic anti-war activists. Björk, *Vägen till Indokina*, 154–157.

[34] *Expressen* 22 Feb. 1968; *Dagens Nyheter* 22 Feb. 1968. See also Kim Salomon, *Rebeller i takt med tiden* (Stockholm: Rabén & Sjögren, 1996) 177–178.

[35] DFFG, *Rapport om Vietnamarbetet i Sverige 1965-1967. Till DFFG:s Kongress 21–23 Juni 1968*. DFFG. A:5 Blandade protokoll m.m. 1967–1973. Vol 1. See also Hammar-ström, FNL i Sverige, 61.

[36] For a specific illustration, see Yngve Holmberg as cited in the *New York Times* 17 March 1968. See also Gösta Bohman, *Inrikes utrikespolitik* (Stockholm: Geber, 1970).

[37] Gun Rehnberg, "Efter Gävle och Sergels torg" in Lars Svedgård, *Palme* (Stockholm: Rabén & Sjögren, 1970) 158–167. For specific examples, see editorials in *Vimmerby Tidning* 22 Feb. 1968, *Svenska Dagbladet* 23 Feb. 1968, *Expressen* 2 March 1968, *Jönköpings-Posten* 11 March 1968 and *Gotlands Allehanda* 13 March 1968.

[38] *Dagens Nyheter* 22 March 1968. Some Liberal papers, however, approved of Palme's conduct exactly because of its domestic implications, arguing that it was crucial that the Vietnam issue not be exploited by the far left. See, for instance, editorial in *Kvällsposten* 24 Feb. 1968.

[39] For specific illustrations, see Tage Erlander as cited in *Riksdagsprotokollet* # 13, 21 March 1968, 32. and Olof Palme as cited in *Aftonbladet* 21 April 1968.

[40] See, for instance, editorials in *Arbetet* 2 March 1968, *Västerbottens Folkblad* 11 March 1968, *Dala-Demokraten* 13 March 1968 and *Aftonbladet* 16 March 1968.

[41] 6 March 1968. Political Division FM. Wilhelm Wachtmeister. Memo. Re: Today's meeting between Tage Erlander and William W. Heath. Avd HP. Grupp 1. Mål Ua. Politik Allmänt. USA. # 221.

[42] 11 March 1968. US Ambassador to Sweden 1967–1969. William W. Heath. Memo. Re: Today's meeting with Torsten Nilsson. Central Foreign Policy File 1967–1969. Political and Defense. Sweden. RG 59.

[43] 27 Feb. 1968. William W. Heath. Telegram to State. Central Foreign Policy File 1967–1969. Political and Defense. Sweden. RG 59; 11 March 1968. Special Assistant to the President Marvin Watson. Memo to the President. Office Files of Marvin Watson. Box # 32. L.B.J. Library.

[44] 28 Feb. 1968. Secretary of State. Dean Rusk. Telegram to William W. Heath. Central Foreign Policy File 1967–1969. Political and Defense. Sweden. RG 59. See also William W. Heath. Oral History Interview. L.B.J. Library. 25 May 1970. Tape # 2, 15–16.

[45] UD, *Sverige i utlänsk press 1968*, 20–22.

[46] See, for example, the *Washington Post* 10 March 1968, *New York Times* 13 March 1968 and *US News & World Report* 18 March 1968.

[47] For specific illustrations, see Yngve Möller as cited in *Riksdagsprotokollet* # 11, 13 March 1968, 31–32. and C-H Hermansson as cited in *Svenska Dagbladet* 13 March 1968.

[48] 9 March 1968. Wilhelm Wachtmeister. Memo. Re: Meeting with William W. Heath on 8 March 1968. Avd HP. Grupp 1. Mål Ua. Politik Allmänt. USA. # 222. See also unidentified US State Department official as cited in the *Washington Evening Star* 9 March 1968.

[49] 7 May 1966. US Ambassador to Sweden 1961–1967. J. Graham Parsons. Telegram to State. Subject Numeric Files 1964–1966. Political and Defense. Sweden. RG 59; 8 July 1966. J. Graham Parsons. Telegram to State. Subject Numeric Files 1964–1966. Political and Defense. Sweden. RG 59.

[50] 26 Oct. 1965. J. Graham Parsons. Letter to Vice-President Hubert Humphrey. Subject Numeric Files 1964–1966. Political and Defense. Sweden. RG 59; 24 May 1966. J. Graham Parsons. Telegram to State. Subject Numeric Files 1964–1966. Political and

Defense. Sweden. RG 59; 16 June 1967. William W. Heath. Memo. US Policy Assessment – Sweden 1967. Central Foreign Policy File 1967–1969. Political and Defense. Sweden. RG 59; 25 April 1969. *Chargé d'affairs* US Embassy Stockholm. Cameron Turner Jr. Telegram to State. Central Foreign Policy File 1967–1969. Political and Defense. Sweden. RG 59; Undated (ca. April 1970). European Section Dept. of State. Unsigned. Memo. Briefing Material for Ambassador Holland's Arrival in Stockholm – April 1970. Subject Numeric Files 1970–1973. Political and Defense. Sweden. RG 59; 23 Aug. 1972. U.S Ambassador to Sweden 1970–1972. Jerome Holland. Telegram to State. US Policy Assessment – Sweden 1972. Subject Numeric Files 1970–1973. Political and Defense. Sweden. RG 59.

[51] 22 Nov. 1967. First Secretary Political Division FM. Jean-Christophe Öberg. Memo. Re: Meeting with William W. Heath on 21 Nov. 1967 Avd HP. Grupp 1. Mål Ua. Politik Allmänt. USA. # 219; 6 Dec. 1967. Unsigned. Telegram to the Swedish Ambassador in the US Hubert de Besche. Re: US Embassy officials increasing irritation at Social Democratic Vietnam policy. Avd HP. Grupp 1. Mål Ua. Politik Allmänt. USA. # 220.

[52] 12 Jan. 1965. First Secretary Political Division FM. Jean-Christophe Öberg. Memo. Re: Impressions of recent visit to Saigon. Avd HP. Grupp 1. Mål Xv. Politik Allmänt. Vietnam. # 1189; 15 March 1965. Swedish Ambassador to China. Lennart Petri. Memo. Avd HP. Grupp 1. Mål Xv. Politik Allmänt. Vietnam. # 1189.

[53] Magnus Jerneck, *Kritik som utrikespolitiskt medel* (Lund: Dialogus, 1983) 27–44. See also Lennart Petri, *Sverige i stora världen* (Stockholm: Atlantis, 1996) 387–399, 418.

[54] 23 Sept. 1964. *Chargé d'affairs* ad interim US Embassy Stockholm. Alfred S. Jenkins. Telegram to State. Subject Numeric Files 1964–1966. Political and Defense. Sweden. RG 59.

[55] 17 Aug. 1965. J. Graham Parsons. Telegram to State. Subject Numeric Files 1964–1966. Political and Defense. Sweden. RG 59.

[56] 6 Oct. 1967. William W. Heath. Telegram to State. Central Foreign Policy File 1967–1969. Political and Defense. Sweden. RG 59; 7 Nov. 1967. Special Assistant to the President. Frederick Panzer. Memo to the President. Office Files of Frederick Panzer. Box 218. L.B.J. Library.

[57] Undated (ca. April 1967). European Section Dept of State. Unsigned. Memo. Sweden. Briefing Paper for New Ambassador William Heath. Central Foreign Policy File 1967–1969. Political and Defense. Sweden. RG 59; 6 Sept. 1969. Cameron Turner Jr. Telegram to State. Central Foreign Policy File 1967–1969. Political and Defense. Sweden. RG 59.

[58] 23 March 1970. USIA. Office of Research and Assessment. Memo. Swedish Public Opinion of the United States. USIA. Office of Research. Special Reports. 1964–1982. Box 8. S # 50.

[59] 23 Feb. 1968. Thomas L. Hughes. Memo to the Secretary of State. Central Foreign Policy File 1967–1969. Political and Defense. Sweden. RG 59; 28 April 1969. Cameron Turner Jr. Telegram to State. Central Foreign Policy File 1967–1969. Political and Defense. Sweden. RG 59; 20 Aug 1972. Jerome Holland. Memo. The Program of the US Embassy in Sweden April 1970–Sept. 1972. Subject Numeric Files 1970–1973. Political

and Defense. Sweden. RG 59. See also US Press Attaché, William Gordon as cited in in *Folket* 15 Feb. 1966; and J. Graham Parsons as cited in *Aftonbladet* 7 March 1967.
[60] 14 Jan. 1966. USIA Head. Leonard Marks. Memo to the White House. Office Files of Frederick Panzer. Box 218. L.B.J. Library; 16 Feb. 1967. J. Graham Parsons. Letter to Torsten Nilsson regarding a recent article in *Arbetet*. Avd HP. Grupp 1. Mål Ua. Politik Allmänt. USA. # 217. See also Oral History Interview. William W. Heath. L.B.J. Library. 25 May 1970. Tape # 2, 17.

[61] For specific illustrations, see Sven Wedén's op-ed in *Dagens Nyheter* May 1966 and Göran Lindahl's op-ed in *Svenska Dagbladet* 30 May 1972. These types of accusations have also been voiced after the fact. See, for instance, Per Ahlmark, *Vänstern och tyranniet* (Stockholm: Timbro, 1994) 193–196. and Thede Palm, "Vietnamkriget i historien" *Svensk Tidskrift* 1981(3): 173–178.

[62] Jörgen Westerståhl, "Vietnam i Sveriges Radio" (University of Gothenburg, 1968); Jan. E. Karlsson, "Vietnamkonfliktens Behandling i TT:s utgående material under perioden 11.2 – 9.3 1968" (University of Gothenburg, 1968); Jan Bjurström and Christer Isaksson, "Vietnamkonfliktens behandling i sju svenska morgon tidningar under peridoen 12 Feb. – Mars 1969" (University of Gothenburg, 1969). See also Olof Rydbeck, *I maktens närhet* (Stockholm: Bonnier, 1990) 214–219. and Johan Romin, *Desertören och Vietnamkriget* (Stockholm: Prisma, 2008) 170.

[63] Eva Queckfeldt, *"Vietnam."* (Lund: Gleerup, 1981) 73, 90–91; Åke Ortmark, *De okända makthavarna* (Stockholm: Wahlström & Widstrand, 1969) 375–376.

[64] For specific illustrations, see the article series by Erik Eriksson and Sara Lidman in *Aftonbladet* on 7 Jan. 1969, 9 Jan. 1969, 11 Jan. 1969 and 12 Jan. 1969, or Lasse Lindström's article in *Expressen* on 29 April 1971. See also editorial in *Arbetet* 13 June 1969.

[65] Dag Ryen, "Misted Mirrors" (University of Kentucky, 1992) vi–viii, 95–96, 100; Caroline Page, *US Official Propaganda during the Vietnam War* (London: Leicester University Press, 1996) 130–148.

[66] Eva Block, *Amerikabiliden i svensk dagspress 1963-1968* (Lund: Glennstrup, 1976) 122–131; Kjell Östberg, *1968* (Stockholm: Prisma, 2002) 57–60, 86–87, 158–159.

67 Birgitta Stene, "The Swedish Image of America" in Sven Hakon Rossel, *et al.*. (eds.), Images of America in Scandinavia (Atlanta: Rodopi, 1998) 180–188.

[68] Olof Petersson, *Väljarna och världspolitiken* (Stockholm: Norstedt, 1982) 11, 23, 43–45, 55–57, 100–101; Henry Bäck, *Den utrikespolitiska dagsordningen* (Stockholm: Gotab, 1979) 57–58.

[69] Sven-Olof Josefsson, *Året var 1968* (Dissertation. University of Gothenburg, 1996) 255–259. For specific examples, see various NLF-activists as cited in *Aftonbladet* 1 Nov. 1966 and *Svenska Dagbladet* 29 Jan. 1967.

[70] Petersson, *Väljarna och världspolitiken*, 53, 102.

[71] Yvonne Hirdman, *Vi bygger landet* (Stockholm: Tiden, 1988) 303; Nordin, *Fackföreningsrörelsen i Sverige*, 349. For specific examples, see *Aktuellt* # 16 1967, 8–9. and *Tiden* # 6 1968, 257–261.

[72] For specific examples, see Inga Thorsson, *Att internationalisera Sverige* (Stockholm: Tiden, 1971) 137–140. and Yngve Möller, *Mina tre liv* (Stockholm: Tiden, 1983) 249–271.

[73] A 1973 poll showed that Social Democrats under 30 years old were twice as likely to disapprove of US foreign policy than Social Democrats over 30. Petersson, *Väljarna och världspolitiken*, 57. For a specific example, see SSU Chairman Bosse Ringholm as cited in Svedgård, *Palme*, 122–123.

[74] 14 June 1968. William W. Heath. Telegram to State. Central Foreign Policy File 1967–1969. Political and Defense. Sweden. RG 59; 23 March 1970. USIA. Office of Research and Assessment. Memo. Swedish Public Opinion of the United States. USIA. Office of Research. Special Reports. 1964–1982. Box 8. S # 50.

[75] 24 May 1966. J. Graham Parsons. Telegram to State. Subject Numeric Files 1964–1966. Political and Defense. Sweden. RG 59; 28 Jan. 1967. Cameron Turner Jr. Memo. Re: Notes for the Ambassador's Consultations with the Secretary of State. Central Foreign Policy File 1967–1969. Political and Defense. Sweden. RG 59.

[76] See, for example, *Dagens Nyheter* 18 Oct. 1967, *Svenska Dagbladet* 29 Feb. 1968 and *Expressen* 17 April 1970.

[77] See, for instance *Aftonbladet* 1 Nov. 1966, *Dagens Nyheter* 30 Jan. 1967, *Folket* 24 Nov. 1970 and *Göteborgs-Posten* 3 Jan. 1971.

[78] 8 July 1968. Scandinavian Desk Dept. of State. Paul Hughes. Memo. Inspectors Briefing Material Embassy Stockholm. Central Foreign Policy File 1967–1969. Political and Defense. Sweden. RG 59.

[79] Holland as cited in *Newsweek* 27 June 1972.

[80] Suzanne Brown-Fleming, "Ambassador George Crews McGhee and the Vietnam Crisis" *SHAFR Newsletter* 26 (4)1995: 22–25.

[81] Page, US Official Propaganda during the Vietnam War, 298–307.

[82] Richard Barnett, *The Alliance* (New York: Simon and Schuster, 1983) 290–291; H.W. Brands, *The Wages of Globalism* (Oxford: Oxford University Press, 1995) 254–255.

[83] 11 June. 1968. William W. Heath. Memo. US Policy Assessment – Sweden 1968. Central Foreign Policy File 1967–1969. Political and Defense. Sweden. RG 59; 3 Dec. 1970. Jerome Holland. Memo. US Policy Assessment – Sweden 1970. Subject Numeric Files 1970–1973. Political and Defense. Sweden. RG 59; 23 Aug. 1972. Jerome Holland. Memo. US Policy Assessment – Sweden 1972. Subject Numeric Files 1970–1973. Political and Defense. Sweden. RG 59.

[84] 8 March 1968. William W. Heath. Memo to the Assistant Secretary for European Affairs Dept. of State John Leddy. Central Foreign Policy File 1967–1969. Political and Defense. Sweden. RG 59; 1 April 1968. David M. McKillop. Memo to John Leddy. Central Foreign Policy File 1967–1969. Political and Defense. Sweden. RG 59.

[85] SOU, *Fred och säkerhet* (SOU 2002: 108) 320–328.

[86] 2 May 1969. Scandinavian Desk Dept. of State. George Mason Ingram. Memo. Central Foreign Policy File 1967–1969. Political and Defense. Sweden. RG 59.

[87] Fredrik Logevall, "The Swedish–American Conflict over Vietnam" *Diplomatic History* 1993 17 (3): 430–433.

[88] See, for instance, Bengt Håkansson as cited in *Svenska Dagbladet* 14 April 1968 and Göran Agrell as cited in *Sydsvenska Dagbladet* 10 May 1968.

[89] The same point can be made about the Nixon administration. See, for instance, Carl Rowan as cited in *Aftonbladet* 16 April 1969.

[90] 25 July 1969. Edelman International Corp. "Review of Public Relations Program of the Swedish–American Chamber of Commerce," 3. (Courtesy of Edward Burton.) See also Anders Pers as cited in *Dagens Nyheter* 5 Dec. 1971.

[91] 29 Jan. 1969. Turner Cameron Jr. Telegram to State. Central Foreign Policy File 1967–1969. Political and Defense. Sweden. RG 59. Cameron cautions that any economic sanctions against Sweden are likely to backfire against the United States. The Assistant Secretary for Congressional relations in the Dept. of State, David Abshire, similarly advised Senator Lowell Weicker that trade sanctions targeting Sweden in protest against the Social Democrats' Vietnam policy would only harm the United States as the latter enjoyed a positive trade balance with Sweden. Undated (ca. spring 1970). David M. Abshire. Letter to Senator Lowell Weicker. US Dept. of State. Bureau of European Affairs. Office of Northern Affairs. Records relating to Sweden 1957–1975. RG 59.

[92] For a specific illustration, see Senator Warren Magnuson as cited in the Congr., Rec. # 90th Congr., 2nd Sess., 28 May 1968: 6571.

[93] Burton Kaufman, "Foreign Aid and the Balance-of-Payments Problem" in Robert Devine (ed.), *The Johnson Years. Vol III.* (Lawrence: University of Kansas Press, 1987) 88–91.

[94] Krister Wahlbäck, "Från kritiker till medlare" *Internationella Studier* 1973 (3): 93.

[95] Lyndon B. Johnson, *The Vantage Point* (New York: Holt, Rinehart & Winston, 1971) 23. See also Walt W. Rostow, *Diffusion of Power* (New York: MacMillan, 1972) 399.

[96] Thomas Schwartz, *Lyndon Johnson and Europe* (Cambridge: Harvard University Press, 2003) 209; Frank Costigliola, "The Vietnam War and Challenges to American Power in Europe" in Lloyd C. Gardner and Ted Gittinger (eds.), *International Perspectives on Vietnam* (College Station: Texas A & M University Press, 2000) 146–147.

[97] 17 Feb. 1967. Special Assistant to the President. Nicolas Katzenbach. Memo to the President. WHCF. Country File. CO 277. Box 68. L.B.J. Library; 27 April 1967. Director of the USIA. Leonard Marks. Memo to President. White House Country File 277. Box 68. L.B.J. Library; 5 Jan. 1968. President's Evening Reading. NSF. Agency File. Box 50. L.B.J. Library.

[98] Walt. W. Rostow. Special Assistant to the President, interview with author 29 May 2002. See also Lars-Göran Stenelo, *The International Critic* (Lund: Studentlitteratur, 1984) 53–54.

[99] Jussi Hanhimäki, *Scandinavia and the United States* (New York: Twayne Publishers, 1997) 121; Thomas Schwartz, "Lyndon Johnson and Europe: Alliance Politics" in H.W. Brands (ed.), *The Foreign Policies of Lyndon Johnson* (College Station: Texas A & M University Press, 1999) 40.

[100] See, for instance, Eugenie Blang, *To Urge Common Sense on the Americans* (Dissertation. College of William and Mary, 2000) 9–10, 260–262, 266., Frank Costigliola,

"L.B.J., Germany, and the End of the Cold War" in Warren Cohen and Nancy Bernkopf (eds.), *Lyndon Johnson Confronts the World* (Cambridge: Cambridge University Press, 1994) 210. and Kaufman, "Foreign Aid and the Balance-of-Payments Problem," 79–112. For two exceptions to this rule, see Brands, *The Wages of Globalism*, 258. and Schwartz, *Lyndon Johnson and Europe*, 4–8, 225–237.

[101] Fredrik Logevall, *Choosing War* (Berkeley: University of California Press, 1999) 133, 149–153, 178–183, 274–275, 372–373; Barnett, *The Alliance*, 264–265.

[102] Blang, *To Urge Common Sense on the Americans*, 97–102, 129–132.

[103] Fredrik Logevall, "America isolated" in Andreas Daum, *et al.* (eds.), *America, Vietnam and the World* (Cambridge: Cambridge University Press, 2003) 175–196. See also Henry Kissinger, *The White House Years* (Boston: Little Brown, 1979) 424–425.

[104] Donald Sassoon, *One Hundred Years of Socialism* (London: IB Touris Publishers, 1996) 327. Sassoon points out that the US would never have accepted the Swedes' vocal criticism from one of the larger, more important, West European states.

[105] Logevall, "The Swedish–American Conflict over the Vietnam War," 444.

[106] 29 Dec. 1969. Scandinavian Desk Dept. of State. Patrick Nieburg. Memo to Albert Hamsing Assistant Director of USIA Europe. US Dept. of State. Bureau of European Affairs. Office of Northern Affairs. Records relating to Sweden 1957–1975. RG 59.

[107] Hanhimäki, *Scandinavia and the United States*, 139.

[108] William Cromwell, *The United States and the European Pillar* (New York: St. Martins Press, 1992) 70–83; Franz Schurman, *The Foreign Policies of Richard Nixon* (Berkeley: University of California Press, 1987) 314–327.

[109] Costigliola, "The Vietnam War and Challenges to American Power in Europe," 148; Schurman, *The Foreign Policies of Richard Nixon*, 314–321, 374–380.

[110] Lawrence S. Kaplan, *NATO and the United States* (New York: Twayne Publishers, 1994) 72–109; Costigliola, "The Vietnam War and the Challenges to American Power in Europe," 143–144.

[111] For a specific illustration, see *Stuttgarter Zeitung* 2 March 1968.

[112] 21 May 1970. Memo to the President from the Secretary of State William Rogers. Re: Planned Palme Visit to the US Nixon Project. NSC. Country File. "Palme Visit – June 1970." Box 938.

[113] This was something that American officials were repeatedly worried about. 1 April 1968. Scandinavian Desk Dept. of State. David McKillop. Memo to John Leddy. Central Foreign Policy File 1967–1969. Political and Defense. Sweden. RG 59; 30 Jan. 1969. Secretary of State. Telegram to US Embassy Stockholm. Central Foreign Policy File 1967–1969. Political and Defense. Sweden. RG 59; 17 Jan. 1970. Martin Hillenbrand. Memo to the Secretary of State. Re: Planned Palme Visit to the US Subject Numeric Files 1970–1973. Political and Defense. Sweden. RG 59.

[114] For specific illustrations in the Scandinavian press, see editorials in *Information* (Den) 9 March 1968, *Päivän Sanomat* (Fin) 10 March 1968, *Politiken* (Den) 10 March 1968, *Helsingin Sanomat* (Fin) 11 March 1968, *Arbeiderbladet* (Nor) 12 March 1968 and *Dagbladet* (Nor) 12 March 1968. Regardless of their respective feelings about Swedish

Vietnam policy, all of these papers strongly criticized Washington's behavior towards Stockholm, viewing this as evidence of superpower arrogance.

[115] Olav Riste, *Norway's Foreign Relations* (Olso: Universitetsförlaget, 2001) 228–230; Ib Faurby, "Danish Alliance Policy 1967–1993" in Carsten Due Nielson and Nikolay Petersen (eds.), *Adaptation and Activism* (Copenhagen: Dansk Udenrigspolitik Institut, 1995) 60.

[116] 6 Jan. 1970. Henry Kissinger. Memo to the President. Re: Swedish Prime Minister Announces Private Visit to the US In this memo Kissinger advises the President about several different courses of action that the US could take in reaction to Palme's planned visit. In the margin of the memo Nixon scribbled: "just completely ignore his [Palme's] visit." Nixon Project. NSC. Country File. "Palme Visit – June 1970." Box 938.

[117] 21 Jan. 1970. White House Staff. William Cargo. Memo to the Secretary of State William Rogers. Nixon Project. NSC. Country File. "Palme Visit – June 1970." Box 938; 4 May 1970. Head of European Section Dept. of State Martin Hillenbrand. Memo to the Secretary of State. Re: Planned Palme Visit to the US Subject Numeric Files 1970–1973. Political and Defense. Sweden. RG 59; 21 May 1970. Secretary of State, William Rogers. Secret Memo to the President. Nixon Project. NSC. Country File. "Palme Visit – June 1970." Box 938. This assessment was seconded by the American Ambassador to Sweden, Jerome Holland, who warned that it was not in America's best interest to allow the Swedes to cast themselves in the role of David versus Goliath. 25 May 1970. Jerome Holland. Telegram to State. Subject Numeric Files 1970–1973. Political and Defense. Sweden. RG 59.

[118] 11 March 1968. William W. Heath. Telegram to John Leddy. Central Foreign Policy File 1967–1969. Political and Defense. Sweden. RG 59.

[119] 9 April 1968. Cameron Turner Jr. Telegram to State. Central Foreign Policy File 1967–1969. Political and Defense. Sweden. RG 59; 11 June. 1968. William W. Heath. Memo. US policy assessment – Sweden. Central Foreign Policy File 1967–1969. Political and Defense. Sweden. RG 59; 4 Nov. 1968. Unsigned. Scandinavian Desk Dept. of State. Country Situation Paper – Sweden. Central Foreign Policy File 1967–1969. Political and Defense. Sweden. RG 59.

[120] Logevall, "Swedish–American Conflict over Vietnam," 433–434.

[121] 28 March 1968. Cameron Turner Jr. Letter to William W. Heath. Central Foreign Policy File 1967–1969. Political and Defense. Sweden. RG 59; 1 April 1968. David H. McKillop. Memo to John Leddy. Central Foreign Policy File 1967–1969. Political and Defense. Sweden. RG 59.

[122] See, for instance, Heath as cited in *Dagens Nyheter* 21 April 1968.

[123] Tage Erlander as cited in *Dagens Nyheter* 9 March 1968; Torsten Nilsson as cited in *Dagens Nyheter* 12 March 1968.

[124] See, for example, Palme as cited in *Aftonbladet* 9 March 1968.

[125] See, for instance, Tage Erlander as cited in the *Washington Post* 27 March 1968.

[126] Tag Erlander. *Aktuellt*. TV 1. 8 March 1968. Television. See also Olof Palme's remarks as cited in *Expressen* 11 March 1968.

[127] Jerneck, *Kritik som utrikespolitiskt medel*, 56–57, 159, 164. For specific examples, see Sten Andersson as cited in *Riksdagsprotokollet* # 21, 29 April 1970, 102–103. and Krister Wickman as cited in *Riksdagsprotokollet* # 48, 21 March 1973, 51. See also Olof Palme as cited in the *New York Times* 8 Jan. 1973.

[128] For specific illustrations, see *Expressen* 27 Aug. 1965, *US News & World Report* 10 Nov. 1969 and *Sydsvenska Dagbladet* 19 Jan. 1973. See also Conservative representative Ivar Virgin as cited in *Riksdagsprotokollet* # 33, 29 Oct. 1969, 17.

[129] 23 Oct. 1969. US Information Agency. Unsigned. Memo. Re: Sept. 1969 Gallup poll in Sweden. USIA. Office of Research. Special Reports. 1964–1982. Box 8. S # 50; Undated (ca. April 1970) European Section Dept. of State Unsigned. Memo. Briefing Material for Ambassador Holland's Arrival in Stockholm – April 1970. Subject Numeric Files 1970–1973. Political and Defense. Sweden. RG 59; 12 May 1972. USIA Director. Henry Loomis. Memo to the Minister of Defense Alexander Haig. US Dept. of State. Bureau of European Affairs. Office of Northern Affairs. Records relating to Sweden 1957–1975. RG 59.

[130] 23 Feb. 1968. Director of Intelligence and Research Dept. of State. Thomas L. Hughes. Central Foreign Policy File 1967–1969. Political and Defense. Sweden. RG 59; 24 May 1972. Jerome Holland. Telegram to State. Subject Numeric Files 1970–1973. Political and Defense. Sweden. RG 59.

[131] 11 March 1968. William W. Heath. Telegram to State. Central Foreign Policy File 1967–1969. Political and Defense. Sweden. RG 59; 28 March 1968. Cameron Turner, Jr. Letter to William W. Heath. Central Foreign Policy File 1967–1969. Political and Defense. Sweden. RG 59. See also article in *Svenska Dagbladet* 13 March 1968.

[132] 9 May 1966. J. Graham Parsons. Telegram to State. Subject Numeric Files 1964–1966. Political and Defense. Sweden. RG 59; 30 July 1971. Jerome Holland. Telegram to State. Subject Numeric Files 1970–1973. Political and Defense. Sweden. RG 59; 4 Jan. 1973. Arthur Olsen. Telegram to State. Subject Numeric Files 1970–1973. Political and Defense. Sweden. RG 59.

[133] Such public expressions of support were particularly evident in the aftermath of the attacks that Jerome Holland had endured when he first arrived in Sweden. *Expressen* 9 June 1970; *Dagens Nyheter* 11 June 1970; *Vestmalands Läns Tidning* 17 Sept. 1970. See also Holland as cited in *Aftonbladet* 15 April 1970.

[134] *Expressen* 31 March 1968.

[135] Center Party leader Gunnar Hedlund and Center Party representative Johannes Antonsson as cited in *Riksdagsprotokollet* # 13, 21 March 1968, 35–37, 104–105. Out of all of the Center Party's representatives, Torsten Bengtsson expressed the biggest misgivings about Palme's conduct. Bengtsson as cited in *Riksdagsprotokollet* # 13, 21 March 1968, 38–39.

[136] For specific examples, see Liberal representative Olof Dahlén and Conservative Party leader Yngve Holmberg as cited in *Riksdagsprotokollet* # 13, 21 March 1968, 18–19, 28, 30–37.

[137] *Svenska Dagbladet* 12 March 1968; *Dagens Nyheter* 13 March 1968.

[138] Holmberg as cited in *Kvällsposten* 9 March 1968.

[139] Gustaf Olivencrona, *Hur väljarna vanns* (Stockholm: Wahlström & Widstrand, 1968) 125–127.

[140] See, for example, Gösta Bohman as cited in *Riksdagsprotokollet* # 13, 21 March 1968, 59. See also Gösta Bohman, *Så var det* (Stockholm: Bonnier, 1983) 94, 164.

[141] For a specific example, see Center Party leader, Gunnar Hedlund as cited in *Aftonbladet* 12 March 1968.

[142] See editorials in *Arbetet* 13 March 1968, *Sydöstra Sveriges Dagblad* 13 March 1968 and *Folket* 14 March 1968.

[143] See editorials in *Expressen* 9 March 1968, *Sundsvalls Tidning* 10 March 1968, *Skånska Dagbladet* 13 March 1968 and *Hudiksvalls Tidning* 13 March 1968.

[144] Björk, *Vägen till Indokina*, 158.

[145] See, for instance, Torsten Nilsson, Olof Palme, John Lundberg and Ingvar Carlsson as cited in *Riksdagsprotokollet* # 13, 21 March 1968, 52, 56, 62, 80–81, 124–126, 132–133. See also Tage Erlander cited in *Dagens Nyheter* 17 March 1968.

[146] See editorials in *Kronobergaren* 11 March 1968, *Piteå-Tidningen* 12 March 1968, *Dagbladet Nya Samhället Sundsvall* 13 March 1968, *Arbetet* 17 March 1968 and *Aftonbladet* 22 March 1968.

[147] For specific illustrations, see Olof Palme as cited in *Veckojournalen* # 11 1968, 18–21, and Social Democratic representative Torsten Hansson as cited in *Riksdagsprotokollet* # 13, 21 March 1968, 103–104. See also *Tiden* # 4 1968, 257–261. and *Fackföreningsrörelsen* # 7 1968, 205–207.

[148] After the election, it was widely believed that Liberal Party leader Sven Wedén's stance on Vietnam had harmed the party. See, for example, Olle Svenning's column in *Dagens Nyheter* 11 Nov. 1968.

[149] 26 March 1968. Letter to the SAP headquarters from a Social Democratic party activist in Hagsätra. The letter's author proposes that the party should use the opposition's response to Heath's recall to its own advantage, arguing that it offers an excellent way for the party to distinguish itself against the opposition. The author adds that the government's handling of the Vietnam issue is bound to bolster the SAP's standing among younger voters. In a return letter, dated 28 March 1968, Sten Andersson (the SAP Party Secretary) agrees with this assessment saying that this question should be employed against the non-socialist opposition during the election campaign. SAP. Handlingar rörande andra länder. Vietnam. Vol. 10. See also *Tiden* # 5 1968, 310–312.

[150] Olof Palme as cited in *Aftonbladet* 1 April 1968; Tage Erlander as cited in *SSKF Kongressprotokoll*. 12:e Kongressen, 5–8 May 1968, 9; Torsten Nilsson as cited in *SAP Kongressprotokoll*. 23:e Kongressen. 9–15 June 1968, 239. See also *Tiden* # 3 1968, 189–191.

[151] 22 March 1968. Cameron Turner Jr. Telegram to State. Central Foreign Policy File 1967–1969. Political and Defense. Sweden. RG 59; 1 April 1968. David H. McKillop. Memo to John Leddy. Central Foreign Policy File 1967–1969. Political and Defense. Sweden. RG 59.

[152] Editorial in *Expressen* 10 March 1968.

[153] Editorial in *Expressen* 31 March 1968.

[154] See, for instance, letters to the editor in *Aftonbladet* 11 April 1968 and 21 April 1968.

[155] For example, in an informal telephone poll conducted among *Aftonbladet*'s readers, 3 out of 4 respondents defended Palme's conduct. *Aftonbladet* 12 March 1968. For accounts about how warmly Palme apparently was received by Social Democratic audiences in the wake of this episode, see articles in *Folket* 18 March 1968, *Arbetet* 23 March 1968 and *Värmlands Folkblad* 25 March 1968.

[156] Resolutions in support of Palme sent into the government from, among others, Lisa Mattson, the Chairwoman of the SSKF (11 March 1968), Eskilstuna SAP arbetarekommun (12 March 1968), SSSF Göteborg (12 March 1968), Nässjö SAP arbetarekommun (13 March 1968), Älvsborgs Södra Socialdemokratiska Kvinnodistrikt (13 March 1968) and Medelpads Socialdemokratiska Kvinnoförbund (27 March 1968). Avd HP. Grupp 1. Mål O. Opinionsyttringar. Vietnam. # 111. See also SKSF Chairman, Evert Svensson's op-ed in *Göteborgs handels- och sjöfartstidning* 3 April 1968.

[157] *Dagens Nyheter* 10 March 1968. See also Daniel Fleming as cited in *SAP Kongressprotokoll*. 23:e Kongressen. 9–15 June 1968, 268.

[158] For specific illustrations, see *Stockholms arbetarekommun Mötesprotokoll*. 11 March 1968. Appendix # 3. and *SAP VU-protokoll* 24 April 1968. Appendix # 43. See also *Aktuellt* # 5 1968, 26. and *Tiden* # 5 1968, 257–261.

[159] SAP. Olof Palmes Arkiv. Brevsamling 3:2 Vol. 31–33. "Brev angående Vietnamtalet 1968." These kinds of messages had likewise arrived following Palme's Gävle speech, but not in the same volume.

[160] SAP. Olof Palmes Arkiv. brevsamling 3:2 Vol. 31–33. "Brev angående Vietnamtalet 1968."

[161] In an informal poll of 190 young people conducted by *Arbetet*, a clear majority (140) rejected Holmberg's call for Palme to resign – though they did not always approve of Palme's behavior. Among those respondents who identified themselves Social Democrats, however, his participation in the Sergels torg demonstration was universally endorsed (*Arbetet* 14 March 1968). In comparison, the previously mentioned *Expressen* poll showed that in the age group of 18 to 24 year olds, 39% approved of Palme's conduct whereas 47% disapproved. In other words, even a majority among this demographic group expressed reservations about Palme's participation in the rally. That said, his approval rating within this slice of the electorate was considerably higher than it was among older groups of voters. For instance, among 25 to 29 year olds, only 27% endorsed Palme's actions. *Expressen* 31 March 1968.

[162] 20 March 1968, Letter from SKfV Chairman Gunnar Myrdal to Tage Erlander. Svenska kommittén för Vietnam, Laos och Kambodja. 1568/E/1/2 Korrespondens. Vol 1967–1968. 3077.

[163] SKfV press release 12 March 1968. Svenska kommittén för Vietnam, Laos och Kambodja. 1568/B/1/1 Utgående handlingar. Vol 1967–1989. 3077.

[164] 12 March 1968. Letter from SKfV General Secretary, Bertil Svanström to Olof Palme. Svenska kommittén för Vietnam, Laos och Kambodja. 1568/E/1/2 Korrespondens. Vol 1967–1968. 3077. See also *Expressen* 11 March 1968 and *Dagens Nyheter* 26 March 1968.

[165] Palme as cited in *Aftonbladet* 9 March 1968.

[166] Yngve Möller as cited in *Riksdagsprotokollet* # 11, 13 March 1968, 37; Tage Erlander as cited in *Jönköpings-Posten* 11 March 1968.

[167] Torsten Nilsson as cited in *SAP Riksdagsgruppens protokoll* 12 March 1968; Tage Erlander as cited in *SAP Riksdagsgruppens protokoll* 7 May 1968.

[168] See, for example, editorials in *Arbetet* 2 March 1968 and *Aftonbladet* 9 March 1968.

[169] See, for instance, editorials in *Norrländska Socialdemokraten* 23 Feb 1968, *Arbetarbladet* 24 Feb. 1968, *Västgöta-Demokraten* 26 Feb 1968 and *Smålands Folkblad* 28 Feb. 1968.

[170] *Arbetet* 14 March 1968; 17 March 1968; 20 March 1968. *Arbetet* claimed that it had received over 1,000 letters in support of Palme.

[171] *Aftonbladet* 9 March 1968, 10 March 1968 and 11 March 1968.

[172] *SSKF Årsberättelse 1968*, 26; SSU/Verdandi, *Utblick # 8. USA-kriget i Vietnam* (Stockholm: Frihets Förlag, 1968.) See also Frans Nilsson as cited in *SAP Kongressprotokoll.* 23:e Kongressen. 9–15 June 1968, 249–250.

[173] Svedgård, *Palme*, 12, 22–23, 86; Svensson, *I maktens labyrinter*, 169–170. See also editorials in *Gotlänningen* 13 March 1968 and *Dagens Nyheter* 23 March 1968.

[174] Tage Erlander as cited in Svedgård, *Palme*, 12–13.

[175] Olof Palme's arkiv. Palme's brevsamling 3:2 Vol. 31–33. "Brev angående Vietnamtalet 1968."

[176] Christer Isaksson, *Palme privat* (Stockholm: Ekerlids, 1995) 135–138; Svedgård, *Palme*, 12, 22–23, 86.

[177] *Aftonbladet* 15 March 1968. In this poll, Palme received 117 votes, whereas Gunnar Sträng and Krister Wickman only received 39 and 18 votes, respectively. Although this poll was by no means scientifically conducted, its results at least indicate the level of support that Palme enjoyed among *Aftonbladet's* readers, who presumably mostly identified with the party's left wing.

[178] SIFO poll results as cited in *Aftonbladet* 5 Dec. 1968.

[179] Ortmark, *Maktspelet i Sverige*, 59–63, 234–235; Isaksson, *Palme privat*, 135–136.

[180] Svedgård, Palme. En presentation, 17, 22; Svensson, I maktens labyrinter, 170.

[181] *SAP Riksdagsgruppens protokoll* 23 April 1968; *SAP PS-protokoll* 6 Aug. 1968. See also Sten Andersson, *I de lugnaste vatten...* (Stockholm: Tiden, 1985) 314–337.

[182] Svensson, *I maktens labyrinter*, 169. See also Gösta Bohman, *Inrikes utrikespolitik* (Stockholm: Geber, 1970) 38–39.

[183] Haste, Boken om Palme, 45; Björk, Vägen till Indokina, 163.

[184] For specific examples, see *Libertas* # 2 1968, 2. and *Tiden* # 5 1968, 257–261. See also editorial in *Aftonbladet* 7 June 1968.

[185] For a specific illustration, see Teddy Arnberg, *et al.*, *Vietnam i dokument* (Stockholm: Prisma, 1968) 10. This view was also shared by the big Social Democratic papers. See, for example, editorials in *Aftonbladet* 23 April 1968 and *Arbetet* 14 June 1968.

[186] See, for example, *Stockholms arbetarekommun. Årsmötesprotokoll.* 27–28 April 1968. Motioner # 1–19, 69; and *SSKF Kongressprotokoll.* 12:e Kongressen. 5–8 May 1968, 407–408.

[187] *Aftonbladet* 2 May 1968; *Stockholms arbetarekommun. Verksamhetsberättelse 1968*, 4–7. See also Olof Palme, *Att vilja gå vidare* (Stockholm: Tiden, 1974) 203–205, 209–210.

[188] Torsten Nilsson as cited in *SAP Kongressprotokoll.* 23:e Kongressen. 9–15 June 1968. 439–440. See also *Aktuellt* # 9 1968, 21.

[189] *SAP VU-protokoll* 19 March 1968 Appendix # 14. See also *Frihet* # 1 1968, 5., *Tiden* # 4 1968, 211. and *Tiden* # 6 1968, 377–378.

[190] Hammarström, *FNL i Sverige*, 58–81.

[191] Ludvig Rasmusson, *Fyrtiotalisterna* (Stockholm: Norstedt, 1985) 120; Salomon, *Rebeller i takt med tiden*, 78.

[192] Stig Hadenius, *Svensk politik under 1900-talet* (Stockholm: Tiden Athena, 1996) 146; Sverker Oredsson, *Svensk oro* (Lund: Nordic Academic Press, 2003) 90–91. For a specific example, see *Tiden* # 6 1968, 321–324.

[193] Åke Kilander, *Vietnam var nära* (Stockholm: Leopard, 2007) 138–145; Salomon, *Rebeller i takt med tiden*, 152–156. See also Torbjörn Säfve, *Rebellerna i Sverige* (Stockholm: Författarförlaget, 1971) 11–71.

[194] Lars Åke Augustsson and Stig Hansén, *De svenska maoisterna* (Göteborg: Lindelöws, 2001) 53–56. See, for example, Sköld Peter Mattis' op-ed in *Aftonbladet* 10 Sept. 1968.

[195] See, for instance, Olof Palme as cited in *Visby Tidningen* 26 July 1968.

[196] For specific illustrations, see Olof Palme as cited in *Barometern* 22 April 1968 and Torsten Nilsson as cited in UD, *Sverige och Vietnamfrågan*, 80–81.

[197] Torsten Nilsson. *Dagens Eko*. 24 July 1968. Radio. See also editorial in *Aftonbladet* 25 July 1968.

[198] See, for instance, SSU chairman, Bosse Ringholm as cited in *SAP Kongressprotokoll.* 23:e Kongressen. 9–15 June 1968, 254–255. See also *Tiden* # 5 1968, 257–261. and *Tiden* # 7 1968, 388–389.

[199] Bohman, *Inrikes utrikespolitik*, 38–39. See also editorials in *Expressen* 25 July 1968, *Dagens Nyheter* 26 July 1968 and *Upsala Nya Tidning* 26 July 1968.

[200] 22 March 1968. Cameron Turner Jr. Telegram to State. Central Foreign Policy File 1967–1969. Political and Defense. Sweden. RG 59; 5 July 1968.William W. Heath. Telegram to State. Central Foreign Policy File 1967–1969. Political and Defense. Sweden. RG 59.

[201] Bo Hammar, *Ett långt farväl till kommunismen* (Stockholm: Bromberg, 1993) 87–88; Hermansson, *C-H Minnen* (Stockholm: Arena, 1993) 245, 248–251.

[202] Kent Lidman, "Vietnamdebatten i Sverige" (University of Umeå, 1973) 17; Olivencrona, *Hur väljarna vanns*, 77, 165–166.

[203] For specific illustrations, see Lars Werner as cited in *Riksdagsprotokollet* # 13, 21 March 1968, 60–63, and C-H Hermansson as cited in *Riksdagsprotokollet* # 13, 21 March 1968, 60–70. See also E. Bondeson's column in *Ny Dag* 8 August 1968.

[204] Information furnished by SIFO January 1999 (Courtesy of Ed Burton.)

[205] James Waite, "Sweden and the Vietnam Criticism" *Southeast Asia* 2 4 (1973): 457. See also Torsten Nilsson, *Åter Vietnam* (Stockholm: Tiden, 1981) 141.

[206] 24 July 1968. William W. Heath. Telegram to State. Central Foreign Policy File 1967–1969. Political and Defense. Sweden. RG 59; 27 Aug. 1968. Paul Hughes. Memo to John

Leddy. Central Foreign Policy File 1967–1969. Political and Defense. Sweden. RG 59; 11 Sept. 1968. Thomas L. Hughes. Memo. Re: SAP fights to hold on to Power in the Swedish Election. Central Foreign Policy File 1967–1969. Political and Defense. Sweden. RG 59.

[207] Peter Esaiasson and Sören Holmberg *De folkvalda* (Stockholm: Bonnier, 1988) 208–211; Stig Hadenius, *et al, Sverige efter 1900* (Stockholm: Bonnier, 1993) 250–252.

[208] Tage Erlander and Torsten Nilsson as cited in UD, *Utrikesfrågor 1968*, 168–175.

[209] Peter Esaiasson, *Svenska valkampanjer 1866–1988* (Stockholm: Allmäna Förlaget, 1990) 249–250; Olivencrona, *Hur väljarna vanns*, 167–169.

[210] Tage Erlander, *60-talet* (Stockholm: Tiden, 1982) 288; Nilsson, *Åter Vietnam*, 140–141; Hermansson, *C-H Minnen*, 248–251, 264; Hammar, *Ett långt farväl till kommunismen*, 87–88.

[211] See, for instance, Olof Palme as cited in *Time Magazine* 29 Jan. 1973.

[212] Svante Lundberg, *Sextioåttor* (Stockholm: Symposium AB, 1993) 19–21, 180–181. For a specific illustration, see Armas Lappalainen, *Om socialismen* (Stockholm: Prisma, 1969) 42–85.

[213] Nils Elvander, *Skandinavisk arbetarrörelse* (Stockholm: Liber, 1980) 125; Östberg, *1968*, 101–103.

[214] Enn Kokk, *Vitbok* (Stockholm: Hjalmarson & Högberg, 2001) 41. For a specific example, see Olof Palme as cited in *Dagens Nyheter* 31 May 1968.

[215] Leif Lewin, *et al.*, *The Swedish Electorate 1887–1968* (Stockholm: Almqvist & Wiksell, 1972) 255; Bo Särlvik, *Riskdagsmannavalen 1965–1968. Del 2* (Stockholm: SCB, 1970) 93–100.

[216] Olof Ruin, *I välfärdsstatens tjänst* (Stockholm: Tiden, 1986) 22–23; Svensson, *I maktens labyrinter*, 168–170.

[217] Olivencrona, *Hur väljarna vanns*, 127–128; Ortmark, *Maktspelet i Sverige*, 230.

[218] Olof Petersson and Bo Särlvik, *Valet 1973. Del 3* (Stockholm: SCB, 1974) 88–89, 94; Särlvik, *Riskdagsmannavalen 1965–1968. Del 2*, 78.

[219] *SAP PS-protokoll* 24 Sept. 1968. See also *Tiden # 8* 1968, 435–454. and *Fackföreningsrörelsen # 20* 1968, 148.

[220] Tage Erlander as cited in *SAP Riksdagsgruppens protokoll* 16 Oct. 1968. See also Rune Nordin, *Den svenska arbetarrörelsen* (Stockholm: Tiden, 1983) 130–131.

[221] 16 Sept. 1968. John Leddy. Memo to the Secretary of State Dean Rusk. Central Foreign Policy File 1967–1969. Political and Defense. Sweden. RG 59; 1 Oct. 1968. William W. Heath. Telegram to State. Central Foreign Policy File 1967–1969. Political and Defense. Sweden. RG 59.

[222] 27 Feb. 1969. Scandinavian Desk Dept. of State. Paul Hughes. Memo. Briefing Paper – Sweden. Central Foreign Policy File 1967–1969. Political and Defense. Sweden. RG 59; 25 Sept. 1969. Director of Intelligence and Research Dept. of State. George C. Denny. Memo to the Secretary of State, Dean Rusk. US Dept. of State. Bureau of European Affairs. Office of Northern Affairs. Records relating to Sweden 1957–1975. RG 59.

[223] Kurt Törnqvist, *Svenskarna och omvärlden* (Stockholm: Beredskapsnämnden för psykologiskt försvar, 1969) 21–25.

[224] Bohman, *Så var det*, 160–162.

[225] 18 Aug. 1965. Political Division FM. Jan af Sillén. Memo of Conversation. Re: Today's meeting between Torsten Nilsson and the American Ambassador, J. Graham Parsons. UD. Avd HP. Grupp 1. Mål Ua. Politik Allmänt. USA. # 210

[226] 17 Sept. 1965. George R. Andrews. Telegram to State. Subject Numeric Files 1964–1966. Political and Defense. Sweden. RG 59; 22 April 1967. Turner Cameron Jr. Telegram to State. Central Foreign Policy File 1967–1969. Political and Defense. Sweden. RG 59.

[227] Möller, *Sverige och Vietnamkriget*, 111–113.

[228] Sundgren, "Splittrad solidaritet," 149–152. For a specific example, see *Info från SKfV 1972*. Svenska kommittén för Vietnam, Laos och Kambodja. 1568/B/1/1 Utgående handlingar. Vol 1967–1989. 3077.

[229] Dahl, "Solidaritetsarbetet för Vietnam," 194–195; Möller, *Sverige och Vietnamkriget*, 360–361; Björk, *Vägen till Indokina*, 191, 200–204.

[230] 29 Jan. 1969. Letter from Bertil Svanström, the SKfV's General Secretary, to Jean-Christophe Öberg. Re: Recent contacts between the SKfV and NLF representatives. Avd HP. Grupp 1. Mål Xv. Politik Allmänt. Vietnam. # 1203; 22 Oct. 1970. Jean-Christophe Öberg. Memo. Re: SKfV hosting meeting between NLF representatives and Swedish parliamentarians. Avd HP. Grupp 1. Mål Xv. Politik Allmänt. Vietnam. # 1207. See also *Dagens Nyheter* 23 June 1969 and *Arbetet* 10 Nov. 1971.

[231] 4 Oct. 1971. Swedish Ambassador to the DRV. Jean-Christophe Öberg. Memo. Re: Birgitta Dahl's Visit to North Vietnam between 24 Sept. to 20 Oct. 1971. Avd HP. Grupp 1. Mål Xv. Politik Allmänt. Vietnam. # 1208.

[232] 30 Sept. 1968. Letter from Bertil Svanström, the SKfV's General Secretary, to Alva Myrdal (Acting Foreign Minister). Re: SKfV invite to the NLF to open an information office in Stockholm. UD. Avd HP. Grupp 1. Mål Xv. Politik Allmänt. Vietnam. # 1202; 3 Oct. 1968. First Secretary Swedish Embassy Moscow. Rune Nyström. Telegram to FM. Re: Today's conversation with an unidentified NLF representative about the SKfV's invite to open an information office in Sweden. Avd HP. Grupp 1. Mål Er. Politik Allmänt. Sovjetunionen. # 309. See also *Svenska Dagbladet* 15 Oct. 1968 and *Vietnam nu* # 11 1968, 2.

[233] Gunnar Jarring, *Utan glasnost och perestrojka* (Stockholm: Bonnier, 1989) 127–129.

[234] Robert K. Brigham, *Guerilla Diplomacy* (Ithaca: Cornell University Press, 1999) 80. See also Jean-Christophe Öberg, *Varför Vietnam?* (Stockholm: Rabén & Sjögren 1985) 131.

[235] *Arbetet* 28 Aug. 1968.

[236] Björk, *Vägen till Indokina*, 191.

The Deserter Question 1967–1973:
A Case Study in Domestic Foreign Policy

The unstated quid pro quo that evolved between the Social Democratic hierarchy and *Svenska Kommittén för Vietnam* (SKfV) – the committee's loyalty in return for concessions – was put to its first real test in conjunction with the highly publicized arrival of four American sailors on 30 December 1967. The so-called "Intrepid Four" (named after the aircraft carrier they had served on) had originally deserted in Japan, and from there they were smuggled into the USSR. Once the Soviets felt that the sailors had outlived their propaganda purpose, contact was established with the SKfV and the midshipmen were subsequently shuttled on to Sweden.[1]

On its own initiative, the SKfV had extended an invitation to the deserters to come to Sweden, and informed Rune Johansson, the Minister of the Interior, that it had advised the sailors not to request visas in order to avoid placing the government in the embarrassing position of having to refuse them entry. The committee reasoned that the Social Democratic administration would be faced with significant domestic dissent if it tried to block the Intrepid Four from coming into the country, so it was better to present the cabinet with this situation as a *fait accompli*.[2]

When the Intrepid Four landed at Arlanda International Airport in Stockholm, they were greeted by the SKfV along with the international media.[3] As added insurance, the SKfV had orchestrated this public reception as a means to put pressure on the government to provide sanctuary for the four sailors.[4] The SKfV's wish was soon fulfilled.

Swedish immigration officials rapidly processed the men's asylum requests, and on 9 January 1968, the Intrepid Four were granted temporary visas on "humanitarian grounds." Other deserters immediately followed in their wake, and before long Sweden began to receive a steady flow of deserters arriving from all corners of the globe.[5] Sweden would eventually become home to one of the largest deserter colonies outside of North America – as some 800 young Americans officially found refuge there between 1967 and 1973.[6]

Asylum for "The Intrepid Four" and American Displeasure

Sweden was not the only Western European country to harbor American deserters, but along with France it was the only place where they could live openly without fear of being returned to US military control. Elsewhere these fugitives typically were forced to live more or less underground, and were at best tolerated by the local authorities. The deserters in Sweden, in contrast, were given official refugee status, work permits and, like all other immigrants, some modest welfare benefits.[7] What really set the country apart from the other host countries, however, was the extremely public and enthusiastic welcome that first greeted the deserters in Sweden. In comparison, Canada and France – which were the other two main sanctuaries for American deserters – treated this matter with a much greater degree of official discretion and they kept the deserters on a much tighter leash. In addition, both the Canadians and the French were much quicker than the Swedes to expel so-called "undesirable elements" among the Americans, and the French government furthermore explicitly prohibited the latter from engaging in anti-war activities while on French soil.[8]

This was not the case in Sweden, where the Social Democratic administration's generous treatment of the deserters instantly became a major source of American discontent. US officials found the deserters' highly visible presence in Sweden to be exceptionally galling and regarded this as tantamount to indirectly encouraging desertion.[9] To many in Washington, not least on Capitol Hill, Sweden's harboring of military fugitives was a much more serious matter than its strident criticism of the war. Sweden's vocal protests could simply be ignored, whereas its sheltering of American deserters and draft resisters directly undermined the war effort. Prior to this, the Congress and the American press had actually paid very little attention to Swedish Vietnam policy.[10]

State Department officials voiced their displeasure at this latest development, sparking speculations in both the American and Swedish press that the welcoming of these men had significantly contributed to the decision to recall Ambassador Heath.[11] US diplomats further warned their Swedish counterparts that abetting American military fugitives was likely to resonate far beyond the beltway, awakening the ire of the American public.[12]

In truth, what the average American actually thought about this practice was not so straightforward, for, as we shall see later, opinions were somewhat divided on this subject. The initial reaction from the American press, however, was less ambiguous. The arrival of the Intrepid Four to Sweden (and of other deserters in the early part of 1968) generated a tremendous amount of attention in the American media, and the majority of this coverage was quite negative.[13] In the most extreme instances, Sweden's deserter policy was declared to be a violation of the country's traditional policy of neutrality.[14]

The most indignant American reaction probably came from the leadership of the International Longshoreman's Union, whose chairman, Thomas Gleason, threatened a boycott against Swedish exports in retaliation for sheltering these men.[15] Although this threat was never carried out, it still illuminates the strong passions that the deserter issue evoked in some quarters in the United States.[16]

The possibility of economic reprisals gave rise to anxiety among Swedish business interests whose livelihood depended on trade with the United States,[17] and a few members of the non-socialist opposition articulated these same fears.[18] Other non-socialist politicians, meanwhile, questioned the wisdom of giving sanctuary to American deserters because this appeared to needlessly provoke Washington. Those who challenged the government's handling of this matter mostly did so out of a concern about this policy's long-term implications for Swedish–American relations,[19] and they griped that this decision seemed to be domestically motivated.[20]

Complaints to this effect could be heard on the other side of the Atlantic as well, and especially in the American conservative press, which accused the Social Democrats of utilizing this issue to court the youth vote in the upcoming election.[21] Not unexpectedly, US diplomats entertained similar suspicions, seeing this development as yet another illustration of the SAP leadership caving in to radical opinion. Well prior to the appearance of the Intrepid Four, American diplomats in Stockholm had already anticipated that the Social Democratic cabinet might be susceptible to domestic agitation in relation to American deserters, and hence the news that these four sailors had been granted asylum did not really take them by surprise.[22] On multiple occasions, US officials, moreover, let it be known that they strongly objected to the Social Democratic administration employing this issue to its own political ends.[23]

In the face of such accusations, Social Democratic spokesmen steadfastly rejected the notion that the decision to grant asylum to the deserters was governed by party tactical considerations.[24] They even denied that this policy was part of the government's stance against the war.[25] Social Democratic officials instead charged that it was the party's parliamentary opponents – left and right – that were trying to politicize this errand.[26] Yet, in hindsight, several leading Social Democrats have been less emphatic on this point, readily acknowledging that the deserters were indeed a significant component of the government's broader Vietnam policy.[27]

Swedish diplomats appear to have had substantial reservations about the government's politicization of this issue. This was partially because they had not been consulted about the decision to open Sweden up to American GIs, and this clearly lessened their enthusiasm for this policy. Most senior diplomats seem to have regarded these men as an unwelcome burden on the two countries' historically amicable relationship. In early 1968, Swedish Embassy officers in Washington repeatedly expressed unease about the adverse reaction that Sweden's acceptance of the deserters had evoked among the American public and press alike.[28] The Swedish Ambassador, Hubert de Besche, reported that he was incessantly asked about this subject, and he was personally alarmed by the amount of negative publicity that this matter had received in the American media.[29] De Besche's concerns were shared by some of his colleagues in Stockholm, who additionally worried about the prospect of Sweden being overrun by American military fugitives.[30] It is plain that many, if not all, high-ranking members of the Foreign Ministry viewed this policy as a severe handicap for Sweden in its dealings with the United States, although they simultaneously recognized that the current political climate in Sweden would not allow for any drastic revisions of the government's current course of action with regard to these men.[31]

Under these circumstances, the best the Swedish diplomatic corps could do was to try to mitigate the unfavorable impact that this policy was having on Sweden's reputation in the United States. The Foreign Ministry sought to neutralize this issue by instructing its staff to call attention to the fact that Sweden was not the only country to grant refuge to American military offenders. It further advised Swedish diplomats to stress that the decision to grant asylum to this group of men should not be interpreted as a hostile act directed against Washington. According to the Foreign Ministry, the government was merely following already established norms pertaining to the acceptance of foreign deserters.[32] Social Democratic spokesmen repeatedly made the same arguments, insisting that the opening of Sweden's borders to American military fugitives was informed solely by Swedish immigration law and accepted practice.[33]

Washington of course was not very persuaded by these disclaimers, but American officials realized that there was not much they could do. First of all, the 1961 Swedish–American extradition treaty explicitly did not apply to military offenses. (Swedish officials liked to empasize that if the situation had been reversed the US would have been obliged to behave in the exact same way.) Due to the limited scope of this earlier agreement, the State Department had no grounds on which to issue a formal diplomatic protest. Secondly, Washington could not officially request that Stockholm expel these fugitives because it would be considered bad form to try to overtly influence the implementation of another country's asylum practices. While never impressed by the Swedes' justifications, the Americans thus could do little except denote their continued disapproval of this policy.[34]

American skepticism about the Social Democratic administration's explanation for why it was supposedly compelled to harbor these men was hardly unwarranted. The latter's reference to previously established practice was little more than a convenient pretext, and it certainly was not an accurate characterization of how Sweden had historically dealt with foreign military offenders. Although it is true that Sweden had provided a sanctuary for foreign deserters as early as the Second World War, and that it had received French military fugitives during the Algerian war, no actual *legal* precedent existed at the time when the first American servicemen arrived in late 1967 and early 1968. This was only added retroactively in October 1968, when Swedish immigration law was revised to include a clause concerning foreign deserters' rights to humanitarian asylum.[35] In other words, the Social Democratic contention that its present acceptance of American deserters was in accordance with traditional legal norms regarding asylum errands was at best a half-truth. (In 1991, this clause was revoked in response to Swedish fears of being inundated with soldiers fleeing the Yugoslavian civil war.)

At the same time it should be stressed that it is improbable that the cabinet would have created a completely new precedent in connection with the arrival of the Americans, as such a move would simply have been viewed as too brazen. This was a delicate issue, and party tactical considerations had to be weighed against Swedish national interests, which called for a workable, if not always absolutely amicable, relationship with Washington. This meant that any Social Democratic challenge to the US had to be cloaked in proper decorum, and hence this fictitious reasoning provided an excuse for why the government had handled the issue in this way. (As was discussed in the preceding chapter, these kinds of theatrics also had a domestic dimension because the Social Democratic administration did not want to overly antagonize latent pro-American sympathies at home.)

The politicized nature of the government's deserter policy was revealed by the very lenient manner in which all of the defectors' asylum requests were originally processed. If the Social Democratic administration had really wanted to keep these men out of Sweden, then it could have either explicitly, or implicitly, encouraged the State Alien Commission to take a much harsher stance against the deserters, but evidently it did not wish to do so. As one contemporary critic pointed out, various legal technicalities could have been invoked to deny entry to most, if not all, of these young men. All foreign asylum seekers were, for example, legally required to apply for entry visas prior to their arrival in Sweden – and if they did not they were at least theoretically subject to instant expulsion. This stipulation was never adhered to in the Americans' case, nor was the standard demand that all aliens must be able to provide legal identification upon entering the country applied to them. (A majority of the deserters showed up without such documentation, having destroyed their military ID papers on route to Sweden.) Lastly, while these GIs could not be legally deported solely on the grounds of having deserted, many of them could have been denied entry for other types of offences. Yet none of these rules were enforced by Swedish immigration authorities (at least not initially.) Consequently, Swedish immigration law was interpreted very generously in favor of the Americans.[36] This reality was also recognized by the government's own supporters, who agreed that if the Social Democratic administration had genuinely been committed to preventing these men from finding sanctuary in Sweden, then it could easily have hidden behind assorted legal formalities.[37]

It is, moreover, apparent that the country's asylum policy toward foreign military fugitives in this period was applied rather selectively and differed from one nationality to the next. For instance, while both American and Portuguese deserters were welcomed with open arms, it was only with great hesitancy that Sweden eventually admitted a handful of Israeli draft resisters. In the late 1960s the Swedish Social Democrats were still on friendly terms with the Labor government in Israel, which presumably explains their reluctance to accept Israeli defectors. Conversely, the SAP leadership's hostility vis-à-vis the Salazar regime and its opposition to US Vietnam policy unquestionably accounted for its willingness to shelter both Portuguese and American military fugitives. The inconsistent manner in which Swedish asylum practices were implemented highlights that this policy was subject to political dictates, not uniform legal standards.

This discrepancy in implementation, taken together with the charitable treatment that the American defectors at first received, only underscores the extent to which this errand was being shaped by domestic political considerations. This, in turn, suggests that the cabinet was directing how this matter should be handled from behind the scenes. Swedish government officials, however, always denied this, and the diplomatic corps consistently emphasized that the State Alien Commission was completely autonomous and that its work was free from outside interference. The implication of this assertion was therefore that the government had no direct influence over how this errand was being handled.[38]

According to established norms, this was correct. In theory, the State Alien Commission had the authority to make its own decisions about all asylum-related errands. But in cases that would potentially influence other future ones, or that could be considered sensitive for foreign policy reasons, the Commission was expected to consult the government for specific directions. Nor was it uncommon for the cabinet to issue verbal instructions to the State Alien Commission about how certain errands should be handled. And once such government directions had been provided, the Commission was obliged to follow them.[39]

The first American deserter, Ray Jones III, fled to Sweden in April 1967, and he was granted temporary humanitarian asylum shortly thereafter. At the time, the State Alien Commission affirmed that the Jones case should not be regarded as a legal precedent.[40] A few months later, in October and November, two more American deserters appeared, but unlike in the Jones' errand the State Alien Commission postponed making a decision about these two additional cases. None of these first three military fugitives elicited substantial domestic or international attention.[41] It was only with the high-profile arrival of the Intrepid Four that the State Alien Commission was finally obligated to publicly articulate its policy toward American deserters.

Although the exact decision-making process surrounding the determination to grant the Intrepid Four temporary asylum cannot be definitively established, it is highly probable that the government instructed the State Alien Commission how to deal with this matter.[42] Several factors support this conclusion. First, it is extremely unlikely that the Commission would have acted unilaterally on an issue carrying such a high potential for political fallout without prior consultation with the government.[43] Second, the decision to provide the Intrepid Four with humanitarian asylum seems to have set a de facto precedent for how all subsequent deserter errands should be settled. In the first six months of 1968, every single deserter who applied for asylum received it.[44] Third, there are some signs that the State Alien Commission was opposed to granting refuge to any additional deserters but was overruled by the government.[45] A final indicator of direct government interference was the speed with which the four sailors' asylum requests were processed. It normally took approximately six weeks for the State Alien Commission to render a verdict on any individual case, but in this instance the sailors only waited ten days until their errands were settled.[46]

In this context, it is also noteworthy that the State Alien Commission inexplicably reversed its original instruction prohibiting the Intrepid Four from engaging in political propaganda while in Sweden.[47] This sudden change of heart, within the span of only a few days, suggests direct government intervention. Here it should be added that the question of whether or not it was appropriate for these Americans to participate in anti-war activities in Sweden was a potentially delicate one that was immediately questioned by some non-socialist politicians.[48] American diplomats also raised this exact objection because they were extremely annoyed that the deserters were allowed to make public appearances against the war.[49] To US officials, Sweden's refusal to muzzle the defectors positively proved that the Social Democrats' approach to this question was politically motivated.[50] Though when they confronted their Swedish colleagues about this topic, the latter evasively responded that the country's immigration laws did not prevent non-citizens from pursuing political activities.[51] Left unsaid was that the State Alien Commission had the legal right to revoke a foreigner's asylum status if his conduct was "deemed to be contrary to the best interests of the Swedish state." In short, a gag order could have been placed on the Americans if Swedish authorities had so wished. This is also exactly what happened to the French deserters that had arrived in Sweden a decade earlier, as they had not been permitted to voice publicly their opposition to the Algerian War.[52]

The bottom line was that the Social Democratic administration had no interest in muzzling the American deserters because domestic – and particularly Social Democratic – anti-war opinion would not have tolerated it.[53] At this juncture, the SKfV was still actively recruiting deserters to speak out against the American war effort,[54] and the SKfV also encouraged the deserters to form their own political organization in Sweden, which led to the establishment of the American Deserters Committee (ADC) in February 1968.[55] That the ADC was permitted to set up an office in Stockholm is in itself quite remarkable considering that this opportunity had previously been denied to US deserters by other West European governments.[56] The government's reluctance to offend domestic opinion by hushing the deserters was underscored by Torsten Nilsson's subsequent boast that the defectors enjoyed political liberties in Sweden that they were deprived of elsewhere.[57]

When these fugitives first appeared in Sweden they were hailed as heroes by the anti-war movement.[58] The newly arrived Americans were considered to be champions of the anti-imperialist cause, and many Swedes felt that they should be commended for their resolute refusal to participate in an immoral war.[59] Not only did the deserters receive a great deal of sympathy in the big Liberal and Social Democratic dailies,[60] but they also had support among most liberal-left leaning groups in Swedish society. Within such circles, either housing or personally knowing one of the fugitives carried a certain prestige.[61] In less than a month after the Intrepid Four's arrival, some forty different grass-roots organizations had joined forces to provide monetary aid and shelter for the deserters.[62] The State Alien Commission's decision to grant the deserters humanitarian asylum was met with universal approval by the Swedish left,[63] and the government's handling of this issue was also very popular among the Social Democratic faithful.[64]

Presumably the SAP leadership felt that this question would help the party to shore up support among young voters going into the election. This seems like a reasonable assumption, especially now that it has been confirmed that the party hierarchy did indeed view the deserter issue as a part and parcel of its broader Vietnam profile. Regardless of this question's actual electoral potential (or its final electoral impact), this policy was undeniably an asset as far the Social Democratic establishment was concerned. This was chiefly because it pleased the party's own anti-war activists and those affiliated with the SKfV specifically.[65] The decision to provide sanctuary for the deserters helped to cement the SKfV's allegiance to the Social Democratic administration. As a reward for its loyalty, the committee's influence over Swedish Vietnam policy was greatly enhanced, but at the expense of the government's own freedom of maneuver.

Domestic Political Conflict: Deserters, Resisters, and the Campaign for Political Asylum

In late winter and early spring of 1968, the deserter issue was front and center of the Vietnam question in Sweden, and the SKfV made it a priority to assist the Americans[66] to the point of establishing this as a main objective in its new charter.[67] With good reason, the SKfV would later also take credit for having compelled the government to grant asylum to the deserters.[68] In return for this assistance, the deserters were induced to participate in various functions sponsored by the committee.[69]

The NLF-groups were likewise quick to enlist the fugitives in their own anti-war activities.[70] Similarly to the SKfV, the DFFG set out to help the deserters to get situated in Sweden and created its own sub-committee to aid the Americans.[71] Maoist anti-war activists had thus also been energetically involved with the deserters from the very beginning,[72] and as a result the Americans were soon drawn into the conflict between the SKfV and the DFFG.[73] It did not take long before the deserters' own organization, the American Deserter Committee (ADC), formally aligned itself with the NLF-movement,[74] and because of this it too became embroiled in a nasty public dispute with SKfV. The ADC and SKfV promptly became bitter adversaries, and within only a couple months the ADC was echoing the NLF-groups' criticism of the Social Democratic administration.[75]

That the ADC ended up siding with the DFFG against the SKfV and the government unquestionably cooled the Social Democratic hierarchy's attitude towards the deserters. Though this might have been a mere coincidence, contemporary observers on both sides of the Atlantic nevertheless noticed that the government's treatment of the deserters appeared to become more restrictive in the wake of the Social Democrats' landslide victory in September 1968.[76] For the first time, the State Alien Commission now rejected the asylum requests of a handful of deserters, and it further recommended that a couple of others be deported.[77] This led the ADC and its allies on the far left to accuse the cabinet of having reversed its position on this question. ADC spokesmen protested that now that the Social Democrats had won the election, the deserters had become politically expendable.[78] (American officials incidentally made the same inference.)[79]

The Social Democratic administration and the State Alien Commission naturally dismissed such allegations as baseless.[80] Although this accusation may have been unjustified, it was still clear that the official Swedish attitude toward the deserters had begun to chill. In all probability, this less lenient treatment was partially rooted in the fear that Sweden now risked being overrun by American deserters, and a stricter interpretation of the nation's immigration law was thus intended to signal that there were limits to the country's hospitality.[81] As for the first deportation orders, they were a by-product of a rising number of deserters who had recently run afoul with the law – mostly for minor infractions such as petty theft, hashish possession, etc. In addition, there were troubling signs that quite a few of the Americans were failing to assimilate and were being relegated to the margins of Swedish society.[82] This turn of events swiftly propelled both the SKfV and the DFFG into action to aid these men.[83]

The petty criminality and adjustment problems exhibited by some of the deserters, along with the seemingly harder government line against them, rapidly gave birth to a mounting campaign to secure political asylum for the Americans.[84] The deserters themselves worried that their temporary asylum would be revoked, or alternatively that they might be repatriated to the US as soon as the war ended. For this reason, their Swedish advocates proposed that political asylum, as opposed to humanitarian asylum, would provide the Americans with better protection against any future deportations.[85]

Editorials in several of the big Liberal and Social Democratic dailies appealed for clearer guidelines in the government's asylum policy and demanded that more needed to be done to help the deserters integrate into Swedish society.[86] From the point of view of the government's Marxist detractors, the country's immigration policy seemed to be driven by politics (i.e., the fear of American retaliation) instead of by humanitarian and moral concerns.[87]

Throughout the late fall and the early winter, the campaign for political asylum continued to gain momentum, peaking in the third week of February 1969. According to the ADC and the DFFG, desertion was a politically motivated offense and hence political refugee status was appropriate.[88] Many of the deserters' sympathizers within the parliamentary left agreed,[89] and numerous editorials appeared in the Communist, Liberal, and Social Democratic press in favor of upgrading the Americans' asylum status.[90] By mid-February a broad coalition had been formed to put pressure on the government.[91] The demand for political asylum was, among others, backed by the SKfV, SKSF, and the SSU.[92] This campaign reached its zenith on 19 February when the NLF-groups in collaboration with the ADC sponsored a large demonstration in Stockholm. Meanwhile, representatives from over 30 different religious and political groups (many of which were Social Democratically affiliated) received a personal audience with the new Minister of the Interior, Eric Holmqvist, in order to plead the deserters' case.[93]

In light of the broad support that this cause enjoyed, especially among the Social Democratic rank and file, it is not terribly astonishing that the government acquiesced to most of the requests put forth by the deserters' backers. In reaction to this outpouring of sympathy for the deserters, the Social Democratic administration either overruled the State Alien Commission outright or postponed indefinitely most of the deportations that the Commission had ordered.[94]

On 21 February the campaign for political asylum finally culminated when the government announced that, in the future, only those Americans convicted of "serious" crimes would be expelled. It furthermore guaranteed permanent asylum to any American refugee who risked being sent to a theater of war, which, in effect, extended asylum to draft resisters as well. The cabinet likewise promised that the deserters' asylum requests would be processed in a more expedient manner, and it promised that the government would work to improve the exiles' socio-economic situation by offering them more extensive aid in the form of improved job training programs, etc.[95] (Needless to say, the domestic political dimension of this announcement did not escape the attention of the non-socialist press.)[96]

The government maintained that these new guidelines would increase the defectors' sense of security, but the declaration conspicuously stopped short of granting them political refugee status.[97] Having rejected the call for political asylum, the Social Democratic administration insisted that the deserters' formal status was irrelevant as long as their quality of life improved.[98]

The government's response seems to have satisfied most Swedish antiwar activists,[99] but not the Maoists.[100] The latter protested that refugees from the Eastern bloc were immediately granted political refugee status, while the Americans were not. In the eyes of the far left, this decision proved that Swedish immigration law was being shaped by political calculations rather than by legal prescriptions. The Communists likewise held that formal political refugee status was denied to the deserters because the government feared Washington's negative reaction[101] – an opinion that was also seconded by a handful of Social Democratic critics.[102]

This accusation was not without merit, and the Swedish Foreign Ministry was anxious about what the American response would be should the government extend formal political refugee status to the deserters.[103] US officials had continuously opposed the prospect of Sweden conferring the deserters with political asylum status,[104] although they also resented that these men were granted "humanitarian asylum" instead. To American diplomats, this implied that the deserters had been subjected to inhumane treatment at the hands of US military authorities.[105] Holmqvist admitted that this was an unfortunate formulation,[106] and on his initiative the phrase "humanitarian asylum" was soon phased out in favor of "asylum due to special circumstances."[107] The changed formulation was therefore intended to appease Washington.

As indicated by these examples, the Social Democratic government's deserter policy, while rooted in domestic considerations, was nonetheless also always restrained by the official US reaction.[108] In the long run, there was little reason for the government to antagonize Washington over the

wording of Swedish policy, particularly because moderate Social Democratic opinion appeared to accept the terms put forth by the government
on 21 February 21.[109] Although a few Social Democrats at first still wanted
the deserters be given political refugee status,[110] in the end most party
members did not press this demand any further.[111] For its part, the SKfV
expressed the hope that political asylum might be attained at a later date but
thanked the government for its recent efforts on behalf of the deserters.[112]

The DFFG, in contrast, tried to keep the campaign for political asylum
alive for the next few months,[113] but for all intents and purposes this issue
was now dead – at least from a Social Democratic perspective. This question
was buried for good at the 24th SAP Congress in October. The Congress
entertained no fewer than five separate motions demanding political asylum
for the deserters (all of which had been submitted in January and early
February), yet none of the delegates objected when the cabinet stood firm
by its earlier decision.[114] This is an excellent illustration of the SAP hierarchy's skill at disarming radical motions presented to the Congress. Satisfied by the contents of the 21 February declaration, the Social Democratic
cadre appeared ready to leave this entire errand behind it, and to most
Social Democrats this matter had effectively been laid to rest.[115] Nor did the
SKfV show any real interest in pursuing this matter any further. Consequently, this issue was no longer of much concern to the SAP leadership.

To be sure, the ADC and their friends on the extraparliamentary left
struggled on in their quest to obtain political asylum, but to no avail.[116]
Without the political backing of the Social Democratic faithful, the ADC
and the NLF-groups simply did not have the necessary clout to compel the
government to revise its decision. By late 1969, even the Communists, who
briefly had seized upon this question, had seemingly lost all interest in it.[117]
While the latter hypothetically remained committed to securing political
asylum for the deserters, the VPK now abandoned this cause as well.[118]

Deserters Lose Support in Sweden

There are several reasons why the deserters squandered the political
allegiance of both the Communists and the Social Democrats. First, as 1969
came to a close, public interest in the Americans' plight had begun to dis-
sipate.[119] Accordingly, this question was of less political relevance to the parliamentary left. Second, most of the deserters were not political enough to
meet the demands of the Swedish anti-war movement – in fact, the majority

of the deserters showed little interest in politics. As a result, a lot of Swedes who had at first embraced these men grew progressively disillusioned, eventually turning their backs on them.[120]

Worse yet, the public's growing indifference rapidly turned into open hostility as more and more deserters were arrested in Sweden on a variety of criminal charges. Even though the overwhelming majority of these crimes were rather petty in nature, this topic attracted a lot of scrutiny, and fairly or not, in the minds of the general public, the deserters increasingly became associated with a negative stereotype as drug addicts and criminals.[121]

Some within the non-socialist camp quickly seized upon these developments to embarrass the Social Democratic administration. Conservative representative Gunnar Hübinette, for example, chastised the government for its failure to protect Sweden's youth from these drug-dealing Americans.[122] Such polemics could likewise be heard in parts of the non-socialist press, which dismissed the deserters as welfare-dependent drug addicts.[123] These domestic critics did not hide their glee at the chance to humiliate the Social Democrats about this issue, and it was one of the rare occasions when the non-socialist opposition was able to score political points by challenging the government's Vietnam policy.[124]

The Social Democratic administration was understandably defensive in the face of this criticism, and Eric Holmqvist was repeatedly forced to account for the cabinet's handling of this situation. He pointed toward various extenuating circumstances; among other things, Holmqvist stated many of these men came from poverty-stricken backgrounds, which probably accounted for their criminal behavior.[125] At the same time, Holmqvist was compelled to concede that perhaps the government had been a bit naive and that Swedish hospitality had, at least in some instances, been abused. He further promised to heed the Conservative call for stricter background checks on all future deserters entering Sweden.[126] From early 1970 on, Swedish immigration policy with regard to the American refugees did become more restrictive.[127]

Even more troubling to the SAP hierarchy was that this animosity towards the deserters had also spread to the party's own constituents.[128] While the Social Democratic administration's opposition to the war itself remained popular at the grassroots level within the SAP, sympathy for the deserters continued to erode and they became more and more of a political burden for the cabinet.[129]

A final factor that served to alienate ordinary Social Democrats from the deserters was the strident political posture of the American Deserter

Committee, not least its vehement attacks against the government and its dispute with the SKfV. The conflict with SKfV began brewing in June 1968, and then simmered to a boil in May 1969 after the release of the film *Deserter USA*, which was a collaborative project between the ADC and two young radical Swedish filmmakers.[130] *Deserter USA* condemned the cabinet's failure to provide political asylum and generally maligned the SKfV, dismissing the committee as a lapdog of big capital. Several bitter exchanges between the ADC and the SKfV followed the film's release.[131] Thereafter, the breach between the two organizations was irreconcilable, leaving the SKfV openly hostile towards the ADC and seemingly more ambivalent about the deserters in general.[132]

Not only had the ADC managed to alienate many of its original and more politically moderate supporters, by this point its own supposed constituents likewise deemed the organization to be completely irrelevant.[133] Failing even to mobilize its fellow exiles and lacking the patronage of the SKfV and parliamentary left, the ADC did not have enough political muscle to effectively oppose the government's hardening stance against the deserters.

The American Deserter Committee's political impotence became painfully evident as it sought to prevent the deportation of the first deserter slated for repatriation to the United States. The ADC and the NLF-groups launched a last ditch effort to halt the extradition of Joseph Parra, an American deserter who had served a 17-month prison sentence for narcotics distribution.[134] In spite of having staged various demonstrations and even a hunger strike, they were unable to prevent his expulsion from Sweden.[135] On 25 November 1970, Parra was forcibly repatriated, and a handful of other deportations soon followed.[136]

In the wake of Parra's repatriation, the ADC and its far left allies threatened to launch mass demonstrations to halt further extraditions.[137] In the words of one ADC supporter, Parra's deportation was "an indefensible act on the part of the Social Democratic government," protesting that "the deserters were now being treated more like political liabilities than refugees."[138] The ADC, along with the rest of the extraparliamentary left, believed that this new tougher attitude toward the deserters was a ploy by the Social Democratic administration to improve its relations with Washington.[139]

The DFFG-sponsored protests that followed Parra's expulsion,[140] however, did nothing to dissuade the cabinet from allowing the other slated deportations to proceed, for at this juncture there was little incentive for the SAP leadership to overturn them. Although the SKfV nominally supported the campaign to stop Parra's extradition,[141] it did not appear willing to throw its full prestige behind this endeavor. The same could be said for the Communists, and in the end neither the SKfV nor the VPK made any significant effort to intervene on Parra's behalf. Perhaps more importantly, there were no visible signs that the Social Democratic cadre disapproved of the government's handling of this errand.

All in all, popular sympathy for the deserters' cause had hit an all-time low, and this being the case the government stood to gain little by over-ruling drug-related deportation orders. Indeed, to do so at this stage would only have invited domestic protests. Olof Palme likely captured the public mood when he remarked, "If these deserters were really sincere about their not wanting to hurt anyone in Vietnam, they surely wouldn't be selling narcotics."[142] By now the Americans had become an albatross around the neck of the Social Democratic administration.

The government's tougher posture against these men therefore appears to have been driven by changing domestic political realities, and not, as the deserters themselves thought, by the Social Democratic administration's desire to appease the United States, for at this juncture the deserters were no longer a source of serious friction between Stockholm and Washington. As early as January 1969, the Swedish Embassy reported that the State Department had apparently ceased to view Sweden's acceptance of these men in a severely negative light.[143] This assessment was subsequently confirmed during both the Swedish Ambassador to the US Hubert de Besche and Torsten Nilsson's individual meetings with Nixon's new Secretary of State, William Rogers, in April and October of 1969. On both occasions, Rogers emphasized this question's decreased significance for Swedish–American relations.[144] Henceforth the deserters would not return as a major sticking point between the two countries.

US-Swedish Relations and Changing Attitudes to Deserters

By late 1968 and early 1969, then, American officials had put this issue behind them. Realizing that it was not in a legal position to challenge Sweden's deserter policy, the State Department revised its strategy. American diplomats grasped that this was a highly politicized question in Sweden, and for this reason a confrontational approach was only likely to backfire. Accordingly, the State Department never overtly pressured Sweden to expel the deserters, but instead focused on repatriating those men who voluntarily wanted to return to the United States, which over the years rose to be a sizable number.[145]

Originally, American officials made it a priority to assist those fugitives who chose to turn themselves in because from a propaganda standpoint it was important to show that the men who had fled to Sweden had become disillusioned and wanted to return home. However, by early 1969 this was no longer as crucial, considering that the deserters had seemingly become more of a public relations problem for the Social Democratic government than they were for the United States. At this point, their troubles were so well publicized that discouraging other soldiers from fleeing to Sweden was deemed to be less urgent.[146]

In time the repatriation issue became such a low priority that the State Department even contemplated cutting the funding that paid for transport of these fugitives back to the United States because the sheer volume of returnees was beginning to strain the department's budget. On the advice of the American Embassy in Stockholm, however, these plans were shelved. The latter cautioned that for domestic political reasons, the US government could ill afford to give the impression that it did not care about what happened to these men,[147] although this was probably not very far from the truth. This argument ultimately won out, and American Embassy officials continued to assist any deserter who desired to surrender himself to US military authorities. This policy became established practice[148] and remained in effect for the rest of the war.

While the Embassy concentrated on facilitating the repatriation process, it simultaneously kept a close eye on those fugitives who had opted to stay on in Sweden.[149] In no small part this was because the State Department suspected the Soviets of secretly having a hand in encouraging American servicemen to desert.[150] This matter greatly preoccupied other US government agencies as well, and the CIA, the FBI, the Army's Criminal Investigation Division, and the Navy's Criminal Investigative Service all monitored the American deserter colony in Sweden. Although these organizations devoted most of their attention to the ADC, to a lesser degree they were also interested in the deserters' Swedish sympathizers.[151]

As for intelligence specifically pertaining to the deserters, the Embassy received continual updates from the State Alien Commission about all newly arrived deserters and draft resisters. This discreet (though not secret) working arrangement proved to be a valuable source of data for American officials, providing them with the name, rank, and date of birth of each new military fugitive that was given asylum.[152] Otherwise, the bulk of the information that US authorities had about the deserters in Sweden appears to have been gathered from interviews with those GIs who had undergone voluntary repatriation because they were routinely debriefed upon their return to American military control.[153]

Materials obtained via the Freedom of Information Act make clear that US officials also had access to other sources of confidential information, including informants within the American peace movement.[154] However, because these documents are so heavily censored, the exact identity of these sources remain unclear to this day. The available evidence does, however, indicate that the CIA, unlike the other American intelligence agencies, also had its own informants on the ground in Sweden.[155]

The deserters were not unaware that American authorities were monitoring them, and they further believed that their own ranks had been infiltrated by US intelligence officers acting as agent provocateurs. To some, this ostensibly also accounted for the American Deserter Committee's extreme behavior.[156] In this context it is of interest that the original leadership of the ADC had played a key role in disseminating the idea that the deserter colony was being penetrated by American agents, denouncing some of their peers as US government informants. The ADC's scare propaganda, in turn, convinced many of their fellow deserters that the CIA was directing various plots against them.[157] While these fears were definitely overstated, they were probably not entirely unfounded in light of what we have since come to know about the agency's clandestine activities during these years.[158]

Since this time, it has additionally been revealed that Swedish intelligence officers passed on information about the deserters to CIA operatives in Stockholm.[159] Apparently both SÄPO (the regular Swedish secret police)[160] and IB (the Social Democratic Party's own clandestine intelligence organization) secretly collected intelligence about the deserters. This was part of both organizations' broader surveillance of the Swedish far left.[161]

In this period it was not completely unknown that Swedish authorities collaborated with the CIA,[162] but had the news come out then that the government was covertly turning information about the deserters over to the US this would have been extremely embarrassing for the SAP leadership. This is because the Social Democratic faithful would have had great difficulty accepting this total disjuncture in government policy. On one hand, the Social Democratic administration rolled out the red carpet for the deserters, and on the other, it went behind their backs providing intelligence about them to the CIA. Given that some members of the cabinet were quite knowledgeable about IB's activities, it seems very unlikely that they were wholly ignorant of this practice – and even if they were, this was presumably only because they intentionally did not want to know. All in all, this represents one of the most flagrant examples of the Social Democratic administration's double-dealings during the war.

In addition, this provides us with yet another striking illustration of how Swedish–American tensions at the government-to-government level over Vietnam did not necessarily preclude close cooperation in most other areas. The Swedes' continued willingness to pass along this type of data to the US probably also does much to explain why the State Department eventually ceased to view the deserter issue as a grave impediment to the two countries' relationship.

Many conservatives on Capitol Hill, however, were not so forgiving;[163] and Sweden's acceptance of American deserters was the subject of continuous Congressional interest and indignation.[164] Senator Strom Thurmond, for instance, complained, "Sweden's policy of refusing to extradite deserters is part of her hostility toward us [the US] in our attempts to defend the West, including Sweden, against Communist aggression… I call upon the State Department to take stronger measures and to use every diplomatic means at our command, including the use of whatever sanctions may be necessary, to force Sweden to adopt a policy for the common good."[165] Democratic representative John Rarick seconded Senator Thurmond's call for sanctions. According to Rarick, harboring American deserters proved that Sweden was actively siding against the US in the Vietnam conflict.[166]

Yet not everyone in the US was of this same opinion,[167] and many American peace activists certainly applauded the Social Democratic administration's decision to shelter these men.[168] Such nuances in American public opinion notwithstanding, throughout the war the Swedish diplomatic corps continued to regard the deserter issue as a serious liability for the country's image in the United States.[169] In fact, as late as January 1973 Hubert de Besche advised that this question remained a potentially grave handicap for Sweden in its relationship to the American public in a way that neither its diplomatic recognition of Hanoi nor its criticism of the war had been.[170] A subsequent diplomatic report concluded that this question had the single most damaging impact on popular perceptions of Sweden because to the average American Sweden's acceptance of the deserters was both humiliating and insulting.[171]

While the accuracy of this general characterization cannot be established definitively, the Social Democratic administration still had good reason to believe that it was more or less correct. From the very start, the deserter issue had infected the Swedes' relationship with the American press, and Social Democratic spokesmen were quickly forced to acknowledge that this was an extremely sensitive topic in the United States.[172] In early 1969, Torsten Nilsson expressed frustration about the enormous amount of attention that the country's acceptance of deserters had received in the American media, and he felt that this policy had been completely misunderstood on the other side of the Atlantic. He additionally griped that Sweden had been unfairly singled out for criticism despite the fact that many other nations had also provided sanctuary for American deserters.[173] This question would continue to dog the Social Democratic administration in its dealings with the American public and media.[174]

At no time was this as apparent as during Palme's 1970 visit to the United States, at which point Palme faced a barrage of questions about the deserters.[175] On two separate occasions he was also confronted by hostile demonstrations organized by the International Longshoreman's Union, which remained angry with the Swedish government for harboring American military fugitives.[176] Palme sought to neutralize the issue by calling attention to the fact that the number of American military offenders in Sweden paled in comparison to the number of deserters that had arrived from the Eastern bloc. He further insisted that this matter had been totally blown out of proportion by the US media.[177]

The American fixation with this subject was undoubtedly frustrating to Palme. Instead of being afforded an opportunity to explain why he and his government opposed the war, he spent much of his trip defending Sweden's deserter policy, an issue that probably was not of much interest to him personally anymore. Even prior to this trip, Palme had lamented publicly that he could not understand the amount of criticism that this policy had elicited in the United States. Noticeably irritated, he declared, "It is not a question whether or not we [Swedes] like the deserters, but a question of whether or not we maintain our humanitarian standards"[178] – hardly a resounding endorsement of the deserters on Palme's part.

As suggested by the above comments, by 1969/1970 the Social Democratic administration had come to regard the deserters as an encumbrance. Even though Swedish Foreign Ministry officials had likely exaggerated the negative impact that this question had on the country's image, it is still indisputable that this whole affair had, at least temporarily, generated unprecedented hostility toward Sweden among certain segments of the American public.

* * *

It is equally transparent that this question had become a public relations liability for the Social Democratic administration at home. The opening of Sweden to American deserters in 1968 had ostensibly helped to deliver the anti-war vote to the SAP in the September elections, thereby indirectly contributing to the party's landslide election victory. Yet, it did not take long before the deserters' various troubles appeared to begin to outweigh their political value to the Social Democrats. The government's increasingly restrictive posture vis-à-vis these men was unmistakably a result of the public's mounting aversion toward them. Thus, when the country finally closed its borders to American military fugitives in late March 1973 in conjunction with the signing the Paris Peace Accords,[179] this was not, as the deserters themselves asserted, an attempt by the Social Democratic administration to buy American goodwill.[180] As has already been established, Washington had at this point long since stopped being overly concerned about this matter. Rather, this move was almost certainly motivated by the fear that Sweden might become a refugee for thousands of military fugitives who had been hiding underground elsewhere in the world. Politically, the Social Democratic government did not stand to gain anything more from the deserter issue – quite to the contrary, they had much to lose.

That the deserters now had outlived their political purpose in Sweden was definitely not lost upon American commentators. As early as September 1971, a report by the House of Representatives' Subcommittee on Europe observed that "the Social Democratic government has received the publicity it wanted with the Intrepid Four and now wished the deserters and their personal problems would quietly leave."[181] Accusations to this effect were by no means unprecedented.

Indeed, US officials had always privately believed that the Social Democratic administration was exploiting the deserters for its own political ends.[182] Some of the deserters were of the same opinion. This sentiment was maybe best exemplified by American deserter John Ashley, who in a letter to his parents, likened the Americans' presence in Sweden to that of Afro-Americans invited to white liberal cocktail parties in the United States – in both cases they were solely there to bolster the progressive credentials of their hosts.[183] Ashley's judgment was seconded by his fellow deserter, Larry Tipton, who bitterly determined that "the Swedes received us [the deserters] for their own propaganda needs, not out of the goodness of their hearts."[184]

The deserters' advocates in Sweden often harbored likeminded suspicions. Thomas Hayes (an American Episcopal Minister who served as a spiritual advisor to the deserter colony in Sweden between 1969 and 1970) concluded, "Sweden wanted all the credit for accepting the American exiles, but little responsibility for job training, housing, and schooling."[185] Desmond Carragher, a former peer counselor to the American deserters, offers a slightly more generous interpretation of the Social Democratic administration's deserter policy, stating that in hindsight it is plain to see that the decision to shelter these men was not very well thought out by Swedish authorities. At first, the deserters were treated principally as political symbols, and little consideration was given to what kinds of troubles they were likely to experience in Sweden (or to bring with them for that matter.) No effective programs were initially in place to help the Americans adjust to life in exile, which in part explains why many deserters ran into a variety of difficulties in Sweden.[186]

Even if one accepts this more charitable view of Swedish deserter policy, this still highlights the rather shortsighted, and at times patently opportunistic nature of the Social Democrat's Vietnam policy. The deserters were let into Sweden in order to satisfy domestic anti-war opinion – and above all to please the SKfV. This was done without a careful assessment of the potential problems that might result from this policy. In particular, this policy's ramifications for Sweden's reputation in the US do not seem to have been given sufficient consideration.

Unlike Sweden, France and Canada both avoided these pitfalls. By handling this issue with a great deal more discretion (and by keeping the deserters under stricter control), neither the Canadians nor the French suffered as many adverse political consequences as the Swedes did. However, in all three instances the decision to provide refuge for American deserters was done with an eye towards domestic opinion, and it was a policy that directly played to indigenous anti-American and nationalistic sentiments.[187] Thus, in neither the French, Canadian, nor Swedish case did this policy appear to originate solely (or even primarily) out of a genuine sense of empathy for the deserters.

The Social Democratic administration's policy toward North Vietnam was born out of a comparable political impulse. As we shall see in the next chapter, the Swedish decision to extend diplomatic recognition, and financial assistance, to the DRV was not principally rooted in a sense of solidarity with the Vietnamese people; instead, it was chiefly a byproduct of internal Social Democratic party tactical calculations. Similarly to its deserter policy, Stockholm's dealings with Hanoi were repeatedly tempered by Washington's reactions. In both instances, the government's Vietnam stance was shaped by the ever shifting "push and pull" interaction between domestic political expediency and the preservation of Sweden's own long-term interests.

Chapter 4: Notes

[1] 29 Nov. 1967. Telegram to the SKfV from four American Deserters in Moscow. (Hans Göran Franck. Handlingar rörande amerikanska Vietnam-desertörer/-veteraner. Vol 1.) Michael Lindner, one of the Intrepid Four, confirmed this narrative of events. Lindner written correspondence with the author 15 Jan. 2000.

[2] 28 Dec. 1967. Letter to the Minister of the Interior, Rune Johansson, from the General Secretary of the SKfV. Bertil Svanström. Svenska kommittén för Vietnam, Laos och Kambodja. 1568/E/1/2 Korrespondens. Vol 1967–1968. 3077.

[3] The Intrepid Four as cited in Robert Manning, "We couldn't swing with it" in Robert Manning and Michael Janeway (eds.), Who We Are (Boston: Little Brown, 1969) 229–246.

[4] Bertil Svanström as cited in Michael Richard, "American Deserters in Stockholm" Interplay 12 (1970): 28–37.

[5] Statens Utlänningsnämnd. Protokoll och föredragningspromemorior. F:2 A. April 1967–March 1973. Vol. 37–48. Most of the deserters went AWOL from American bases in West Germany, and then fled to Sweden via Denmark.

[6] SCB, Data Om Invandrare (Stockholm: SCB, 1981). Although both Swedish and US official discourse typically referred to all of the American exiles in Sweden as deserters, approximately one third of these men were actually draft resisters, not deserters. Moreover, the official estimate of 800 men does not include those Americans who never reported their presence to Swedish immigration authorities. The real number was probably closer to 1,000 men. Jim Walch interview with the author 2 July 1999. During the war, Walch served as a counselor and advocate for the American deserters in Sweden.

[7] Devi Prasad, Love it, or leave it (London: War Resisters International, 1971) 17–47; Jim Walsh, "USA:s Flyktingar" Tiden # 9 1972, 504–511.

[8] John Hagan, Northern Passage (Cambridge: Harvard University Press, 2001) 48–58. See also The International Herald Tribune 28 June 1967.

[9] 30 Sept. 1968. Assistant Chief of Staff Intelligence. Dept of the Army. Unsigned. Memo. "Desertion Propaganda and Its Effect on US Army Europe." (Dept. of Army. FOIPA Carl-Gustaf Scott January 2002); 25 May 1970. Interview. William W. Heath, US Ambassador to Sweden 1967–1969. L.B.J. Library. Oral History Project. Tape # 2, 25.

[10] Magnus Jerneck, Kritik som utrikespolitiskt medel (Lund: Dialogus, 1983) 79–80, 109–110, 115–117, 187, 209–210, 217, 229. For a specific example, Senator Carl Curtis as cited in Svenska Dagbladet 9 Jan. 1968.

[11] Aftonbladet 9 March 1968; New York Times 17 March 1968.

[12] 5 Jan. 1968. European Section Dept. of State. Walter Stoessel. Telegram to the US Embassy Stockholm. Re: Today's discussion with the Swedish Ambassador to the US Hubert de Besche. Central Foreign Policy File 1967–1969. Political and Defense. Sweden. RG 59; 11 March 1968. Political Section FM. Wilhelm Wachtmeister. Memo. Re: March 6 meeting between Tage Erlander and the US Ambassador to Sweden William W. Heath. Avd HP. Grupp 1. Mål Ua. Politik Allmänt. USA # 222.

[13] See, for instance, *Lincoln Star* 23 Jan. 1968 and *Houston Post* 16 March 1968.

[14] *The Frank McGee Report*. NBC. 25 Feb. 1968. Television. (Transcript as found in Avd HP. Grupp 1. Mål Ua. Politik Allmänt. USA # 222.)

[15] *Wall Street Journal* 12 April 1968. Even though Gleason did not follow through on his boycott threat, the International Longshoreman's Union would continue to protest Sweden's acceptance of American deserters. Gleason as cited in *Expressen* 5 June 1970.

[16] Gordon Coates, a retired factory worker from St. Louis, for instance, launched a one-man campaign, urging his fellow Americans to stop buying Swedish goods in protest against Sweden's harboring of US military fugitives. *Expressen* 10 May 1968. Similar calls were also heard in the Congress. *Dagens Nyheter* 29 April 1969.

[17] 8 April 1968. Hubert de Besche. Telegram to FM. Avd HP. Grupp 1. Mål Ua. Politik Allmänt. USA # 222; 17 April 1968. Sven Frychius. Telegram to FM. Avd HP. Grupp 1. Mål Ua. Politik Allmänt. USA # 222. Both telegrams provide an overview of undated discussions that Embassy officials had recently had with leading Swedish businessmen in the United States. According to de Besche and Frychius, the latter were very concerned about the negative impact that the government's Vietnam stance might have on Swedish exports in the United States. See also *Svenska Dagbladet* 14 April 1968.

[18] For a specific illustration, see comments by Conservative representative Henrik Åkerlund as cited in *Riksdagsprotokollet* # 13, 26 March 1969, 92–93.

[19] See, for instance, Center Party representative, Torsten Bengtsson as cited in *Riksdagsprotokollet* # 13, 21 March 1968, 39. See also Liberal representative Erik Boheman's op-ed in *Dagens Nyheter* 18 April 1968.

[20] For specific examples, see Conservative municipal politician Birger Horndal as cited in *Falu-Kuriren* 11 March 1968 and Conservative representative Gunnar Hübinette's exchange with Eric Holmqvist as cited in *Riksdagsprotokollet* # 20, 23 April 1970, 8–9. Similar sentiments were also expressed by a number of prominent Swedish businessmen. See, for instance, Axel Iveroth, Chairman of the Association of Swedish Industrialists, as cited in *Aftonbladet* 28 April 1969.

[21] *US News & World Report* 19 Feb. 1968; *Washington Evening Star* 18 March 1968.

[22] 8 Dec. 1967. Cameron Turner Jr. Telegram to State. Central Foreign Policy File 1967–1969. Political and Defense. Sweden. RG 59; 5 Jan. 1968. Cameron Turner Jr. Telegram to State. Central Foreign Policy File 1967–1969. Political and Defense. Sweden. RG 59.

[23] 5 Jan. 1968. Walter Stoessel. Telegram to US Embassy Stockholm. Re: Today's discussion with the Swedish Ambassador to the US Hubert de Besche. Central Foreign Policy File 1967–1969. Political and Defense. Sweden. RG 59; 11 March 1968. Wilhelm Wachtmeister. Memo. Re: Meeting between Erlander and US Ambassador to Sweden William Heath on 6 Jan. 1968. Avd HP. Grupp 1. Mål Ua. Politik Allmänt. USA # 221; 15 March 1968. Hubert de Besche. Telegram to FM. Re: Lunch with the Head of European Section Dept. of State John Leddy on 13 March 1968. Avd HP. Grupp 1. Mål Ua. Politik Allmänt. USA # 222.

[24] For a specific illustration, see the Minister of the Interior, Eric Holmqvist as cited in *SAP Kongressprotokoll*. 24:e Kongressen. 28 Sept.–4 Oct. 1969, 563–564. See also Torsten Nilsson, *Åter Vietnam* (Stockholm: Tiden, 1981) 152.

[25] See, for instance, Torsten Nilsson as cited in UD, *Utrikesfrågor 1969* (Stockholm: UD, 1969) 43. and Olof Palme as cited in UD, *Utrikesfrågor 1970* (Stockholm: UD, 1970) 49.

[26] Eric Holmqvist as cited in *Riksdagsprotokollet* # 6, 28 February 1969, 149; Eric Holmqvist as cited in *Riksdagsprotokollet* # 20, 23 April 1970, 8–9.

[27] Torsten Nilsson and Krister Wickman as cited by Jerneck, *Kritik som utrikespolitiskt medel*, 70, 217. This was also confirmed by Sverker Åström, the Swedish Under Secretary of State 1972–1977. Åström interview with author 20 July 1999.

[28] 5 Feb. 1968. Political Section FM. Lennart Alvin. Memo. Re: US press coverage of Sweden's acceptance of the deserters. Avd HP. Grupp 1. Mål Ua. Politik Allmänt. USA # 221; 26 March 1968. Sven Frychius. Letter to Sten Sundfelt FM. Avd HP. Grupp 1. Mål Ua. Politik Allmänt. USA # 222.

[29] 11 Feb. 1968. Hubert de Besche. Telegram to FM Avd HP. Grupp 1. Mål Ua. Politik Allmänt. USA # 221; 12 March 1968. Hubert de Besche. Telegram to FM. Avd HP. Grupp 1. Mål Ua. Politik Allmänt. USA # 221.

[30] 17 Jan. 1968. Press Secretary FM. Sten Sundfelt. Memo. Avd HP. Grupp 1. Mål Ua. Politik Allmänt. USA # 220. See also anonymous Foreign Ministry official as cited by Walch, "Regeringen och Vietnamkrigsvägarna" in *Tiden* # 5 1971, 292–301.

[31] For example, in response to the Swedish Embassy staff in Moscow's complaints that the Soviets did not ask for permission before sending American deserters on to Sweden, the Foreign Ministry in Stockholm instructed the Embassy staff not to broach the issue with Soviet authorities. The Foreign Ministry stated such a protest would be meaningless because domestic political opinion in Sweden would not permit the repatriation of American deserters to the USSR. 6 June 1968. Head of the Legal Section FM. Love Kellberg. Telegram to the Swedish Embassy in Moscow. Avd HP. Grupp 1. Mål Er. Politik Allmänt. Sovjetunionen. # 306.

[32] 19 March 1968. Love Kellberg. Telegram to all Swedish delegations in the United States. Avd HP. Grupp 1. Mål Ua. Politik Allmänt. USA # 222; 25 Nov. 1970. Political Division FM. Leif Leifland. Telegram to all Swedish delegations in the United States. Avd HP. Grupp 1. Mål Ua. Politik Allmänt. USA # 238. Swedish government spokesmen adopted a similar line of argumentation. See, for example, Torsten Nilsson as cited in *Dagens Nyheter* 18 March 1968.

[33] Olof Palme. *The Today Show*. NBC. 9 June 1970. Television. (Transcript as found in Avd HP. Grupp 1. Mål Ua. Politik Allmänt. USA # 236.) See also Nilsson, *Åter Vietnam*, 151–152.

[34] 25 May 1970. William W. Heath. L.B.J. Library. Oral History Project. Tape # 2, 28. Congress was of the same opinion. US Senate: Committee on the Armed Services. Report to the Subcommittee on Treatment of Military Deserters. "Treatment of Deserters from Military Service." 91st Cong., 1st Sess., 6 March 1969, 10.

[35] *Kungl. Maj:ts proposition 142,* 4 Oct. 1968, 114. Avd R. Grupp 191. Mål K. Svensk visitering. Förrymda krigsfångar, militärarbetare, desertörer, m.m. May 1967–Nov. 1986. # 6.

[36] Klas Lithner, "De amerikanska desertörerna" *Svensk Tidskrift* 55 (1968): 86–90.

[37] For a specific illustration, see SKfV Chairman Gunnar Myrdal's op-ed in *Dagens Nyheter* 25 Jan. 1968.

[38] The first such instructions were sent out in early 1968, and they were continuously revised. 19 March 1968. Love Kellberg. Telegram to all Swedish delegations in the United States. Avd HP. Grupp 1. Mål Ua. Politik Allmänt. USA # 222; 25 Nov. 1970. Leif Leifland. Telegram to all Swedish delegations in the United States. Avd HP. Grupp 1. Mål Ua. Politik Allmänt. USA # 238.

[39] Ingmar Källberg interview with the author 20 July 1999. Källberg first worked as a lawyer within the Ministry of Interior and then later in the Ministry of Immigration. Bengt Ranland also confirmed this. Starting in 1970, Ranland was a Department Head within the Ministry of Immigration. Ranland written correspondence with the author 23 Sept. 1999.

[40] *Svenska Dagbladet* 18 Sept. 1967. Over the next two years, the State Alien Commission repeatedly reiterated that no precedent existed with regard to the American deserters and that every case would be treated individually based on the merits of each case. This would later give Swedish immigration officials leeway to enforce a more restrictive interpretation of the country's asylum policy toward these men.

[41] That said, their presence in Sweden did not go entirely unnoticed. *London Times* 17 Aug. 1967; *Aftonbladet* 26 Oct. 1967.

[42] At that time, no official protocol was taken down during cabinet meetings, but, as far as Eric Holmqvist can recall, the government as a whole never discussed this issue. In early 1968, Holmqvist was still the Minister of Agriculture, and he did not become the Minister of the Interior until 1969, but he was good friends with Rune Johansson, who then was the Minister of the Interior. Holmqvist, however, has no recollection of Johansson ever discussing the deserter question. (Holmqvist written correspondence with the author 15 Oct. 1999.) The most probable scenario is that Erlander and Palme, in conjunction with Nilsson and Johansson, jointly made a decision about how this issue should be handled by the State Alien Commission. Unfortunately, neither Tage Erlander's diary, nor Nilsson's memoir *Åter Vietnam* shed any light on this question, and to date Rune Johansson's personal papers remain unsorted. Yet according to Sverker Åström, it is very likely that Palme played a key role in making this decision. Åström interview with the author 20 July 1999.

[43] Given the sensitive nature of this particular errand, both Bengt Ranland and Ingmar Källberg agree that it is very likely that the government either directly or indirectly let the Commission know how it would like to see this matter handled. Källberg interview with the author 20 July 1999; Ranland written correspondence with the author 21 Sept. 1999.

[44] For example, the asylum requests of the two deserters that arrived after Ray Jones III in the late fall of 1967 were not decided in their favor until the decision to extend

159

humanitarian asylum to the Intrepid Four had already been announced. 23 Jan. 1968. Statens Utlänningnämnd Protokoll. A:1 Vol. 37.

[45] 21 Dec. 1967. Letter from the State Alien Commission to the High Command of the Swedish Armed Forces. (Statens Utlänningskommission Protokoll. Hemliga Arkivet. E:8 1953-1969. Vol 1.) In this unsigned letter, the Commission expresses its ambivalence about Sweden becoming a prospective safe haven for American deserters. The Commission further asks the High Command to find out what punishment a deserter might expect if he were to be repatriated to the United States. The unsigned letter also states that if a deserter is returned forcibly to the US (and then is given a severe punishment) a 'certain pressure' will appear in Sweden to oppose any such deportations. Gunnar Sommarin, the Press Secretary of the State Alien Board, points out that it is not very surprising that the members of the State Alien Commission would have been opposed to granting asylum to American deserters given that they were not political appointees. He adds that in this period most Swedish lawyers still tended to be politically conservative. Sommarin interview with the author 6 July 1999. See also the op-ed by Gösta Johansson, the State Alien Commission's Press Secretary, in Dagens Nyheter 20 Feb. 1969. Johansson's reservations about this policy are unmistakable, as he notes that: "some were using the deserters as 'political exhibits.'"

[46] Dagens Nyheter 10 Jan. 1968. While direct government intervention cannot be proven beyond a doubt, at a minimum the cabinet did not choose to overturn the Commission's decision to provide asylum to the American deserters.

[47] 3 Jan. 1968. Press release. Statens Utlänningskommission. Avd R. Grupp 191. Mål K. Förrymda krigsfångar, militärarbetare, desertörer, m.m. # 6; 9 Jan. 1968. Press release. Statens Utlänningskommission. Avd R. Grupp 191. Mål K. Förrymda krigsfångar, militärarbetare, desertörer, m.m. # 6. This first statement made clear that the Commission expected the deserters to refrain from any overt political activity, whereas the second press release completely contradicted the contents of the first, declaring that the deserters were by no means forbidden to engage in political agitation. See also Arbetet 29 Dec. 1967, Svenska Dagbladet 3 Jan. 1968 and Aftonbladet 10 Jan. 1968.

[48] For a specific illustration, see Center Party leader Gunnar Hedlund as cited in Dagens Nyheter 12 March 1968. Likeminded reservations were also heard from parts of the non-socialist press. See editorials in Vestmanlands Läns Tidning 3 Jan. 1968, Norrköpings Tidningar 4 Jan. 1968 and Västerbottens-Kuriren 20 Feb. 1968.

[49] 16 Jan. 1968. William W. Heath. Telegram to State. Central Foreign Policy File 1967–1969. Political and Defense. Sweden. RG 59; 4 April 1968. Hubert de Besche. Telegram to FM. Re: Recent undated conversation with John Leddy Head of the European Section Dept. of State. Avd HP. Grupp 1. Mål Ua. Politik Allmänt. USA # 220.

[50] 5 Jan. 1968. Hubert de Besche. Telegram to FM. Re: Today's meeting with Walter Stossel. Avd HP. Grupp 1. Mål Ua. Politik Allmänt. USA # 220; 9 April 1969. Political Counselor US Embassy Stockholm. Arthur Berg. Letter to Paul Hughes Scandinavian Desk Dept. of State. Central Foreign Policy File 1967–1969. Political and Defense. Sweden. RG 59.

[51] 20 March 1968. Political Section FM. Unsigned. Telegram to all Swedish delegations in the United States. Avd HP. Grupp 1. Mål Ua. Politik Allmänt. USA # 222. The telegram instructs the delegations how to best reply to this specific American objection.

[52] In 1953, Torsten Nilsson's predecessor, Östen Undén, explicitly declared that foreigners were prohibited from engaging in political propaganda while on Swedish soil. Undén as cited in UD, Utrikesfrågor 1953 (Stockholm: UD, 1953) 90–91. He subsequently made sure that the French deserters abided by this guideline.

[53] For specific illustrations of Social Democratic support for the deserters, see editorials in Dagbladet Nya Samhället Sundsvall 3 Jan. 1968, Folkbladet Östgöten 5 Jan. 1968 and Aftonbladet 10 Jan. 1968.

[54] See, for instance, Ray Jones as cited in SKfV, "Röster för Vietnam" (Stockholm: SKfV, 1968) 14.

[55] Bertil Svanström apparently approached Mike Vale about creating an independent political forum for the newly arrived deserters. Vale, a radical American political activist who at the time was residing in Sweden, was subsequently instrumental in setting up the ADC. Desmond Carragher written correspondence with the author 18 Dec. 1999. Carragher was a peer counselor and advocate for the deserters during the war.

[56] Martin Schiff, "The United States and Sweden" American Scandinavian Review 1973 61(4): 369.

[57] Torsten Nilsson as cited in Expressen 12 Nov. 1969.

[58] Gunnar Myrdal. Aktuellt. TV 1. 21 March 1968. Television. See also Sara Lidman's op-ed in Aftonbladet 10 Sept. 1968 and NLF-activist Cecila Wennerström's op-ed in Gaudeamus 10 April 1969.

[59] For a specific example, see Vilhelm Moberg, Den okända släkten (Stockholm: PAN/Norstedt, 1968) 130.

[60] For specific illustrations, see editorials in Dagens Nyheter 30 Dec. 1967, Expressen 3 Jan. 1968, Aftonbladet 2 Jan. 1968 and Arbetet 11 Jan. 1968.

[61] Mrs. Olsson (a social worker that worked exclusively with newly arrived immigrants) as cited in Ulla Davidsson, et al., "Amerikanska desertörer i Sverige" (University of Stockholm, 1970) 58.

[62] Aftonbladet 12 Jan. 1968; Expressen 10 March 1968.

[63] For a specific illustration, see editorial in Norrskensflamman 11 Jan. 1968.

[64] SSSF. Årsmöte protokoll 23–24 Feb. 1968. Motion # 4. For additional examples, see "Vi 5" in Aftonbladet 2 Jan. 1968 and letter to the editor from "Fredsvänlig" in Folket 3 Jan. 1968.

[65] Op-ed by Gunnar Myrdal in Dagens Nyheter 25 Jan. 1968. According to Myrdal, the government's decision to shelter to the deserters disproved the NLF-groups' contention that the Social Democratic administration was susceptible to American pressure.

[66] Among other things, the SKfV formed a group specifically aimed at helping the deserters to get settled in Sweden, which was known as "Arbetsgruppen för stöd åt Vietnamkrigsvägare." Hans Göran Franck. Handlingar rörande amerikanska Vietnam-desertörer/-veteraner. Vol 1.

[67] Undated (ca Jan. 1968). SKfV, "Appell för Vietnams folk." Svenska kommittén för Vietnam, Laos och Kambodja. Handlingar rörande Indokina. Vol 1967–1971. 3077.

[68] 1972. "Info från SKfV." Svenska kommittén för Vietnam, Laos och Kambodja. 1568/F/1/9. Vol 1967–1973. 3077; 1973. "Stöd Indokinas Folk." Svenska kommittén för Vietnam, Laos och Kambodia. 1568/F/1/9. Vol 1967–1973. 3077. See also Bertil Svanström as cited in Richard, "American Deserters in Stockholm," 28–37.

[69] SKfV, "Röster för Vietnam," 14. See also Ray Jones Jr. as cited in Tommy Hammarström, *FNL i Sverige* (Stockholm: AB Solidaritet, 1975) 90–91, and former SKfV activist, Maud Sundquist, as cited in the *Philadelphia Inquirer* 10 Feb. 1985.

[70] Thomas Hayes, *American deserters in Sweden* (New York: Association Press, 1971) 71; Åke Kilander, *Vietnam var nära* (Stockholm: Leopard, 2007) 147.

[71] Rapport från de Förenade FLN-Gruppernas kommitte för USA-krigsvägrare. May 1968. De Förenade FLN-Grupperna. A:5. Bla protokoll m.m. 1967–1973. Vol 1. After the fact, the NLF-groups also claimed to have helped to open Sweden up to American deserters. For a specific illustration, see Ulf Hellberg's op-ed in *Folkbladet Östgöten* 12 May 1969.

[72] Hammarström, *FNL i Sverige*, 42, 83–84, 90–92; Kilander, *Vietnam var nära,* 146–147.

[73] The DFFG, for instance, suggested that the SKfV was not as committed to helping the deserters as it was. Rapport om Vietnamarbetet i Sverige. Till DFFG:s Kongress 21–23 June 1968. De förenade FLN-Grupperna. A:5. Bla protokoll m.m. 1967–1973. Vol 1.

[74] ADC spokesmen, Bill Jones speech on 29 March 1968. (transcript in) De Förenade FLN-Grupperna. A:5. Bla protokoll m.m. 1967–1973. Vol 1. In this speech, Jones thanks the DFFG for all of its help, adding that it was the only organization in Sweden that has faithfully stood by the deserters' side.

[75] Bill Jones and Bertil Svanström as cited in the *New York Times* 9 June 1968. Jones accused the SKfV of reneging on a promise of financial aid to the ADC, and Svanström, in turn, condemned the ADC for being extremists.

[76] *Aftonbladet* 1 Oct 1969; *New York Times* 20 Oct. 1968.

[77] *Arbetet* 9 Oct. 1968.

[78] For a specific illustration, see Bill Jones and Sara Lidman as cited in *Aftonbladet* 28 Oct. 1968.

[79] 15 Oct. 1968. William W. Heath. Telegram to State. Central Foreign Policy File 1967–1969. Political and Defense. Sweden. RG 59; 5 Nov. 1968. William W. Heath. Memo. "Status report on US deserters in Sweden." (Dept. of State. FOIPA Carl-Gustaf Scott March 2002.)

[80] *Dagens Nyheter* 29 Oct. 1968.

[81] Op-ed by Jim Walch in *Dagens Nyheter* 2 June 1971.

[82] Carl-Gustaf Scott, "Sweden might be a haven, but it's not heaven" *Immigrants & Minorities* 33 2015.

[83] SKfV, Mötesprotokoll. Arbetsgruppen för stöd åt Vietnamkrigsvägrare 23 Oct. 1968 (Hans Göran Franck. Handlingar rörande amerikanska Vietnam-desertörer/-veteraner.

Vol 2); "Uprop till stöd för den Amerikanske Vietnamkrigsvägararen Warren Hammerman" *The Second Front Review* # 7, 1969, 21–22.

[84] The demand for political asylum had actually been raised by the NLF-groups as early October 1967, that is, well prior to the arrival of the Intrepid Four. Dagens Nyheter 22 Oct. 1967. The Communists were likewise early supporters of this cause. See, for instance, the editorial in Norrskensflamman 11 Jan. 1968. See also Kilander, Vietnam var nära, 146–147.

[85] For specific illustrations, see *Tidsignal* # 6 1969, 2. and *The Second Front Review* # 7 1969, 11–13. Under Swedish immigration law at that time, political refugees were provided with more extensive social benefits, and greater legal protections, than non-political refugees. Humanitarian asylum status therefore only put the American exiles on par with so-called "economic immigrants." *Kungl. Maj:ts proposition 142,* 4 Oct. 1968, 114.

[86] See, for instance, editorials in *Expressen* 28 Oct. 1968 and *Aftonbladet* 29 Oct. 1968. See also Bengt Söderström and Lars Wiklund's op-ed in *Dagens Nyheter* 15 Feb. 1969.

[87] For a specific illustration, see Åsa Moberg's column in *Aftonbladet* 6 Dec. 1968.

[88] 9 Dec. 1968. Facklig Vietnamaktion. "Politisk Asyl åt Vietnamkrigsvägare" (Hans Göran Franck. Handlingar rörande amerikanska Vietnam-desertörer/-veteraner. Vol 2.) See also *Vietnambulletinen* # 1 1969, 23. and *The Second Front Review* # 7, 1969, 2–3.

[89] Hans-Göran Franck as cited in Hammarström, *FNL i Sverige*, 83–89. See also Communist leader CH Hermansson as cited in *Riksdagsprotokollet* # 1, 14 Jan. 1969, 21–22.

[90] *Ny Dag* 30 Jan. 1969; *Dagens Nyheter* 12 Feb. 1968; *Norrskensflamman* 15 Jan. 1969; *Aftonbladet* 14 Feb. 1969; *Expressen* 20 Feb. 1968; *Folket* 21 Feb. 1969.

[91] In a petition published in *Dagens Nyheter* on 19 Feb. 1968, at least 20 different organizations, political clubs, and unions endorsed this cause. The signatories of the petition represented a diverse range of interest groups: everything from temperance and Christian organizations to VPK and *Sveriges Socialdemokratiska Studentförbund*, SSSF (the Association of Social Democratic Students.)

[92] 18 Feb. 1969. Letter from the SSU to the Ministry of the Interior. (Inrikesdepartementet. Konseljakter avseende utlänningsärenden); 20 Feb. 1969. Letter from SKfV to the Ministry of the Interior. Svenska kommittén för Vietnam, Laos och Kambodja. 1568/E/1/2 Korrespondens. Vol 1969. 3077. See also SKSF, *Program. Årsberättelse. Motioner. 1969,* 21. and Hans-Göran Franck, "Vietnamkrigsvägare i Sverige" in *Vietnam-69* (Stockholm: Rabén & Sjögren, 1969) 130–138.

[93] *Dagens Nyheter* 20 Feb. 1969.

[94] Mr. Weibo (a Department Secretary within the Ministry of the Interior) as cited in Davidsson, *et al.,* "Amerikanska desertörer i Sverige," 31. See also *Svenska Dagbladet* 22 Feb. 1969.

[95] Press release. The Ministry of the Interior. 21 Feb. 1969. Avd R. Grupp 191. Mål K. Förrymda krigsfångar, militärarbetare, desertörer, m.m. # 7.

[96] See, for example, editorials in *Blekinge Läns Tidning* 22 Feb. 1969, *Göteborgs-Posten* 23 Feb. 1969 and *Svenska Dagbladet* 23 Feb. 1969.

[97] Eric Holmqvist as cited in *Dagens Nyheter* 22 Feb. 1969. American Embassy officials surmised that the SAP leadership wanted to mollify internal left wing agitation without opening Sweden up to a flood of new deserters. 28 Feb. 1968. Turner Cameron Jr. Telegram to State. Central Foreign Policy File 1967–1969. Political and Defense. Sweden. RG 59.

[98] Eric Holmqvist as cited in *Svenska Dagbladet* 1 March 1969.

[99] For a specific illustration, see editorial in *Dagens Nyheter* 26 Feb. 1969.

[100] *Vietnambulletinen* # 2 1969, 22–23; *Vietnambulletinen* # 3 1969, 12.

[101] For specific illustrations, see *Ny Dag* 27 Feb. 1969 and *Tidsignal* # 5 1969, 6–7.

[102] For a specific example, see the editorial by SSSF Chairman, Bengt Liljenroth in *Libertas* # 5/6 1969, 2.

[103] Anonymous sources within the Foreign Ministry as cited in *Dagens Nyheter* 21 Feb. 1969. The Foreign Ministry additionally worried that conferring the Americans with formal political refugee status would only encourage more deserters to flee to Sweden. 18 Feb. 1969. Political Division FM. Rolf Lindholm. Memo. Avd R. Grupp 191. Mål K. Förrymda krigsfångar, militärarbetare, desertörer, m.m. # 7.

[104] 18 Jan. 1968. William W. Heath. Telegram to State. Central Foreign Policy File 1967–1969. Political and Defense. Sweden. RG 59.

[105] Undated (ca. Jan. 1968.) Legal Division FM. Lennart Myrsten. Memo. Re: Meeting with Jerome Holloway, the Head of the Political Section at the American Embassy in Stockholm on Jan. 10, 1968. Avd HP. Grupp 1. Mål Ua. Politik Allmänt. USA # 220. According to the memo, Holloway complained that the very term 'humanitarian asylum' suggested that the deserters had been mistreated, or even tortured, while serving in the US Armed Forces. See also Ambassador William Heath as cited in the *Austin American* 27 June 1968.

[106] Eric Holmqvist as cited in *Dagens Nyheter* 22 Feb. 1969.

[107] Eric Holmqvist as cited in *Svenska Dagbladet* 29 April 1970. The actual phrase change occurred on 1 July 1969 when the State Alien Commission was replaced by the newly created Ministry of Immigration.

[108] Even apologists of the government's deserter policy were not blind to this fact. See, for instance, editorial in *Dagens Nyheter* 22 Feb. 1969.

[109] For a specific example, see editorial in *Arbetarbladet* 25 Feb. 1969.

[110] For a specific illustration, see Hans-Göran Franck as cited in *Upsala Nya Tidning* 5 March 1969. See also editorial in *Aftonbladet* 25 Feb. 1969.

[111] *Stockholms arbetarekommun. Årsmötesprotokoll.* 19–20 April 1969. Motioner och utlåtande. # 11–12: A – 11–12:E. These two motions demanding political asylum for the deserters were submitted by SSSF Stockholm and SSU Libertas. Both motions were defeated.

[112] 4 March 1969. Letter from the SKfV to the Ministry of the Interior. Svenska kommittén för Vietnam, Laos och Kambodja. 1568/E/1/2 Korrespondens. Vol 1969. 3077.

[113] *Vietnambulletinen* # 3 1969, 25. See also letter to the editor from a NLF-activist in *Arbetarbladet* 29 April 1969.

[114] Eric Holmqvist as cited in SAP Kongressprotokoll. 24:e Kongressen. 28 Sept.–4 Oct. 1969, 563–564; SAP Kongressprotokoll. Motioner. 24:e Kongressen. 28 Sept.–4 Oct. 1969, 313–322.

[115] That said, there was some isolated grumbling on the party's left wing about this issue even after this. See, for instance, Bo Digné as cited in Stockholms arbetarekommun. Mötesprotokoll. 10 Nov. 1969, 3.

[116] The American Deserter Committee Newsletter 24 April 1969, 1–2; Vietnambulletinen # 1 1971, 4.

[117] For example, immediately following the government's February 21 declaration CH Hermansson had severely criticized the cabinet for not extending political asylum to the deserters. Exchange between Hermansson and Eric Holmqvist as cited in Riksdagsprotokollet # 6, 28 Feb. 1969, 139–150.

[118] That said, a few prominent Communists, such as Sara Lidman and John Takman, personally continued to advocate for the deserters even hereafter. Ny Dag 25 Nov. 1970; Dagens Nyheter 7 June 1971.

[119] Mr. Weibo as cited in Davidsson, et al., "Amerikanska desertörer i Sverige," 41.

[120] In the words of Jim Walch: "a lot of people expected the Americans to be more politically polished, to be basically anti-war activists who had said 'no' to the war and who could formulate an anti-war position. And some people were, but most were not." Walch as cited in Sofia Gustafsson-McFarland, "Americans, Once in Exile, Now at home in Sweden" (New York University 1990) 10.

[121] Scott, "Sweden might be a haven, but it's not heaven" Immigrants & Minorities 33 2015.

[122] Gunnar Hübinette and Eric Holmqvist as cited in Riksdagsprotokollet # 20, 23 April 1970, 3–7.

[123] For specific illustrations, see editorials in Nya Wermlands-Tidningen 22 Feb. 1969 and Vestmanlands Läns Tidning 20 March 1970. For an illustration of a more general criticism of the government's handling of the deserter issue, see editorial in Vimmberby Tidning 15 Oct. 1969.

[124] See, for example, Liberal representative Karl Kilsmo as cited in Riksdagsprotokollet # 13, 26 March 1969, 57–58.

[125] Holmqvist as cited in Riksdagsprotokollet # 20, 23 April 1970, 3–7. See also Holmqvist as cited in Svenska Dagbladet 29 April 1970.

[126] Holmqvist. Rapport. TV 2. 24 April 1970. Television.

[127] That the Swedish stance towards the deserters stiffened after 1969 was confirmed by all of the former immigration officials that I contacted. Bengt Ranland written correspondence with the author September 1999; Ingmar Källberg interview with the author 20 July 1999; Gunnar Sommarin interview with the author 6 July 1999.

[128] Undated (ca. Sept. 1969.) Letter to the Ministry of the Interior from a Social Democratic constituent in Malmö. (Inrikesdepartementet. Konseljakter avseende utlänningsärenden.) This letter serves as an excellent illustration of the growing antipathy that some Social Democrats harbored toward the deserters. The letter, signed by an "old party friend," asks why the Americans are permitted to commit crimes with seeming

impunity, and the letter's author demands that they be repatriated to 'wherever they came from.' See also editorial in *Dala-Demokraten* 20 Feb. 1969.

[129] Undated (ca. October 1969.) Letter to Torsten Nilsson signed "F.S." (SAP. F:2 D. Handlingar rörande andra lander. Vietnam. Vol 12.) "F.S." objects to the deserters' criminality and calls for them to be expelled from Sweden.

[130] According to the filmmakers, the intent of *Deserter USA* was to reveal the hypocrisy of the Social Democratic administration's deserter policy and to expose the government and the SKfV as lackeys of American imperialism. Lars Lambert and Olle Sjögren as cited in *Chaplin 88* 2 (1969): 52–54.

[131] For a specific illustration, see the exchange debate between the two organizations' spokesmen in the op-ed pages of *Aftonbladet* on 2 May 1969, 16 May 1969, and 29 May 1969.

[132] Bertil Svanström as cited in Richard, "American Deserters in Stockholm," 28–37; Gunnar Myrdal as cited in *The New Yorker* 23 May 1970.

[133] Even though the ADC was never was able to mobilize a majority of the exile community, it still enjoyed considerable influence among the Americans in 1968 and into early 1969. By 1970, however, the ADC had completely discredited itself in the eyes of most exiles. Carragher written correspondence with author 18 Dec. 1999.

[134] DFFG petition to the SAP leadership demanding that the decision to deport Parra be reversed. Appendix. *SAP VU-protokoll* 2 Dec. 1970.

[135] *Svenska Dagbladet* 15 Nov. 1970; *Dagens Nyheter* 23 Nov. 1970; *Aftonbladet* 25 Nov. 1970.

[136] *Dagens Nyheter* 27 Nov. 1970. As of late March 1971, six deserters had been expelled from Sweden and another 28 had been denied asylum. Press Release. Ministry of Immigration 20 April 1971. Avd R. Grupp 191. Mål K. Förrymda krigsfångar, militärarbetare, desertörer, m.m. # 8.

[137] *Ny Dag* 11 Dec. 1970.

[138] William Males as cited in the *Los Angles Times* 10 Dec. 1970.

[139] For specific illustrations, see the DFFG's open letter to Palme in protest against the deportations in *Ny Dag* 25 Nov. 1970 and ADC spokesmen, Mike Powers, as cited in *Vietnambulletinen* # 1 1971, 6.

[140] *Dagens Nyheter* 13 Dec. 1970.

[141] *Ny Dag* 25 Nov. 1970.

[142] Palme as cited in the *Washington Evening Star* 27 Dec. 1970.

[143] 20 Jan. 1969. Sven Frychius. Memo. Re: Lunch with Robert McCloskey, the new Deputy Assistant Secretary of State for Public Affairs on 17 Jan. 1969. Avd HP. Grupp 1. Mål Ua. Politik Allmänt. USA # 227. According to Frychius, McCloskey stated that although the deserter issue had originally caused some irritation in the State Department this was no longer seen as a serious impediment to Swedish–American relations.

[144] 25 April 1969. Hubert de Besche. Telegram to FM. Re: Meeting with William Rogers the US Secretary of State on 23 April 1969. Avd HP. Grupp 1. Mål Ua. Politik Allmänt. USA # 229; 20 Oct. 1969. Jean-Christophe Öberg. Memo. Today's meeting between

Torsten Nilsson and William Rogers the US Secretary of State. Avd HP. Grupp 1. Mål Ua. Politik Allmänt. USA # 232.

[145] 31 Oct. 1968. George Ingram. Memo to George Springsteen, Deputy Ass. Secretary of State for European Affairs Central Foreign Policy File 1967–1969. Political and Defense. Sweden. RG 59; 7 Feb. 1969. Arthur Berg. Memo to Paul Hughes, Scandinavian Desk Dept. of State. Central Foreign Policy File 1967–1969. Political and Defense. Sweden. RG 59.

[146] 10 March 1969. Paul Hughes. Letter to Turner Cameron Jr. Central Foreign Policy File 1967–1969. Political and Defense. Sweden. RG 59; Undated (ca. Jan. 1971.) European Section Dept. of State. Unsigned. Memo. Briefing on Palme's views as expressed in Public Statements about S.E. Asia. Subject Numeric Files 1970–1973. Political and Defense. Sweden. RG 59. This last memo states that: "we [the US] still wish that Sweden did not find it necessary to offer hospitality to military deserters...However, we must admit that Sweden is relieving the US military forces and society of several hundred misfits, many of whom use and traffic drugs and commit other crimes."

[147] 14 March 1969. Cameron Turner Jr. Telegram to State. Central Foreign Policy File 1967–1969. Political and Defense. Sweden. RG 59; 9 April 1969. Arthur Berg. Memo to Paul Hughes. Central Foreign Policy File 1967–1969. Political and Defense. Sweden. RG 59.

[148] 30 March 1970. Ass. Secretary of State for European Affairs. Martin Hillenbrand. Memo to William Rogers Secretary of State. Re: The Secretary's upcoming courtesy call with the new US Ambassador to Sweden, Jerome Holland. Subject Numeric Files 1970–1973. Political and Defense. Sweden. RG 59.

[149] 5 Nov. 1968. William W. Heath. Memo. "Status Report on US deserters in Sweden." (Dept. of State. FOIPA Carl-Gustaf Scott March 2002.)

[150] 18 March 1969. Cameron Turner Jr. Telegram to State. Central Foreign Policy File 1967–1969. Political and Defense. Sweden. RG 59.

[151] 15 Nov. 1967. CIA. Unsigned. Memo. "International Connections of U.S Peace groups (CIA. FOIPA Carl-Gustaf Scott March 2002); 21 Nov. 1969. Dept of Army US Army Intelligence. Unsigned. Untitled Memo. Re: Debriefing of US Army Deserter who had returned from Sweden. (Dept. of Army. FOIPA Carl-Gustaf Scott Jan. 2002.) These two memos only represent a tiny sample of the trove of documents that I obtained via the Freedom of Information Act from the FBI (Dec. 2001), Dept. of the Army (January 2002), the CIA (March 2002), Dept. of State (March 2002) and Dept. of the Navy (April 2002.) A central theme in the reports from all of these different intelligence agencies was their interest in establishing whatever international connections may have existed between the deserters and the far left in Europe, Asia, and the United States.

[152] 7 Feb. 1968. Head of Political Division FM. Wilhelm Wachtmeister. Memo. Re: Recent undated lunch conversation with Cameron Turner Jr. Avd HP. Grupp 1. Mål Ua. Politik Allmänt. USA # 221; 28 Feb. 1969. Turner Cameron Jr. Telegram to State. Central Foreign Policy File 1967–1969. Political and Defense. Sweden. RG 59.

[153] 3 Nov. 1970. Dept of Navy. Navy Criminal Investigation Service. Unsigned. Memo Re: Debriefing of a recently returned naval deserter from Sweden. (Dept. of Navy. FOIPA Carl-Gustaf Scott April 2002.) This is just one of many memos of this nature that

I examined. The overwhelming majority of the documents that I received via FOIPA from the CIA, FBI, Army, and Navy are the based on debriefings of the returnees.
[154] 17 Sept. 1968. CIA. Unsigned. Memo. Re: The ADC's activities during the Ninth World Youth Festival in Sofia, Bulgaria, 28 July–6 Aug. 1968 (CIA. FOIPA Carl-Gustaf Scott March 2002.) The nature of the information contained in this report makes it clear that the CIA had an informant among the US delegation in Sofia, who reported back his observations about the deserters. This is only one of several examples of this type of sources that I found.
[155] 27 April 1972. CIA. Unsigned. Untitled Memo. (CIA. FOIPA Carl-Gustaf Scott March 2002); 20 Dec. 1972. CIA. Unsigned. Untitled Memo. (CIA. FOIPA Carl-Gustaf Scott March 2002); 13 March 1973. CIA. Unsigned. Untitled Memo. (CIA. FOIPA Carl-Gustaf Scott March 2002.) All of these memos describe the inner workings of, the conflicts within, and the major personalities involved with the ADC (which later changed its name to Up from Exile) in such detail that there can be no doubt that someone (or several people) closely associated with the ADC/Up from Exile was (were) providing firsthand information to American intelligence agents. The documents, however, do not allow one to draw any firm conclusions about the informant(s) identity.
[156] This issue is discussed at great length in a 1997 TV documentary about the exile colony in Sweden, *Hell no we won't go!* TV 2. 24 April 1997. Television.
[157] For a specific illustration, see Bill Jones, "Förföljelser av desertörerna efter avslöjandet av agenterna" *Tidsignal* # 4 1968, 3–4. See also Richard, "American Deserters in Stockholm," 28–37.
[158] The materials that I obtained via the Freedom of Information Act neither confirm nor disprove the existence of agent provocateurs among the deserters in Sweden. Lawrence Baskir and William Strauss (the two principal scholars of Vietnam era draft and military offenders), however, call attention to the fact that the placement of such agents would have been consistent with the CIA's operations during the war. Operation CHAOS was a CIA project aimed at monitoring and discrediting radical American expatriates, and in 1968 the program was explicitly expanded to include draft and military fugitives living abroad. Lawrence Baskir and William Strauss, *Chance and Circumstance* (New York: Vintage Books, 1978) 196. In 1990, following the recommendation of the so-called "Rockefeller Commission", virtually all the documents pertaining to Operation CHAOS were destroyed; and unless other sources of evidence are found the exact nature of the CIA's activities in relation to exile colony in Sweden will remain unknown.
[159] Svenska Dagbladet 3 Dec. 1998.
[160] "ADC/Deserters folder 1968–1970" (SÄPO archive.) See also Magnus Hjort, *Den farliga fredsrörelsen* (SOU 2002: 90) 230–233.
[161] Försvarets underrättelsenämnd, Redovisning av vissa uppgifter om den militära underrättelse- och säkerhetstjänsten, 26 Nov. 1998, 38, 52.
[162] For specific examples, see *Aftonbladet* 9 Jan. 1969 and *FIB/Kulturfront* # 9 1973, 2–5.
[163] Indeed, as late as 1970, conservative politicians continued to voice their displeasure about the Social Democratic administration's decision to give sanctuary to US military

fugitives. 17 April 1970. Congressman Albert Watson. Letter to Secretary of State, William Rogers. Subject Numeric Files 1970–1973. Political and Defense. Sweden. RG 59. See also House Representative, Mendel Rivers as cited in the Congr. Rec. 91st Congr., 2nd Sess., 29 April 1970: 13385.

[164] While several Congressional studies examined Swedish deserter policy, the Sub-committee on Treatment of Military Deserters' report of March 1969 was by far the most critical of the Swedes. It concluded that that the decision to accept American defectors was optional, rather than mandatory, under Swedish law. In the postscript, the report further concurred "with the widespread American resentment against Sweden for pro-viding a sanctuary for American deserters." US Senate: Committee on the Armed Ser-vices. Report to the Subcommittee on Treatment of Military Deserters. "Treatment of Deserters from Military Service." 91st Congr., 1st Sess., 6 March 1969, 10.

[165] Thurmond as cited in the Congr. Rec. 91st Congr., 1st Sess., 20 Nov. 1969: 35116.

[166] Rarick as cited in the Congr. Rec. 91st Congr., 1st Sess., 15 April 1969: 9255. For another example along the same lines, see John McCormack, the Speaker of the House, as cited in *Göteborgs-Posten* 4 May 1969.

[167] A 1973 study showed that 43% of the American public felt that Sweden should not have accepted US deserters, whereas only 27% approved of Swedish policy. The remain-der either had mixed feelings or no opinion on this matter. "Knowledge of, and attitudes toward Sweden. Nationwide Studies Among the American public by Response Analysis 1973." (Courtesy of Edward Burton.)

[168] 27 Oct. 1968. Press Release by CALCAV (Hans Göran Franck. Handlingar rörande amerikanska Vietnam-desertörer/-veteraner. Vol 2.) Organizations, like the Clergy and Laymen Concerned about the Vietnam War, Vietnam Veterans against the War, and Students for a Democratic Society all endorsed Sweden's policy of accepting American deserters. *The New Yorker* 23 May 1970. See also Dr. William Davidson as cited in *Dagens Nyheter* 24 March 1968.

[169] 5 Feb. 1968. Lennart Alvin. Memo. Re: American press coverage of Sweden's accep-tance of American deserters. Avd HP. Grupp 1. Mål Ua. Politik Allmänt. USA # 221; 18 March 1969. Hubert de Besche. Telegram to FM. Avd HP. Grupp 1. Mål Ua. Politik Allmänt. USA # 228. See also Wilhelm Wachtmeister, *Som jag såg det* (Stockholm: Norstedt, 1996) 176.

[170] 8 Jan. 1973. Hubert de Besche. Memo. Avd HP. Grupp 1. Mål Ua. Politik Allmänt. USA # 255.

[171] 2 March 1973. *Chargé d'affairs* Swedish Embassy Washington. Leif Leifland. Memo. Avd HP. Grupp 1. Mål Ua. Politik Allmänt. USA # 257.

[172] Torsten Nilsson as cited in *Dagens Nyheter* 12 March 1968; Olof Palme as cited in *Baltimore Sun* 3 April 1968.

[173] Torsten Nilsson as cited in *Riksdagsprotokollet* # 13, 26 March 1969, 74, 83, 85.

[174] A good example of this was when Olof Palme was interviewed on the CBS Nightly News. Among other things, Palme was asked whether he thought that Sweden's acceptance of deserters was really compatible with the country's neutrality. Needless to

say, Palme was probably not particularly thrilled to get this question, at least not when phrased in this manner. Palme. *CBS Nightly News*. CBS. 19 Oct. 1969. Television. (Transcript as found in Avd HP. Grupp 1. Mål Ua. Politik Allmänt. USA # 232.)

[175] The International Herald Tribune 5 June 1970.

[176] *Dagens Nyheter* 7 June 1970; *Aftonbladet* 11 June 1970.

[177] For specific illustrations, see Palme as cited in UD, *Utrikesfrågor 1970* (Stockholm: UD, 1970) 49. and Palme as cited in the *New York Times* 5 June 1970.

[178] Palme as cited in the *Washington Evening Star* 20 Sept. 1969.

[179] *New York Times* 2 April 1973.

[180] For a specific illustration, see George Corrano, a spokesman for "Up from Exile," as cited in *Aftonbladet* 1 April 1973. See also article by Ulf Nilsson in *Expressen* 2 April 1973.

[181] House Committee on Foreign Affairs. "American Deserters in Sweden." [Unpublished] Report of a Staff Study by the House Subcommittee on Europe. 92nd Congr., 2nd Sess. Sept 1971. Bureau of European Affairs. Office of Northern Affairs. Records relating to Sweden 1957–1975. RG 59.

[182] 5 Jan. 1968. Turner Cameron Jr. Telegram to State. Central Foreign Policy File 1967–1969. Political and Defense. Sweden. RG 59. See also US House of Representatives. Committee on the Armed Services. Report of the Special Subcommittee on National Defense Posture. "Review of the Vietnam Conflict and Its Impact on US Military Commitments abroad." 90th Congr., 2nd Sess., 24 Aug. 1968, 79. This report specifically complained about the fact that the deserters in Sweden were being utilized for political reasons.

[183] Letter by Ashley as cited in *Dagens Nyheter* 4 Feb. 1969.

[184] Larry Tipton. *Jimmy*. TV 2. 16 May 1971. Television.

[185] Hayes, *American Deserters in Sweden*, 73.

[186] Desmond Carragher written correspondence with the author 18 Dec. 1999.

[187] Renée Kasinsky, *Refugees from Militarism* (New Brunswick, NJ: Transaction Books, 1976) 125–126; Marianna Sullivan, *France's Vietnam Policy* (London: Greenwood Press, 1978) xi–xiii.

Swedish Diplomatic Recognition and Humanitarian Aid to the Democratic Republic of Vietnam 1969–1970: A Case Study in Domestic Foreign Policy

In 1957 Sweden had voted to induct South Vietnam into the United Nations. In essence this meant that the Swedes had *de jure* recognized the GVN, even though relations between the nations were not officially established until 1960. Sweden, however, had not extended the same courtesy to North Vietnam, instead abstaining when asked to vote on UN membership for the Democratic Republic of Vietnam (DRV). As a result, no formal contacts were ever erected between Stockholm and Hanoi. Prior to 1965, the absence of such ties had not been subject to any real debate in Sweden, but demands to recognize the Ho Chi Minh state quickly arose in the wake of mounting domestic protests against the American war effort in Indochina.

It did not take long before these demands created a real headache for the Social Democratic administration. The cabinet was apprehensive about giving in to such agitation because it was known that Washington would react negatively to such a move – and because no other Western country had yet done so. The Social Democratic government initially hid behind a variety of pretexts to avoid taking this step, and then later – when the domestic pressure to recognize the DRV had grown too strong to ignore – it simply sought to postpone this action as long as possible.

The call to extend official ties to North Vietnam was first raised by radical Social Democratic students in March 1965,[1] but the Communists promptly overtook this cause. Throughout the rest of 1965, Sveriges Kommunistiska Parti monopolized this question, making it a centerpiece in the party's new international platform.[2] They repeatedly cited the government's failure to recognize Hanoi as evidence of the Social Democrats' reluctance to antagonize Washington,[3] and they sought to use this issue to broaden their appeal among younger radical voters. The Communists' aggressiveness on this topic would in time place the SAP leadership in a compromised position vis-à-vis the entire anti-war movement.[4]

The Communists had therefore identified a good question for them to exploit, and in 1966 the SKP vastly expanded its propaganda in favor of erecting diplomatic relations with North Vietnam. The party also sharpened its attacks on the government, attributing the latter's refusal to recognize the DRV to its fear of offending the Americans.[5]

At this juncture, such sentiments were also being seconded by more and more Social Democratic anti-war activists. Egged on by Communist agitation, in early 1966 the party's left wing had likewise stepped up its efforts to induce the cabinet to cultivate closer ties with Hanoi.[6]

Pressure To Recognize the Democratic Republic of Vietnam

By April 1966 internal dissatisfaction with the Social Democratic administration's stance towards North Vietnam had noticeably intensified,[7] and the government's position was openly challenged during the annual gathering of *Stockholms arbetarekommun* on 23–24 April. At this meeting Torsten Nilsson was forced to defend the cabinet's refusal to upgrade relations with the DRV, arguing that to do so now would be harmful, and would only hurt the credibility of Swedish neutrality. Nilsson further claimed that if such ties were presently established, this would jeopardize any future mediating role for Sweden in the Vietnamese conflict. Neither explanation satisfied Nilsson's critics,[8] and it was rather transparent that the SAP leadership was using the country's potential mediating function as an alibi to avert conflict with Washington.

The notion that a future mediating role prevented the government from a taking a more assertive position on this question had first been put forth by the SAP hierarchy during the bi-annual parliamentary debate on foreign policy on 23 March,[9] and Social Democratic spokesmen had continuously reiterated this argument thereafter.[10] This line of reasoning, however, never impressed the Communists, nor did it neutralize Social Democratic lobbying in favor of recognizing the DRV.[11] Not even the SAP leadership's attempt to ban this errand from being raised during the party's 1 May celebrations served to quell rising internal agitation.[12] If anything, the Social Democratic rank and file's support for extending diplomatic relations to North Vietnam flourished in the next few months.[13] The government's cautiousness was increasingly questioned by Social Democratic anti-war activists, putting the cabinet more and more on the defensive.[14]

That the Social Democratic administration was under escalating pressure to revise its standpoint was plain to US officials. The Americans frankly did not expect the cabinet to be able to withstand this level of intense lobbying indefinitely, given how strongly the Communists were pushing this question. Although Washington had no formal grounds on which to protest an official Swedish opening to North Vietnam, US diplomats let it be known that they were deeply opposed to any movement in that direction.[15] The Swedes, in turn, tried to reassure their American counterparts that the government had no intention of giving in to this pressure.[16] US Embassy officers in Stockholm did not have much faith in these assurances, however, and concluded that the Social Democratic administration was gradually losing control over this issue.[17]

While this errand briefly lost some of its earlier prominence in the immediate aftermath of the 1966 elections, the Communists resurrected it in 1967,[18] introducing legislation in parliament to institute diplomatic relations with the DRV.[19] These bills were defeated by the Social Democratically controlled Foreign Affairs Committee without being put to a vote,[20] but not before the cabinet was obliged to justify its position on this question. Again, the government rationalized its inaction in terms of a desire to preserve a future mediating role for Sweden – although Nilsson added that there was no real need to establish an official relationship with the North Vietnamese at this stage because Stockholm and Hanoi already enjoyed a satisfactory, albeit informal, rapport with each other.[21]

Needless to say, Nilsson's explanation did little to placate either the SKP-oriented left[22] or the Maoists, who by early 1967 had likewise joined in the effort to compel the government to recognize the DRV.[23] The DFFG demanded that the government revise its stance toward North Vietnam, and it further attacked the cabinet's current policy.[24] Once the NLF-groups threw their weight behind this cause, it added a much stronger extraparliamentary dimension to the campaign. Henceforward, the Social Democratic administration's refusal to move forward on this errand was challenged on three separate fronts: in the streets, in the parliament, and internally within the SAP.

The NLF-groups' deepening involvement with this question appears to have mobilized radical Social Democrats, who in the first months of 1967 demonstrated a strengthened resolve to induce the government to formalize its relationship with the Ho Chi Minh state.[25] As was discussed in Chapter 2, the SAP leadership tried to defuse this issue during the meeting of *Stockholms arbetarekommun* in mid April when it announced that the government had decided to downgrade diplomatic relations with South Vietnam.[26] The latter clearly hoped that this announcement would take the wind out of the sails of the campaign to establish official relations with the DRV.

Despite denials to the contrary,[27] the SAP hierarchy was still unwilling to disturb its relations with Washington over this matter. For this reason, the Social Democratic administration sought to find a compromise that would please its own rank and file without alienating the Americans. On this occasion, the cabinet deferred to the Foreign Ministry's judgment, which still firmly maintained that Sweden should keep North Vietnam at a safe distance.[28] Social Democratic Vietnam policy did not yet possess the full bravado that often characterized it in later years. The trouble was that it did not take long before it became manifest that this compromise solution had failed to produce the desired results.

To many Social Democrats, the government's gesture at dissociating Sweden from South Vietnam did not make up for its continued reluctance to extend diplomatic recognition to North Vietnam. In fact, internal support for establishing such relations only grew stronger, even within the party's more conservative trade union wing.[29] This is because this issue continued to gain traction among the Social Democratic faithful during the summer and fall of 1967,[30] and it was also brought up at the SAP Extra Congress in October.[31]

The spread of such sentiments into the party's more centrist core was replicated within society at large, for by mid-1967 anti-war activists of all political stripes agreed that Sweden should go ahead and recognize the DRV.[32] This development was especially evident among younger left-leaning elements within both the Liberal and Center Party, some of whom already favored such action.[33] Indeed, in 1967 the Center Party introduced its own bill in parliament calling for the establishment of full relations with Hanoi.[34] At this juncture, therefore, the Social Democratic administration's unwillingness to reconsider its policy toward North Vietnam had become more and more out of step, not just with its own cadre, but also with most mainstream opponents of the war.

The government's refusal to budge on this subject played into the hands of the Communists who used this as a trump card in their efforts to court the anti-war vote. Beginning in the spring and throughout the remainder of 1967, the reformulated Communist Party – now known as the VPK – intensified its criticism of the government's handling of this errand.[35]

The cabinet responded by repeating a familiar litany of excuses, maintaining that at this moment there was no pressing need for such action because Sweden already had a cordial working relationship with the North

Vietnamese. Torsten Nilsson additionally asserted that the situation in Indochina was very precarious, and consequently it would be unwise for Sweden to take any action that might rashly endanger the prospect of an eventual peace agreement. Nilsson also reiterated that any move toward recognizing the DRV would likely make a Swedish mediating role impossible. The Communists were of course not swayed by this logic,[36] and their agitation continued unabated.

In early 1968, the VPK once more submitted bills in parliament advocating that Sweden upgrade relations with North Vietnam,[37] and over the next several months Communist spokesmen repeatedly denounced the government's failure to act on this question.[38] Such complaints were likewise leveled by the NLF-groups.[39] According to the DFFG's propaganda, the Social Democratic administration's passive approach to this errand supposedly proved its complicity in propping up US imperialism.[40] To put pressure on the Social Democratic establishment, the NLF-groups sponsored a series of "public meetings" across the country demanding that the government immediately extend diplomatic relations to North Vietnam.[41]

This paralleled a VPK-initiated write-in campaign to the same end, which was embraced by a wide variety of radical groupings, such as *Socialistiska Förbundet* and *Unga Filosopher*, as well as by a handful of NLF-chapters. More significantly, this latter effort was endorsed by many prominent left-leaning Social Democrats like Bengt Liljenroth, Folke Isaksson, and Eric Ericsson. In addition, the effort was backed by a number of local SSU and SSSF chapters and even by some members of the Liberal and Center Parties' youth associations. In the end, over 9,000 people, representing approximately 70 different organizations, took part in this initiative.[42] By early 1968, then, the call to recognize the DRV enjoyed widespread support among more moderate anti-war activists, including much of the Social Democratic rank and file.

Spurred on by Communist and Maoist activism, Social Democratic radicals bolstered their own efforts to persuade the government to reassess its policy toward North Vietnam,[43] and at this stage *Aftonbladet* also came out in favor of the cause.[44] Internal impatience with the government's position was now becoming quite palpable. This restlessness was very manifest during *Stockholms arbetarekommun's* meeting on 8 January 1968, at which time several delegates questioned the validity of the cabinet's approach to this matter. Nilsson's attempt to account for the government's position did little to impress his critics. Nilsson's detractors noted that the possibility of Sweden playing a future mediating role in Vietnam no longer seemed credible, and accordingly there remained no valid reason not to move forward with this errand.[45]

Over the winter of 1967–1968, Social Democratic leaders had clung to the earlier cited rationalizations for not extending diplomatic relations to North Vietnam,[46] but by the spring of 1968 the plausibility of these explanations no longer rang true. This was in no small part due to the fact that peace talks between Washington and Hanoi had at last gotten underway, which ostensibly removed the need for a continued low-key Swedish approach to this issue. The Social Democratic hierarchy, however, was still reluctant to confer diplomatic status upon the DRV, stressing the sensitive nature of the negotiations in Paris as a pretext to not yet alter Swedish policy.[47] Government spokesmen tenaciously stuck to the contention that there was no rush to address this matter in view of the satisfactory state of Swedish–North Vietnamese relations in recent years.[48] Although the cabinet managed to turn back renewed Communist initiatives on this front, by this point its justification for doing so had lost much of its original legitimacy[49] – even in the eyes of most Social Democratic anti-war activists.[50]

When *Stockholms arbetarekommun* convened for its big annual gathering on 27–28 April 1968, no lfewer than 20 motions called upon the government to establish official relations with North Vietnam. Torsten Nilsson was narrowly able to head off these motions, but only on the condition that *Stockholms arbetarekommun* would recommend that the government review its current policy. The Stockholm SAP district, moreover, declared that it would welcome closer relations between Hanoi and Stockholm in the near future.[51] Following this gathering, internal agitation in favor of recognizing the DRV only intensified.[52]

By the late spring of 1968, sentiments to this effect had taken a strong hold within the party, and they were even in evidence inside the trade union movement.[53] At this juncture, the SAP leadership's longstanding opposition to making such a move finally began to crumble. On 1 May, Nilsson for the first time hinted that Swedish recognition of the DRV might not be far off,[54] and the very next day, he confirmed that the government intended to take this step as soon as circumstances permitted it to do so.[55] When asked about the cabinet's sudden about-face, Nilsson acknowledged that there had been strong internal lobbying with regard to this question, but he insisted that this had not played a part in this reversal.[56]

Social Democratic anti-war activists were quite pleased by the government's revised attitude, while still pressing for it to formally recognize the DRV.[57] This matter was subject to considerable debate at the SAP Congress in June, where three different motions favoring such action were presented.[58] In response to these proposals, Nilsson was once more obliged to account for the cabinet's continued reluctance to amend its present position, citing the fragility of the Paris peace talks as the main deterrent against any Swedish initiative on this front. Nilsson explained that for the time being Swedish policy would stay the same, although he reiterated that it might soon change. All of this was met with substantial skepticism (and even outright hostility) by some members of *Stockholms arbetarekommun*.[59]

In the end, however, Nilsson got his wish, and the SAP Congress rejected these motions, but not without first making a major concession to radical internal opinion by promising to provide 10 million crowns in humanitarian aid to North Vietnam.[60] This was one of the most enthusiastically applauded announcements during the Congress,[61] and it temporarily neutralized the demand to recognize the DRV.

This announcement obviously was not well received in Washington, which immediately objected to the aid package.[62] Still, one might surmise that American officials were simultaneously somewhat pleased that the Social Democratic administration had not gone ahead and established full relations with North Vietnam. US diplomats had feared that the latter might do this at the SAP Congress in light of Nilsson's recent public statements. The Americans were well aware that internal agitation had been steadily building over the last several months and that the SAP leadership's ability to withstand additional pressure on this issue was rapidly deteriorating. Washington consequently had begun to prepare itself for this eventuality. In the Americans' view, an official Swedish opening to North Vietnam appeared to be inevitable, particularly because it was not likely to harm the Social Democrats at the polls.[63]

This assessment was more or less correct because by 1968 the Center Party was promoting this issue almost as hard as the Communists.[64] At this point, therefore, the SAP risked being outflanked both to its right and its left on this question. Indirectly, this also meant that the Social Democrats had nothing to lose electorally by recognizing North Vietnam. In fact, after the SAP Congress, *Aftonbladet* worried that the party had missed an excellent opportunity to distinguish itself on this issue heading into the upcoming election.[65]

Apparently this argument was not enough to persuade the SAP leadership to change course because following the Congress it stood firm. The government stated anew that it was not yet appropriate for the country to revise its present stance towards North Vietnam,[66] although by now this did little to stem sustained internal unrest. Rather than having a calming effect, Nilsson's repeated suggestions that Sweden would soon recognize the DRV only encouraged increased Social Democratic activism on this issue.[67]

While this question momentarily became less visible in the immediate aftermath of the SAP's spectacular election victory in September, it reappeared in the second week of November when Einar Larsson, a member of the Center Party, challenged the government's handling of this errand in the parliament.[68] Larsson's inquiry at once ignited a massive outpouring of support for recognizing the DRV,[69] not least from various Social Democratic sources,[70] including those closely associated with the SKfV.

On 11 November, the SKfV received a personal audience with Nilsson, hoping to present a strong case for upgrading relations with Hanoi. *Svenska Kommittén för Vietnam* had inherited this cause from its predecessor the SVK, and for this reason it was also centrally featured in the SKfV's founding charter.[71] When the SKfV met with Nilsson, it argued that there no longer existed any justifiable reason to delay establishing official ties with North Vietnam because a Swedish mediating role was by now completely out of the question.[72] Nilsson conceded that this was true, but he maintained that to do so at this point could still potentially harm the Paris peace talks. He did, however, reveal that the cabinet was essentially already prepared to act on this errand and that it might do so even before a formal peace agreement had been signed by all of the belligerent parties.[73] Three days later, on 14 November, in response to Einar Larsson's earlier query, Nilsson reaffirmed that the government was now in principle positive to recognizing the DRV, stating that the time for this was rapidly approaching.[74]

Nilsson's insinuation that an opening on this front was just around the corner set off an avalanche of lobbying. Most of this activity emanated from Social Democratically affiliated organizations and unions,[75] though over the next two months the call to upgrade relations with North Vietnam was also heard from many other quarters as well.[76] Even prior to mid-November, Nilsson and his closest associates had started to discuss when the cabinet should act on this matter.[77] The SAP hierarchy unquestionably realized that this could not be put off much longer because domestic agitation was sure to escalate. In sum, the political burden of not recognizing the DRV was simply becoming too heavy to bear.

This development was readily apparent to American diplomats, who grasped that it was only a matter of time before Stockholm took this step.[78] However, the fact that US officials were prepared for this possibility did not mean that they approved of it.[79] From an American point of view, Swedish recognition of the DRV would be an unwelcome propaganda boost for the North Vietnamese, which, in turn, was bound to make Hanoi more intransigent during the peace talks.[80] That said, US officials privately acknowledged that Washington did not possess any leverage to prevent the Swedes from taking this step, and therefore the best it could do was just to try to get the Social Democratic administration to postpone any such action.[81]

In hindsight it is nevertheless plain to see that the anticipated American reaction was the sole obstacle to Sweden moving forward on this issue.[82] On a number of different occasions, Torsten Nilsson discussed his concerns about the prospect of an adverse American response,[83] and this anxiety was, at times, also publicly articulated.[84] In addition, this fear would likewise determine the exact timing of the government's recognition of the DRV.

A Matter of Timing: Sweden's Recognition of the DRV and the Political Aftermath

In theory, Sweden's recognition of new states was subject to universal legal standards, but internal Foreign Ministry documents reveal that the decision on whether or not to establish relations with any given country was ultimately political in nature. North Vietnam had from the outset met the formal criteria guiding Swedish recognition policy; namely, the Ho Chi Minh state exercised complete political control over its own territory. Still, Stockholm had declined to establish official relations with Hanoi. Originally, this was mostly because the Swedes did not want to be perceived as siding with the Communist world against the West.[85] Such cautiousness was not just discernable in relation to North Vietnam, for Sweden's policy towards new states was customarily subject to this kind of pragmatic *Realpolitik*. Most notably, the government had rejected recognizing East Germany – this in spite of growing domestic pressure for it to do so. Considering the country's vital political and economic ties to the Federal Republic of Germany, the cabinet was not about to jeopardize the nation's own well-being for the sake of upholding some abstract legal principle. Furthermore, the government's policy toward the two divided German states was in equal measure a reflection of Sweden's generally prudent approach to European affairs, and the cabinet certainly had no intention of establishing relations with the DDR until the rest of the West was ready to do so.[86] Sweden's new "activist" policy in foreign affairs was thus chiefly applicable in relation to the developing world and had little to no bearing on its policies closer to home in Europe.[87]

Indeed, the Social Democratic administration's refusal to extend diplomatic relations to East Germany is very instructive and demonstrates the limits of Swedish autonomy in world affairs. This illustration additionally reveals that Social Democratic party tactical considerations always had to be weighed against (and if need be subordinated to) the country's long-term economic and security needs.

In late 1968, the logic of this approach demanded that the cabinet find a way to placate domestic opinion without recklessly endangering relations with Washington. Because the Americans were expected to vehemently oppose a Swedish opening to North Vietnam, the Social Democratic administration concluded that the best time to do this would be during the transition period between the Johnson and Nixon administrations. Because no one was formally in charge in Washington during this interim phase, the Swedes surmised that there would be no severe US reaction if they acted at this moment. The SAP leadership additionally gambled that the Americans' attention would be preoccupied with the transition process itself.[88] The choice of timing, then, was a very carefully calculated act.

After the fact, however, Nilsson dismissed the notion that there had been any correlation between the timing of the Swedish recognition of the DRV on 10 January 1969 and the transition between the two presidential administrations.[89] Because Sweden was the first Western country to take this step, it was a big international news story. The Swedish and foreign press alike remarked upon the obvious disingenuousness of Nilsson's explanation,[90] though some papers simultaneously praised the Social Democratic administration's for its tactical acumen in selecting this particular moment.[91]

Officially, the government motivated the timing of its decision on the grounds that the Paris peace talks had finally made enough progress that Swedish recognition of Hanoi would not disrupt the negotiations.[92] In truth, the Swedes had not received any information to support this optimistic conclusion; instead, most sources with direct insight into the talks had indicated that the exact opposite was true.[93] As late as the first week of January 1969, the North Vietnamese Ambassador to Poland, Dô Phat Quang, confided to his Swedish interlocutors that the discussions in Paris were currently deadlocked. In Quang's opinion, the war would probably have to continue before the negotiations could advance.[94]

Nilsson appears to have been just as duplicitous when he further explained that this decision had been made in order to facilitate a future

Scandinavian collaborative reconstruction effort in Vietnam.[95] Although such a project was already being planned between Sweden, Norway, and Denmark, Danish officials denied that the implementation of this scheme first required the establishment of full diplomatic relations with North Vietnam.[96] Had the Social Democratic administration's primary ambition really been to advance these joint Nordic preparations, then its failure to give the Danes and Norwegians prior notice of its intention to recognize the DRV would have been totally inexplicable. Norway and Denmark were actually quite resentful about having been kept in the dark about this decision, feeling that the Swedes' behavior had undermined their collaborative effort to assist the Vietnamese.[97]

Nor were Danes and Norwegians the only ones who were unhappy about the Social Democratic administration's unilateral recognition of North Vietnam, and such discontent was also manifest among many senior Swedish diplomats, in part because they too had not been previously consulted about this decision.[98] Nilsson had expected most top Foreign Ministry officials to disapprove of this move, so he had intentionally excluded them from this decision-making process. There were of course some within the Foreign Ministry who backed this initiative (such as Jean-Christophe Öberg), but this group appears to have been a minority.[99] Those who objected to this policy did so for a variety of reasons: a few because they feared that it would isolate Sweden politically, while others worried that it would have a prejudicial effect on Sweden's relations towards the two German states because this decision would almost certainly also intensify domestic lobbying to recognize the DDR.[100] Yet, more than anything else, their misgivings were rooted in a concern about this decision's negative ramifications for Swedish–American relations.[101]

These apprehensions did not prove to be totally unwarranted. For even though the Americans did not invoke economic sanctions against Stockholm (which had been the government's main worry),[102] the Swedish announcement did receive a very cool reception in Washington.[103] This also ensured that the Swedes got off on the wrong foot with the incoming Nixon administration.[104] American officials protested that Sweden's recognition of the DRV would not help the peace negotiations,[105] decrying it as yet another example of the Social Democrats' increasingly pro-Communist bias. Specifically, the Americans felt that Sweden had strengthened the North Vietnamese position at the peace table,[106] and they also saw this as yet more evidence of a progressively anti-American slant in Swedish foreign policy.[107]

181

The Social Democratic administration's reaction was to vehemently deny that its handling of this errand had been motivated by any hostility towards the United States. In addition, it strove to tone down the significance of this decision, stating that it was merely a natural outgrowth of the intensified ties that had developed between Stockholm and Hanoi in recent years.[108]

These sorts of explanations, however, did little to appease the new presidential administration in Washington. The Nixon White House saw this decision as a direct affront to the United States, and it retaliated by not appointing a new ambassador to Stockholm and by closing the American consulate in Gothenburg.[109]

Throughout the remainder of 1969 and into 1970, the US kept the Ambassador post in Stockholm vacant to denote its dissatisfaction with the Social Democrats' Vietnam stance. While American diplomats never publicly confirmed that this was the objective of this policy, they never explicitly denied it either.[110] The implication of the Nixon administration's behavior certainly did not escape the notice of contemporary observers, and this topic was discussed at length in both the Swedish and American press.[111] When Richard Nixon at last decided to appoint a new Ambassador to Sweden, he shrewdly sent Jerome Holland, an Afro-American, whose mere presence it was thought would help to subdue the "progressive" and "racially conscious" Swedes.[112] When Holland finally arrived in Sweden in April 1970, the US Embassy in Stockholm had been without an Ambassador for nearly 15 months (that is, ever since William Heath's departure on 23 January 1969.)

American diplomats were apparently satisfied with this strategy, feeling that the Social Democrats had understood that the United States' patience had run out and that it had had enough of Swedish shenanigans. They calculated that this new approach would cause the SAP leadership to become more deferential towards Washington.[113] While this policy did (at least briefly) seem to have the desired effect, the reality was that withholding the appointment of a new Ambassador was a rather inconsequential rebuke. And beyond this, Washington did not enact any other substantial retaliatory measures. This was not necessarily because the Nixon administration was fundamentally adverse to this idea – in fact, it undoubtedly would have preferred to take much stronger action,[114] but for all of the reasons already discussed in Chapter 3, the White House found that it simply did not have many other suitable forms of punishment at its deposal.

These political practicalities did not stop conservatives on Capitol Hill from calling for a tougher stance against Sweden in the wake of this announcement,[115] and similar sentiments were also expressed in the American press.[116] According to Swedish officials in Washington, the Social Democratic government's decision to establish diplomatic relations with North Vietnam had, with few exceptions, elicited a very hostile response in the American media.[117] This was true even in the case of many liberal dailies, such as the *Washington Post*, which otherwise were generally supportive of the Swedes' outspoken opposition to the war.[118] Above all, many American papers complained that this action had helped the Vietnamese Communists.[119]

This negative publicity was a cause for concern among Swedish businessmen, who feared that it would harm the country's industrial exports in America.[120] They were quick to express their anxiety to the cabinet, cautioning that the government's new assertive profile in world affairs should not be permitted to jeopardize Swedish trade.[121] Identical protests were also heard from some members of the non-socialist opposition who accused the Social Democrats of hurting the country's national interests in their relentless pursuit of short-term party tactical objectives.[122]

Even though the non-socialist parties declared that they were not in principle against recognizing the DRV, this did not prevent several prominent Liberal and Conservative politicians from raising a series of technical objections to this decision.[123] First and foremost, they griped that the government had failed to inform Sweden's Nordic neighbors as well as the other parliamentary parties prior to moving forward on this issue.[124] Some also questioned the appropriateness of the timing of this decision, arguing that Sweden should have waited until a final peace agreement had been reached before taking this step.[125] Grievances to this effect were naturally also vented in the Conservative press.[126]

Looking back, one cannot help but be struck by how timid the opposition's overall reaction to this decision was. There are several likely explanations for this. First, by early 1969 the non-socialist parties had already grasped that they did not stand to gain much by fervently opposing the Social Democrats' Vietnam policy because this strategy had mostly backfired on them so far. Second, this particular question was a potentially divisive one for the opposition given that the Center Party was also firmly committed to recognizing the DRV.[127] This being the case, a too forceful condemnation of the government by either the Liberal or Conservative leadership was almost certain to create a fissure within the non-socialist camp. One might also add that an overly aggressive stance on this question was not really advisable for the Liberal Party as it was bound to create turmoil within the party. This was because a majority of the party's younger members had embraced the decision to establish diplomatic relations with North Vietnam,[128] as had many Liberal papers.[129]

The Social Democratic establishment evidently anticipated an impotent response from the opposition because during the internal discussions that led up to this move Nilsson made it known that he intended to disregard their protests.[130] Once the decision had been announced, the SAP leadership deflected the opposition's objections without undue difficulty, again skillfully playing the nationalism card. The government also defended itself by declaring that it was not formally required to consult with either the domestic opposition or with other nations before recognizing new states. Last but not least, the Social Democratic administration emphatically denied that its approach to this errand had been shaped by party tactical calculations.[131]

Needless to say, these disclaimers did not satisfy the government's domestic detractors who chided the Social Democrats for caving in to radical pressure.[132] To them, the government's recognition of the Ho Chi Minh state merely underscored the SAP's continued readiness to use the Vietnam issue for its own political ends,[133] and it was for this exact reason that even some Liberal papers took issue with this decision.[134]

Much of the American press similarly interpreted Stockholm's opening to Hanoi as a byproduct of Social Democratic party tactical considerations, and this was also the dominant view among the US diplomatic corps.[135] The Americans' suspicions in this regard were seemingly verified by unidentified sources within the Swedish Foreign Ministry. These sources specifically stated that the decision to recognize the DRV had principally been born out of the Social Democratic establishment's desire to placate young firebrands within the party. The SAP hierarchy supposedly wanted to preempt this issue prior to the opening of the next parliamentary session, at which time a new group of young radical Social Democrats was expected to enter the *Riksdag*.[136] Although the identity of the above-mentioned sources cannot yet be definitely established, there was no shortage of Swedish diplomats who believed that this decision was mainly rooted in Social Democratic party tactical calculations.[137] Even Jean-Christophe Öberg, who was one of the most vocal backers of this policy, insinuated that this policy had a domestic dimension to it, telling an American official that it had "taken the wind out of the sails of the far left."[138]

Afterwards, several people who had direct insight into the decision-making process have likewise confirmed the domestic origins of this decision.[139] In this context, it is of interest that both Torsten Nilsson and Krister Wickman subsequently affirmed that this initiative had been part and parcel of the government's Vietnam policy.[140] This admission completely undercuts the Social Democratic administration's original insistence that its recognition of the DRV was just a "routine errand."[141] In other words, this move was very much a demonstrative act intended to signal the party's posture on the war. Nor can there be any doubt that the timing of the decision was partially determined by the SAP's political objectives. Nilsson apparently wanted to make sure that Sweden took this step before the US did; if the Social Democratic administration failed to do so, then the potential domestic benefits of this decision would be lost.[142]

Everyone who has examined this subject agrees that the government's decision-making process in this instance was at least indirectly influenced by the domestic agitation that had preceded it[143] – yet the present work is the only study that emphasizes the absolute primacy of domestic politics. This book contends that the decision to recognize North Vietnam can only be understood within the particular circumstance of the SAP leadership's two-fold ambition to pacify internal unrest while at the same time repulsing its Marxist adversaries.

The campaign to establish diplomatic ties between Stockholm and Hanoi had by and large been driven by political elites, and these ties enjoyed the strongest support within radical educated circles. The general electorate, in contrast, appears to have been far less passionate about this initiative.[144] This divergence in opinion was also seemingly confirmed by the results of a public opinion poll taken in the fall of 1968, which showed that only 30 per cent of the general public wanted Sweden to recognize North Vietnam (whereas a full 48 per cent were opposed.)[145] These figures further suggest there was little incentive for the Social Democrats to make this issue into a big part of their electoral strategy. On the other hand, there is nothing to indicate that the government's handling of this errand in any way harmed the party's standing among the voting public. (Polls taken right before and right after the recognition of the DRV show no discernable shift in the party's popularity.)[146] In truth, most voters probably did not regard this as a decisive issue, and in all likelihood this policy was mostly aimed at an internal Social Democratic audience – though to a lesser extent it was also meant to appeal to young radical voters.[147] From this, one might further deduce that the Social Democrats had no intention of resting on their laurels or of allowing the VPK to recoup its previous gains among this segment of the electorate.

Hence, in the short term, one of the major immediate benefits of this decision was that it neutralized this question politically, thereby depriving the

VPK of a valuable source of propaganda. Communist spokesmen understandably welcomed the decision to recognize the DRV, though they highlighted their own role in bringing this about and complained that this should have happened much earlier.[148] Thus, while the establishment of diplomatic relations with North Vietnam did not produce a huge victory for the Communists, it was still a great illustration of how the far left's agenda on Vietnam was absorbed by the Social Democrats and was then eventually transformed into official state policy.

The DFFG was also quick to highlight its own contribution to this decision. It declared that recognition of the DRV was a triumph for Swedish anti-war opinion, adding that the government had only taken this step under pressure from the NLF-groups.[149] This assertion was somewhat surprisingly seconded by parts of the Social Democratic press, which likewise paid tribute to the NLF-groups' pivotal contribution to this campaign.[150]

Generally speaking, the decision to establish formal relations with North Vietnam was very popular among the Social Democratic faithful,[151] and this decision certainly received a resounding endorsement from the Social Democratic press.[152] Not without reason, many Social Democrats felt that their efforts to bring this decision about should likewise be recognized, and such sentiments were especially felt by those Social Democrats who were directly affiliated with the SKfV.[153] The SKfV took full credit for having prodded the government into taking this step,[154] but it simultaneously made sure to commend the cabinet for having had the courage to be the first Western government to do so.[155]

All in all, the decision to extend full diplomatic relations to North Vietnam was indisputably a political asset for the Social Democratic administration, but at the same time this initiative was not without drawbacks because it de facto encouraged additional pressure in relation to Vietnam. The SKfV and the DFFG were both noticeably energized by this decision, and they immediately launched their own respective campaigns to compel the cabinet to also recognize the newly created Provisional Revolutionary Government of South Vietnam (PRR) the political wing of the Communist-controlled NLF.[156] This cause was similarly embraced by the VPK and SAP's left wing,[157] and over the next few years it become a major preoccupation for all Swedish anti-war activists. In the end, extending diplomatic relations to the DRV did not have the calming effect the SAP leadership had originally hoped for. Instead, this issue was merely replaced by another one that would cause just as many (if not worse) headaches for the cabinet. The question of whether or not to recognize the PRR would remain a thorn in the side of the Social Democratic administration until the Saigon regime finally fell in April 1975, at which point Sweden became one of the first countries to establish formal relations with the new revolutionary government of South Vietnam.[158]

The Politicization of Swedish Aid to North Vietnam

In the short term, the official opening between Stockholm and Hanoi was at once followed in 1969 by intensified domestic agitation for Sweden to provide massive economic assistance to North Vietnam.[159] The Social Democratic press insisted that this decision would surely help to speed up Swedish reconstruction efforts in Indochina.[160] Here it is worth recalling that Torsten Nilsson had himself cited the need to facilitate such aid as one of the main reasons behind the cabinet's decision to recognize North Vietnam.[161]

The possibility of aiding in the reconstruction of both Vietnamese states once the war was over had first been proposed in April of 1966, although planning for this eventuality did not begin in earnest until the second half of 1967. While the Swedes had been the ones to propose this scheme, it had initially been conceptualized as a collaborative endeavor between all of the Nordic states (except for Iceland).[162] Plans for postwar reconstruction (as well as for more immediate short-term humanitarian assistance) were presumably adopted because they were a relatively safe outlet for Swedish Vietnam policy. Such proposals allowed the Social Democratic administration to demonstrate its solidarity with the Vietnamese people in a manner that was tolerable to Washington, as the latter was not likely to object to these sorts of efforts so long as this assistance was given to both Vietnamese states. One can safely assume that these schemes appealed to the other three Nordic governments for precisely the same reason because they all also faced mounting domestic pressure in relation to the war.[163]

In Sweden the aid question had first appeared in the spring/summer of 1965 when the Communists placed it on the domestic political agenda by demanding that the government provide direct humanitarian assistance to the Vietnamese people.[164] This issue swiftly became a key point in the SKP's new international platform, and in early 1966 the Communists intensified their efforts on this front by sponsoring two parliamentary bills demanding such aid.[165] By now interest in this question had spread to the left wing of the Social Democratic Party as well, with the latter asking for Sweden to make greater efforts to ease the plight of the Vietnamese civilian population.[166]

Initially the Social Democratic leadership tried to avoid addressing the question by stating that this kind of errand was best dealt with by the Red Cross, proclaiming that unilateral government aid to either side in the Vietnamese conflict would be incompatible with Swedish neutrality.[167] In 1966, the SAP hierarchy, however, sought to satisfy these demands by endorsing the previously discussed *Nationalinsamlingen*,[168] that consequently had a dual purpose; in addition to counteracting the Maoists' collection campaign on behalf of the NLF, it was also designed to respond to (and implicitly deflect) the increasing calls for the government to devote greater economic resources to humanitarian efforts in Indochina.

The creation of *Nationalinsamlingen* in itself did little to defuse the demands for heightened unilateral Swedish assistance to Vietnam, which hereafter only grew more intense. The Communists, in particular, aggressively promoted this cause, and in 1967 they reintroduced a bill in the parliament requesting such monies.[169] The government once again opposed such a move on the grounds that the Swedish Red Cross was already giving this type of humanitarian help to the Vietnamese,[170] and the bill was defeated.[171] Nilsson, however, offered a compromise, pledging to provide substantial state funds for the Red Cross' work in Vietnam.[172]

The problem was that it almost instantly became apparent that the Social Democratic administration's offer to fund a greater share of the Red Cross's activities was not sufficient to quiet internal agitation favoring unilateral Swedish aid to North Vietnam.[173] This topic later became the subject of lively debate during the SAP's Extra Congress in October, at which time it was decided that the party would not only back plans for postwar reconstruction in Indochina, but that it would also formally take over the SSU's collection fund for the NLF.[174] It was within this context – and only at this point – that the government began to plan in earnest for postwar reconstruction, appointing a study committee for this purpose in November. This was soon followed by another generous government grant to Vietnam in January 1968.[175]

Encouraged by this latest aid promise, as well as by the resolutions that had been adopted during the SAP Congress, Social Democratic anti-war activists stepped up their campaign to secure even more funding for the DRV.[176] The SAP leadership responded by reiterating its commitment to help rebuild Vietnam, underscoring that significant progress had already been made in the planning for this.[177] Concomitantly it was decided to give the NLF an additional 25,000 crowns directly out of the party's own treasury.[178] Throughout the rest of the spring of 1968, Torsten Nilsson repeatedly returned to this subject,[179] and the aid issue received prominent attention in his 1 May speech.[180] This new emphasis left little doubt that assistance to Vietnam had become a central component in the party's election strategy. Although the main purpose of these aid proposals was without question to rally the party cadre, they were almost certainly also targeted at capturing the youth anti-war vote.

Consequently it is not very surprising that this question was centrally featured during the SAP Congress in June. Not only did the party leadership announce that the Social Democrats had established their own fund for the NLF (as had been decided at the preceding Congress), but it was further revealed that the government intended to offer an additional 10 million Swedish crowns to North Vietnam.[181] (This distinguished the initiative from Sweden's earlier assistance packages, which had also given the Saigon government a share of the monies.) Although these announcements were presumably meant to temper demands that Sweden recognize the DRV, these aid initiatives were potent political propaganda in their own right.

The SAP's need to strengthen its position in this area was not solely about fending off continued Communist agitation,[182] but it was equally an attempt to counteract the Liberal and Center Parties' maneuvers in relation to this question. The latter two parties had first expressed interest in this topic in 1966,[183] and by 1968 they had both begun to call for Sweden to make a substantial contribution to Vietnam's postwar rehabilitation.[184] After this both the Center and Liberal Parties,[185] along with the Communists, continued to champion this cause in the parliament.[186]

Thus by 1969 a broad domestic coalition had in effect been established in favor of rebuilding Vietnam, and at this juncture even the Conservatives expressed nominal support for such a scheme.[187] Indeed, all of the parliamentary parties now agreed that Sweden should provide aid to the two Vietnamese states once the war was over, and this assistance should be given within the framework of a pan-Nordic collaborative project.[188]

This did not prevent Social Democratic radicals from drawing up their own proposal for Sweden to give 20 million crowns in interest-free credits to the DRV within the next year. This initiative was approved by *Stockholms arbetarekommun*, which agreed to submit it as a motion at the upcoming SAP Congress. This was done in spite of the party district leaders' reservations about the unilateral character of this proposal, as the latter still preferred to keep Swedish aid within the confines of a joint-Nordic project.[189] As it turns out they need not have worried because it rapidly became clear that the other Nordic governments were not yet ready to move forward with this proposal. At this stage, neither Finland, Denmark, nor Norway was willing to take any action that was likely to upset either superpower.[190]

The Swedes therefore decided to go it alone in proceeding with their own plan to assist the North Vietnamese. The reality was that even if the Social Democratic administration had wanted to abandon this project, it would have been very difficult for it to do so. This is because a retreat on this issue would not only have opened the SAP up to attacks from both its parliamentary and extraparliamentary opponents, but it would also have had a severely demoralizing effect on the party cadre. For by now the Social Democratic faithful were firmly committed to this cause,[191] and as the summer of 1969 faded into the fall, internal agitation in favor of such assistance to the DRV showed no signs of dissipating.[192]

Enthusiasm for this initiative was especially strong among those party activists who were personally involved with the SKfV,[193] and in late 1968 and early 1969 the committee had intensified its efforts to secure assistance for North Vietnam.[194] (The SKfV would later also boast about its own role in bringing this aid package about.)[195] The campaign thus largely followed the same pattern that had preceded the decision to recognize the DRV. This question had likewise first been advanced by the Communists, and it had then eventually made its way into official government policy owing to the intense lobbying of the party's left wing and the SKfV.

In a bid to placate this internal agitation, on 30 September 1969 Torsten Nilsson announced to the SAP Congress that the government intended to give more than 200 million crowns in reconstruction aid to the Hanoi regime. This offer was in response to the earlier mentioned motion submitted by *Stockholms arbetarekommun*, which had called for a massive aid package to the DRV. In its final form, this proposal promised that Sweden would unilaterally provide North Vietnam with a combination of loans and credits over a three-year period.[196] The Congress greeted the unveiling of this initiative with a standing ovation.[197]

Nilsson's decision to make this announcement during the Congress was unmistakably motivated by party tactical considerations, and his conduct on this occasion was consistent with the SAP hierarchy's historical tradition of using this particular forum to rally the party cadre.[198] The political subtext of Nilsson's behavior was accentuated by the fact that he had made a special point to insure that his staff finished the proposal in time for the Congress.[199] Also, in order to make the most of this announcement, Nilsson had tried to keep it a secret leading up to the Congress. (Even Sweden's foreign diplomatic missions had not been informed about these plans, so this news took them by complete surprise as well.)[200] This announcement was clearly meant to galvanize the party faithful heading into the 1970 general election, which it seemingly did, as was evidenced by the enormously positive reaction that it received from the Social Democratic cadre and press alike.[201]

The party's left wing regarded this announcement as a victory, as it had long sought to redirect Swedish developmental aid to so-called "progressive regimes." Radical elements within the SAP specifically wanted North Vietnam to become a principle beneficiary of Swedish developmental aid,[202] which in time also occurred.[203] The radicalization of the political climate in Sweden had the effect of politicizing the country's developmental assistance, and Swedish assistance to Vietnam would remain a contentious issue for many years to come.[204]

This clash began almost immediately as a few members of the non-socialist opposition complained that Nilsson's speech had implied that this assistance was now only going to be offered to the North Vietnamese.[205] The non-socialist parties protested that this went against the earlier parliamentary agreement, which had unambiguously stipulated that Swedish assistance would be provided to South Vietnam as well.[206] The original text of Nilsson's address to the Congress said that aid would also be given to the GVN, but due to the stir caused by the standing ovation Nilsson inadvertently skipped over this point in his speech.[207]

Nor was this the sole misunderstanding created by Nilsson's announcement, for many outside observers had additionally taken Nilsson's comments to mean that Swedish reconstruction aid to North Vietnam would begin in July 1970 – regardless of whether a formal peace agreement had been reached by that point or not.[208] While Nilsson's original intentions are impossible to determine after the fact, his personal secretary Jean-Christophe Öberg informed the press that the cabinet in effect considered hostilities to be over in North Vietnam, and therefore Swedish assistance could proceed to the DRV the very next year.[209] The significance of Öberg's remarks was that if his interpretation of the situation had been acted upon, this clearly would have violated Swedish neutrality because the international laws relating to the conduct of neutral states explicitly forbid them from providing credits to nations that presently are engaged in armed conflict. Humanitarian assistance to North Vietnam would conversely have been considered permissible, but not the kind of unilateral aid that had been outlined in Nilsson's proposal to the Congress.[210]

Nilsson later blamed the media for this confusion, and furthermore accused his domestic critics of intentionally misinterpreting the government's plans.[211] In reality, Nilsson's troubles – albeit with some help from Öberg – were of his own making.[212] (Here it should be pointed out that many Social Democrats had understood Nilsson's announcement in the exact same way as the non-socialist opposition – that is, that Swedish reconstruction aid would begin the very next year.)[213] Although Nilsson indisputably could have done a much better job of communicating his intentions, a large share of the blame also belongs to those few senior diplomats who had been consulted about this initiative prior to the Congress[214] because they arguably should have anticipated the extremely adverse response that this announcement would elicit in the United States.

Indeed, the American reaction to the unveiling of these plans was generally very negative, not least in the US press.[215] This anger towards Sweden was perhaps best exemplified by the renewed threats of the International Longshoremen to boycott all Swedish imports.[216] Such action was only averted through the personal intervention of Arne Geijer, the LO Chairman who managed to persuade his American counterpart George Meany, the President of the AFL/CIO, to cancel the boycott.[217]

Calls for economic sanctions against Sweden were likewise raised on Capitol Hill.[218] Republican Senator William Scherle, for example, demanded that the Swedes be disqualified from receiving any American loans in the future.[219] This turn of events was highly unsettling to Swedish diplomats, who were worried that such Congressional indignation might also put American military exports to Sweden at risk.[220]

While neither the State Department nor the White House was ultimately willing to heed these demands for economic sanctions, Swedish diplomats still advised that Washington was incensed with Stockholm.[221] This was a pretty accurate diagnosis because, unbeknownst to the Swedes, President Nixon had just instructed the State Department "to cut anything we [the US] can with Sweden."[222] Although this order was never acted upon, it illuminates the Americans' rising antipathy towards the Social Democratic administration. However, such far-reaching punitive measures proved to be unnecessary because the mere threat of American financial punishment was enough to get the Social Democratic administration to back off from its proposed aid package to the DRV.[223]

As soon as the news of Nilsson's aid announcement became known in America, the US Export-Import Bank initiated an investigation into whether or not the Swedish plan to grant financial assistance to North Vietnam was in violation of the bank's bylaws. These bylaws explicitly prohibited it from lending money to any nation that was assisting a third party presently engaged in an armed conflict with the United States. This inquiry would not affect the bank's previous loans to Sweden, but it might determine whether a new (already planned) loan of 200–300 million dollars could still be given to Scandinavian Airlines.[224] The implied threat behind this investigation was certainly not lost upon the Swedes, who correctly interpreted it as an attempt to stifle the government's Vietnam criticism.[225]

Not unexpectedly, Swedish industrial interests expressed great alarm about this turn of events,[226] with some claiming that their companies had lost orders as a consequence of the negative publicity that the government's aid package had created in the United States.[227] While these allegations did not have much merit, anxieties to this effect were nevertheless understandable under the circumstances. For this reason, spokesmen for the Swedish Industrialist and Export Federation also asked the cabinet to clarify its intentions to Washington.[228]

A lot of the government's domestic critics seconded this demand for clarification. Although parts of the opposition (and especially the Center Party) had at first endorsed the government's aid package,[229] many others within the non-socialist camp soon grumbled that the Social Democratic administration's short-sightedness had put Swedish trade in jeopardy and had further undermined the credibility of the country's neutrality.[230] Moreover, the Conservatives and the Liberals (as well as the Conservative and Liberal press) viewed the government's conduct with considerable skepticism, complaining that it had chiefly been informed by a desire to mollify internal agitation,[231] which was something the Social Democrats of course denied.[232] Initially, the government's detractors had not challenged the aid proposal per se, though they had questioned some select aspects of it. In particular, they criticized the Social Democratic administration's failure to consult with the other Nordic governments prior to moving forward with its own plan to aid North Vietnam.[233]

In retrospect, many of those with direct knowledge of the events that surrounded this decision-making process agree that this errand was poorly handled by the government,[234] although they differed about who was to blame.[235] At the time, the Swedish diplomatic corps was internally divided about how Sweden should respond to the threat of economic sanctions, with some younger diplomats apparently advocating that Stockholm should defy Washington and keep its promises to Hanoi.[236] It perhaps goes without saying that the senior leadership of the Foreign Ministry vetoed this approach. The latter rapidly disavowed the aid proposal in the wake of the American protests, citing the necessity of protecting Swedish trade. In an attempt to patch things up with the United States, Wilhelm Wachtmeister, the Swedish Undersecretary of State, ghostwrote an op-ed in *Dagens Nyheter* for Torsten Nilsson. In this piece, Wachtmeister explained that the cabinet never had any intention of providing reconstruction aid to the DRV until a formal peace agreement had been reached, though humanitarian aid (which the Americans did not object to) would continue to go forward as it had previously.[237]

"Nilsson's clarification" in *Dagens Nyheter* was followed by several other government statements, all of which affirmed that Sweden would not give anything but humanitarian assistance to the North Vietnamese prior to a final cessation of hostilities.[238] Torsten Nilsson, for one, made a personal pledge to this effect to the new US Secretary of State, William Rogers, during a private meeting between the two men in New York on 20 October 1969.[239] Combined with Arne Geijer's personal appeal to George Meany, these various government declarations appeared to allay Washington's immediate concerns.[240]

Social Democratic spokesmen, however, denied that Sweden was under any direct American pressure, and they also categorically rejected the idea that the cabinet had backpedaled in the face of US threats.[241] Instead, SAP officials averred that Swedish foreign policy would not be influenced by outside interference, nor would it be subjugated to the country's commercial needs.[242] Such claims notwithstanding, it was plain to domestic and American observers alike that the government had backed off from its original proposal.[243] This was apparent even to most Social Democrats,[244] who at the time pleaded with the government not to renege on its pledge to help the North Vietnamese.[245]

Parts of the non-socialist opposition naturally sought to exploit the government's retreat, seizing upon it as a rare (and golden) opportunity to score political points by discrediting the administration's Vietnam policy.[246] Conversely, the Social Democrats sought to turn the tables on their critics, asserting that it was the three non-socialist parties that were trying to politicize this issue. They additionally accused the latter of being overly sensitive to the American point of view;[247] though this was one of the few instances that the Social Democrats' attempt to play the nationalism card could not entirely negate the opposition's objections.

On this occasion, this tactic could not be employed effectively because identical accusations were concurrently being leveled against the Social

Democrats by their Marxist rivals, who could not be credibly dismissed as American pawns. Happy to capitalize on the government's backpedaling, the VPK[248] and the DFFG were both quick to condemn the Social Democratic administration for caving in to US pressure.[249]

The other principal reason that the nationalism card could not be successfully utilized was simply because no amount of Social Democratic denials to the contrary could hide the reality that the government had retreated in the face of American economic threats.[250] Even if one is willing to accept the Social Democratic leadership's claim that it never intended to provide anything but humanitarian aid to North Vietnam before the war's end, it is irrefutable that the government acquiesced to the Americans' wishes about how this assistance should be delivered and exactly what kind of assistance was deemed to be permissible. The Export-Import Bank had made it clear that it would only accept continued Swedish aid to North Vietnam on two specific conditions: one, that it was transferred exclusively via the Red Cross and thus not unilaterally from government to government as Nilsson had initially outlined, and two, that chemical fertilizers should not be made available to the DRV because these fertilizers could ostensibly be used to make bombs.[251] In hindsight, there is no doubt that the Social Democratic administration surrendered to the Export-Import Bank's proscriptions.

This angered many Social Democrats who wanted this assistance to be given directly to North Vietnam and not via the Red Cross. Their opposition to utilizing the Red Cross stemmed from the latter's narrow definition of humanitarian aid. The Red Cross was not willing to pass along either chemical fertilizers or paper products to the DRV, both of which were at the top of the North Vietnamese wish list.[252]

The government dismissed these objections, insisting that the Red Cross was a perfectly suitable instrument for facilitating Swedish aid, adding that the North Vietnamese were perfectly happy with this arrangement. As for the chemical fertilizers, the Social Democratic administration claimed that this was not an issue because Hanoi was no longer interested in this type of assistance.[253]

In reality, the government's assertions were total fabrications. To begin with, the North Vietnamese repeatedly made it known to Swedish officials that they did not want this assistance to go via the Red Cross, precisely because of the organization's limited definition of humanitarian aid.[254] Secondly, they still very much wanted the chemical fertilizers that the Swedes had previously pledged to provide.[255]

Once it became clear that the Swedes would not budge on these two issues, the North Vietnamese were forced to accept this. While the latter were not very happy about this development, they said that they understood the government's position and made it clear that they had no intention of publicly embarrassing the Social Democratic administration.[256] The North Vietnamese in fact repeatedly defended the government's Vietnam policy against the Swedish far left's attacks.[257] The SAP hierarchy, in turn, employed the DRV's gratitude as a means to neutralize internal and external criticism, alleging that Hanoi was completely satisfied with the aid package. Because the North Vietnamese were gracious enough to play along with this claim,[258] there was – according to the SAP leadership – no merit to the allegation that the government had betrayed the DRV.[259]

This line of argumentation did little to mollify radical detractors of the government's Vietnam policy who continued to assail the cabinet's retreat on the aid issue well into 1970. This bitterness was especially pronounced among Social Democratic anti-war activists.[260] Although the Social Democratic administration was eventually forced to deal with this problem (a point to which we will return in the next chapter), its first priority now was to patch things up with Washington.

The cabinet's handling of this errand once again illuminates the limits of the Social Democratic administration's ability to pursue an entirely independent course in world affairs. The SAP hierarchy was only willing to challenge Washington – and thereby accommodate domestic anti-war sentiment – to the point that it did not endanger Sweden's fundamental national interests. As was highlighted by this episode, the mere prospect of American reprisals was enough to invoke Swedish self-censorship. As soon as Washington was satisfied that the Swedes had conformed to its dictates, the threat of economic sanctions disappeared.

In the months immediately following the DRV aid debacle, the Social Democratic administration worked hard to set US-Swedish relations on a better footing again. In November and December 1969, Olof Palme and Tage Erlander, for example, both went out of their way to declare that the Swedes wanted to be on good terms with Washington, with Erlander professing his personal admiration for America's sacrifices during the two World Wars.[261] Erlander also subsequently traveled to the US in order to "clear up any misunderstanding" between the two countries.[262] This new conciliatory attitude continued into 1970, and was only briefly interrupted by the government's condemnation of the American invasion of Cambodia in early May.[263]

This renewed criticism of the US was born out of domestic political necessity, so its significance should not be exaggerated. This is not to say that the SAP leadership was not genuinely opposed to the invasion, yet considering the level of popular outrage that the invasion had ignited in Sweden,[264] not least within the SAP's own ranks,[265] it would have been basically impossible for the government to remain silent on this subject. With the exception of the Conservatives, all the other parliamentary parties also objected to the expansion of American military operations into Cambodia,[266] and for this reason the SAP did not risk anything domestically by opposing the United States. Nor did Social Democratic criticism in this instance have serious repercussions for Swedish–American relations because it was lost in the international choir of protests against the invasion.[267] This short outburst was therefore an isolated episode, and it did not signify a reversal of the government's new, more temperate, public posture vis-à-vis Washington.

Once the initial domestic reaction to the invasion dissipated, Social Democratic rhetoric once again became much more judicious.[268] This new-found moderation was especially manifest during Olof Palme's private visit to the US in June 1970.[269] Palme's trip presumably had a dual purpose: the first was to mend fences with the Americans (if not with the Nixon administration itself, then at least with the American media and public).[270] Its second purpose was seemingly related to the need to reassure moderate swing voters at home that a Social Democratic government under Palme would not undertake any radical departures in foreign policy that would endanger either the country's international reputation or gravely rupture its relations with the United States.

The Social Democratic establishment's attempt to smooth things over with Washington did not go unnoticed by contemporary observers,[271] and the Swedish far left denounced Palme's visit to the United States as an act of blatant appeasement.[272] Nor were the SAP's efforts to make amends lost upon American diplomats.[273] Above all, it was evident that the Social Democratic administration was trying to regain American goodwill by interceding on behalf of American prisoners of war in Vietnam. While this initiative did not produce any dramatic results, Washington seems to have genuinely appreciated it.[274]

* * *

By late 1970, both sides agreed that the two countries' relationship had improved,[275] and this was mostly because the Social Democratic administration had toned down its criticism of the United States. This led to a thaw in Swedish–American relations, which would more or less remain intact for the next year and a half.[276]

This pattern of Social Democratic "provocations" followed by phases of moderation vis-à-vis the United States was repeated over and over again, so in this sense the ebb and flow of Swedish Vietnam policy followed a certain predictable logic (even if it was not exactly premeditated). On every occasion that the Swedish–American diplomatic conflict threatened to spiral out of control, the Social Democratic administration was noticeably quick to ameliorate American anger by once again temporarily adopting a more judicious approach to the Vietnam issue.

The thaw in Swedish–American relations that had become perceptible by late 1970 was helped along by Nixon's Vietnamization of the war as well as by the ongoing peace talks in Paris, which made the situation in Indochina of less immediate concern in Sweden. Yet, as we shall see, as soon as domestic mobilization against the war returned in force, so did the SAP hierarchy's attacks against the United States. The domestic and foreign dimensions of the government's Vietnam policy were thus always intertwined, and in 1970 this meant that the Social Democratic administration would be forced to deal with the domestic fallout that had resulted from its recent efforts to placate Washington.

Chapter 5: Notes

[1] 15 March 1965. Letter to Torsten Nilsson from the SSSF Chairperson, Anna-Greta Leijon. Avd HP. Grupp 1. Mål O. Opinionsyttringar. Vietnam # 110. See also *Aftonbladet* 16 March 1965.

[2] Communist leader CH Hermansson as cited in *Riksdagsprotokollet* # 40, 9 Dec. 1965, 39. See also Demokratisk Ungdom, "Dagens Ungdom – politisk ungdomsrevy" # 3 1965, 6.

[3] See, for instance, Per Francke's op-ed in *Ny Dag* 10 Sept. 1965.

[4] For a specific illustration, see CH Hermansson and Torsten Nilsson as cited in *Riksdagsprotokollet* # 33, 2 Nov. 1965, 61–62, 71–73.

[5] CH Hermansson, *CH Minnen* (Stockholm: Arena, 1993) 269. For specific illustrations, see editorial in *Norrskensflamman* 25 Aug. 1966 and Sara Lidman's op-ed in *Aftonbladet* 13 Dec. 1966.

[6] Enn Kokk, "Laboremus 1902–1987" in Tuula Eriksson (eds.), *Framtidsutmaningar. Socialdemokratin inför 90-talet* (Uppsala: Laboremus, 1987) 31. For a specific example, see *SSSF Verksamhetsberättelse 1966*, 11.

[7] *Stockholms arbetarekommun. Årsmötesprotokoll*, 23–24 April 1966. Motioner # 4–7. See also the editorial in *Aftonbladet* 14 April 1966 and Folke Isaksson's op-ed in *Dagens Nyheter* 17 April 1966.

[8] *Stockholms arbetarekommun. Årsmötesprotokoll*. 23 April 1966, 7–8; *Stockholms arbetarekommun. Årsmötesprotokoll*. 24 April 1966, 1–4.

[9] Tage Erlander as cited in *Riksdagsprotokollet* # 12, 23 March 1966, 80–81.

[10] Yngve Möller, *Sverige och Vietnamkriget* (Stockholm: Tiden, 1992) 61–62.

[11] 23 May 1966. Letter to government from SSSF. Avd HP. Grupp 1. Mål O. Opinionsyttringar. Vietnam # 110. See also CH Hermansson as cited in *Riksdagsprotokollet* # 30, 1 Nov. 1966, 50.

[12] *Dagens Nyheter* 2 May 1966; *Ny Dag* 6 May 1966.

[13] 1 Nov. 1966. Letter to the government from the Social Democratic Student Club in Stockholm. Avd HP. Grupp 1. Mål O. Opinionsyttringar. Vietnam # 110; *SAP VU-protokoll* 20 June 1966. Appendix # 45. See also *Frihet* # 5 1966, 16–19.

[14] See, for example, Allan Björk and Hjalmar Mehr's exchange in the editorial pages of *Aftonbladet* on 23 May 1966 and 26 May 1966.

[15] 22 April 1966. US Ambassador to Sweden 1961–1967. J. Graham Parsons. Telegram to State. Subject Numeric Files 1964–1966. Political and Defense. Sweden. RG 59; 25 April 1966. *Chargé d'affairs* US Embassy Stockholm. Turner Cameron Jr. Telegram to State. Subject Numeric Files 1964–1966. Political and Defense. Sweden. RG 59.

[16] 23 May 1966. Head of Political Division FM. Richard Hichens-Bergström. Memo. Re: Today's visit with U.S Ambassador, J. Graham Parsons. Avd HP. Grupp 1. Mål Ua. Politik Allmänt. USA # 215; 12 Aug. 1966. Political Division FM. Jean-Christophe

Öberg. Memo. Re: Meeting with the Second Secretary of US Embassy George Andrews on 11 Aug. 1966. Avd HP. Grupp 1. Mål Ua. Politik Allmänt. USA # 216.

[17] 17 Aug. 1966. 1966. J. Graham Parsons. Telegram to State. Subject Numeric Files 1964–1966. Political and Defense. Sweden. RG 59.

[18] See, for instance, Sara Lidman's op-ed in *Aftonbladet* 11 Feb. 1967 and editorial in *Norrskensflamman* 10 March 1967.

[19] Bill # 185 submitted by Lars Werner in the First Chamber of parliament; Bill # 239 submitted by CH Hermansson, et al., in the Second Chamber of parliament. *Riksdagsprotokollet 1967.* Motioner.

[20] *Riksdagsprotokollet 1967.* Utrikesutskottets utlåtande # 3 1967, 3–4.

[21] CH Hermansson, Torsten Nilsson, and Social Democratic representative Stig Alemyr as cited in *Riksdagsprotokollet* # 12, 8 March 1967, 43–45, 48–49, 63. Nilsson would reiterate this justification throughout the rest of 1967. For a specific example, see Nilsson cited in *Dagens Nyheter* 2 July 1967.

[22] See, for example, Socialistiska Förbundet, *Program för socialism* (Stockholm: Bonnier, 1967) 45–49.

[23] Resolutions sent to the government from Västmalands NLF-group (30 March 1967) and Umeå NLF-group (7 April 1967). Avd HP. Grupp 1. Mål O. Opinionsyttringar. Vietnam # 110.

[24] See, for example, *Smålands Folkblad* 21 Oct. 1967 and *Göteborgs-Posten* 23 Oct. 1967.

[25] *Stockholms arbetarekommun. Årsmötesprotokoll,* 15–16 April 1967. Motioner # 6, # 8. See also *Frihet* # 4 1967, 4–5. and *Aftonbladet* 27 Feb. 1967.

[26] *Ny Dag* 28 April 1967.

[27] Torsten Nilsson. *Aktuellt.* TV 1. 17 April 1967. Television.

[28] Kaj Björk, *Vägen till Indokina* (Stockholm: Atlas, 2003) 138.

[29] The demand that Sweden recognize the DRV had first been raised by a handful of trade unionists in conjunction with the LO Congress in September 1966. *LO Kongressprotokoll.* 17:e Kongressen. 3–9 Sept. 1966, 549–556.

[30] *SSU Kongressprotokoll.* 18:e Kongressen. 12 June 1967, 82–83, 89–108; *Aktuellt* # 7 1967, 7–9. See also Leif Dahlberg, *Över folkets huvud* (Stockholm: Bonnier, 1967) 85–88.

[31] *SAP Kongressprotokoll.* Motioner. Extra Kongress 1967, 233–235.

[32] Survey of Swedish anti-war activists as cited in *Dagens Nyheter* 2 July 1967. See also Möller, *Sverige och Vietnamkriget,* 82.

[33] For specific illustrations, see Rune Johansson's op-ed in *Aftonbladet* 28 Feb. 1967 and *Liberal Debatt* 1967, 15–32.

[34] Bill # 465 in the First Chamber of Parliament by Nils-Eric Gustafsson; Bill # 591 in the Second Chamber of parliament by Einar Larsson and Claes Elmstadt. *Riksdagsprotokollet 1967.* Motioner.

[35] Letters to the government from *Stockholms Läns Kommunistiska Partidistrikt* (23 April 1967), *Vänsterpartiet Kommunisternas Ungdomsförbund* (18 June 1967), *Svenska Kvinnors Kommunistiska Vänsterförbund Göteborg* (17 Sept. 1967), and *Kalmar Kommunistiska arbetarekommun* (8 Nov 1967.) Avd HP. Grupp 1. Mål O. Opinionsyttringar.

Vietnam # 110. In May 1967, the SKP officially changed its name to *Vänsterpartiet Kommunisterna* (VPK).

[36] See, for instance, CH Hermansson and Torsten Nilsson as cited in *Riksdagsprotokollet* # 50, 7 Dec. 1967, 89–99. See also Torsten Nilsson, *Åter Vietnam* (Stockholm: Tiden, 1981) 125.

[37] Bill # 52 by Lars Werner in the First Chamber of parliament; Bill # 49 by C-H Hermansson, *et al.* in the Second Chamber of parliament. *Riksdagsprotokollet 1968.* Motioner. See also *Riksdagsprotokollet 1968.* Utrikesutskottets utlåtande # 1, 28 Feb. 1968.

[38] See, for instance, Communist representative Lars Werner as cited in *Riksdagsprotokollet* #13, 21 March 1968, 62. See also *Ny Dag* 2 Feb. 1968, 1 March 1968 and 11 July 1968.

[39] *Aftonbladet* 22 Feb. 1968; *Eskilstuna-Kuriren* 22 April 1968.

[40] *Vietnambulletinen* # 1 1968, 4.

[41] Resolutions calling upon the government to recognize the DRV adopted following "public meetings" in Karlstad (7 Jan. 1968), Göteborg (27 Feb. 1968), Växsjö (19 April 1968), and Karlskrona (21 April 1968.) Avd HP. Grupp 1. Mål O. Opinionsyttringar. Vietnam # 111.

[42] *Tidssignal* 2 Feb. 1968; *Expressen* 3 April 1968. See also Olof Kleberg's op-ed in *Aftonbladet* 16 Feb. 1968.

[43] *SSSF Årsmöte protokoll 1968.* Motion # 4; SSSF Förslag till Handlingsprogram. Internationell politik A1–A3; *Stockholms arbetarekommun. Mötesprotokoll.* 8 Jan. 1968. Motion # 2; *SAP VU-protokoll* 19 March 1968. Appendix # 5.

[44] Editorial in *Aftonbladet* 4 Jan. 1968.

[45] Ingemar Josefsson, Pierre Vinde, Torsten Nilsson, Lars Anell and Jan Mild as cited in *Stockholms arbetarekommun. Mötesprotokoll.* 8 Jan. 1968, 2–3.

[46] For a specific illustration, see Torsten Nilsson as cited in *Riksdagsprotokollet* # 50, 7 Dec. 1967, 89–99. See also Nilsson, *Åter Vietnam*, 125.

[47] Communist representative Lars Werner and Social Democratic representative Yngve Möller as cited in *Riksdagsprotokollet* # 11, 13 March 1968, 29–34. See also Torsten Nilsson as cited in *Dagens Nyheter* 4 April 1968.

[48] Torsten Nilsson as cited in UD, *Utrikesfrågor 1968* (Stockholm: UD, 1968) 121.

[49] See, for instance, Communist representative, Sven Hector as cited in *Riksdagsprotokollet* # 21, 2 May 1968, 5.

[50] Undated (ca. May 1968). Letter to Tage Erlander from Laboremus, the Social Democratic student organization in Uppsala. Avd HP. Grupp 1. Mål O. Opinionsyttringar. Vietnam # 110. The letter declared that because the peace negotiations in Paris had begun, Sweden would not be needed as a potential mediator, and consequently there no longer existed a logical justification for not recognizing the DRV.

[51] *Stockholms arbetarekommun. Årsmötesprotokoll*, 27–28 April 1968. Utlåtande över motionerna 1–19, 69.

[52] See, for example, *Frihet*, # 3 1968, 5l. and *Libertas* # 2 1968, 2.

[53] Letters to the government from Papersindustriarbetarförbundet Avd # 15 (ca March 1968), Byggarbetarförbundet Avd # 35 (ca March 1968) and Deje FCO:s Vietnamkommitte (3 April 1968) Avd HP. Grupp 1. Mål O. Opinionsyttringar. Vietnam # 111.

[54] Torsten Nilsson as cited in *Utrikesfrågor 1968*, 131–132.

[55] Torsten Nilsson and Sven Hector as cited in *Riksdagsprotokollet* # 21, 2 May 1968, 5.

[56] Torsten Nilsson. *Kvällsekot*. P 1. 2 May 1968. Radio.

[57] For a specific illustration, see editorial in *Aftonbladet* 7 June 1968.

[58] *SAP Kongressprotokoll*. Motioner. 23:e Kongressen. 9–15 June 1968, 45–51. Motioner # 16, 18–19.

[59] Daniel Fleming, Mats Hult, Ronald Morell and Torsten Nilsson as cited in *SAP Kongressprotokoll*. 23:e Kongressen. 9–15 June 1968, 262–265, 273–277.

[60] Torsten Nilsson as cited in *SAP Kongressprotokoll*. 23:e Kongressen. 9–15 June 1968, 439–440. Per Anger apparently told US Embassy officials that the aid announcement had been informed by domestic political calculations. 21 June 1968. William W. Heath. U.S Ambassador to Sweden 1967–1969. Telegram to State. Re: Conversation with Per Anger, the Director of International Developmental Aid on 18 June 1968. Central Foreign Policy File 1967–1969. Political and Defense. Sweden. RG 59.

[61] *Aktuellt* # 9 1968, 21.

[62] 20 June. 1968. Wilhelm Wachtmeister. Memo. Re: Today's meeting with the American Ambassador, William H. Heath. Avd HP. Grupp 1. Mål Ua. Politik Allmänt. USA # 223.

[63] 5 Jan. 1968. Cameron Turner Jr. Telegram to State. Central Foreign Policy File 1967–1969. Political and Defense. Sweden. RG 59; 10 May 1968. William W. Heath. Telegram to State: Re: Probable Swedish Recognition of the DRV. Central Foreign Policy File 1967–1969. Political and Defense. Sweden. RG 59.; 5 June 1968. Director of Intelligence and Research Dept. of State. Thomas L. Hughes. Memo to Secretary of State Dean Rusk. Re: Swedish Social Democrats may announce Recognition of the DRV at Party Congress. Central Foreign Policy File 1967–1969. Political and Defense. Sweden. RG 59.

[64] See, for example, and Jorma Enochsson, *Den Unga Centern* (Stockholm: Norstedt, 1969) 79–81. See also Eva Queckfeldt, *"Vietnam"* (Lund: Glennstrup, 1981) 32, 35.

[65] Editorial in *Aftonbladet* 13 June 1968.

[66] See, for instance, Torsten Nilsson as cited in *Arbetet* 28 Aug. 1968.

[67] *SAP VU-protokoll* 26 June 1968. Appendix # 57 k–o. See also *Dagens Nyheter* 22 Oct. 1968.

[68] Larsson as cited in *Rikdagsprotokollet* # 35, 7 Nov. 1968, 25.

[69] See, for example, editorial in *Ny Dag* 14 Nov. 1968.

[70] 8 Nov. 1968. Letter to the government from SSU Lucidor. Avd HP. Grupp 1. Mål O. Opinionsyttringar. Vietnam # 110. See also editorials in *Aftonbladet* 12 Nov. 1968 and *Örebro-Kuriren* 12 Nov. 1968.

[71] Undated (ca. Jan. 1968). SKfV, "Appel för Vietnams folk." Svenska kommittén för Vietnam, Laos och Kambodja. 1568/B/1/1 Utgående handlingar. Vol 1967–1989. 3077. See also Erik Tängestad, "Att organisera ett engagemang" (University of Stockholm, 1988) 25.

[72] 11 Nov. 1968. Letter to Erlander from the SKfV. Svenska kommittén för Vietnam, Laos och Kambodja. 1568/E/1/2 Korrespondens. Vol 1967–1968. 3077. See also *Aftonbladet* 12 Nov. 1968 and 16 Nov. 1968.

[73] Torsten Nilsson. *Dagens Eko.* P 1. 11 Nov. 1968. Radio. See also *Dagens Nyheter* 12 Nov. 1968.

[74] Nilsson and Larsson as cited in *Riksdagsprotokollet* # 37, 14 Nov. 1968, 5–6.

[75] Resolutions sent to the government from Gotlands SSU (17 Nov. 1968), Stockholm FCO (21 Nov 1968), SSSF (26 Nov. 1968), Typografiska Föreningen Stockholm (26 Nov. 1968), Enskede SAP (10 Dec. 1968), SAP Stockholms Län (11 Dec. 1968), and a joint resolution from Sv. Fabriksarbetarförbundet # 7, Träindustriarbetarförbundet # 20 and Svenska Byggarbetarförbundet # 1 (19 Dec. 1968.) Avd HP. Grupp 1. Mål O. Opinionsyttringar. Vietnam # 110.

[76] Resolutions sent to the government from VPK Hällefors (16 Nov. 1968), Sveriges Arbetares Centralorganisation (26 Nov. 1968), VPK Örebro Läns Distrikt (1 Dec. 1968), and Liberala Klubben Uppsala (5 Dec. 1968) Avd HP. Grupp 1. Mål O. Opinionsyttringar. Vietnam # 111. See also Lars Herlitz in *Ny Dag* 19 Dec. 1968.

[77] Jean-Christophe Öberg, *Varför Vietnam?* (Stockholm: Rabén & Sjögren, 1985) 132.

[78] 22 Nov. 1968. William W. Heath. Telegram to State. Central Foreign Policy File 1967–1969. Political and Defense. Sweden. RG 59.

[79] American officials made this directly known to the Swedes on several different occasions. 12 Aug. 1966. Jean-Christophe Öberg. Memo. Re: Meeting with the Second Secretary of the US Embassy George Andrews on 11 Aug 1966. During this conversation, Andrews warned that Washington was sure to interpret a Swedish recognition of the DRV as an "unfriendly act." Avd HP. Grupp 1. Mål Ua. Politik Allmänt. USA # 216; 10 June 1968. Political Division FM. Unsigned. Telegram to Swedish Embassy in Washington. Re: Visit by First Secretary of US Embassy Jerome Holloway on 7 June 1968. Avd HP. Grupp 1. Mål Ua. Politik Allmänt. USA # 223. Holloway apparently expressed "concern" about the prospect of Sweden recognizing the DRV during the upcoming SAP Congress.

[80] 7 June 1968. US Secretary of State Dean Rusk. Telegram to the US Ambassador of Sweden, William W. Heath. Central Foreign Policy File 1967–1969. Political and Defense. Sweden. RG 59.

[81] 16 Nov. 1968. William W. Heath. Telegram to State. Central Foreign Policy File 1967–1969. Political and Defense. Sweden. RG 59.

[82] Ann-Marie Ekengren, *Av hänsyn till folkrätten?* (Stockholm: Nerenius & Santérus, 1999) 233–244. This fact was certainly not lost on the government's detractors. See, for example, Dahlberg, *Över folkets huvud*, 85–88.

[83] Öberg, *Varför Vietnam?* 123–124, 133–134.

[84] Nilsson as cited in *Stockholms arbetarekommun. Årsmötesprotokoll.* 23 April 1966, 7–8; Nilsson as cited in *SAP Kongressprotokoll.* 23:e Kongressen. 9–15 June 1968, 274–277.

[85] 16 Sept. 1963. Political Division FM. Sverker Åström. Letter to Swedish Ambassador to China, Lennart Petri. Avd HP. Grupp 12. Mål Xv. Erkännande av stater och regeringar.

Vietnam # 63; 4 June 1968. Leif Leifland. Memo. Avd HP. Grupp 12. Mål Xv. Erkännande av stater och regeringar. Vietnam # 63.

[86] Ekengren, *Av hänsyn till folkrätten?*, 118–127, 238–242, 268–289.

[87] Carl-Gustaf Scott, "Swedish Vietnam Criticism Reconsidered" *Cold War History* 2009 9 (2): 243–266.

[88] Unidentified Swedish diplomat as cited by Magnus Jerneck, *Kritik som utrikespolitiskt medel* (Lund: Dialogus, 1983) 67. See also Öberg, *Varför Vietnam?*, 133–134. and Nilsson, *Åter Vietnam*, 142.

[89] See, for instance, Nilsson as cited in *Svenska Dagbladet* 11 Jan. 1969.

[90] See, for example, *Le Monde* 10 Jan. 1969, *Frankfurter Rundscheau* 11 Jan. 1969 and *Uusi Soumi* 11 Jan. 1969.

[91] See, for instance, *Dagens Nyheter* 11 Jan.1969, *New York Times* 11 Jan. 1969 and *Berliner Morgonpost* 11 Jan. 1969.

[92] 10 Jan. 1969. Foreign Ministry Press release as cited in UD, *Utrikesfrågor 1969* (Stockholm: UD, 1969) 120–121.

[93] 19 Dec. 1968. Head of the Swedish OECD Delegation in Paris. Carl Henrik von Platen. Telegram to FM. Re: Yesterday's meeting with the US Ambassador at Large, Averell Harriman. Avd HP. Grupp 1. Mål Ua. Politik Allmänt. USA # 226. According to Harriman, the Saigon regime was dragging its feet, which made it impossible to make any substantial progress in the talks.

[94] 9 Jan. 1969. Jean-Christophe Öberg. Memo. Re: Recent undated meeting between William Wachtmeister and Dô Phat Quang. Avd HP. Grupp 1. Mål Xv. Politik Allmänt. Vietnam # 1203.

[95] Nilsson as cited in *Svenska Dagbladet* 11 Jan. 1969.

[96] 17 Jan. 1969. William W. Heath. Telegram to State. Re: Conversation with unnamed Danish Embassy official in Stockholm on 14 Jan. Bureau of European Affairs. Office of Northern Affairs. Records relating to Sweden 1957–1975. RG 59. According to this Danish source, formal relations with the DRV were not a necessary prerequisite for joint Nordic reconstruction planning.

[97] 10 Jan. 1969. Swedish Ambassador to Denmark 1965–1969. Ragnvald Bagge. Memo. Re: Today's conversation with various unnamed Danish government officials. Avd HP. Grupp 12. Mål Xv. Erkännande av stater och regeringar. Vietnam # 61. According to Bagge, the Danes were not only disappointed by the Swedes' lack of prior consultation, but they also were annoyed at Nilsson for citing the joint Nordic reconstruction plans as a justification for Sweden's conduct. Similar complaints were heard from the Norwegians as well. 14 Jan. 1969. Swedish Ambassador to Norway 1968–1973. Richard Hichens-Bergström. Telegram to FM. Re: Norwegian government's negative reaction to Sweden's recognition of the DRV. Avd HP. Grupp 12. Mål Xv. Erkännande av stater och regeringar. Vietnam # 61.

[98] See, for instance, Lennart Petri, *Sverige i stora världen* (Stockholm: Atlantis, 1996) 422–425. and Åke Sjölin, "Torsten Nilsson om Vietnam" *Svensk Tidskrift* 1985 (1): 45.

[99] Ekengren, *Av hänsyn till folkrätten?*, 233–236. See also Öberg, *Varför Vietnam?*, 124–126, 134.

[100] 2 Sept. 1966. Swedish Ambassador to Thailand. Åke Sjölin. Letter to Richard Hichens-Bergström. Avd HP. Grupp 12. Mål Xv. Erkännande av stater och regeringar. Vietnam # 63; 4 June 1968. Political Division FM. Leif Leifland. Memo. Avd HP. Grupp 12. Mål Xv. Erkännande av stater och regeringar. Vietnam # 63.

[101] See, for instance, the Head of the Swedish Consulate in New York, Tore Tallroth, as cited in *Blekinge Läns Tidning* 28 March 1969.

[102] Ekengren, *Av hänsyn till folkrätten?*, 193, 206–218, 240.

[103] 11 Jan. 1969. Secretary of State. Dean Rusk. Telegram to the US Embassy in Stockholm. Central Foreign Policy File 1967–1969. Political and Defense. Sweden. RG 59. Dean instructed the Embassy to inform the Swedish government that Washington found the latter's decision to recognize the DRV to be both "unwise and unhelpful."

[104] 13 Jan. 1969. White House Staff. Robert Murphy. Memo to the President-Elect Richard Nixon. Nixon Project. White House Special Files. 1969–1974. Country File: Sweden. Murphy proposes that the time has finally come for the US to mark its disapproval of Swedish Vietnam policy. Murphy specifically recommended that the Nixon Administration not approve a new Ambassador to Stockholm until the Social Democratic administration demonstrated a more "cooperative attitude." The new administration's animosity toward Sweden was also readily apparent to Swedish diplomats in Washington. 18 March 1969. The Swedish Ambassador to the US 1963–1972. Hubert de Besche. Telegram to Torsten Nilsson. Avd HP. Grupp 1. Mål Ua. Politik Allmänt. USA # 228.

[105] State Department Press spokesmen, Robert McClosky as cited in *Dagens Nyheter* 11 Jan. 1969.

[106] 13 Jan. 1969. William W. Heath. Telegram to State. Re: Today's meeting with Swedish Foreign Minister, Torsten Nilsson. Central Foreign Policy File 1967–1969. Political and Defense. Sweden. RG 59; 18 Jan. 1969. Hubert de Besche. Telegram to FM. Re: Recent undated conversations with several different White House officials. Avd HP. Grupp 1. Mål Ua. Politik Allmänt. USA # 227. According to de Besche, Walt Rostow, in particular, seemed to be very bitter about the Swedish decision to recognize the DRV, regarding this as a de facto endorsement of the Communist cause.

[107] 24 Feb. 1969. European Section Dept. of State. Paul Hughes. Memo Re: Today's meeting between the new Undersecretary of State, U. Alexis Johnson and the Swedish Ambassador to the US Hubert de Besche. Central Foreign Policy File 1967–1969. Political and Defense. Sweden. RG 59.; 26 May 1969. Hubert de Besche. Telegram to FM. Re: Today's conversation with Head of the USIA, Frank Shakespeare. Avd HP. Grupp 1. Mål Ua. Politik Allmänt. USA # 229. According to Shakespeare, the Nixon administration interpreted Sweden's recognition of the DRV as being directed against the United States.

[108] 13 Jan. 1969. Jean-Christophe Öberg. Memo. Re: Today's meeting between Torsten Nilsson and US Ambassador William W. Heath. Avd HP. Grupp 1. Mål Ua. Politik

Allmänt. USA # 227. See also Torsten Nilsson as cited in *Rikdagsprotokollet* # 2, 22 Jan 1969, 8–21.

[109] 16 Jan. 1969. Assistant Secretary for European Affairs Dept. of State. John Leddy. Memo to Acting Secretary of State. Central Foreign Policy File 1967–1969. Political and Defense. Sweden. RG 59; 24 April 1969. Paul Hughes. Scandinavian Desk Dept. of State. Memo to Martin Hillenbrand Assistant Secretary for European Affairs Dept. of State. Central Foreign Policy File 1967–1969. Political and Defense. Sweden. RG 59.

[110] See, for instance, US Ambassador, Jerome Holland as cited by James Waite, "Sweden and the Vietnam criticism" *South East Asia* 1973 2 (4): 457.

[111] See, for instance, *Svenska Dagbladet* 13 Jan. 1969, *Washington Post* 24 Jan. 1969, *Expressen* 21 April 1969 and *New York Times* 14 Oct. 1969.

[112] For specific illustrations, see the *Daily Telegraph* 14 Jan. 1970 and *Washington Evening Star* 19 Jan. 1970. See also Ruth Link, "Ambassador Holland and the Swedes" *Crisis* 1971 78 (2): 43–48.

[113] 26 April 1969. Cameron Turner Jr. Telegram to State. Central Foreign Policy File 1967–1969. Political and Defense. Sweden. RG 59; 29 April 1969. Secretary of State. William Rogers. Telegram to US Embassy Stockholm. Central Foreign Policy File 1967–1969. Political and Defense. Sweden. RG 59.

[114] 13 Jan. 1969. Robert Murphy. Memo to the President-Elect Richard Nixon. Nixon Project. White House Special Files. 1969–1974. Country File: Sweden. Box 9. In this memo, Murphy suggests that the Nixon administration should seriously consider taking more concrete retaliatory measures against Sweden, such as enacting trade sanctions.

[115] For specific illustrations, see House Representative John Rarick as cited in the Congr. Rec. 91st Congr., 1st Sess., 13 Jan. 1969: 185, 454. and House Representative Edward Derwinski as cited in the Congr. Rec. 91st Congr., 1st Sess., 2 April 1969: 8539.

[116] See, for example, Elmer Raessner's column in the *New York Daily News* 21 Jan. 1969.

[117] 20 Feb. 1969. Swedish Embassy Washington. Mats Olander. Memo. Re: American press coverage of the Swedish recognition of North Vietnam. Avd HP. Grupp 1. Mål Ua. Politik Allmänt. USA # 227; 28 Feb. 1969. Sven Frychius. Telegram to FM. Avd HP. Grupp 1. Mål Ua. Politik Allmänt. USA # 227.

[118] The *Washington Post* 14 Jan. 1969.

[119] See, for instance, editorials in the *Washington Evening Star* 11 Jan. 1969, *Minneapolis Tribune* 13 Jan. 1969 and *Houston Post* 19 Jan. 1969.

[120] See, for instance, interviews with leading Sweden businessmen, such as Axel Iveroth and Lars Åkerman, as cited in *Kvällsposten* 15 May 1969.

[121] Letters to the government from Nordengren Patenter AB (15 Jan. 1969); Sveriges Redareförbund (7 Feb. 1969), Sveriges Allmänna Exportförening (4 March 1969), and a group of 40 Swedish businessmen in California (10 March 196.) Avd HP. Grupp 1. Mål O. Opinionsyttringar. Vietnam # 111.

[122] See, for instance, the exchange between Torsten Nilsson, Liberal representative Karl Kilsmo, and Conservative representatives Henrik Åkerlund and Allan Hernelius as cited

in *Riksdagsprotokollet* # 2, 22 Jan. 1969. 8–21. See also Erik Boheman's op-ed in *Göteborgs-Posten* 24 Jan. 1969.

[123] Sven Wedén, Gunnar Hedlund and Yngve Holmberg as cited in *Dagens Nyheter* 11 Jan. 1969.

[124] See, for instance, Liberal representative Olof Dahlén and Conservative representative Ivar Virgin as cited in *Riksdagsprotokollet* # 13, 26 March 1969, 36–37, 75. See also Clas G. Johnson, *Ny giv – Samtal med Yngve Holmberg* (Stockholm: Almqvist & Wiksell, 1969) 120–121.

[125] For a specific illustration, see Conservative representative, Henrik Åkerlund as cited in *Riksdagsprotokollet* # 2, 17 Jan. 1969, 3–4. See also Erik Boheman, *Tankar i en talmansstol* (Stockholm: Norstedt, 1970) 204.

[126] See, for instance, editorials in *Barometern* 13 Jan. 1969, *Borås Tidning* 14 Jan. 1969 and *Svenska Dagbladet* 17 Jan. 1969.

[127] Gunnar Hedlund as cited in *Svenska Dagbladet* 11 Jan. 1969. That said, some Center Party representatives, like Torsten Bengtsson and Sven Wahllund, would later also complain about the government's failure to inform the opposition about its intent to recognize the DRV. Torsten Bengtsson as cited in *Riksdagsprotokollet* # 13, 26 March 1969, 21, 77. and Sven Wahlund as cited in *Riksdagsprotokollet* # 13, 26 March 1969, 69.

[128] See, for instance, Per Ahlmark as cited in *Expressen* 10 Jan. 1969.

[129] See, for example, editorials in *Expressen* 10 Jan.1969, *Sundsvalls Tidning* 11 Jan. 1969, *Dagens Nyheter* 13 Jan. 1969 and *Nerikes Allehanda* 23 Jan. 1969.

[130] Öberg, *Varför Vietnam?*, 134.

[131] Torsten Nilsson as cited in *Riksdagsprotokollet* # 4, 5 Feb. 1969, 14, 57–60; Arne Geijer and Torsten Nilsson as cited in *Riksdagsprotokollet* # 13, 26 March 1969, 33–34, 67–69, 74, 78.

[132] For a specific illustration, see Lars De Geer's op-ed in *Dagens Nyheter* 26 Feb. 1969.

[133] Conservative representative Allan Hernelius as cited in *Rikdagsprotokollet* # 2, 22 Jan. 1969, 17–19; Gösta Bohman as cited in *Riksdagsprotokollet* # 13, 26 March 1969, 79–80.

[134] See, for instance, editorials in *Göteborgs-Posten* 11 Jan. 1969, *Upsala Nya Tidning* 11 Jan. 1969 and *Kvällsposten* 11 Jan. 1969. Similar complaints were obviously also voiced in a number of Conservative papers, see editorials in *Vimmerby Tidning* 10 Jan. 1969, *Smålandsposten* 13 Jan. 1969 and *Barometern* 24 Jan. 1969.

[135] 16 Jan. 1969. John Leddy. Action Memo to Acting Secretary of State. Central Foreign Policy File 1967–1969. Political and Defense. Sweden. RG 59; 27 Feb. 1969. Paul Hughes. Memo. Briefing paper – Sweden. Central Foreign Policy File 1967–1969. Political and Defense. Sweden. RG 59.

[136] 17 Jan. 1969. William W. Heath. Telegram to State. Re: Recent undated conversations with a number of unidentified Swedish Foreign Ministry officials. Central Foreign Policy File 1967–1969. Political and Defense. Sweden. RG 59.

[137] Tore Tallroth as cited in *Blekinge Läns Tidning* 28 March 1969. See also Petri, *Sverige i stora världen*, 425.

[138] 14 Feb. 1969. Scandinavian Desk Dept. of State. George Ingram. Memo. Re: Today's meeting with Jean-Christophe Öberg at the US Embassy in Stockholm. Central Foreign Policy File 1967–1969. Political and Defense. Sweden. RG 59.

[139] Lennart Klackenberg, a retired specialist on Swedish development aid within the Swedish Ministry of Finance, interview with the author, 8 May 2003. See also Björk, *Vägen till Indokina*, 169.

[140] Torsten Nilsson and Krister Wickman as cited by Jerneck, *Kritik som utrikespolitisktmedel*, 70, 217.

[141] Torsten Nilsson as cited in *Utrikesfrågor 1969*, 121–123; Olof Palme as cited in the *New York Times* 5 June 1970.

[142] Ekengren, *Av hänsyn till folkrätten?*, 238–242. See also Petri, *Sverige i stora världen*, 422.

[143] Margareta Ström, "Norska Reaktioner på Sveriges Erkännande av Nordvietnam" (University of Stockholm, 1969) 5; Kent Lidman, "Vietnamdebatten i Sverige" (University of Umeå, 1973) 16; Ekengren, *Av hänsyn till folkrätten?*, 141–143, 195.

[144] Ekengren, *Av hänsyn till folkrätten?*, 124, 134,141–143, 199.

[145] Kurt Törnqvist, *Svenskarna och omvärlden* (Stockholm: Bredskapsnämnden för psykologiskt försvar, 1969) 13–20.

[146] Between December 1968 and March 1969, the SAP's share of the electorate ranged from 50.4% to 52.5% (that is, well within the margin of error). Sören Holmberg and Olof Petersson, *Inom felmarginalen* (Stockholm: Liber, 1980) 246.

[147] The above-mentioned poll also revealed that support for establishing relations with North Vietnam was slightly more popular among young voters than it was among older ones. Among voters between 20 to 24 years old, 39% favored recognizing the DRV, whereas 47% were opposed to doing so. Törnqvist, *Svenskarna och omvärlden*, 13–20.

[148] See, for instance, CH Hermansson as cited in *Expressen* 10 Jan. 1969. See also editorials *Norrskensflamman* 11 Jan. 1969 and *Ny Dag* 16 Jan. 1969.

[149] See, for example, *Vietnambulletinen* # 1 1969, 7. See also DFFG spokesperson, Åsa Hellström, as cited in *Aftonbladet* 11 Jan. 1969.

[150] *Aftonbladet* 10 Jan. 1969; *Värmlands Folkblad* 11 Jan. 1969; *Nya Norrland* 11 Jan. 1969.

[151] See, for instance, *Tiden* # 8 1969, 450. See also *Aftonbladet* 12 Jan. 1969.

[152] See, for example, editorials in *Arbetet* 11 Jan. 1969, *Örebro-Kuriren* 13 Jan. 1969 and *Arbetarbladet* 16 Jan. 1969.

[153] See, for instance, *Libertas* # 1 1969, 2.

[154] 11 March 1969. SKfV. "Uprop" Signed by Bertil Svanström. Svenska kommittén för Vietnam, Laos och Kambodja. 1568/B/1/1 Utgående handlingar. Vol 1967–1989. 3077. See also *Vietnam nu* # 1 1969, 1.

[155] 23 Jan. 1969. Letter to the government from the Chairman of the SKfV. Gunnar Myrdal. Svenska kommittén för Vietnam, Laos och Kambodja. 1568/E/1/2 Korrespondens. Vol 1969. 3077.

[156] Christopher Sundgren, "Splittrad Solidaritet" in Maj-Lis Eriksson, *et al.* (eds.), *Med eller mot strömmen* (Stockholm: Sober, 1980) 146–149. For a specific example, see *Vietnambulletinen* # 4 1969, 24.

[157] See, for instance, Torsten Nilsson and CH Hermansson as cited in *Riksdagsprotokollet* # 33, 29 Oct. 1969, 95, 103–104. See also editorials in *Aftonbladet* 26 June 1969 and 19 Sept. 1969.

[158] Ekengren, *Av hänsyn till folkrätten?*, 139, 143; Björk, *Vägen till Indokina*, 199–201, 207–208.

[159] For specific illustrations, see Erik Eriksson's op-ed in *Aftonbladet* 12 Jan. 1969 and *Tiden* # 1 1969, 63. See also *SSU Kongressprotokoll*. 19:e Kongressen. 3–8 May 1970. *Politik i SSU 1967–1969*, 38–40.

[160] See, editorials in *Arbetet* 11 Jan. 1969, *Östra Småland* 13 Jan. 1969 and *Gotlands Folkblad* 15 Jan. 1969.

[161] See, for instance, Nilsson cited in *Svenska Dagbladet* 11 Jan. 1969.

[162] Möller, *Sverige och Vietnamkriget*, 174.

[163] Öberg, *Varför Vietnam?*, 151.

[164] See, for instance, Communist representative Sven Hector as cited in *Riksdagsprotokollet* # 20, 29 April 1965, 52. See also *Ny Dag* 4 June 1965 and 18 Aug. 1965.

[165] Bill # 377 in the First Chamber of parliament submitted by Lars Werner; Bill # 446 in the Second Chamber of parliament submitted by Sven Hector, *et al. Riksdagsprotokollet 1966*. Motioner.

[166] *Stockholms arbetarekommun. Årsmötesprotokoll*, 23–24 April 1966. Motioner # 4–7. See also SSSF, *Verksamhetsberättelse 1966*, 11.

[167] *Stockholms arbetarekommun. Årsmötesprotokoll*, 23–24 April 1966. Utlåtande över motioner # 4–7. See also Torsten Nilsson as cited in *Riksdagsprotokollet* # 26, 20 May 1965, 5.

[168] See, for instance, Torsten Nilsson as cited in *Riksdagsprotokollet* # 12, 23 March 1966, 58.

[169] Bill # 51 in the Second Chamber of parliament submitted by Sven Hector, *et al. Riksdagsprotokollet 1967*. Motioner.

[170] See exchange between Torsten Nilsson and C-H Hermansson as cited in *Riksdagsprotokollet* # 4, 26 Jan. 1967, 93–94.

[171] *Riksdagsprotokollet 1967*. Statsutskottets utlåtande # 53, 31.

[172] Nilsson as cited in Utrikesdepartementet, *Sverige och Vietnamfrågan* (Stockholm: UD, 1968) 36–67.

[173] If anything this campaign had only continued to gain momentum between the spring and fall of 1967. *Stockholms arbetarekommun. Årsmötesprotokoll*. 15–16 April 1967, 14–15, 18–21. Motioner # 2–5, 13–21; *SSU Kongressprotokoll*. 17:e Kongressen. 12 June 1967, 99–108. Motion # 47. See also *Aktuellt* # 7 1967, 7–8.

[174] *SAP Kongressprotokoll*. Extra Kongress. 21–23 Oct. 1967. 457–458; *SAP Kongressprotokoll*. Motioner. Extra Kongress 1967, 233–235.

[175] Björn Elmbrant and Erik Eriksson, *Det bidde en tumme* (Stockholm: Prisma, 1970) 18–21.

[176] SSSF, *Årsmöte protokoll*, 22–25 Feb. 1968. Förslag till handlingsprogram, A 3; *Stockholms arbetarekommun. Verksamhetsberättelse 1968*, 5. See also Social Democratic representative Oskar Lindqvist as cited in *Riksdagsprotokollet* # 7, 14 Feb. 1968, 22.

[177] For a specific illustration, see Tage Erlander as cited in *Riksdagsprotokollet* # 13, 21 March 1968, 10.

[178] *SAP VU-protokoll* 26 March 1968.

[179] Nilsson as cited in *Rikdagsprotokollet* # 15, 18 April 1968, 55; Nilsson as cited in *Riksdagsprotokollet* # 21, 3 May 1968, 53–54.

[180] Nilsson as cited in UD, *Sverige och Vietnamfrågan* (Stockholm: UD, 1968) 80–81.

[181] Anders Thunborg as cited in *SAP Kongressprotokoll. 23:Kongressen. 9–15 June 1968*, 248; Tage Erlander and Torsten Nilsson as cited in *SAP Kongressprotokoll. 23:Kongressen. 9–15 June 1968*, 440.

[182] For a specific example, see *Riksdagsprotokollet* # 21, 3 May 1968, 56–57. See also Elmbrant and Eriksson, *Det bidde en tumme*, 27.

[183] Bill # 3 submitted by Center Party representatives John Eriksson and Bengt Börjesson in the Second Chamber of parliament in January 1966. (*Riksdagsprotokollet 1966. Motioner.*) See also Liberal Leader, Bertil Ohlin as cited in *Riksdagsprotokollet* # 12, 23 March 1966, 39.

[184] See, for example, Center Party representative Einar Larsson as cited in *Riksdagsprotokollet* # 10, 7 March 1968, 150. and Liberal representative Ingrid Segerstedt-Wiberg as cited in *Riksdagsprotokollet* # 21, 3 May 1968, 70. See also Lennart Widing's op-ed in *Dagens Nyheter* 8 Feb. 1968.

[185] See, for instance, Liberal representative Olof Dahlén as cited in *Riksdagsprotokollet* # 13, 26 March 1968, 76. See also Bill # 461 submitted by Center Party representative Johannes Antonsson in the Second Chamber of parliament in January 1969. *Riksdagsprotokollet 1969. Motioner.*

[186] Bill # 99 and Bill # 171 submitted by Lars Werner in the First Chamber of parliament in January 1969. (*Riksdagsprotokollet 1969. Motioner.*) See also CH Hermansson as cited in *Riksdagsprotokollet* # 13, 26 March 1969, 47.

[187] See, for instance, Yngve Holmberg as cited in *Riksdagsprotokollet* # 13, 26 March 1969, 32.

[188] For specific illustrations, see Torsten Nilsson as cited in *Riksdagsprotokollet* # 13, 26 March 1969, 68–69. See also *Riksdagsprotokollet 1969. Statsutskottets utlåtande* # 82 1969 and *Riksdagsprotokollet 1969. Utrikesutskottets utlåtande* # 15 1969.

[189] *Stockholms arbetarekommun. Mötesprotokoll.* 21 March 1969. Motion # 14. See also Social Democratic representative Mats Hellström as cited in *Riksdagsprotokollet* # 13, 26 March 1969, 93.

[190] Möller, *Sverige och Vietnamkriget*, 174–176. See also Öberg, *Varför Vietnam?*, 151–155.

[191] For example, during the party's 1 May demonstration in Stockholm, there were several sections entirely devoted to the aid question. *Stockholms arbetarekommun. Verksamhetsberättelse 1969*, 7.

[192] See, for instance, the editorial in *Aftonbladet* 25 Aug. 1969 and *Aktuellt* # 14/15 1969, 24–25.

[193] 10 Sept. 1969. Letter to Torsten Nilsson from Social Democratic trade unionist and SKfV board member, Erik Alderin. Svenska kommittén för Vietnam, Laos och Kambodja. 1568/E/1/2 Korrespondens. Vol 1969. 3077.

[194] 20 May 1969. SKfV Press Release. Svenska kommittén för Vietnam, Laos och Kambodja. 1568/B/1/1 Utgående handlingar. Vol 1967-1989. 3077.

[195] Undated (ca. 1972.) SKfV, "Info från SKfV." Svenska kommittén för Vietnam, Laos och Kambodja. 1568/B/1/1 Utgående handlingar. Vol 1967-1989. 3077.

[196] Nilsson as cited in SAP Kongressprotokoll. 24:e Kongressen. 28 Sept.-4 Oct. 1969, 247-248.

[197] Birgitta Dahl, "Solidaritetsarbetet för Vietnam" in Enn Kokk (ed.), Var blev ni av ljuva drömmar? (Stockholm: Ordfront, 2002) 187.

[198] Jan Pierre, Partikongresser och regeringens politik (Lund: Kommunalfakta Förlag, 1986) 289.

[199] Öberg, Varför Vietnam?, 159-161.

[200] Lennart Klackenberg interview with author 8 May 2003.

[201] See, for instance, Georg Johansson as cited in SAP Kongressprotokoll. 24:e Kongressen. 28 Sept.-4 Oct. 1969, 258. See also editorials in Aftonbladet 1 Oct. 1969, Arbetarbladet 1 Oct. 1969 and Arbetet 2 Oct. 1969.

[202] Harald Lundberg, Broderskapsrörelsen(s) i svensk politik och kristenhet 1930-1980 (Stockholm: Broderskaps Förlag, 2004) 232-233; Elmbrant and Eriksson, Det bidde en tumme, 28-32.

[203] Eivor Samuelsson, Nord Vietnam (Stockholm: Utbildningsförlaget, 1972) 110-111.

[204] Susan Holmberg, "Welfare Abroad: Swedish Developmental Assistance" in Bengt Sundelius (ed.), The Committed Neutral (Boulder: Westview Press, 1989) 134-143; Ulf Bjereld and Marie Demker, Utrikespolitiken som slagfält (Stockholm: Nerenius & Santérus, 1995) 277-306.

[205] For a specific illustration, see Sven Wedén's op-ed in Dagens Nyheter 7 Oct. 1969.

[206] Riksdagsprotokollet 1969. Utrikesutskottets utlåtande # 15.

[207] Nilsson as cited in SAP Kongressprotokoll. 24:e Kongressen. 28 Sept.- 4 Oct. 1969, 247-248. See also Möller, Sverige och Vietnamkriget, 179-180.

[208] See, for example, Yngve Holmberg as cited in Svenska Dagbladet 3 Oct. 1969.

[209] Elmbrant and Eriksson, Det bidde en tumme, 38-39; Björk, Vägen till Indokina, 175-178. According to Kaj Björk, Nilsson was perfectly clear on the point that this aid would not be given to North Vietnam until the war was over. So it was Öberg's press conference that had created this confusion.

[210] Försvarsdepartementet, Folkrätten i krig (SOU 1984: 56) 266-268. See also Per Cramér, Neutralitetsbegreppet (Stockholm: Norstedt, 1989) 99.

[211] See, for instance, Nilsson as cited in Dagens Nyheter 15 Oct. 1969 and Nilsson as cited in Riksdagsprotokollet # 33, 29 Oct. 1969, 99-102, 113.

[212] Elmbrant and Eriksson, Det bidde en tumme, 42.

[213] See, for example, editorials in *Norrländska Socialdemokraten* 1 Oct. 1969 and *Arbetet* 2 Oct. 1969. See also Dahl, "Solidaritetsarbetet för Vietnam," 188.

[214] Björk, *Vägen till Indokina*, 176–178.

[215] For specific examples, see editorials in the *Oregonian* 3 Oct 1969, *Orlando Sentinel* 11 Oct 1969, and *Chicago Tribune* 15 Oct. 1969.

[216] *Dagens Nyheter* 15 Oct. 1969; *Svenska Dagbladet* 21 Oct. 1969.

[217] Geijer as cited in *Svenska Dagbladet* 23 Oct. 1969. See also *New York Times* 15 Oct. 1969 and *Baltimore Sun* 16 Oct. 1969.

[218] See, for instance, Representative John Rarick as cited in 91st Congr., 1st Sess., 13 Oct. 1969: 29781. and 15 Oct. 1969: 30262–30264. and Senator Strom Thurmond as cited in 91st Congr., 1st Sess., 20 Nov. 1969: 35116.

[219] Senator William Scherle as cited in 91st Congr., 1st Sess., 3 Oct. 1969: 28403–28404. Congressional bitterness toward Sweden due to its support for the DRV would linger well into 1970. See Senator Herman Talmadge as cited in 91st Congr., 2nd Sess., 27 Jan. 1970: 1275. and Representative Mendel Rivers as cited in 91st Congr., 2nd Sess., 29 April 1970: 13385.

[220] 28 Oct. 1969. Hubert de Besche. Telegram to FM. Avd HP. Grupp 1. Mål Ua. Politik Allmänt. USA # 232. See also SOU, *Fred och säkerhet* (SOU 2002:108) 324–326.

[221] 8 Oct. 1969. Hubert de Besche. Telegram to FM. Re: Today's meeting with Martin Hillenbrand. Avd HP. Grupp 1. Mål Ua. Politik Allmänt. USA # 231; 28 Oct. 1969. Hubert de Besche. Telegram to FM. Avd HP. Grupp 1. Mål Ua. Politik Allmänt. USA # 232.

[222] 3 Oct. 1969. White House Staff. Ken Cole. Memo to Henry Kissinger. Re: President's instructions. Nixon Project. White House Special Files. 1969–1974. Country File: Sweden. Box 9. This was followed by an extensive discussion about what other forms of retaliation could be employed to punish Sweden. 6 Oct. 1969. Ken Cole. Memo to Henry Kissinger. Re: Discuss with President what measures that State suggests that we should take against Sweden. Nixon Project. White House Special Files. 1969–1974. Country File: Sweden. Box 9.

[223] State Department spokesman Carl Bartch as cited in the *Washington Post* 14 Oct. 1969. Bratch disclosed that the Nixon administration was contemplating implementing economic sanctions against Sweden in retaliation for its assistance to the DRV.

[224] *Dagens Nyheter* 4 Oct. 1969; *Washington Post* 9 Oct. 1969; *New York Times* 14 Oct. 1969.

[225] For a specific illustration, see editorial in *Aftonbladet* 14 Oct. 1969.

[226] *Dagens Nyheter* 4 Oct. 1969. See also Möller, *Sverige och Vietnamkriget*, 199.

[227] *Dala-Demokraten* 9 Oct. 1969; *Svenska Dagbladet* 10 Oct. 1969; *Aftonbladet* 13 Oct. 1969.

[228] *Kvällsposten* 10 Oct. 1969; *Dagens Nyheter* 16 Oct. 1969.

[229] Åke Pettersson, "Centeridéer i utrikespolitiken" in Centerpartiet, *Samarbete och skiljelinjer* (Stockholm: LT:s Förlag, 1970) 160–161; David Wirmark, "Solidaritet för en mänskligare värld" in Folkpartiet, *För ett mänskligare samhälle* (Stockholm: Folk och samhälle, 1970) 209. See also editorials in *Expressen* 1 Oct. 1969, *Dagens Nyheter* 1 Oct. 1969, and *Skånska Dagbladet* 1 Oct. 1969.

[230] For a specific example, see Conservative representative Ivar Virgin as cited in *Riksdagsprotokollet* # 33, 29 Oct. 1969, 17–19. See also editorials in *Helsingborgs Dagblad* 11 Oct. 1969, *Vestmalands Läns Tidning* 14 Oct. 1969, *Bohuslänningen* 16 Oct. 1969 and *Barometern* 23 Oct. 1969.

[231] For specific illustrations, see Yngve Holmberg as cited in *Svenska Dagbladet* 3 Oct. 1969 and Conservative representative Leif Cassel as cited in *Dagens Nyheter* 27 Oct. 1969. See also editorials in *Göteborgs-Posten* 10 Oct. 1969, *Smålandsposten* 16 Oct. 1969, *Blekinge Läns Tidning* 20 Oct. 1969, and *Norrköpings Tidningar* 13 Nov. 1969. It is worth noting that the Communists also complained that the government was using the DRV aid package for own political ends. See, for example, CH Hermansson as cited in *Riksdagsprotokollet* # 33, 29 Oct. 1969, 103, 110–111.

[232] See, for instance, exchange between Torsten Nilsson and Sven Wedén as cited in *Riksdagsprotokollet* # 33, 29 Oct. 1969, 105–106, 108–110.

[233] See, for instance, Sven Wedén's op-ed in *Dagens Nyheter* 7 Oct. 1969 and Yngve Holmberg as cited in *Svenska Dagbladet* 10 Oct. 1969.

[234] Lennart Klackenberg interview with author 8 May 2003. See also Björk, *Vägen till Indokina*, 176–178; Öberg, *Varför Vietnam?*, 188.

[235] Kaj Björk, for example, blames Jean-Christophe Öberg for this incident. (Björk, *Vägen till Indokina*, 162, 172–178, 180–186.) Whereas Öberg instead criticizes the senior hierarchy within the Foreign Ministry. Öberg, *Varför Vietnam?*, 162–165, 175–176.

[236] Elmbrant and Eriksson, *Det bidde en tumme*, 42–43.

[237] Dagens Nyheter 8 Oct. 1969. See also Möller, *Sverige och Vietnamkriget*, 187. and Björk, *Vägen till Indokina*, 183.

[238] Olof Palme. "Face the Nation." CBS. 19 Oct. 1969. Television. (Transcript as found in Avd HP. Grupp 1. Mål Ua. Politik Allmänt. USA # 232.) See also Palme's comments as cited in *Svenska Dagbladet* 15 Oct. 1969.

[239] 20 Oct. 1969. Jean-Christophe Öberg. Memo of Conversation. Re: Today's meeting between Torsten Nilsson and William Rogers. Avd HP. Grupp 1. Mål Ua. Politik Allmänt. USA # 232. See also *Dagens Nyheter* 20 Oct. 1969 and *Aftonbladet* 21 Oct. 1969.

[240] *The Washington Post* 22 Oct. 1969. This effort was supplemented through private visits to Washington by the well-known Swedish industrialist Marcus Wallenberg, the SAP's International Secretary Anders Thunborg, and the Swedish Commander and Chief Stig Synnergren. In the late fall of 1969, all three men were sent as government envoys to soothe the Americans' irritation. SOU, *Fred och säkerhet*, 277–278.

[241] Olof Palme as cited in *Svenska Dagbladet* 15 Oct. 1969; Sven Anderson as cited in *Aftonbladet* 16 Nov. 1969.

[242] Olof Palme as cited in *Stockholms arbetarekommun. Mötesprotokoll.* 10 Nov. 1969, 2; Torsten Nilsson as cited in *Expressen* 12 Nov. 1969.

[243] See, for instance, Peter Weiss's op-ed in *Dagens Nyheter* 19 Oct. 1969 and Erik Norlander's article in *Veckojournalen* # 43 1969, 24–25. See also the *Houston Chronicle* 9 Oct. 1969, *New York Times* 19 Oct. 1969 and *US News & World Report* 10 Nov. 1969.

²⁴⁴ For specific illustrations, see the editorial in *Aftonbladet* 9 Oct. 1969 and Leif Dahlberg's op-ed in *Dagens Nyheter* 19 Oct. 1969. See also Dahl, "Solidaritetsarbetet för Vietnam," 188.

²⁴⁵ Letters to the government from SSSF Chairman, Bengt Liljenroth (ca Oct. 1969); 1:a kretsen Stockholms arbetarekommun (12 Nov. 1969), Borås arbetarekommun (18 Nov. 1969) and Umeå arbetarekommun (28 Nov. 1969) Avd HP. Grupp 1. Mål O. Opinionsyttringar. Vietnam # 111. See also editorials in *Arbetet* 11 Oct. 1969 and *Nya Norrland* 20 Oct. 1969.

²⁴⁶ For specific illustrations, see Sven Wedén as cited in *Riksdagsprotokollet* # 31, 16 Oct. 1969, 11. and Ivar Virgin as cited in *Riksdagsprotokollet* # 33, 29 Oct. 1969, 17–19. See also editorials in *Dagens Nyheter* 8 Oct. 1969, *Katrineholms-Kuriren* 15 Oct. 1969, *Smålands Allehanda* 16 Oct. 1969 and *Expressen* 20 Oct. 1969.

²⁴⁷ See, for instance, Torsten Nilsson as cited in SAP, "Vietnam i debatten" SAP partistyrelsens informationstjänst # 7 1969, 3–11. See also editorials in *Arbetarbladet* 11 Oct. 1969, *Västgöta-Demokraten* 13 Oct. 1969 and *Norrländska Socialdemokraten* 15 Oct. 1969.

²⁴⁸ See, for instance, CH Hermansson as cited in *Riksdagsprotokollet* # 33, 29 Oct. 1969, 102–104, 110–111. and Sara Lidman's op-ed in *Aftonbladet* 18 Oct. 1969.

²⁴⁹ Åke Kilander, *Vietnam var nära* (Stockholm: Leopard, 2007) 312; Hammarström, *FNL i Sverige*, 82. See also *Dagens Nyheter* 16 Nov. 1969.

²⁵⁰ Bjereld och Demker, *Utrikespolitiken som slagfält*, 281. For a specific example, see Torsten Nilsson as cited in *Riksdagsprotokollet* # 33, 29 Oct. 1969, 100–101, 108.

²⁵¹ Öberg, *Varför Vietnam?*, 153–154.

²⁵² Elmbrant and Eriksson, *Det bidde en tumme*, 73, 77, 109. For specific illustrations, see Leif Dahlberg's open letter to Torsten Nilsson in *Aftonbladet* 3 Jan. 1970 and SSSF Chairman, Bengt Liljenroth's op-ed in *Aftonbladet* 4 April 1970.

²⁵³ Torsten Nilsson as cited in *Stockholms arbetarekommun. Årsmötesprotokoll.* 17–19 April 1970, 13–15, 21–23; Olof Palme as cited in *SAP Riksdagsgruppens protokoll* 21 April 1970.

²⁵⁴ 20 Jan. 1970. Leif Leifland. Memo. Re: Today's conversation between Ole Jödahl and Nguyen Tho Chan the North Vietnamese Ambassador. Avd HP. Grupp 1. Mål Xv. Politik Allmänt. Vietnam # 1206; 12 Jan. 1970. Jean-Christophe Öberg. Memo. Re: Yesterday's conversation with Nguyen Tho Chan. Avd HP. Grupp 1. Mål Xv. Politik Allmänt. Vietnam # 1206.

²⁵⁵ 30 Oct. 1969. Jean-Christophe Öberg. Memo. Re: Today's meeting between Torsten Nilsson and Nguyen Tho Chan. Avd HP. Grupp 1. Mål Xv. Politik Allmänt. Vietnam # 1205; 24 Dec. 1969. Swedish Ambassador to Moscow. Gunnar Jarring. Telegram to UD. Re: Today's conversation with Nguyen Tho Chan. Avd HP. Grupp 1. Mål Xv. Politik Allmänt. Vietnam # 1206.

²⁵⁶ 8 Jan. 1970. Jean-Christophe Öberg. Memo. Re: Today's meeting between Torsten Nilsson and Nguyen Tho Chan. Avd HP. Grupp 1. Mål Xv. Politik Allmänt. Vietnam # 1206; 20 Jan. 1970. Leif Leifland. Memo. Re: Today's conversation between Ole Jödahl and Nguyen Tho Chan. Avd HP. Grupp 1. Mål Xv. Politik Allmänt. Vietnam # 1206.

[257] 25 Sept. 1971. Swedish Ambassador to the DRV. Jean-Christophe Öberg. Memo. Re: Recent undated conversation with the N. Vietnamese Ambassador to Sweden, Nguyen Tho Chan. Avd HP. Grupp 1. Mål Xv. Politik Allmänt. Vietnam # 1208. Chan stated that on several different occasions he had defended the government's Vietnam policy during his meetings with Swedish NLF sympathizers. According to Chan, the latter came across as naïve and lacking sound political instincts. He specifically criticized their failure to comprehend that their continual attacks against Social Democratic Vietnam policy by extension also harmed the Vietnamese Communist cause.

[258] North Vietnamese Ambassador Nguyen Tho Chang remarks as cited in *Dagens Nyheter* 6 Sept. 1970. Chang appeared side by side with Palme during the 1970 election campaign, expressing North Vietnamese gratitude for the Swedish aid package.

[259] Sten Andersson as cited in *SAP PS-protokoll* 17 March 1970; Torsten Nilsson as cited in UD, *Utrikesfrågor 1970* (Stockholm: UD, 1970) 120–122.

[260] Erik Svanfeldt, "Svenska kommittén för Vietnam" (University of Uppsala, 1990) 25; Dahl, "Solidaritetsarbetet för Vietnam," 188–189.

[261] Palme as cited in *Göteborgs handels- och sjöfartstidning* 21 Nov. 1969; Erlander as cited in *Dagens Nyheter* 12 Dec. 1969.

[262] Tage Erlander as cited in *Svenska Dagbladet* 10 Dec. 1969.

[263] Torsten Nilsson and Olof Palme as cited in UD, *Utrikesfrågor 1970*, 116–118.

[264] For specific examples, see Sara Lidman's op-ed in *Aftonbladet* 7 May 1970 and *Fackföreningsrörelsen*, # 11 1970, 360–361.

[265] SSKF *Årsberättelse 1970*, 43; Stockholms arbetarekommun, *Aktuell information* # 4 1970.

[266] Yngve Holmberg, CH Hermansson, Gunnar Hedlund and Gunnar Hélen as cited in *Svenska Dagbladet* 4 May 1970.

[267] 31 Dec. 1970. Hubert de Besche. Memo. Swedish–American Relations during 1970. Avd HP. Grupp 1. Mål Ua. Politik Allmänt. USA # 239.

[268] See, for instance, Olof Palme as cited in *Expressen* 3 June 1970.

[269] Jerneck, *Kritik som utrikespolitikt medel*, 159–164; Möller, *Sverige och Vietnamkriget*, 251–253.

[270] *Kvällsposten* 6 June 1970; *Svenska Dagbladet* 7 June 1970.

[271] See, for example, Stig Ramel, the Chairman of the Association of Swedish Exporters, as cited in *Värmlands Folkblad* 31 July 1970. See also *Vietnam nu* # 4 1970, 2.

[272] For a specific illustration, see CH Hermansson as cited in *Dagens Nyheter* 4 May 1970. See also Hammarström, *FNL i Sverige*, 102.

[273] 13 Dec. 1969. Turner Cameron Jr. Telegram to State. Central Foreign Policy File 1967–1969. Political and Defense. Sweden. RG 59; Undated (ca. March 1970.) European Section Dept. of State. Unsigned. Briefing Material for Ambassador Holland's Arrival in Stockholm – April 1970. Subject Numeric Files 1970–1973. Political and Defense. Sweden. RG 59.

[274] 7 Nov. 1969. William Rogers. Letter to Torsten Nilsson: Re: American appreciation for Swedish efforts on behalf of the US POWs. Avd HP. Grupp 1. Mål Ua. Politik All-

mänt. USA # 232; 6 Nov. 1970. Henry Kissinger. Memo to President Richard Nixon. Nixon Project. White House Special Files. 1969–1974. Country File: Sweden. Box 9.

[275] 3 Dec. 1970. US Ambassador to Sweden 1970–1972. Jerome Holland. Memo. US Policy Assessment – Sweden 1970. Subject Numeric Files 1970–1973. Political and Defense. Sweden. RG 59; 31 Dec. 1970. Hubert de Besche. Memo. Swedish–American Relations in 1970. Avd HP. Grupp 1. Mål Ua. Politik Allmänt. USA # 239.

[276] Fredrik Logevall, "The Swedish–American Conflict over Vietnam" *Diplomatic History* 1993 17 (3): 438.

Dénouement 1970–1974:
Conflict and Stalemate on Both Fronts

By early 1970, the Social Democratic administration had already made substantial strides toward improving relations with Washington. The SAP leadership's strident condemnation of the Cambodian invasion notwith-standing, the next two years witnessed a de-escalation in Swedish–American tensions that would last until the spring of 1972. However, the new Palme government's rapprochement with the Americans simultaneously provoked internal dissent.

As was discussed in Chapter 5, it was transparent to Swedes of all political persuasions that the Social Democratic administration had retreated in the face of US economic threats.[1] This was very difficult for some Social Democrats to accept and resulted in considerable bitterness. Though others defended the cabinet's handling of the DRV aid package, the aid debacle nevertheless placed virtually all Social Democratic anti-war activists in a bind,[2] and *Aftonbladet* openly worried that this issue would cost the party votes to the left.[3]

Palme personally faced a similar dilemma. Prior to becoming Prime Minister in late 1969, he had been identified principally with the SAP's left wing, but his new responsibilities required that he also represent more conservative constituents, both within the party and among the electorate at large. Palme's problem consequently was that he needed to satisfy his radical base without alienating moderate mainstream opinion. As was evidenced by the government's backpedaling on the DRV aid package, these two objectives were not always compatible, and once his administration gave precedence to protecting Swedish trade this inevitably led to dis-enchantment among some of his more radical supporters.[4] (The government's sharp criticism of the Cambodian invasion must be understood in this context, as this was clearly meant to ameliorate internal discontent arising from its sudden reversal on the aid package.) In sum, Palme's quandary was that his original radical image had created expectations that he was not able to live up to when he took over the helm of the government and the Social Democratic Party.[5]

Managing Domestic Criticism

Tensions over the withdrawn assistance to the DRV lingered on in to the winter and finally came to a head in the late spring of 1970[6] when the leadership of *Sveriges Socialdemokratiska Studentförbund* (SSSF) went as far as to suggest that the government should resign in light of its broken promise to the North Vietnamese.[7] At this juncture, the SAP hierarchy decided that it had had enough of such insubordination. It steadfastly refuted the claim that the cabinet had caved in to American pressure, and it further demanded that the cadre fall in line behind the government.[8] The party hierarchy's effort to squash this rebellion was finally set in motion during *Stockholms arbetarekommun's* annual meeting in mid-April, at which time the party district issued a strong vote of confidence in the cabinet's handling of this matter. The district cited North Vietnam's appreciation of Swedish policy, and it chastised those within the party who intimated that the government had let itself be intimidated by the Americans.[9] *Stockholms arbetarekommun's* decree in effect signaled the end of any such continued dissent,[10] and the SSSF was subsequently punished for its defiance. Some of its members were expelled from the SAP while the rest of the organization was dismantled and forcibly incorporated into the *Sveriges Socialdemokratiska Ungdomsförbund* (SSU).[11] Thereafter, internal discipline was strictly enforced, and a massive public relations effort was mounted in defense of the official party line.[12]

Though the SAP hierarchy was at last able to reassert its authority over its own flock, it was still powerless to prevent the Communists and the Maoists from continuing to capitalize upon the government's mishandling of the aid package. Throughout the spring of 1970, the VPK aggressively sought to use this issue to its own ends as the party attempted to recoup its losses among young voters.[13] The war's significance to the Communists was additionally enhanced by the Maoists' foray in to electoral politics, compelling the VPK for the first time to be concerned about being outflanked to its left by the KFML.[14] Either directly or via the DFFG, the Maoists in the KFML were similarly quick to exploit the DRV aid fiasco, citing this as proof of the government's hypocrisy and the Social Democrats' lack of genuine commitment to the Vietnamese people.[15]

The Maoists' attempt to utilize this issue to broaden their electoral appeal, however, was almost instantly undermined by their own belligerent behavior. The worst self-inflicted wound occurred in April during a DFFG-led protest against the newly arrived American Ambassador, Jerome Holland. Afterwards, Holland claimed to have been called a "nigger" by one of the demonstrators,[16] and although spokesmen for the NLF-groups vigorously denied that they had made any such comments, their protestations of innocence seem to have fallen on deaf ears.[17] This episode was soon also followed by several other attacks on Holland, including one in which the Ambassador was pelted with eggs.[18] Together all of these incidents generated a lot of negative publicity for the DFFG and put the Maoists on the defensive.[19]

The Social Democrats adroitly seized upon these events as a means to discredit the DFFG, and in April the party launched an aggressive counter-offensive against the Maoists.[20] This assault was spearheaded by Palme, who decried the NLF-activists' behavior as profoundly undemocratic.[21] These Social Democratic attacks continued for the next several months,[22] and the Vietnam issue would subsequently remain at the heart of SAP and KFML's conflict on the campaign trail.[23]

Both parties believed that they would electorally benefit from their opposition to the war.[24] The Vietnamese conflict was of course exceptionally important to the KFML, which enlisted the DFFG in its propaganda work. Unlike in 1968, the NLF-groups actively participated in the 1970 election campaign, and even though they did not officially endorse the KFML, their support for the latter was nevertheless obvious in light of their bellicose critique of SAP and VPK's respective Vietnam positions.[25] The KFML had high hopes leading up to the election, convinced that they were gathering momentum.[26] Their optimism was not entirely unwarranted, for in 1969 the Maoists' 1 May demonstrations had actually been larger than the Social Democratic ones in a few smaller cities.[27] While it is probably fair to assume that the Social Democratic establishment was not overly concerned about the KFML's potential electoral impact, the SAP hierarchy worried enough about it to issue a special brochure instructing the party's election workers on how to best deflect Maoist criticism of the government's Vietnam policy.[28]

The Social Democrats faced pressure from the SKfV as well, which likewise sought to turn the war into a major election issue. The SKfV specifically demanded that each party make clear its stand on future Swedish assistance to North Vietnam.[29] The aid question's importance during the campaign was bolstered by the publication of Björn Elmbrant and Erik

Eriksson's book *Det bidde en tumme* (*It Didn't Amount to Much*), which offered a stinging left-wing critique of the government's handling of the DRV aid package.[30]

Now the SAP was also attacked from the right in relation to Vietnam, and this definitely raised the political temperature on the campaign trail.[31] This critique was most famously elaborated by Gösta Bohman in his earlier-mentioned book *Inrikes utrikespolitik. Det handlar of Vietnam* (*Domestic Foreign Policy: It is About Vietnam*), which dismissed the government's Vietnam stance as pure political pandering.[32] That having been said, the war was predominantly a factor in the competition between the Social Democrats and its two Marxist rivals; otherwise, the election campaign was mostly pre-occupied with domestic matters rather than with international affairs.

While the war's role in the 1970 election campaign should not be exaggerated, it was still a substantial issue. From a Social Democratic point of view, this question's primary value was largely related to its contribution to the party's overall ideological profile. Heading into the election, the party's electoral strategy was principally aimed at mobilizing its own voters. The SAP hierarchy hoped to accomplish this by embracing a radical political vision that gave special emphasis to international solidarity and greater domestic equality. Given that Social Democratic strategists specifically identified young voters as one of the most vital groups for the party to get out to the polls,[33] this, in effect, bolstered the Vietnam issue's significance.

Taken as a whole, the 1970 campaign was informed by the radicalized political environment of the time, and this also shaped the main contest between the SAP and the Center Party whose election propaganda similarly emphasized greater domestic egalitarianism.[34] These general tendencies were given an additional boost with the outbreak of a series of wildcat strikes at the end of 1969.[35] Such labor unrest had the effect of pushing the SAP in an even more radical direction,[36] while concomitantly boosting the electoral hopes of the party's Marxist rivals, who now believed that the political climate in Sweden was decisively turning in their favor.[37]

This prediction proved to be true for the Communists at least, who – to the detriment of the SAP – appear to have profited electorally from the strikes, as the VPK was one of the major winners in the 1970 election. The party enlarged its share of the electorate by 1.8 per cent, giving it 4.8 per cent of the total vote.[38] This result, in turn, secured the VPK's continued presence in the parliament, which in itself was an impressive feat in light of the internal chaos that the party had experienced in the aftermath of the 1968 election.[39]

The VPK's improved electoral standing aside, the Center Party was indisputably the election's biggest winner, raising its share of the popular vote to nearly 20 per cent (a net gain of 4 per cent). Part of this increase had come at the expense of the Social Democrats, who even though they managed to stay in power suffered a considerable setback. The Social Democrats' support had shrunk by 5 per cent since the last election (down to 45.3 per cent). While the SAP had lost votes to the right and the left alike,[40] during its post-election analysis it was determined that the party's greatest losses had been to the left, some of it to the Maoists in the KFML, but most of it to the VPK. The Social Democratic leadership surmised that this could largely be attributed to many of its own adherents voting strategically in order to ensure the VPK's future political survival.[41] With this in mind, one might guess that the VPK's modest gains were tolerable to the Social Democrats because they now had become implicitly dependent upon Communist backing in the parliament to stay in power.

This new situation, however, basically guaranteed that the Social Democratic administration would remain committed to a Hanoi-friendly course because a pro-DRV/NLF position was an effective (and relatively politically risk-free) way for the Social Democrats to reward the Communists for their loyalty in parliament. The election result likewise spoke against a revision of the government's current Vietnam stance for the simple reason that the SAP once again had to fret about being outflanked by the Communists on this issue. Between 1968 and 1970, the latter had been so politically marginalized that the VPK had basically become an afterthought for the SAP. This being the case, during this brief two-year interlude, the government's Vietnam posture was therefore presumably mostly directed at satisfying internal anti-war agitation and not by the need to fend off external Communist subversion. The VPK's electoral resurgence in 1970 changed this, not least because the Social Democrats' losses to their left could partially be attributed to the government's reversal on the DRV aid package[42] (as was exemplified by Lars Rudebeck's subsequent defection to the Communists).[43] Thus, VPK's resurrection ensured that the war would continue to figure prominently in Swedish domestic politics.

The Communists' electoral rebound was unquestionably rather unnerving to the Social Democrats, especially in view of their own weakened standing among first-time voters. The 1970 election outcome demonstrated that the SAP's support among this segment of the electorate of had dropped to 44 per cent, whereas the VPK had captured approximately 10 per cent of the vote in the 20–22-year-old bracket. (The party's position within this demographic bracket was thus essentially twice as strong as it was among the general electorate.) The VPK, furthermore, did particularly well with younger educated voters, i.e., the anti-war vote. The SAP, in contrast, squandered the advantage that it had enjoyed among this specific demographic group in 1968.[44]

These losses were naturally a matter of serious concern to the SAP hierarchy, which for the next several years repeatedly lamented the party's eroding position among the young intellectual left.[45] This development was to a large degree offset by its continued solid standing among younger blue-collar workers,[46] for neither the Communists nor the Maoists had made any significant headway among this category of voters, as was underscored by the outcome of the 1970 election. In addition, the election had made it clear that the Maoists did not pose much of an electoral threat to the SAP.

The KFML had only garnered 0.4 per cent of the total vote, and while its message had appealed to many university students, the party had received essentially no backing from the Swedish working class.[47] Hence, it appears that the Social Democrats' standoff with the Maoists resulted in a draw. On the one hand, SAP was never able to secure the allegiance of the most militant members of the baby-boom generation, but on the other hand KFML's attempt to make inroads among blue-collar voters did not fare much better. In all likelihood, this outcome was acceptable to the Social Democrats.

KFML's dismal electoral performance in 1970 did not completely eliminate it as a source of anxiety, and at least in relation to the Vietnam issue the far left continued to be a threat long after the 1970 election. Accordingly, the Social Democratic hierarchy was determined to keep up the offensive against the Maoists and Communists alike, and it concluded that the party's Marxist adversaries would be most effectively disarmed by maintaining a radical political profile.[48] Such calculations kept the party wedded to a militant position on Vietnam because it was well aware that both VPK and KFML were going to continue to try to capitalize on popular opposition to the war.[49]

Although the Social Democrats' apprehensions were not totally unfounded, in the long run the Maoists ended up being much more of a problem for the VPK than for the SAP. VPK's gains among the young intellectual left had insured its electoral survival, but at a steep price. By 1973, the VPK had been almost completely transformed into a party of the urban intelligentsia, and the influx of these young militants would destabilize the party for a long time to come.[50] Moreover, once this group became its main constituency, VPK was constantly forced to look over its shoulder so as to not be outmaneuvered by the Maoists. (The Communists had, in fact, lost their youth organization, *Vänsterpartiets Ungdomsförbund*, to the Maoists in the midst of the 1970 election campaign.)[51]

This turn of events of course suited the Social Democrats[52] because they were arguably the main beneficiaries of the disintegration of the far left that took place after 1969. The next decade witnessed a blossoming of new groupings to the left of VPK, most of which were Maoist, though some were also Trotskyite. The early 1970s were subsequently characterized by recurring splits as well as endemic infighting within the Swedish far left. These clashes, in turn, sharply curtailed the revolutionary left's forward momentum and made it less of an immediate concern to the Social Democrats.[53]

Out of all of these conflicts, the most important one by far was the one between KFML and *Kommunistiska Förbundet Marxist-Leninisterna Revolutionärerna* (KFML(r). The latter had split off from the former following the 1970 election in a dispute over the party's future direction.[54] This quarrel by extension served to break the revolutionary branch of the anti-war movement into two rival factions. While the overwhelming majority of the local NFL-chapters stayed affiliated with the KFML, the KFML(r) established its own Vietnam group, *Solidaritetsfronten för Indokinas folk* (SFIF, the Solidarity Front for the People of Indochina). SFIF, however, was never able to unseat DFFG's dominant position within the revolutionary anti-war movement. Still, for the next year or so, DFFG's face-off with KFML(r)/SFIF consumed much of the organization's energy and greatly reduced its effectiveness.[55] The balkanization of the militant branch of the anti-war movement (the Trotskyites soon also founded their own anti-war organization)[56] by default gave the parliamentary left, and the Social Democratic leadership in particular, increased breathing room.

It would take DFFG well over a year to recover from the chaos created by KFML(r)'s defection, causing it to turn inward and temporarily reducing its political efficacy. The NLF-movement was likewise briefly pushed out of the domestic political limelight due to new developments relating to the war itself. As was indicated at the end of the last chapter, the Paris peace talks, in conjunction with Nixon's Vietnamization program, relegated the Vietnamese conflict to the back pages, and consequently popular interest in South East Asia started to dwindle. Once the initial uproar surrounding the invasion of Cambodia had dissipated, the far left, the general public, and the Social Democratic establishment all increasingly concentrated on other international issues (mostly relating to the Middle East), as well as on the worsening economic situation at home.

The Swedish Anti-War Movement, the Christmas Bombings, and Diplomatic Crisis

Yet in contrast to what happened in many other Western countries – including the United States – the anti-war movement in Sweden did not fade away after 1970. In spite of the war's reduced domestic significance, neither the revolutionary nor the reformist branches of the anti-war movement disappeared, and both retained a visible, if slightly less prominent, presence in Swedish politics. The Vietnam issue itself was kept alive by the combination of persistent external attacks against the government and internal Social Democratic agitation. Above all, it was the ongoing competition between the DFFG and the SKfV that continuously re-energized each side. From 1970 on, both branches of the anti-war movement largely directed their efforts at trying to get the government to recognize the Provisional Revolutionary Government of South Vietnam (PRR) and this cause also found a voice in parliament via Social Democratic and Communist members of the SKfV.[57]

The Social Democratic administration, however, managed to stave off these demands, in no small part because the war's recently diminished importance made it easier for the government to withstand the anti-war movement's lobbying. Although the cabinet did protest the American invasion of Laos in early February 1971, such criticism of the US was the exception rather than the rule in these years as the Social Democratic cabinet's rhetoric concerning events in Indochina grew considerably more muted. As a result, by late 1971 and early 1972 the situation in South East Asia had by and large receded as a topic of severe contention between Stockholm and Washington. This is not to say that the war had completely vanished as a source of friction, but it was now less of a burden on Swedish–American relations than it had been in 1968 and 1969.[58]

This uneasy respite was not to last. As soon as the Americans resumed bombing the DRV in February 1972 (in response to the North Vietnamese spring offensive), the Social Democratic administration once again found itself under intense domestic pressure to speak out against the war,[59] which it did repeatedly over the next few months.[60] The escalation in hostilities propelled both sides of the anti-war movement back into action, and the NLF-groups' bi-annual Vietnam Week in mid-April attracted its biggest crowds ever (approximately 50,000 people in 170 different locations across Sweden.) In Stockholm alone, somewhere between 11,000 and 12,000 demonstrators partook in the week's concluding rally, making it the largest anti-war protest in Sweden so far.[61]

As was made manifest by the size of these demonstrations, after a two-year lull, the Swedish anti-war movement had quickly regained its stride. Indeed, in the next year it grew by leaps and bounds, peaking at the turn of 1972/1973. During the final year leading up to the Paris peace agreement in April 1973, Sweden arguably had the proportionately largest and most powerful anti-war movement in the entire Western world. [62] Save for a few Conservative holdouts,[63] the Swedish public also basically appeared to share the far left's view of the Vietnamese conflict.[64] As a consequence, there was considerable sympathy for the Vietnamese Communists,[65] and it is probably safe to say that the latter's popularity in Sweden was unrivaled in the Western world.

Under these circumstances, it behooved the cabinet to be attentive to the country's anti-war activists, who continued to push the government to recognize the PRR. Pressure to do so had steadily been building over the past two years,[66] and this also explains why Nguyen Van Thien, the PRR's chief's negotiator at the Paris peace talks, was invited to address the Social Democrats' 1 May rally in Stockholm.[67] For this same reason, the PRR's Foreign Minister, Madame Thin Binh, was the main guest speaker at the SAP's party Congress a few months later in early October. For her part, Binh thanked the Congress for Sweden's assistance to the NLF, though she simultaneously embarrassed the government by calling upon it to recognize the PRR.[68] Overall, the war was centrally featured during the Congress as party leaders not only repeatedly castigated US Vietnam policy, [69] but for the third time in less than a year the cabinet also pledged additional financial aid to both the DRV and the PRR.[70] The Congress, in turn, adopted its most militant Vietnam resolution ever, expressing complete support for the PRR's peace plan while at the same time characterizing the American war effort as "a human rights violation."[71] The Congress was punctuated by an anti-war demonstration that was jointly organized by *Stockholms arbetare-kommun* and the SKfV.[72]

Looking back, there can be no doubt that the SAP hierarchy once again successfully employed the Vietnam issue as a means to direct internal radical energies away from the domestic status quo where these sorts of impulses might have hurt the party at the polls. In the end, the party hierarchy was even able to skillfully placate internal calls for the recognition of the PRR by promising to do so at some future point,[73] thereby turning this errand into a symbolic gesture that required no concrete government action.[74]

At the time, the Social Democratic establishment likewise appears to have embraced the Vietnam issue because it could be utilized to mobilize its own cadre heading in to the next election. It must be remembered that the party's support in the polls had fallen precipitously since the last election, and rising inflation and unemployment figures did not make its electoral prospects any brighter.[75] This being the case, the situation in South East Asia was unquestionably a welcome distraction and largely accounts for why Vietnam was given so much room at the SAP Congress.

All in all, the SAP Congress seems to have served its intended purpose in energizing the Social Democratic faithful. Anti-war agitation within the party (including the trade union movement) remained intense during the next two months,[76] reaching its zenith in mid-October when Social Democratic, Communist, and Maoist demonstrators marched side by side in a number of different local anti-war demonstrations.[77]

This fervor only abated in early December when the US and North Vietnam at last appeared to be on the verge of reaching a peace agreement. At this point the Social Democratic administration took steps to try to mend fences with Washington,[78] but these efforts were almost instantly cut short by Nixon's decision to resume bombings against the DRV on 18 December 1972.

This aerial attack, which would become known as the Christmas bombings of 1972, was a massive show of force that was intended to compel the North Vietnamese to return to the peace table on American terms. It lasted for the next 12 days, and at the time it was widely reported that the bombings had inflicted a high number of civilian casualties. The reaction to the renewed US aerial assault on North Vietnam was universally negative in Sweden and immediately catapulted both branches of the anti-war movement back into action.[79]

Revulsion against Nixon's action was acutely felt among the Social Democratic faithful,[80] and internal demands, spearheaded by the SKfV, were at once raised for the government to denounce the bombings,[81] which it did. On 19 December, the new Social Democratic Foreign Minister, Krister Wickman, released an official statement criticizing the American resumption of hostilities against North Vietnam.[82] Had the Swedish protest stopped with this pronouncement, the subsequent diplomatic crisis with the Americans would have been averted, but this is not what happened.

On 23 December, Olof Palme instead issued his most strident rebuke of the US to date in which he compared the American bombings to the earlier atrocities at Katyn, Sharpsville, and Treblinka. He added that there was no plausible military justification for the current aerial attack, and consequently it could only accurately be characterized as "torture."[83] Afterwards practically all attention would focus on Palme's decision to invoke Treblinka, and this statement was later commonly referred to as Palme's Christmas Speech (*jultal*).

The main question is really why Palme felt compelled to react publicly to the Christmas bombings when there was no real reason for him to do so. After all, Wickman's statement would have more than sufficed as an official government response. Although part of the answer can unquestionably be found in Palme's sincere abhorrence of the bombings,[84] this explanation cannot alone account for his behavior.

Rather, Palme's decision to issue a personal protest can only be understood against the backdrop of the fierce domestic – and especially Social Democratic – reaction to the Christmas bombings. There was immense pressure from within *Stockholms arbetarekommun* for Palme, specifically, to address this topic.[85] In this case he could not resort to the previously used tactic of letting a junior member of the SAP leadership, like Ingvar Carlsson, lead the attack against US Vietnam policy,[86] while he himself stayed in the background playing the more genteel role of prime minister.[87] Nor could Palme ignore the reality that his outspokenness against the war had done much to build and fortify his present position within the party and that his own core supporters would presumably have been extremely disappointed if he had remained silent about the renewed US bombings.

It should also be stressed that in late 1972 Palme's authority within the government was quite circumscribed, and he was still surrounded by several senior cabinet members that he had inherited from Erlander. The backing of his own left wing constituents became all the more crucial at a time when he was locked in a power struggle with the very influential Minister of Finance, Gunnar Sträng (a battle that Palme at the time was reportedly losing).[88] It is therefore of some interest that when Palme a year later rearranged his cabinet, he brought several prominent Social Democratic antiwar activists in to the government.[89] Even if one accepts the notion that Palme's condemnation of the Christmas bombings was principally motivated by authentic outrage, there can be little doubt that tactical calculations also contributed to his (and the party's) handling of this issue.

Palme had, however, completely failed to anticipate the strength of the American reaction, which by all accounts took him by surprise.[90] It is obvious that Palme did not fully appreciate the Holocaust's symbolic power in American political discourse, and contemporary observers rightly noted that if not for the Treblinka reference, Palme's protest would largely have been overlooked in the United States.[91] And had Palme not invoked this specific imagery, his Christmas Speech would likely just have been lost in the broader chorus of international dissent.

Palme's parallel to the Holocaust was at the heart of the US response. Not only did this comparison create resentment in the American conservative press and on Capitol Hill, but it also opened Sweden up to negative scrutiny about its policy of accommodation toward the Third Reich during the Second World War. In the eyes of many American critics, Palme's reference to Treblinka was the height of hypocrisy in view of the Swedes' own wartime conduct.[92]

Nixon was personally outraged by the implication of Palme's statement, as was his closest adviser, Henry Kissinger. Because Kissinger himself was of German Jewish descent, he found Palme's rhetoric to be particularly repugnant.[93] In consultation with Kissinger, Nixon instructed the State Department to freeze US–Swedish diplomatic relations if Palme did not publicly retract his comments. Although Sweden did not rank very highly among the Nixon administration's foreign policy concerns, the White House had nevertheless kept a fairly close eye on the Social Democratic administration. Nixon was already known to personally dislike Palme, and this latest episode was the final straw.[94] The State Department had earlier argued for a "cordial, but correct" policy toward Sweden, but now it too agreed that the time had come to remind Stockholm that there were real limits to Washington's patience.[95]

Specifically, the Swedes were told that the US intended to withdraw its *chargé d'affairs* indefinitely, which would leave the American Embassy in Stockholm without a top diplomat. (President Nixon had not yet appointed a new Ambassador to Sweden following Jerome Holland's departure in August 1972.) In addition, the US would not accept a new Swedish Ambassador in Washington to replace Hubert De Besche once he left his post in January 1973 as had been already scheduled. The two countries' embassies would for the time being be left in the hands of lower ranking officials (though they would not be closed).[96]

The freeze consequently did not entail a total severing of diplomatic contacts between the two countries; instead, most day-to-day business was just to be conducted at a lower level. Initially, this did somewhat inhibit the Swedish capacity to get information from the State Department, but otherwise the conflict hardly affected routine interactions between Stockholm and Washington.[97] American policy toward Sweden during the freeze could be summarized as "business as usual, but no unusual business." In concrete terms, this meant that all official high-level diplomatic and military visits were postponed for the time being. Nor was it regarded as a suitable time to initiate any new major collaborative projects between the two states or for Sweden to request any new large-scale military orders (though all pre-existing orders were still honored).[98]

In the final analysis, then, this dispute was mostly about appearances. The freeze was a symbolic act that had virtually no bearing on the bottom line of postwar Swedish-American relations, that is, in terms of trade or scientific and military collaboration. Although genuinely irritated with the Swedes, the White House never contemplated extending the conflict beyond the government-to-government level.[99] Both sides, in fact, went to great lengths to ensure that the current chill in diplomatic relations did not negatively affect other spheres. Throughout the entire duration of the freeze, economic, scientific, and military elites took care to preserve the continuity in their trans-Atlantic contacts. This was a top priority for the Social Democratic administration, which over the course of the next year discreetly sent a number of envoys to Washington to secure continued Swedish access to US military technology. Palme additionally directed the heads of both the Swedish Navy and Army to make sure that the two countries' military relations were not harmed by his present quarrel with Nixon. If anything, Swedish-American military cooperation actually intensified during the freeze.[100]

The main trouble was that the freeze lasted much longer than anyone had at first anticipated, and full diplomatic relations were not restored until May 1974. As has already been noted, this situation could have been avoided altogether had Palme instead chosen to recant, for the Americans had at first not made the sanctions publicly known, thereby leaving the door open for a Swedish retraction. It seems that the Swedish government, including the Foreign Ministry, did not at first appreciate the gravity of the American reaction,[101] though the Swedes did comprehend that something needed to be done. Accordingly on 24 December, under Sverker Åström's guidance, Palme composed a new direct appeal to Nixon to halt the bombings. Somewhat preposterously, Palme offered to debate the President, further explaining that his opposition to the war was rooted in his great admiration of American democracy.[102] The contents of this follow-up message fell well short of either an apology or a disavowal of his earlier denunciation of the bombings, but its tone was certainly much more reconciliatory. This is also confirmed by the message's co-author, Sverker

Åström, who states that Palme's personal message to Nixon was intended as an olive branch.[103]

While some leading Social Democrats hailed Palme's Christmas Speech, others privately questioned the appropriateness of his Treblinka analogy.[104] Not without good reason, many were concerned that Palme had gone too far on this occasion,[105] and this anxiety was naturally shared by most Swedish senior diplomats. Palme's Christmas Speech had been formulated without the prior consultation of the Foreign Ministry, which was quite dismayed by its contents,[106] and the latter would work tirelessly to try to repair Swedish–American relations.[107] However, in the immediate wake of this brewing crisis it advised the government not to shrink in the face of Nixon's ire, feeling that to do so would only undermine Sweden's international standing, not least vis-à-vis the United States.[108] For this reason, Palme's follow-up message had to walk a careful balance of seeking to mollify the Nixon administration without giving the appearance of groveling.[109]

Regardless of Palme's actual intent, the Americans did not fail to notice that his personal appeal to the President was considerably softer in tone than the statement that he had originally delivered on 23 December.[110] From their point of view, however, this was not enough,[111] so after Washington had waited for a few more days, the State Department finally announced its intention to invoke diplomatic sanctions against Sweden. The full story broke in the media on 29 December and caused an enormous stir on both sides of the Atlantic, making the front page of several major American dailies the next day.[112]

Worried about the potential political domestic fallout from this situation, the Social Democratic leadership had held off on making the sanctions public. The decision to sit on this news was also informed by the belief that the Nixon administration was unlikely to follow through on its threat to completely freeze relations. Both Palme and Sweden's top diplomats had incorrectly surmised that once the President's initial anger had dissipated somewhat, Nixon would modify his response. In hindsight, it is clear that this was wishful thinking, and it took the Swedes a while to grasp that this impasse was actually likely to last for some time.[113]

By early March the severity of the situation had began to sink in among Swedish diplomats. In addition, they soon realized that Nixon would personally determine the duration of the freeze, and he did not appear to be in any hurry to patch things up with Sweden.[114] From the very start, American officials made it known that "the ball now rested in the Swedes' court" and that was it up to Stockholm to take the initiative to improve the two countries' relationship.[115] The Nixon administration would stick to this policy and was resolved to not send a new Ambassador to Stockholm until the Swedes demonstrated an "improved attitude."[116]

The Americans eventually ceased to expect a public apology from Palme, recognizing that for domestic reasons this was basically out of the question,[117] and Palme never did formally recant his Christmas Speech. Still, short of apologizing, Palme otherwise did his best to regain American goodwill.[118] Among other things, he avowed that his reference to Treblinka was never intended to be a comparison between the perpetrators (i.e. Nixon and Hitler). Instead, he claimed that he had only sought to draw a parallel between the victims in each instance, adding that he was sorry if this had been misinterpreted.[119] Along with Wickman,[120] Palme also continuously reiterated his desire for good relations with Washington, expressing his great admiration for many aspects of American society.[121] In fact, he insisted that "Sweden was probably the most pro-American country in Europe."[122] (This rhetoric was not just directed at Washington, but ostensibly also at moderate swing voters.)

Although not always possible for domestic reasons,[123] by early 1973 it was nonetheless evident that the Social Democratic administration was trying to avoid any additional criticism of the United States so as to prevent any further deterioration of the two countries' relations. This effort was made easier by the formal cessation of hostilities in Vietnam, and American officials quickly recognized that the Social Democratic administration was trying to patch things up with the United States.[124] For starters, the SAP leadership sent numerous oblique, but unambiguously friendly, public signals to the Americans. Palme likewise let it be known via a variety of different back channels that he was interested in ending the standoff.[125] Surreptitious Social Democratic endeavors to make peace would intensify following the 1973 election, but prior to the end of the election campaign there was only so far Palme could go to atone for his attack on the US without hurting either himself or his party. As it turns out, the freeze would not really cause Palme and the SAP undue problems on the domestic front – quite to the contrary.

The Petition to End Hostilities (Namninsamlingen)
and the Bach Mai Campaign

In reality, Palme's Christmas Speech found fertile soil in Sweden, and in the next few weeks anti-war protests spread rapidly across the country.[126] Condemnations of the bombings were supplemented with calls for heightened assistance to the DRV.[127] Opposition to US policy at times bordered on near religious fervor, as was illustrated by Birgitta Dahl's somewhat outlandish demand that all American television shows should to be taken off the air in retaliation for the bombings.[128] Such hyperbole aside, the Swedish public was now more or less totally united against the American war effort,[129] causing *Aftonbladet* to conclude that domestic opinion had as of late moved in a decisively militant direction – in no small part due to Palme's condemnation of the bombings.[130]

This was probably a pretty accurate reading of the public mood, for at the time Palme's protest was widely heralded domestically. If one examines all of the messages that were sent to Palme from private individuals and organizations in Sweden following his Christmas Speech (and the subsequent fallout), the positive responses outnumbered the negative ones by almost a 5 to 1 ratio (290 to 60). While this type of evidence cannot be utilized as a definitive reading of the public mood, it still indicates that Palme enjoyed extensive public backing. (This is because 290 messages of support is a lot more encouragement than the Prime Minster could normally expect to get about any given issue.) Moreover, when looking through this material one cannot help but notice that quite a bit of this support came from non-socialist voters who stated that they otherwise did not sympathize with Palme.[131]

Remarkably, the leadership of the Center and Liberal Parties also offered a qualified vote of confidence in Palme.[132] To be sure, some Liberal parliamentarians questioned the appropriateness of his Treblinka analogy,[133] but on principal many non-socialist politicians defended Palme's (and Sweden's) right to speak his (its) mind.[134] With the partial exception of the Conservative leader Gösta Bohman – who initially said that he understood Nixon's retaliation against Palme[135] – the American sanctions were generally not well received within the non-socialist camp. This disapproval was quite manifest in the Liberal and Center Party press,[136] and it was especially pronounced in the larger urban Liberal dailies,[137] such as *Dagens Nyheter*, which vehemently argued Palme's case.[138]

Such expressions of support from the non-socialist opposition notwithstanding, Palme's speech naturally received the warmest response from the

Swedish left – including the far left, whose support for Palme only inten-sified once Nixon's sanctions became public knowledge.[139] In the face of Nixon's retaliation, the SKfV immediately rallied around Palme,[140] and so did the Communists, who angrily complained about the Americans' at-tempt to silence Sweden.[141] Palme's protest against the bombings was even endorsed by the DFFG, which declared that the government's Vietnam policy was at last beginning to come around.[142]

The Social Democratic press' enthusiastic backing of Palme's Christmas Speech only increased in the aftermath of the American sanctions.[143] This was also true of the Social Democratic response overall, which likewise was overwhelmingly supportive.[144] A majority of all of the messages that the Prime Minister's office received with regard to Palme's Christmas Speech came either from Social Democratic party districts, auxiliary organizations, voters, party activists, or trade unionists.[145] On 15 January 1973, an editorial in the Social Democratic *Västgöta-Demokraten* proclaimed that the party should take pride in Palme's outspoken stance against the war,[146] and most Social Democrats apparently agreed.

A poll taken in early 1973 revealed that 67 per cent of all Social Dem-ocratic respondents approved of the government's protests against the bom-bings, while only 13 per cent felt that the government had gone too far in its criticism of the Nixon administration. The same poll also showed that 57 per cent believed that the US was pursuing a wrong-headed policy in South East Asia. Internal enthusiasm for the government's position was of course highest among those voters' who strongly sympathized with the DRV/NLF,[147] yet the internal reaction to Palme's Christmas Speech makes clear that the cabinet's Vietnam stance resonated among Social Democrats of all ages and all walks of life. This policy's appeal was therefore no longer solely limited to a radical minority within the party. The events surrounding the Christmas bombings appear to have done much to broaden Palme's support within the SAP and to help him to cement his role as the party's new leader.

This was invaluable to Palme, whose leadership had been questioned following the 1970 election. Not only had he been held responsible for the party's electoral decline in 1970, but he was also held responsible for mounting economic difficulties at home. By early 1972 there were more and more signs of an internal crisis of confidence in Palme,[148] but his response to the Christmas bombings seems to have helped to reaffirm his standing within the party. When one reads through his personal correspondence from Social Democratic voters and party activists, many state that they had never been more proud to be Social Democrats.[149]

In short, this entire situation vastly strengthened Palme's internal stature. Again, this was probably not entirely attributable to Palme's anti-war posture per se, but to the Social Democrats' tradition of circling the wagons around their leader in times when the party was being attacked from without. This episode was no exception, and Nixon's heavy-handed conduct visibly invigorated the party cadre.

The SAP hierarchy, in turn, moved to channel the surge of domestic anti-war sentiments to the party's advantage. To this end, the Party Secretary, Sten Andersson, proposed that all five parliamentary parties join together to issue a joint resolution protesting the bombings.[150] After some haggling, the other parties eventually agreed to back a common declaration asking the US to desist from further military action, while concurrently urging both sides to return to the peace table. This entreaty was supplemented with a telegram to the United Nation's General Secretary, Kurt Waldheim, petitioning him to use his influence to bring about an immediate ceasefire.[151] Both the telegram and the petition were far more cautiously worded than Palme's Christmas Speech had been.

Despite the differences in tone between these various messages, by consenting to back a common resolution the other parties played right in to the Social Democrats' hands, pulling the opposition in behind the government's Vietnam policy. This, in effect, ensured that Palme's conflict with Nixon could not be capitalized upon by the three non-socialist parties because by signing this resolution they too became implicitly responsible for the Social Democratic administration's position on this issue.[152] (It must also be emphasized that the five-party negotiations regarding the resolution were completed before any of the other parties had gotten wind of Nixon's intention to punish Sweden – a point to which we will return.) Equally importantly, this Social Democratic initiative prevented anyone else from becoming the primary beneficiary of popular indignation against the bombings.[153]

This joint resolution calling for an immediate end to hostilities was supplemented with a nationwide campaign to collect signatures backing this demand. *Namninsamlingen*, as this effort was known, got underway on 29 December. In this instance, the SAP was borrowing a page from the DFFG, which had just recently concluded its own signature collection in support of an unconditional American withdrawal from Indochina.[154] The Social Democratic establishment hence was no longer just usurping the NLF-movement's DRV/NLF-friendly message, but also its methods of agitation. By adopting a forward position in response to these events, the SAP once again protected itself from being outflanked by its Marxist rivals.

Besides the five parliamentary parties, *Namninsamlingen* was also backed by the trade union movement, the federation of Swedish employers, and numerous charitable organizations.[155] Perhaps not surprisingly, the SKfV threw its full weight behind the campaign,[156] but so did DFFG – this in spite of the fact that it was not entirely pleased with the wording of the petition, which it considered to be too timid.[157] However, by participating in this effort the NLF-movement arguably let itself become co-opted by the Social Democrats,[158] and in the long run DFFG's energetic contribution to *Namninsamlingen* was almost certainly more of an asset to the Social Democratic establishment than to the Maoists.

Pretty much everyone to the left of the SAP stood behind this effort,[159] save for the Trotskyites and KFML(r) who were basically irrelevant.[160] This consensus, however, also extended to the right side of the political spectrum. Even the King, Gustaf VI Adolf – who was previously known to have disapproved of the government's Vietnam stance – endorsed the campaign.[161] Support for *Namninsamlingen* was also vocalized in vast parts of the non-socialist press, which, like its Social Democratic counterpart,[162] pleaded with its readers to sign the petitions.[163] Several prominent Center Party and Liberal parliamentarians furthermore personally participated in the task of gathering signatures, as did many of their Communist and Social Democratic colleagues, including Palme.[164] The campaign got off to an impressive start, collecting approximately 120,000 signatures the very first day.[165]

Aside from KFML(r) and the Trotskyites, the most vocal opponents of *Namninsamlingen* could be found on the extreme right. Small anti-Communist groups, like the Democratic Alliance, rejected this effort,[166] and in this they were joined by many Evangelical Christians, who – in contrast to the State Church[167] – similarly dissociated themselves from the campaign.[168] More significantly, a lot of Conservatives also harbored grave reservations about *Namninsamlingen*,[169] as did some on the right wing of the Liberal Party.[170] This reluctance was very detectable in the editorial pages of many Conservative papers,[171] which suspected that the petition drive was being shaped by Social Democratic party tactical considerations.[172] Sentiments to this effect were likewise expressed by quite a few Liberal and Center Party papers (even by some papers that had initially backed this effort).[173] Owing to these suspicions, the non-socialist press' attitude toward *Namninsamlingen* in many instances quickly cooled.[174]

Such antipathy was fueled by accusations that the collection process itself was tainted by widespread fraud because some people were allegedly signing the petition repeatedly.[175] There were, moreover, complaints about peer pressure to sign, particularly among school children, many of whom were too young to fully grasp what they were endorsing.[176] The Conservative leader Gösta Bohman rapidly became the main political conduit for this dissent.[177]

Bohman had objected to Palme's Holocaust analogy from the outset,[178] arguing that Palme's polemics had undermined the credibility of Swedish neutrality.[179] This view was soon seconded by the Conservative press, as well as by many right-leaning smaller rural Liberal papers, especially once the American sanctions were made public. The latter often surmised that Palme's Christmas Speech had been principally motivated by domestic considerations, and although none of these papers were willing to defend Nixon's reaction, many of them grumbled that Palme's conduct had done considerable harm to the country's national interests.[180]

As already suggested, such misgivings were especially pronounced among Conservatives. This is because they had entered the five-party talks surrounding the joint resolution with serious apprehensions, and they had only agreed to sign it after some modifications to the text had been made. (Specifically, Gösta Bohman had insisted that the North Vietnamese also be asked to return to the peace table so that the petition would not be unilaterally directed against the United States.) The Conservatives later claimed that this concession was a substantial victory.[181] If so, it was a rather hollow one.

The reality was that the Conservatives had been forced to sign the five-party resolution under duress, a development that the Social Democratic press did not hide its glee about.[182] When the Conservatives at first had wavered, they had been subjected to enormous pressure from the left,[183] and not least from the Social Democratic press.[184] *Aftonbladet* had gone so far as to label Gösta Bohman a security threat because of his supposed sensitivity to the Americans' point of view.[185] The Conservative leadership was indisputably on the defensive, and even some of its own followers demanded that the party sign the joint petition.[186] This put the party hierarchy in a tough position with little choice but to give in. In the current political climate, it would simply have been political suicide to refuse completely to participate in *Namninsamlingen,* and the fact that the Conservatives ultimately endorsed the resolution testifies to the strength of the radical political winds that were blowing across Sweden at the time.

All told, then, the Conservatives' ambivalence about the petition drive was rather understandable, and this feeling was only enhanced when it became known that the Social Democrats had failed to inform them about Nixon's sanctions during the five-party negotiations. The Conservatives deeply resented having been shanghaied by the government,[187] but there was not much that they could really do about it after the fact.

The Social Democrats were for their part quite pleased that their opponents had been forced to capitulate,[188] and they swiftly took to the offensive. The SAP leadership emphatically denied that its handling of this errand had been motivated by party tactical calculations.[189] Several Social Democratic papers expanded upon this assertion, declaring that, if anyone, it was the Conservatives who were playing politics with this issue.[190]

The SAP's intent was to try to politically isolate the Conservatives by seeking to drive a wedge into the non-socialist camp,[191] and to an extent this also impeded the Conservatives' ability to challenge the government's Vietnam stance. The Social Democrats' counter-offensive was greatly assisted by the Liberal press' eagerness to question the Conservatives' reluctance to fall in line behind the government.[192]

Outwardly the SAP leadership stated that it was not concerned about the Conservatives' obstinacy,[193] but privately there were some lingering worries that the non-socialist opposition might be able to exploit the government's falling out with the United States.[194] Behind close doors there was also a bit of anxiety about the Conservatives' contacts with the American Embassy, which Social Democratic officials were well aware of.[195]

Even so, very early on the Social Democrats understood that the Conservatives' criticism of the government was most likely to hurt the other two non-socialist parties.[196] This was mainly because the Center and Liberal Parties' own constituents had a far more negative attitude towards Palme's Christmas Speech than their respective members of parliament did. The earlier cited poll showed that 44 per cent of all Liberal voters and 45 per cent of all Center Party voters disapproved of the Social Democratic administration's general approach to the war. (The corresponding figure for Conservative voters was 68 per cent.) The same poll further made it clear that the average Liberal and Center Party voter was far less sympathetic toward the Vietnamese Communists than their Social Democratic equivalents.[197] This discrepancy consequently gave the Conservatives an opportunity to distinguish themselves vis-à-vis the other two non-socialist parties. Their opposition to the government in this area was also a good issue for the Conservatives because it had galvanized the party's own core supporters,[198] and the SAP hierarchy grasped that the Conservatives' objections to *Namninsamlingen* was mostly aimed at satisfying the party's own right wing.[199]

Although the Conservatives' persistent sniping at the government's Vietnam policy might well have strengthened its position within the non-socialist bloc,[200] it was equally apparent that they were not going to be able to use the diplomatic freeze against the Social Democrats. There were two main reasons for this. To begin with, this dispute had not adversely affected Swedish trade with the United States. Swedish–American commerce actually increased during the freeze,[201] thereby eliminating a potentially potent political weapon that the Conservatives might have utilized against the Social Democratic administration.

The second reason had to do with the Watergate scandal. Like elsewhere in Western Europe, Watergate severely damaged the Nixon's administration's image in Sweden. The combination of Watergate, the Christmas bombings, and the diplomatic freeze caused America's popularity ratings in Sweden to plummet, hitting a postwar low in 1973.[202]

Social Democratic leaders were cognizant that all of these factors had helped to protect the party from being harmed by the freeze.[203] To suggest that Watergate saved Palme would be an exaggeration, but it definitely made his domestic position much less precarious. If this scandal had not prematurely forced Nixon out of office, a prolonged dispute with Washington would surely have become a political burden for the SAP, and by extension also for Palme personally.

In the short term, however, the Social Democratic government's clash with the Nixon administration became almost a badge of honor for the party, particularly in light of Watergate. Nixon was already exceedingly unpopular among the Social Democratic faithful prior to the Christmas bombings,[204] and needless to say the President's popularity dropped even further after this.[205]

This being so, Palme's dispute with Nixon was not likely to harm the SAP electorally. Indeed, a number of different polls measuring the party's popularity ratings at the turn of 1972/1973 showed that popular sympathies for the Social Democrats had risen by several percentage points between November–December of 1972 and January–February of 1973.[206] While one cannot necessarily draw a direct causal connection between Nixon's sanctions and the SAP's improved standing in the polls, at a minimum these poll results suggest that the freeze did not hurt the Social Democrats politically. A survey of one thousand Swedish politicians taken in late February 1973 further revealed that most Social Democratic, Liberal, Communist, and

Center Party politicians believed that the government's Vietnam stance was going to help the SAP in the upcoming election.[207] Hence, it appears that the diplomatic freeze had the exact opposite effect than the one that the Nixon administration had hoped for. Instead of weakening Palme's domestic position, it had rallied the Swedish public behind the government.

Although the White House categorically denied it,[208] Nixon was plainly trying to undercut the Social Democratic administration by keeping the freeze in place until the 1973 election was over.[209] Some prominent Swedish businessmen and non-socialist politicians welcomed this approach, hoping that the freeze would injure the SAP at the polls.[210] Unfortunately for the non-socialist bloc, Nixon's tactics backfired and instead bolstered the Social Democrats' domestic popularity. By turning this into a conflict between the US and Sweden, the White House had inadvertently generated sympathy for Palme, even among many Swedes who normally did not support him.[211]

In this situation, the Conservatives could only go so far to challenge the Social Democrats without risking the appearance of siding with the Americans. Bohman's original expression of "understanding" for Nixon's reaction to Palme's Christmas Speech had placed his Conservative Party in a compromised position that the Social Democrats were quick to seize upon.[212] The SAP expressly sought to impugn the Conservatives' patriotism by characterizing them as susceptible to American pressure and, therefore, as unreliable.[213] Accusations to this effect pushed the Conservatives back on their heels, and Bohman was subsequently compelled to dissociate himself from the American sanctions.[214]

The Social Democrats were likewise successfully able to play the nationalism card directly against the United States,[215] and Nixon's punitive behavior allowed the government to cast itself in the gratifying role of David vs. Goliath.[216] This strategy required some tact so as not to additionally aggravate relations with the Americans, but the Social Democratic rank and file was very receptive to the party leadership's insistence that Sweden alone would determine its own foreign policy.[217] This message became central to the Social Democrats' propaganda throughout the 1973 election campaign.[218]

The idea that the government was standing up to the Americans was generally well received,[219] though it was of course especially popular among the Social Democratic faithful.[220] The SAP hierarchy actively encouraged these nationalist feelings. Olof Palme insisted that Sweden had made a substantial contribution to international opinion against the war, and by so doing the country had also played an instrumental role in bringing an end to the Christmas bombings.[221] Social Democratic spokesmen even ventured so far as to declare that Sweden had had a direct impact upon US Vietnam policy.[222] The party press likewise hailed the nation's supposedly leading role in fomenting worldwide opposition to the war, adding that the Social Democrats' anti-war protests had raised the country's international stature considerably.[223] According to this interpretation of events, Nixon's harsh reaction to Palme's Christmas Speech was evidence of Sweden's alleged importance.[224]

The validity of the above assertions is dubious at best, but at the time this mattered little, at least not for internal Social Democratic purposes. The government's dispute with Washington had re-energized the cadre, and the Social Democratic establishment realized that *Namninsamlingen* had unified the party, which in itself was of enormous value heading in to the upcoming September elections.[225] If anything, the SAP hierarchy believed that this entire chain of events had given the party a bounce in the polls, considerably brightening its electoral prospects. In addition, *Namninsamlingen* offered a welcome respite from a growing sense of economic malaise, and in the eyes of Social Democratic officials this whole episode had also helped to strengthen the party's ideological profile.[226]

For all of these reasons, the SAP leadership urged the party faithful to throw themselves into action in support of *Namninsamlingen*,[227] which they did.[228] A survey conducted by *Sveriges Radio* between 20 and 27 January indicated that 68 per cent of all Social Democratic sympathizers had already signed *Namninsamlingen*, and a full 96 per cent stated that they would do so if given the opportunity. In contrast, close to one-third of all Liberal and Center Party voters said they would not sign it, and the percentage of refuseniks was even higher among the Conservatives' supporters. Analyzing these figures, the SAP hierarchy concluded that *Namninsamlingen* had been an unqualified triumph for the party.[229]

At the time there was little dispute about this fact,[230] and this was also acknowledged by US government officials. Privately, American diplomats conceded that the Social Democrats had managed to turn the dispute with Washington to their advantage and that *Namninsamlingen* in effect had become a referendum in defense of the government's Vietnam position.[231] This interpretation was undoubtedly correct. By any standard *Namninsamlingen* was a colossal success, gathering approximately 2.6 million signatures in approximately one month's time.[232] Even leaving room for multiple signatures, this was a remarkable accomplishment considering that the size of the entire population in 1973 was just a bit over 8 million people.

Namninsamlingen was instantly followed by another Social Democratic initiative to collect money for North Vietnam. The funds would explicitly be used to repair the Bach Mai Children's Hospital in Hanoi that had been damaged by the recent American aerial attack.[233] The primary aim of this collection was to prevent the Social Democratic cadre from losing steam,[234] and in this it positively succeeded as the SAP and the Social Democratic trade union federation, LO, became the driving motor behind this new project.[235] The Bach Mai campaign was warmly received by the Social Democratic faithful[236] and was aggressively promoted by the party press, which pleaded with its readers to eagerly participate in this effort.[237]

This call was seconded by much of the Liberal and Center Party press,[238] and similarly to *Namninsamlingen*, the Bach Mai initiative was also officially co-sponsored by all five parliamentary parties, the trade unions, and by a number of different charitable organizations.[239] This new endeavor likewise received very strong backing from the SKfV and the DFFG.[240]

The Maoists, however, were not blind to the party tactical motives behind the Bach Mai collection.[241] It was also plain to see that the SAP was yet again mimicking DFFG's propaganda methods – or perhaps more precisely, the party was taking back older agitation techniques that had once belonged to the Social Democratic labor movement – and by so doing it diverted resources (and prestige) away from DFFG's collection for the NLF. As with *Namninsamlingen*, the Bach Mai campaign was a huge success, generating nearly 10 million crowns in donations by the time it was formally discontinued in August.[242] From a Social Democratic perspective, the main benefit of this effort was that the party had once more been able to draw Conservatives and Maoists alike in behind the government, thereby guaranteeing that it retained the initiative in relation to the Vietnam issue.[243] The SAP hierarchy moreover took care to satisfy Social Democratic antiwar activists by providing matching funds for the Bach Mai project out of the party's own treasury, as well as by offering additional government assistance to the PRR.[244]

The Bach Mai collection kept the Social Democratic cadre preoccupied for the next several months. Keeping the Vietnamese conflict at the top of the domestic political agenda, however, proved to be far more difficult once the final peace treaty had been signed in Paris at the end of March 1973. As soon as the last Americans withdrew from Saigon, the war was essentially over in most people's minds, and thereafter public interest in South East Asia rapidly waned.[245] The peace treaty therefore greatly reduced the Vietnam issue's domestic significance hereafter. Although Social Democratic leaders never completely stopped talking about Vietnam,[246] by the late spring this question no longer commanded much attention on the campaign trail, and the same can be said about the diplomatic freeze.

The 1973 Election and Making Amends with America

Instead of focusing on international relations and the war in Indochina, the 1973 election campaign highlighted a series of domestic problems, especially unemployment.[247] The SAP's election strategy was focused on beating the Center Party, and during the final months of the election campaign the party hierarchy did not appear to be overly concerned about either the Communists or the Maoists.[248] Generally speaking, Social Democrats' rhetoric was quite restrained, and the radical demands for increased domestic equality that had shaped the 1968 and 1970 election campaigns had now receded into the background. This more cautious approach was rooted in the belief that the election was going to be decided by moderate swing voters.[249] Even though the SAP's support in the polls had risen dramatically over the past year, it was still thought that the non-socialist opposition had a legitimate chance of unseating the Social Democrats, and the election was expected to be unusually close.[250]

The three non-socialist parties fell just short, and the election produced a 50/50 split between the two blocs, which constitutionally allowed the SAP to remain in office. However, the 1973 election proved be a harbinger of what was to come because it was the first tangible sign that the political winds had finally begun to shift rightward again. The Social Democrats would be ousted in the next election, but for now they had managed to hang on, staying in power with a very weak mandate due to continued Communist support in the parliament.[251]

The Conservatives and Center Party both made gains in the election, whereas the Liberals' electoral decline continued. On the left, VPK made modest headway at the Social Democrats' expense, while the two Maoist parties, KFML and KFML(r), had stalled at 0.6 per cent of the total vote. As for the Social Democrats, their share of the electorate had declined by 1.7 per cent since 1970, and the party had done alarmingly poorly among young voters – and especially among young, educated ones.[252] Nonetheless, the Social Democratic establishment considered the election to have been a victory in light of the party's terrible standings in the polls only a year earlier.[253] Foreign policy issues had not played a crucial part in the final outcome,[254] but this did not stop the SAP leadership from believing that its posture on Vietnam had been key to keeping the party in office.[255]

Having narrowly survived the election, the Social Democratic administration slowly set out to improve relations with the United States. By the late fall of 1973, Indochina had not yet completely disappeared from the domestic political horizon, but it had begun to fade more and more in to the background. This had the effect of significantly reducing the anti-war movement's influence, making it much easier for the government to take steps to restoring a better rapport with Washington.

An excellent example of this was the government's decision to prevent the Swedish Ambassador to Chile, Harald Edelstam, from speaking out against Washington's role in the overthrow of Salvador Allende's Socialist government.[256] Silencing Edelstam was a bit of a risky proposition for the Social Democratic administration because it was simultaneously seeking to capitalize upon popular indignation against Augusto Pinochet's coup.[257] In the end, the cabinet decided to prioritize re-normalizing relations with Washington over any short-term domestic gain that the SAP might have accrued from this situation. There could be little doubt now that the attainment of improved relations with the US now required sustained Swedish self-restraint.

Palme also clandestinely sought to regain American goodwill by trying to persuade Iceland to stay in NATO. The Swedes were well aware of the Americans' concerns regarding Iceland's threat to leave the alliance, and at the end of October Palme stressed the necessity of retaining American troops on the island to his Icelandic counterpart. Palme's intervention evidently succeeded, at least in the sense that his attempt to mediate pleased Washington.[258]

Another development that likewise served to ease tensions between Washington and Stockholm was Sven Andersson's appointment as the new Foreign Minister. Following the 1973 election, Palme reshuffled his cabinet, and Sven Andersson replaced Wickman. Anderson was a peculiar choice for the Foreign Minster post given that he was considered to belong to the party's right wing, and his personal relationship with Palme was not very good. He was furthermore known to be pro-American, and evidently disapproved of Palme's Vietnam stance.[259]

Prior to this appointment, Sven Andersson had served as the Minister of Defense from 1957 to 1973, so he was intimately informed about Sweden's clandestine military contacts with NATO.[260] During his tenure as Foreign Minister he did much to repair relations with the Americans,[261] and it is noteworthy that when he was first selected for this post the State Department regarded this as a sign that the Social Democratic administration was trying to make peace.[262] Without question this was an accurate interpretation of Andersson's reassignment, and he himself certainly seemed to have viewed it as such, later covertly passing on intelligence to the US about North Vietnamese troop movements.[263]

Sven Andersson's appointment, along with Palme's mediation attempt in the NATO–Iceland conflict, paved the way for a re-normalization of Swedish–American relations. Unlike Palme, however, Nixon was in no rush to sort this situation out because his energies were directed elsewhere, and, above all, towards saving his presidency from being dragged down by Watergate. Thus, it was only in the face of rising Congressional protests that he at last revised his position on Sweden.[264]

Although Palme's Holocaust analogy had originally put Sweden's friends on Capitol Hill in an awkward position, this became less and less of an issue as Watergate started to take its toll on the Nixon administration. As the President's domestic stature deteriorated, the US Congress stepped up its lobbying to revoke the sanctions against Sweden. Momentum for this end built over the summer and into the fall of 1973,[265] and resolutions were soon passed in both the House and the Senate calling for the freeze to be lifted.[266]

Because this pressure was not likely to disappear, the State Department recommended that full diplomatic relations be restored with Stockholm. In the State Department's judgment, once the Social Democrats had emerged victorious from the 1973 elections, there was little to be gained by sticking to this punitive approach.[267] The State Department's initial irritation with Palme notwithstanding, as 1973 wore on most American diplomats who were directly involved with this errand favored revoking the sanctions. To them, Nixon's behavior increasingly seemed petty, and even counterproductive to American interests.[268] In late November, Henry Kissinger likewise concluded that the time had come to reconsider Washington's present stance toward Stockholm. This assessment mostly stemmed from a desire to remove this issue as a source of conflict between the White House and the Congress, and over the next couple of months he sought to persuade the President to modify his attitude toward Sweden.[269] Apparently, Nixon was still very annoyed with Palme, but because the Congress was not about to relent, he eventually agreed to rescind the sanctions, and full relations between the two countries were finally restored in May 1974.[270]

* * *

Even though Congressional agitation was the principal impetus behind this policy shift, considerations about how the freeze was perceived internationally, and especially in Europe, also figured into the decision to renormalize relations with Sweden. Swedish diplomats had at a very early stage recognized that the Nixon administration's behavior vis-à-vis Sweden was ill at ease with the latter's proclaimed ambition to create a stronger partnership with Western Europe.[271] By the fall of 1973, both the State Department and the White House had also recognized this reality. Internal American diplomatic reports from this period repeatedly pointed out that Nixon's sanctions against Sweden were now a burden for the United States in its dealings with the rest of Western Europe.[272]

Here it has to be remembered that the international reaction to the Christmas bombings had been extremely negative, and the Swedes were by no means the only ones who had objected strongly to them. The resumption of US military operations against North Vietnam had created serious tensions with several other countries as well, particularly with India, Denmark, and Australia, who were all also briefly threatened with diplomatic sanctions. Holland, Finland, New Zealand, and Canada had likewise ended up on Nixon's black list because of their negative responses to the Christmas bombings.[273] In contrast to Sweden, however, these other countries were all soon removed from this list, and with some justification the Swedes felt that they were being singled out by the Nixon administration for the simple reason that it was easier politically for Washington to retaliate against them than against one of the American's formal Western European allies.[274]

Regardless of whether this was the case or not, the political ramifications of Nixon's sanctions towards the Social Democratic administration – both at home and abroad – was considerably reduced by the fact that the bombings had been so ill received elsewhere in Europe. The year 1973 represented the nadir in postwar US–West European relations, as was underscored by the complete fiasco of the White House's "Year of Europe" proposal.[275] In this political atmosphere, Stockholm's dispute with Washington did not harm Sweden's international reputation as much as it would have done under other normal circumstances.

Palme's strident condemnation of the Christmas bombings had received a lot of attention in Europe and had resonated strongly in the rest of Scandinavia where antipathy toward Nixon's Vietnam policy also ran very deep.[276] For this reason, resentment about the sanctions was most intense there, though similar sentiments were in evidence in other parts of the world as well.[277] Still, this did not generally translate into a desire to emulate the Swedish Social Democrats' approach to the war, and why this was so will be discussed in the next and final chapter.

Chapter 6: Notes

[1] Communist leader CH Hermansson as cited in *Riksdagsprotokollet* # 21, 29 April 1970, 71–73; Conservative Representative Ivar Virgin as cited in *Riksdagsprotokollet* # 22, 5 May 1970, 38.

[2] Bengt Liljenroth, "Vietnamrörelsen i Sverige" in Lars Torbiörnsson (ed.), *Tålamodets triumf* (Stockholm: Prisma, 1973) 242–243, 247; Birgitta Dahl, "Solidaritetsarbetet för Vietnam" in Enn Kokk (ed.), *Var blev ni av ljuva drömmar?* (Stockholm: Ordfront, 2002) 188–189.

[3] Editorial *Aftonbladet* 18 April 1970.

[4] According Birgitta Dahl, however, this internal bitterness about the DRV aid fiasco was directed more at Torsten Nilsson than at Palme. Dahl, interview with the author, 27 May 2004. Dahl was the SKfV Chairperson 1971–1977. Be this as it may, Palme was still burdened with this general problem.

[5] Hans Haste, *Boken om Palme* (Stockholm: Tiden, 1986) 49.

[6] Erik Svanfeldt, "Svenska kommittén för Vietnam" (University of Uppsala, 1990) 25; Björn Elmbrant and Erik Eriksson, *Det bidde en tumme* (Stockholm: Prisma, 1970) 99–114, 128–131.

[7] *Liberta*s # 1 1970, 3–5; Bengt Liljenroth's op-ed in *Aftonbladet* 4 April 1970.

[8] Social Democratic representative Lilly Hansson as cited *Riksdagsprotokollet* # 22, 5 May 1970, 88; Olof Palme as cited in *SAP Riksdagsgruppens protokoll* 21 April 1970.

[9] *Stockholms arbetarekommun. Årsmötesprotokoll.* 17–18 April 1970, 13–15, 21–23.

[10] Yngve Möller, *Sverige och Vietnamkriget* (Stockholm: Tiden, 1992) 214.

[11] Lars Bengtsson *et al.*, *Svenska partiapparater* (Stockholm: Bonnier, 1972) 235.

[12] Anna-Lisa Lewén-Eliasson and Torsten Hansson as cited in *SAP Riksdagsgruppens protokoll* 21 April 1970; SKSF, *Årsberättelse 1970*, 37–39. Here it should said that this "stick" had been preceded by "a carrot"– namely, a 50,000 crown party donation to the NLF. *Aftonbladet* 30 March 1970.

[13] CH Hermansson as cited in *Riksdagsprotokollet* # 22, 5 May 1970, 115–116. See also Bill # 366 in the Second Chamber of Parliament, and Bill # 334 in the First Chamber of parliament (*Riksdagsprotokollet. Motioner 1970*).

[14] Peter Esaiasson, *Svenska valkampanjer 1866–1988* (Stockholm: Allmänna Förlaget, 1990) 254–255.

[15] Kim Salomon, *Rebeller i takt med tiden* (Stockholm: Rabén Prisma, 1996) 171.

[16] *Arbetet* 10 April 1970. See also Sherman Adams as cited in *Aftonbladet* 19 April 1970. Sherman, an Afro-American political activist, confirmed that he indeed had referred to Holland as a "house nigger" – though not as a "nigger."

[17] DFFG spokesman, Sköld Peter Matthis as cited in *Svenska Dagbladet* 17 April 1970.

[18] *Dagens Nyheter* 28 April 1970; *Expressen* 24 May 1970.

[19] Åke Kilander, *Vietnam var nära* (Stockholm: Leopard 2007) 352–353.

[20] Mats Hellström, Birgitta Dahl and Olof Palme as cited in *SAP Riksdagsgruppens protokoll* 21 April 1970. See also Kaj Björk, *Vägen till Indokina* (Stockholm: Altas, 2003) 187–189.

[21] Palme cited in *Dagens Nyheter* 30 April 1970; Palme as cited in *Riksdagsprotokollet* # 21, 29 April 1970, 23.

[22] Social Democratic representative Sture Eriksson as cited in *Dagens Nyheter* 2 June 1970; Torsten Nilsson as cited in *Vi* # 37 1970, 14.

[23] Salomon, *Rebeller i takt med tiden*, 174–175.

[24] Sten Andersson and Lars Henriksson as cited in *SAP PS-protokoll* 21 May 1970; KFML, *Vad vill KFML?* (Uppsala: Marxistiskt Forum, 1970) 15–16.

[25] Salomon, *Rebeller i takt med tiden*, 156–157.

[26] Lars-Åke Augustsson and Stig Hansén, *De svenska maoisterna* (Göteborg: Lindelöws, 2001) 56–58.

[27] Christopher Sundgren, "Splittrad Solidaritet" in Maj-Lis Eriksson, *et al.* (eds.), *Med eller mot strömmen?* (Stockholm: Sober, 1980) 148.

[28] SAP, "Fakta och argument i valrörelsen" # 17 (Stockholm: SAP, 1970)

[29] Undated (ca. Aug. 1970.) Letter to the SAP leadership from SKfV Secretary Bertil Svanström. Svanström specifically asked about the party's intentions with regard to the DRV aid package and whether or not the SAP would back Swedish recognition of the PRR, the Provisional Revolutionary Government of South Vietnam. Svenska kommittén för Vietnam, Laos och Kambodja. 1568/E/1/2 Korrespondens. Vol 1970. 3077.

[30] Björk, *Vägen till Indokina*, 192.

[31] For a specific example, see Åke Petersson, "Centeridéer i utrikespolitiken" in Centerpartiet, *Samarbete och skiljelinjer* (Stockholm: LT:s Förlag, 1970) 160–161.

[32] Esaiasson, *Svenska valkampanjer 1866–1988*, 255, 257.

[33] Nils Elvander, *Skandinavisk arbetarrörelse* (Stockholm: Liber, 1980) 228–229.

[34] Esaiasson, *Svenska valkampanjer 1866–1988*, 258.

[35] Stig Hadenius, *Svensk politik under* 1900-*talet* (Stockholm: Tiden Athena, 1996) 162.

[36] Kjell Östberg, *1968* (Stockholm: Prisma, 2002) 126–131.

[37] Augustsson and Hansén, *De svenska maoisterna*, 56–60.

[38] Bo Särlvik, *Almänna valen 1970. Del 3* (Stockholm: SCB, 1973) 67–69; Elvander, *Skandinavisk arbetarrörelse*, 158–159, 180.

[39] Sven Olsson, "VPK 1968–1978" in Jan Engberg (ed.), *Utanför systemet* (Stockholm: Rabén & Sjögren, 1978) 181–184, 190–192. See also CH Hermansson, *CH Minnen* (Stockholm: Arena, 1993) 253–254.

[40] Hadenius, *Svensk politik under 1900-talet*,163; Särlvik, *Almänna valen 1970*. Del 3, 67–69.

[41] *SAP PS-protokoll* 30 Sept. 1970; *SAP PS-protokoll* 26 Nov. 1970. See also Olof Palme as cited in *SAP Riksdagsgruppens protokoll* 16 Oct. 1970.

[42] Enn Kokk, "Vart tog den där elden vägen" in Kokk (ed.), *Var blev ni av ljuva drömmar?*, 42.

[43] Lars Rudebeck "Ord och handling i regeringens Vietnampolitik" in *Tiden* # 8 1970, 457–468. See also Dahl, "Solidaritetsarbetet för Vietnam," 190–191.

44 Särlvik, *Almänna valen 1970. Del 3*, 68-70, 81-82, 95, 102, 105–106.

45 *SAP PS-protokoll* 21 Sept. 1973. See also Enn Kokk, *VPK och SKP* (Stockholm: Tiden, 1974) 89, 110–112.

46 Bosse Ringholm as cited in *SAP Riksdagsgruppens protokoll* 16 May 1972; Lars Engquist as cited in *SAP PS-protokoll* 29 Nov. 1973.

47 Särlvik, *Almänna valen 1970 Del 3*, 67–69, 103. See also Salomon, *Rebeller i takt med tiden*, 194–196.

48 *SAP VU-protokoll* 29 Sept. 1970; Olof Palme and Sten Andersson as cited in *SAP PS-protokoll* 26 Nov. 1970.

49 *SAP VU-protokoll* 24 Nov. 1970.

50 Kent Lindkvist, *Program och parti* (Lund: Studentlitteratur, 1982) 62–83; Olsson, "VPK 1968-1978," 188–197.

51 Bengtsson *et al.*, *Svenska partiapparter*, 292–294.

52 Editorial in *Tiden* # 7 1970, 443–444; Kokk, *VPK och SKP*, 24–27.

53 Östberg, *1968*, 124–125, 143–152; Elvander, *Skandinavisk arbetarrörelse*, 125–126.

54 Lasse Peterson, "KFML(r). På jakt efter en proletär identitet" in Engberg (ed.), *Utanför systemet*, 83–120.

55 Liljenroth, "Vietnamrörelsen i Sverige," 244.

56 Jan Engberg, "RMF/KAF: Visionen om den obefläckade fannan" in Engberg (ed.), *Utanför systemet*, 140–141.

57 Dahl, "Solidaritetsarbetet för Vietnam," 192–193; Svanfeldt, "Svenska Kommittén för Vietnam," 24, 29–33.

58 Magnus Jerneck, *Kritik som utrikespolitiskt medel* (Lund: Dialogus, 1983) 162–163; James Waite, "Sweden and the Vietnam Criticism" *Southeast Asia* 1973 2(4): 455–459.

59 Möller, *Sverige och Vietnamkriget*, 260–271. For a specific example, see *Frihet* # 3 1972, 7.

60 *Utrikesfrågor 1972*, 170–172, 175–186. For specific illustrations, see Ingvar Carlsson as cited in *Dagens Nyheter* 18 May 1972 and Olof Palme as cited in the *New York Times* 8 June 1972.

61 *Dagens Nyheter* 17 April 1972.

62 Tommy Hammarström, *FNL i Sverige* (Stockholm: AB Solidaritet, 1975) 140–147.

63 Conservative representatives Anders Björk, Nils Carlshammre, and Anders Wikjman as cited in *Svenska Dagbladet* 19 April 1972.

64 Salomon, *Rebeller i takt med tiden*, 310–312; Kilander, *Vietnam var nära*, 354–358.

65 Östberg, *1968*, 153, 165. A 1973 poll notably showed that 34% of all Swedish voters thought that the DRV/NLF was the "most right" in the Vietnamese conflict, whereas only 13% felt that the US/GVN was the "most right." The corresponding numbers for Social Democratic respondents were even more favorable to the DRV/NLF – 45% versus 7% for the US/GVN. Olof Petersson, *Väljarna och världspolitiken* (Stockholm: Norstedt, 1982) 78–80.

66 Ann-Marie Ekengren, *Av hänsyn till folkrätten?* (Stockholm: Nerenius & Santérus, 1999) 139, 143.

67 *Stockholms arbetarekommun. Verksamhetsberättelse 1972*, 7–10, 14–16.

[68] Björk, *Vägen till Indokina*, 208.

[69] Olof Palme as cited in *SAP Kongressprotokoll # I*. SAP 25:e Kongress. 30 Sept.–7 Oct. 1972, 13; Torsten Nilsson as cited in *Arbetet* 4 Oct. 1972.

[70] Krister Wickman as cited in *SAP Kongressprotokoll # II*. SAP 25:e Kongress. 30 Sept.–7 Oct 1972, 838–840.

[71] SAP, *Solidaritet för trygghet. Sammanfatting av Socialdemokraternas 25:e ordinarie kongress*. 30 Sept.–7 Oct. 1972, 19.

[72] *Stockholms arbetarekommun. Verksamhetsberättelse 1972*, 19, 39. See also Björk, *Vägen till Indokina*, 208.

[73] For specific illustrations, see Birgitta Dahl as cited in *Arbetet* 3 Oct. 1972 and editorial in *Aftonbladet* 7 Oct. 1972.

[74] For an overview of the motions calling upon the government to recognize the PRR, see *SAP Kongressprotokoll. Motioner II*. SAP 25:e Kongress. 30 Sept.–7 Oct 1972, 744–750.

[75] Hadenius, *Svensk politik under 1900-talet*, 163–164.

[76] For a specific illustrations, see *Tiden # 10* 1972, 545–548. and *Fackföreningsrörelsen # 11* 1972, 2, 7.

[77] *Arbetet* 14 Oct. 1972; *Norrskensflamman* 14 Oct. 1972.

[78] Leif Leifland, *Frostens år* (Stockholm: Nerenius & Santérus, 1997) 19–20, 27–30.

[79] *Ny Dag* 20 Dec. 1972; *Svenska Dagbladet* 21 Dec. 1972.

[80] *SKSF Årsberättelse 1972–1974*, 29–30; *SSKF Årsberättelse 1972*, 90.

[81] 19 Dec. 1972. SKfV Press release. "Open letter to the government." Svenska kommittén för Vietnam, Laos och Kambodja. 1568/F/1/9. Handlingar Rörande Indokina. Vol 1967–1973. 3077. See also the editorial in *Västerbottens Folkblad* 22 Dec. 1972.

[82] Wickman as cited in UD, *Utrikesfrågor 1972* (Stockholm: UD, 1972) 186.

[83] Palme as cited in UD, *Utrikesfrågor 1972*, 186–187.

[84] Harry Schein as cited by Tom Alandh and Birgitta Zachrisson, *Berättelser om Palme* (Stockholm: Norstedt, 1999) 224; Sverker Åström, *Ögonblick* (Stockholm: Bonnier Alba, 1992) 123–124.

[85] Björk, *Vägen till Indokina*, 211.

[86] Just as Palme had earlier acted the part of radical firebrand in relation to Vietnam in Erlander's cabinet, Ingvar Carlsson (and others) would later play a similar role once Palme succeded Erlander. During an anti-war rally in Stockholm on 17 May 1972, Carlsson, for example, excoriated the Nixon administration by stating that the US war effort: "is evidence of America's current state of moral bankruptcy." Carlsson as cited in *Dagens Nyheter* 18 May 1972.

[87] This was confirmed by Sten Andersson, SAP Party Secretary 1963–1982. Andersson states that it would have been impossible for Palme to remain quiet about the bombings in light of the outrage that the attack had provoked within the party. Andersson interview with the author 27 May 2004.

[88] Thage G. Peterson, *Resan mot mars* (Stockholm: Bonnier, 1999) 200–205; Sven Aspling, *Med Erlander och Palme* (Stockholm: Hjalmarson & Högberg, 1999) 155, 158.

[89] Specifically, Bertil Zachrisson became the new Minister of Education, while Palme loyalist Ingvar Carlsson was moved to the Minister of Housing post, and finally Anna-Greta Leijon was made a Minister Without Portfolio. Birgitta Dahl eventually also became a member of Palme's cabinet.

[90] Peterson, *Resan mot mars*, 196–197. See also Sverker Åström's op-ed in *Svenska Dagbladet* 28 April 1997.

[91] See, for example, Alvin Shuster's op-ed in the *New York Times* 9 Jan. 1973.

[92] For specific illustrations, see remarks by Senator Hugh Scott in the Congr. Rec. 93rd Congr., 1st Sess. 11 Jan. 1973: S 736. and Representative Philip Crane in the Congr. Rec. 93rd Congr., 1st Sess. 8 March 1973: E 1414–1416. See also William Buckley Jr's op-ed in the *Washington Evening Star* 11 Jan. 1973.

[93] Henry Kissinger, *The White House Years* (Boston: Little Brown, 1979) 1453.

[94] Staffan Thorsell, *Sverige i Vita Huset* (Stockholm: Bonnier Fakta, 2004) 143–144, 179–180.

[95] Alexis U. Johnson, *The Right Hand of Power* (Englewood Cliffs, NJ: Prentice-Hall, 1984) 539; Leifland, *Frostens år*, 15–17, 41–45.

[96] For an in-depth overview of the chronological narrative of the freeze, see Leifland, *Frostens år*, 76–94. See also Jan Eliasson as cited by Alandh and Zachrisson, *Berättelser om Palme*, 140–141.

[97] 14 Feb. 1974. Leif Leifland. Memo to Sven Andersson. Re: "Frostens år: de svensk-amerikanska förbindelserna under 1973." Avd HP. Grupp 1. Mål Ua. Politik Allmänt. USA # 270.

[98] SOU, *Fred och säkerhet* (SOU 2002: 108) 284–285.

[99] 8 Jan. 1973. Secretary of State. William Rogers. Memo to the President. Nixon Project. White House Special Files. 1969–1974. Country File: Sweden. Box 9. See also Henry Kissinger as cited in Peter Antman and Pierre Schori, *Olof Palme* (Stockholm: Tiden, 1996) 132.

[100] John Owens. Desk Officer for Sweden and Finland 1972–1974. European Section Dept. of State. Georgetown University. Oral History Collection, 57–58; Anders Thunborg, the former SAP International Secretary and Undersecretary of Defense, 1974–1979. Thunborg interview with author 4 May 2003. See also SOU, *Fred och säkerhet*, 268, 285–286.

[101] Leifland, *Frostens år*, 51–54, 61.

[102] Palme's personal message to Nixon as cited in UD, *Utrikesfrågor 1972*, 187.

[103] Sverker Åström, the former Undersecretary of State, interview with the author, 6 May 2000.

[104] Björk, Vägen till Indokina, 211–212; Möller, Sverige och Vietnamkriget, 301, 364.

[105] Anders Thunborg interview with the author 4 May 2003; Åström interview with the author 6 May 2000.

[106] Åström, *Ögonblick*, 124. This was also confirmed by Lennart Klackenberg, a former official within the Ministry of Finance. Klackenberg interview with the author 8 May 2003.

[107] Jan Mårtensson, *Att kyssa ett träd* (Stockholm: Wahlström & Widstrand, 2000) 193–194. See also Hubert de Besche as cited in *Dagens Nyheter* 31 Dec. 1972.

[108] Leifland, *Frostens år*, 159–160.

[109] Sverker Åström interview with the author 6 May 2000.

[110] 5 Jan. 1973. European Section Dept. of State. Russel Fessanden. Memo to the Secretary of State William Rogers. Re: Relations with Sweden. Subject Numeric Files 1970-1973. Political and Defense. Sweden. RG 59.

[111] 13 Jan. 1973. Special Advisor to the President. Henry Kissinger. Memo to the President. Nixon Project. White House Special Files. 1969-1974. Country File: Sweden. Box 9.

[112] New York Times 30 Dec. 1972; Baltimore Sun 30 Dec. 1972; Washington Post 30 Dec. 1972.

[113] Möller, Sverige och Vietnamkriget, 305, 364.

[114] 2 March 1973. Leif Leifland. Telegram to FM. Avd HP. Grupp 1. Mål Ua. Politik Allmänt. USA # 257.

[115] 3 Jan. 1973. Hubert de Besche. Telegram to FM. Re: Today's meeting with Alexis U. Johnson. Avd HP. Grupp 1. Mål Ua. Politik Allmänt. USA # 255.

[116] 13 Jan. 1973. Henry Kissinger. Memo to the President. Nixon Project. White House Special Files. 1969-1974. Country File: Sweden. Box 9; 2 March 1973. Leif Leifland. Memo. Re: Meeting with State Department Officer Richard Pedersen on 28 Feb. 1973. Avd HP. Grupp 1. Mål Ua. Politik Allmänt. USA # 257.

[117] 22 March 1973. Arthur Olsen. Telegram to State. Subject Numeric Files 1970-1973. Political and Defense. Sweden. RG 59; 21 Aug. 1973. Walter Stoessel, Jr. Memo to the Secretary of State. Subject Numeric Files 1970-1973. Political and Defense. Sweden. RG 59.

[118] Möller, Sverige och Vietnamkriget, 323.

[119] Palme as cited in Time Magazine 29 Jan. 1973; Palme as cited in Aftonbladet 18 Aug. 1973.

[120] Wickman as cited in Riksdagsprotokollet # 6, 18 Jan. 1973, 6-7; Wickman as cited in Riksdagsprotokollet # 13, 31 Jan. 1973, 5-7.

[121] Palme. "Today Show." NBC. 17 Aug. 1973. Television. (Trascript as found in Avd HP. Grupp 1. Mål Ua. Politik Allmänt. USA # 264.) See also Palme as cited in Riksdagsprotokollet # 48, 21 March 1973, 51.

[122] Palme as cited in New York Times 8 Jan. 1973.

[123] In the face of Conservative criticsm, Palme felt compelled to reiterate his opposition to the bombings. Palme and Gösta Bohman as cited in Riksdagsprotokollet # 48, 21 March 1973, 31-34, 48-49, 54-58.

[124] John Owens. Georgetown University. Oral History Collection, 55.

[125] SOU, Fred och säkerhet, 283-288; Yngve Möller, Mina tre liv (Stockholm: Tiden, 1983) 306.

[126] Dagens Nyheter 27 Dec. 1972; Värmlands Folkblad 2 Jan. 1973; Söderhamns-Hälsinge-kuriren 2 Jan. 1973.

[127] For a specific illustration, see Center Party politicians Torbjörn Fälldin, Johannes Antonsson and Torsten Bengtsson as cited in Riksdagsprotokollet # 13, 31 Jan. 1973, 13, 83-84, 126.

[128] Dahl as cited in Aftonbladet 26 Dec. 1972.

[129] See, for instance, an anti-war petition signed by 40 prominent Swedish writers in Dagens Nyheter 18 Jan. 1973. See also articles about Church-based opposition to US Vietnam policy in Expressen 11 Jan. 1973 and Vår Kyrka 18 Jan. 1973. Even the King joined in these protests. Gustaf VI Adolf as cited in the New York Times 12 Jan. 1973.

[130] Editorial in *Aftonbladet* 28 Jan. 1973.

[131] Statsministerns Korrespondens. "Brev med anledning av Vietnamuttalandet." Vol. 110–111, 114–119. Statsrådsberedningens Arkiv. E1 1972–1973.

[132] Center Party Leader Torbjörn Fälldin and Liberal Party Secretary Carl Tham as cited in *Aftonbladet* 27 Dec. 1972.

[133] Liberal leader Gunnar Helén as cited in *Riksdagsprotokollet* # 13, 31 Jan. 1973, 30–31. See also Liberal representative Per Ahlmark's op-ed in *Expressen* 6 Jan. 1973.

[134] Krister Wickman and Per Ahlmark as cited in *Rikdagsprotokollet* # 6, 18 Jan. 1973, 6–7; Torbjörn Fälldin and Gunnar Helén as cited in *Riksdagsprotokollet* # 48, 21 March 1973, 16–17, 20–21.

[135] Bohman as cited in *Expressen* Dec. 30 1972.

[136] See editorials in *Hallands Nyheter* 28 Dec. 1972, *Hudiksvalls Tidning* 29 Dec. 1972, *Nerikes Allehanda* 2 Jan. 1973 and *Eskilstuna-Kuriren* 2 Jan. 1973.

[137] See, for instance, editorials in *Göteborgs-Posten* 31 Dec. 1972, *Sydsvenska Dagbladet* 31 Dec. 1972 and *Expressen* 12 Jan. 1973.

[138] Editorials in *Dagens Nyheter* 29 Dec. 1972; 31 Dec. 1972; 3 Jan 1973 and 7 Jan. 1973.

[139] For a specific illustration, see CH Hermansson as cited in *Aftonbladet* 27 Dec. 1972. See also Sara Lidman's op-ed in *Aftonbladet* 11 Jan. 1973 and Evert Kumm's op-ed in *Nerikes Allehanda* 12 Jan. 1973.

[140] *Vietnam nu* # 7–8 1973, 15. See also Svanfeldt, "Svenska Kommittén för Vietnam," 30.

[141] Editorials in *Norrskensflamman* 28 Dec. 1972 and *Ny Dag* 29 Dec. 1972. See also Lars Werner as cited in *Riksdagsprotokollet* # 13, 31 Jan. 1973, 101–102.

[142] DFFG, "Solidaritet Sverige-Vietnam. Vietnamarbetet i Sverige januari-februari 1973." DFFG:s Skriftserie # 15 1973: 3.

[143] See, for instance, editorials in *Norrländska Socialdemokraten* 28 Dec. 1972, *Skånska Dagbladet* 16 Jan. 1973 and *Folkbladet Östgöten* 18 Jan. 1973.

[144] Among those who identified themselves as Social Democrats, I only found one person, "K.J.S." who objected to Palme's speech. This 85-year-old party member specifically worried about Palme's unwillingness to apologize to the United States. 14 Feb. 1973. Statsministerns Korrespondens. "Brev med anledning av Vietnamuttalandet." Vol. 110–111, 114–119. Statsrådsberedningens Arkiv. E1 1972–1973.

[145] Statsministerns Korrespondens. "Brev med anledning av Vietnamuttalandet." Vol. 110–111, 114–119. Statsrådsberedningens Arkiv. E1 1972–1973. See also articles about various local SAP chapters' support for the government's Vietnam stance in *Värmlands Folkblad* 3 Jan. 1973 and March 27 1973.

[146] Editorial in *Västgöta-Demokraten* 15 Jan. 1973. Likeminded sentiments were heard from other Social Democratic papers as well. See, for instance, editorial in *Folket* 25 Jan. 1973.

[147] Petersson, *Väljarna och världspolitiken*, 78–81, 104. Here it should be added that 4% of the party's voters, conversely, thought that the government had *not gone far enough* in its opposition to US Vietnam policy.

[148] Haste, *Boken om Palme*, 48–55.

[149] Statsministerns Korrespondens. "Brev med anledning av Vietnamuttalandet." Vol. 110–111, 114–119. Statsrådsberedningens Arkiv. E1 1972–1973.

[150] Dagens Nyheter 24 Dec. 1972.

[151] Copies of both the petition and the telegram as cited in UD, Utrikesfrågor 1972, 188–189.

[152] Björk, Vägen till Indokina, 212.

[153] Sten Andersson as cited in SAP PS-protokoll 8 Jan. 1973; Olof Palme as cited in SAP Riksdagsgruppens protokoll 10 Jan. 1973.

[154] Dagens Nyheter 31 Oct. 1972.

[155] Sten Andersson as cited in Aktuellt # 1 1973, 21. See also Svenska Dagbladet 29 Dec. 1972.

[156] SKfV Verksamhetsberättelse 1973. Svenska kommittén för Vietnam, Laos och Kambodja. 1568/F/1/9. Handlingar rörande Indokina. Vol 1967–1973. 3077. See also Dagens Nyheter 30 Dec. 1972

[157] DFFG, "Solidaritet Sverige–Vietnam. Vietnamarbetet i Sverige januari–februari 1973." DFFG:s Skriftserie # 15 1973: 14–20.

[158] Sten Andersson, I de lugnaste vatten... (Stockholm: Tiden, 1993) 258–262. Privately, Andersson was quite pleased that the DFFG had fallen in line behind Namninsamlingen.

[159] For examples of Communist support for Namninsamlingen, see Norrskensflamman 28 Dec. 1972 and Ny Dag 5 Jan 1973. For illustrations of KFML and Syndicalist support, see articles in Arbetaren 5 Jan. 1973 and Aftonbladet 6 Jan. 1973.

[160] Editorials in Mullvaden # 17 1973, 1. and Soldattidningen # 2 1973, 2.

[161] Åke Ortmark, De okända makthavarna (Stockholm: Wahlström & Widstrand, 1969) 146–149; Ulf Bjereld and Marie Demker, Utrikespolitiken som slagfält (Stockholm: Nerenius & Santérus, 1995) 280, 395 fn. # 307.

[162] See, for example, editorials in Gotlands Folkblad 3 Jan. 1973 and Smålands Folkblad 16 Jan. 1973.

[163] See, for instance, editorials in Östgöta Correspondenten 28 Dec. 1972, Hudiksvalls Tidning 29 Dec. 1972 and Skånska Dagbladet 2 Jan. 1973.

[164] Se # 2 1973, 16–19.

[165] Aftonbladet 30 Dec. 1972.

[166] Democratic Alliance spokesman Anders Larsson as cited in Dagens Nyheter 30 Dec. 1972.

[167] Arch Bishop Olof Sundby as cited in Dagens Nyheter 29 Dec. 1972. See also editorial in Vår Kyrka 11 Jan. 1973.

[168] Editorial in Dagen 11 Jan. 1973. See also Pastor Lewi Pethrus as cited in Aftonbladet 29 Dec. 1972.

[169] For a specific example, see Gösta Bohman as cited in Riksdagsprotokollet # 13, 31 Jan. 1973, 33–34.

[170] See, for instance, Sven Wedén's op-ed in Eskilstuna-Kuriren 10 Jan. 1973.

[171] Editorials in Nya Wermlands-Tidningen 29 Dec. 1972 and Norrköpings Tidningar 29 Dec. 1972.

[172] Editorials in Barometern 28 Dec 1972, Borås Tidning 29 Dec. 1972 and Svenska Dagbladet 29 Dec. 1972.

[173] Editorials in *Sydsvenska Dagbladet* 7 Jan. 1973, *Göteborgs handels- och sjöfartstidning* 8 Jan. 1973, *Hudiksvalls Tidning* 9 Jan. 1973 and *Gotlänningen* 10 Jan. 1973.

[174] See, for instance, editorials in *Helsingborgs Dagblad* 7 Jan. 1973, *Borås Tidning* 9 Jan. 1973, and *Västernorrlands Allehanda* 12 Jan. 1973.

[175] For a specific illustration, see Ingemar Larsson's op-ed in *Kvällsposten* 10 Jan. 1973.

[176] See, for instance, editorials in *Upsala Nya Tidning* 8 Jan 1973, *Helsingborgs Dagblad* 10 Jan. 1973, and *Barometern* 15 Jan. 1973.

[177] For a specific example, see Bohman's op-ed in *Dagens Nyheter* 13 Jan. 1973.

[178] Bohman as cited in *Dagens Nyheter* 24 Dec. 1972.

[179] Bohman as cited in *Aftonbladet* 27 Dec. 1972.

[180] See, for example, editorials in *Upsala Nya Tidning* 28 Dec. 1972, *Svenska Dagbladet* 31 Dec. 1972, and *Vestmalands Läns Tidning* 2 Jan. 1973.

[181] Gösta Bohman as cited in *Expressen* 29 Dec. 1972.

[182] For specific examples, see editorials in *Länstidningen Östersund* 29 Dec. 1972, *Nya Norrland* 29 Dec. 1972 and *Aftonbladet* 30 Dec. 1972.

[183] For a specific example, see SKfV Chairperson Birgitta Dahl's open letter to Gösta Bohman in *Aftonbladet* 28 Dec. 1972.

[184] See, for example, editorials in *Västgöta-Demokraten* 27 Dec. 1972, *Kronobergaren* 28 Dec. 1972 and *Dagbladet Nya Samhället Sundsvall* 28 Dec. 1972.

[185] Editorial in *Aftonbladet* 28 Dec. 1972.

[186] *Svenska Dagbladet* 29 Dec. 1972. See also Gösta Bohman, *Så var det* (Stockholm: Bonnier 1983) 173.

[187] For a specific example, see Allan Hernelius as cited in *Riksdagsprotokollet* # 13, 31 Jan. 1973, 132–133. See also editorials in *Borås Tidning* 31 Dec. 1972, *Barometern* 2 Jan. 1973. and *Helsingborgs Dagblad* 3 Jan. 1973.

[188] Andersson, *I de lugnaste vatten…*, 258–262.

[189] For specific illustrations, see Olof Palme as cited in *Aftonbladet* 4 Jan. 1973 and Sten Andersson's letter to the editor in *Svenska Dagbladet* 10 Jan. 1973.

[190] Editorials in *Dagbladet Nya Samhället Sundsvall* 29 Dec. 1972 and *Folkbladet Östgöten* 8 Jan. 1973.

[191] See, for instance, Krister Wickman and Olof Palme as cited in *Riksdagsprotokollet* # 48, 21 March 1973, 44–46, 55–62. See also editorials in *Värmlands Folkblad* 3 Jan. 1973 and *Aftonbladet* 12 Jan. 1973.

[192] See, for instance, editorials in *Nerikes Allehanda* 27 Dec. 1972, *Blekinge Läns Tidning* 28 Dec. 1972 and *Dagens Nyheter* 3 Jan. 1973.

[193] Olof Palme as cited in *Dagens Nyheter* 29 Dec. 1972; Sten Anderson as cited in *Aftonbladet* 3 Jan. 1973.

[194] Palme as cited in *SAP PS-protokoll* 26 April 1973; Internal discussion within the SAP hierarchy as cited in *SAP PS-protokoll* 18 June 1973. Even prior to Nixon's sanctions becoming publicly known, Palme specifically wanted make sure that the Conservatives signed the joint manifesto. Palme as cited in *SAP VU-protokoll* 27 Dec. 1972.

[195] Olof Palme as cited in *SAP Riksdagsgruppens protokoll* 10 April 1973. See also *Dagens Nyheter* 3 March 1997.

[196] Sten Andersson as cited in *SAP PS-protokoll* 8 Jan 1973.

[197] Petersson *Väljarna och världspolitiken*, 79. Only 24% of all Center Party voters felt that the DRV/NLF was the "most right" in the Vietnamese conflict. The corresponding figure for Liberal voters was 25%, which was a lot lower level of support than among Social Democrats.

[198] Bjereld and Demker, *Utrikespolitiken som slagfält*, 294–297. See also Bohman, *Så var det*, 160, 184, 195.

[199] Olof Palme as cited in *SAP PS-protokoll* 18 June 1973.

[200] The Conservatives' dissent against the government's Vietnam policy probably helped them to make inroads among more conservative–leaning Liberals. In the 1973 election, the Conservatives' share of the electorate went up by 3.2%, while Liberals' share declined by 6.8%, and it was clear that the Conservatives had made gains at the Liberals' expense. Petersson and Särlvik, *Valet 1973. Del 3*, 66, 68, 79.

[201] Leifland, *Frostens år*, 99–103. Between 1972 and 1974, American exports to Sweden jumped from 2,764 to 4,595 million crowns per year, and Swedish exports to the US increased from 2,937 to 3,742 million crowns per year. *Statistisk årsbok för Sverige 1973*, 154; *Statistisk årsbok för Sverige 1974*, 162.

[202] Sten Ottoson, *Sverige mellan öst och väst* (Stockholm: Utrikespolitiska Institutet, 2003) 38; Mikael Gilljam and Sören Holmberg, *Väljare och val i Sverige* (Stockholm: Bonnier, 1987) 279.

[203] Leifland, *Frostens år*, 158.

[204] For a specific illustration, see poll of *Aftonbladet's* readers in *Aftonbladet* 9 Nov. 1972.

[205] *Aftonbladet* 23 Dec. 1972. See also editorial in *Arbetet* 24 Dec. 1972.

[206] Sören Holmberg and Olof Petersson, *Inom felmarginalen* (Stockholm: Liber, 1980) 246–251.

[207] *Dagens Nyheter* 5 March 1973.

[208] For a specific illustration, see the US Secretary of State, William Rogers as cited in the *Washington Post* 6 June 1972.

[209] Möller, *Sverige och Vietnamkriget*, 323–324.

[210] Leifland, *Frostens år*, 83.

[211] For a specific illustration, see the Director of *Skandinaviska Enskilda Banken*, Lars Eric Thunholm, as cited in *Svenska Dagbladet* 9 Jan. 1973.

[212] See, for example, Gudrun Helto's column in *Aftonbladet* 27 Dec. 1972. See also editorials in *Norrländska Socialdemokraten* 28 Dec. 1972, *Västgöta-Demokraten* 29 Dec. 1972 and *Värmlands Folkblad* 18 Jan. 1973.

[213] Olof Palme as cited in *Riksdagsprotokollet* # 48, 21 March 1973, 55–57. See also *Frihet* # 5 1973, 2–3.

[214] Gösta Bohman as cited in *Riksdagsprotokollet* # 48, 21 March 1973, 31–34, 58.

[215] See, for instance, Olof Palme as cited in *Göteborgs-Tidningen* 31 Dec. 1972 and Krister Wickman as cited in *Svenska Dagbladet* 14 Jan. 1973. For similar arguments in the Social

Democratic press, see the editorials in *Örebro-Kuriren* 29 Dec. 1972, *Nya Norrland* 2 Jan. 1973, and *Dagbladet Nya Samhället Sundsvall* 15 Jan. 1973.

[216] Barbara Haskel, "Det moraliserande Sverige" *Internationella Studier* 1976 (1): 31–32.

[217] For a specific illustration, see the article about the enthusiastic response that Palme received in Malmö on 19 Aug. 1973. *Arbetet* 20 Aug. 1973.

[218] See, for example, Olof Palme as cited in *Aftonbladet* 18 Aug. 1973.

[219] For a specific illustration, see Karl Dovermalm's letter to the editor in *Expressen* 17 Jan. 1973.

[220] See, for example, editorials in *Västgöta-Demokraten* 15 Jan. 1973 and *Folket* 25 Jan. 1973.

[221] Palme cited in the *New York Times* 31 Dec. 1972; Palme as cited in *Expressen* 8 July 1973.

[222] Krister Wickman as cited in *Aftonbladet* 6 Jan. 1973; Sten Andersson as cited in *Aktuellt* # 1 1973, 21.

[223] Editorials in *Västerbottens Folkblad* 4 Jan. 1973, *Aftonbladet* 15 Jan. 1973, *Norrländska Socialdemokraten* 16 Jan. 1973. and *Värmlands Folkblad* 18 Jan. 1973.

[224] See, for example, editorials in *Västerbottens Folkblad* 28 Dec. 1972, *Arbetet* 29 Dec. 1972. and *Folkbladet Östgöten* 2 Jan. 1973.

[225] Sten Andersson and Anna-Lisa Lewén as cited in *SAP VU-protokoll* 27 Dec. 1972; Olof Palme as cited in *SAP Riksdagsgruppens protokoll* 10 Jan. 1973.

[226] Sten Andersson and Olof Palme as cited in *SAP PS-protokoll* 8 Jan. 1973; Sten Andersson and Olof Palme as cited in *SAP PS-protokoll* 16 Feb. 1973. See also Björn Elmbrant, *Palme* (Stockholm: Författarförlaget, 1989) 153.

[227] Olof Palme as cited in *SAP Riksdagsgruppens protokoll* 10 Jan. 1973.

[228] A letter (dated 11 Jan. 1973) to the SAP leadership from *Leksands Socialdemokratiska Kvinnoklubb* is a good example of this collective effort. The letter states that the club's members collected 447 signatures during a recent hockey game. SAP. Handlingar rörande andra länder. Vietnam. 1972–1976.

[229] Sten Andersson and Olof Palme as cited in *SAP PS-protokoll* 16 Feb. 1973. A copy of this survey can be found in SAP. Handlingar rörande andra länder. Vietnam. 1972–1976.

[230] For specific illustrations, see Ebbe Carlsson's column in *Göteborgs handels- och sjöfartstidning* 29 Dec. 1972 and Sture Lindmark's op-ed in *Svenska Dagbladet* 4 Jan. 1973.

[231] 24 Jan. 1973. Arthur Olsen. Telegram to State. Re: Election Year in Sweden – The Prelude. Subject Numeric Files 1970–1973. Political and Defense. Sweden. RG 59; 21 March 1973. Arthur Olsen. Telegram to State. Re: Sweden gears up for September election. Subject Numeric Files 1970–1973. Political and Defense. Sweden. RG 59.

[232] 6 Feb. 1973. Arne Kriström and Sune K. Johansson. "29 Dec. 1972 – 2 Feb. 1973. Sverige för fred i Vietnam." SAP. Handlingar rörande andra länder. Vietnam. 1972–1976.

[233] *Aftonbladet* 19 Jan. 1973.

[234] Sten Andersson and Olof Palme as cited in *SAP PS-protokoll* 16 Feb. 1973; Report by Ingvar Svanberg as found in *SAP Riksdagsgruppens protokoll* 6 March 1973.

[235] *Svenska Dagbladet* 10 Jan. 1973; *Fackföreningsrörelsen* # 5 1973, 4–5.

[236] For a specific example, see *Stockholms arbetarekommun. Verksamhetsberättelse 1973*, 21–22.

[237] See, for instance, editorials in *Dagbladet Nya Samhället Sundsvall* 17 Jan 1973, *Arbetarbladet* 25 Jan. 1973 and *Dala-Demokraten* 10 Feb. 1973.

[238] Editorials in *Skånska Dagbladet* 17 Jan. 1973, *Göteborgs-Posten* 20 Jan. 1973, *Gefle Dagblad* 25 Jan. 1973 and *Hallands Nyheter* 26 Jan. 1973.

[239] *Dagens Nyheter* 25 Jan. 1973; *Ny Dag* 9 Feb. 1973.

[240] Hammarström, *FNL i Sverige*, 172; Svanfeldt, "Svenska Kommittén för Vietnam," 31.

[241] DFFG, "Solidaritet Sverige–Vietnam. Vietnamarbetet i Sverige januari–februari 1973." DFFG:s Skriftserie # 15 1973: 22–24.

[242] 20 Aug. 1973. Kommittén för Bach Mai, "Verksamhetsberättelse och revisionsberättelse." SAP. Handlingar rörande andra länder. Vietnam. 1972–1976.

[243] Sten Andersson as cited in *SAP PS-protokoll* 16 Feb. 1973. See also Andersson, *I de lugnaste vatten...*, 262–264.

[244] Krister Wickman as cited in *SAP Riksdagsgruppens protokoll* 30 Jan. 1973. See also *Aftonbladet* 24 Jan. 1973.

[245] Henry Bäck, *Den utrikespolitiska dagsordningen* (Stockholm: Gotab, 1979) 48–49.

[246] For a specific example, see Olof Palme as cited in *Arbetet* 20 Aug. 1973.

[247] Esaiasson, *Svenska valkampanjer 1866–1988*, 259–260.

[248] *SAP Riksdagsgruppens protokoll* 1 June 1973.

[249] Elvander, *Skandinavisk arbetarrörelse*, 228–229.

[250] Stig Hadenius, *et al.*, *Sverige efter 1900* (Stockholm: Bonnier, 1993) 260–261.

[251] *Ibid.*, 261–262.

[252] Olof Petersson and Bo Särlvik, *Valet 1973. Del 3* (Stockholm: SCB, 1974) 64–67, 79–85, 88–89, 94. The final tally left the SAP with 43.6%, the VPK with 5.3%, the Conservatives with 14.3%, the Liberals with 9.4%, and the Center Party with 25.1% of the total vote. The Center Party was, once again, indisputably the biggest winner, increasing its share of the total electorate by 5%.

[253] Olof Palme as cited in *SAP Riksdagsgruppens protokoll* 30 Oct. 1973. The SAP hierarchy's relief about staying in power notwithstanding, following the election the leadership remained deeply concerned about the party's losses among young, educated voters. *SAP PS-protokoll* 21 Sept. 1973; *SAP PS-protokoll* 14 Feb. 1974.

[254] Petersson, *Väljare och världspolitiken*, 51. Exit polls showed that only 4% out of all Social Democratic voters had cast their ballots for the party because of its foreign policy positions.

[255] Andersson, *I de lugnaste vatten...*, 254. Andersson's claim here should probably be taken with a grain of salt given that he was the main architect behind *Namninsamlingen*.

[256] Harald Edelstam as cited in *Aftonbladet* 28 Feb. 1974. See also Möller, *Sverige och Vietnamkriget*, 327.

[257] Sten Andersson as cited in *SAP PS-protokoll* 21 Sept. 1973; Sten Andersson as cited in *SAP VU-protokoll* 29 Oct. 1973.

[258] Leifland, *Frostens år*, 163–165.

[259] Christer Isaksson, *Palme privat* (Stockholm: Ekerlids, 1995) 205–206; Leifland, *Frostens år*, 163, 180.

[260] Anders Thunborg as cited in *Svenska Dagbladet* 23 March 1998.

[261] Wilhelm Wachtmeister, *Som jag såg det* (Stockholm: Norstedt, 1996) 186–187. See also SOU, *Fred och säkerhet*, 692.

[262] 31 Oct. 1973. Deputy Ass. Secretary of European Affairs. George Springsteen. Memo to Secretary of State. Re: Swedish Cabinet Reshuffle. Subject Numeric Files 1970–1973. Political and Defense. Sweden. RG 59.

[263] Leifland, *Frostens år*, 188–189.

[264] See, for instance, Representative Donald Fraser, Congr. Rec. 93rd Congr., 1st Sess. 27 Feb. 1973: 5719. and Senator Hubert Humphrey, Congr. Rec. 93rd Congr., 1st Sess. 16 April 1973: S 7525–7526.

[265] Lars-Göran Stenelo, *The International Critic* (Lund: Studentlitteratur, 1984) 166–167; Jerneck, *Kritik som utrikespolitiskt medel*, 85–98.

[266] Senate Resolution # 149 (20 July 1973); House Resolution # 531 (2 Aug. 1973); "Hearing before the Subcommittee on Europe of the Committee on Foreign Affairs." House of Representatives. 93rd Cong., 1st Sess., 12 Sept. 1973: 1–7.

[267] 11 Oct. 1973. John Owens. Memo to the Secretary of State. Subject Numeric Files 1970–1973. Political and Defense. Sweden. RG 59; 15 Nov. 1973. Walter Stoessel. Memo to the Secretary of State. Subject Numeric Files 1970–1973. Political and Defense. Sweden. RG 59.

[268] John Owens. Georgetown University. Oral History Project, 55–56.

[269] 26 Nov. 1973. Henry Kissinger. Memo to the President. Nixon Project. White House Special Files. 1969–1974. Country File: Sweden. Box 9.

[270] For a complete overview of the diplomatic end game leading up to the re-normalization of Swedish–American relations, see Leif Leifland, *Frostens år*.

[271] 15 March 1973. Leif Leifland. Telegram to FM. Avd HP. Grupp 1. Mål Ua. Politik Allmänt. USA # 257.

[272] 11 Oct. 1973. Walter Stoessel, Jr. Memo to the Secretary of State. Subject Numeric Files 1970–1973. Political and Defense. Sweden. RG 59; 26 Nov. 1973; 24 Dec. 1973. Henry Kissinger. Memo to the President. Nixon Project. White House Special Files. 1969–1974. Country File: Sweden. Box 9.

[273] Kissinger, *The White House Years*, 1453–1454.

[274] Olof Palme as cited in the *International Herald Tribune* 10 Jan. 1973.

[275] Richard Barnet, *The Alliance: America, Europe, Japan* (New York: Simon and Schuster, 1983) 319–320; Lawrence Kaplan, *NATO and the US* (New York: Twayne Publishers, 1994) 114–119.

[276] Jussi Hanhimaki, *Scandinavia and the United States* (New York: Twayne Publishers, 1996) 104–105.

[277] Möller, *Sverige och Vietnamkriget*, 306–307. For specific examples, see the editorials in *Helsingin Sanomat* 28 Dec. 1972, the *Beirut Daily Star* 31 Dec. 1972, *Arbeiderbladet* 2 Jan. 1973, and the *Bangkok Post* 6 Jan. 1973.

Swedish Vietnam Policy Reconsidered

As was discussed in the preceding chapter, the international reaction to the Christmas bombings was overwhelmingly negative, and in Europe the war had never been very popular to begin with. From the very start, Western European leaders had objected to the American war effort on economic, political, and strategic grounds. These leaders had good reason to oppose the war because it threatened to fundamentally alter the global balance of power while at the same time igniting social unrest at home. Above all, the Vietnamese conflict confronted West European governments with a very difficult predicament, namely, how to placate rising domestic anti-war agitation without seriously jeopardizing relations with Washington. As a rule, they dissociated themselves from the war but avoided any overt public criticism of the United States.[1]

No so with Sweden, which, led by Olof Palme, quickly established itself as the most persistent and vocal non-Communist critique of the war, especially once De Gaulle withdrew from the international stage in 1969. The Social Democratic government additionally distinguished itself through its open sanctuary of American deserters and its economic assistance to, and political support for, the National Liberation Front and the Democratic Republic of Vietnam. Its backing of the Vietnamese Communist cause was unrivaled in the rest of the Western World, and even in Europe the Swedish Social Democrats' radicalness on the war stood out.[2]

Needless to say, the Swedish position on Vietnam was warmly received throughout the Communist world,[3] and many American and European anti-war activists likewise approved of it.[4] Beyond these select circles, how-ever, the Swedes' approach to the war was not viewed in a terribly favorable light elsewhere in Europe.[5] Indeed, even among other Social Democratic Parties, the Swedes' initiatives to aid the NLF/DRV normally found little official support, and on occasion their reaction to Swedish Vietnam policy was rather frosty.[6] Norway and Denmark were really the only exceptions to this rule, and there too sympathy for the Swedish course of action was not entirely unqualified.[7]

Unique in Western Europe: Sweden's Position on Vietnam and the Socialist Democratic Party's Tactics

In retrospect, scholars have attributed the Swedish Social Democrats' exceptional militancy on the Vietnam issue to the country's neutral status,[8] but this explanation alone is insufficient. Sweden's lack of formal political obligations to NATO undeniably gave it greater freedom of maneuver in world affairs than most of its West European neighbors enjoyed, though it must simultaneously be pointed out that no other European neutral country reacted to the war in the same way as Sweden. All of the other neutrals, while also privately skeptical of the American War effort, generally kept these reservations to themselves, and they certainly did not go out of their way to back the Vietnamese Communists.[9]

Sweden's unique response to the war was in all likelihood partially a by-product of its own historical experience of never having been invaded by the Soviet Union. This, for example, was not the case for Finland and Austria, where sympathies for the Vietnamese Communist cause were always bound to be tempered by their own lived experience of occupation. Similar reservations existed in Catholic Ireland where the papacy's fervent anti-Communism was likewise sure to dampen popular approval for the NLF/DRV.[10]

None of these sorts of concerns were present in postwar Sweden, and instead the origins of the Swedish Social Democrats' stance on the war must, first and foremost, be found in Swedish domestic politics. For starters, unlike their German and British counterparts, the Swedish Social Democrats had to contend with a newly revitalized Communist Party that was aggressively courting the young anti-war vote. In relation to the Vietnam issue at least, the Maoists were also a source of real concern because in Sweden the far left had much more of an impact on the public debate about the war than it did elsewhere in Europe. In Sweden, the main domestic argument about the war (at least after 1968) was really about the Maoists' methods of protesting and not so much about the latter's fundamental analysis of the Vietnamese conflict.[11] In other countries, such as West Germany, this was just not the case, and there the political mainstream systematically rejected the views of anti-war radicals.[12]

Also, in contrast to many other West European Social Democratically-oriented parties, including the West German SPD (Sozialdemokratische Partei Deutschlands) and the British Labour Party, the SAP did not have to be as concerned about how moderate swing voters might react if the party assumed an overly critical posture against the war because opinion polls consistently showed that the Swedish public was more deeply opposed to the American war effort than any of its West European counterparts. This was especially true from 1968 onwards, by which time the non-socialist opposition had all but capitulated in relation to the Vietnam issue.

Moreover, in most European countries the war simply was just not anywhere near as high up on the domestic political agenda as it was in Sweden. In Britain, for instance, anxieties over the situation in Northern Ireland were guaranteed to top any concerns about Vietnam, whereas in Italy public attention was predominantly directed at the nearly civil war-like conditions that had taken hold in the country by the late 1960s. Sweden did not have any of these kinds of pressing internal issues of its own, and so the Swedes appear to have been preoccupied with the Vietnamese conflict to an almost obsessive degree.[13]

These divergent European attitudes about the war were additionally rooted in profoundly different political domestic realities. During the 1960s most West European Social Democratic parties had drifted towards the political center in a bid to appeal to more middle class, white-collar professionals, and this more centrist approach usually inhibited a more openly critical stance against the United States. The SAP, however, adopted the exact opposite tact in order to ideologically reinvigorate itself and stay in office. Although it too hoped to expand the party's electoral base beyond blue-collar workers, the SAP did so by shifting leftwards instead. At the time, a radical political wind was blowing across all of the Western World, yet there were few places, if any, where it was felt as strongly as in Sweden. As a result, the entire political spectrum in Sweden was significantly pushed to the left.[14] It is solely in the context of this exceedingly radical political climate that the government's support for the Vietnamese Communists becomes comprehensible. To be sure, the American war effort was enormously unpopular in Norway and Denmark as well, but popular opposition to the war there paled in comparison to Sweden.[15] Only in Sweden did the Social Democrats risk being outflanked to the *right* on the Vietnam issue, and the Liberal and the Center Parties sought to match, if not outdo, VPK and SAP's labors to secure more economic assistance for the Vietnamese Communists. All of these factors thus served to inform the SAP hierarchy's unusual response to the war.

In short, then, the Swedish Social Democrats operated in a very different political atmosphere with regard to this issue than the majority of their Western European neighbors, and accordingly they had to be much more willing to oblige domestic dissent against the war. At the same time, however, this environment was largely of the SAP hierarchy's own making because, by playing to popular anti-war opinion, they also enhanced the Vietnamese conflict's domestic importance.

This peculiar set of political circumstances simply did not exist anywhere else, and this essentially accounts for the radicalness of the Swedish position on the war. It also explains why the Swedish approach to Vietnam did not gain much traction in the rest of Western Europe, save for in Norway and Denmark. Although the latter two countries followed Stockholm's lead on this issue up to a point,[16] neither Oslo nor Copenhagen was ultimately willing to risk open conflict with Washington over the war.[17] With this in mind, the Social Democratic claim that Sweden had made a crucial contribution to building international opposition to the war rings rather hollow.[18]

Even if the Swedish position on the war did not directly impact US policy in a significant way, does this automatically mean that it was a failure, as Yngve Möller has suggested?[19] In the opinion of this study – the answer is no, not necessarily. Here it must first be stressed that no other West European government had any real influence over Washington's handling of the war either.[20] Secondly, and more to the point, influencing US policy was never a main driving impetus behind the Swedish Social Democrats' vocal opposition to the war. This is not to say that the SAP hierarchy's contention that it wanted to render moral support to opponents of the war – both in the US and elsewhere – was completely insincere, but this was hardly the policy's primary purpose. Rather, as already implied, the Social Democratic administration's Vietnam posture was principally motivated by party tactical considerations, and this strategy was undeniably quite successful, at least in the short term.

Again, the SAP's main priority was to stay in power, and its leftward shift – as exemplified by its militancy on the Vietnam issue – helped it to do so initially by keeping the party in sync with the times. The Swedish Social Democrats managed to remain in office all the way up until 1976, whereas their Norwegian and Danish colleagues fell out of power in 1965 and 1968, respectively, largely due to their failure to adjust to the rapidly changing political climate. Equally importantly, the SAP's willingness to accommodate rising domestic radical agitation, including its active courtship of popular anti-war opinion, allowed the party to avert the splits (and subsequent mass defections to new socialist parties) that its Norwegian and Danish sister parties both experienced.[21]

While the SAP's leftward turn in the 1960s could not reverse a long-term trend that spelled the end of class-based voting (and by extension also the Social Democrats' postwar electoral supremacy),[22] between 1960 and 1973 the SAP was still able to increase its membership from approximately 801,000 to 967,000 individuals. This was an impressive feat given that the Danish Social Democrats and the Norwegian Labour Party in the same period lost tens of thousands of members each, a decline that was particularly dramatic in the Danish case.[23]

The Swedish Social Democratic establishment, furthermore, was not only able to forestall the creation of new splinter parties, but it also managed to hold the party together by fending off external subversion. Although the SAP never attained the allegiance of the Maoist anti-war movement, it prevented the far left from monopolizing the Vietnam issue. In addition, the Social Democrats effectively repulsed the KFML's attempt to infiltrate the trade unions, thereby thwarting the latter's efforts to establish a foothold among the SAP's core constituency.[24]

By international standards, the SAP also did a very good job of containing radical anti-war sentiments within the party. The Swedish Social Democratic leadership, for example, wisely avoided the German SPD's and the Norwegian Labour Party's mistake of expelling vast numbers of radicals. Instead, the SAP did its utmost to keep such elements within the party by means of various concessions, not least in regard to the Vietnam question. Even so, the SAP was compelled to banish a handful of younger members and to dismantle its student organization, the SSSF. This setback, however, has to be kept in perspective, for in these years many parties (both in Sweden and elsewhere in Europe) lost either their youth or student groups to the revolutionary left.[25] Unlike, for example, the VPK's loss of its youth organization to the Maoists, the dismantlement of the SSSF was a relatively minor affair, particularly because the majority of the their members were quickly reabsorbed into the SSU.[26]

Additionally, it should be kept in mind that the SSU was far more important to the party than the SSSF – both politically and in terms of absolute member numbers. Throughout the Vietnam era, the SSU acted as a crucial bulwark against the far left, and between 1962 and 1972 the organization was actually able to increase its membership from 49,000 to 70,000 people.[27] In the long run, the Social Democratic Party's combined losses to the Communists and the Maoists were negligible, especially when compared to the mass defections suffered by the Norwegian and Danish Social Democrats.

Taken as a whole, the SAP was consequently much better at harnessing popular opposition to the war than most of its contemporaries within the traditional left in Western Europe. Above all, the SAP retained its customary share of the youth vote (mostly due to the party's continued strong standing among young working-class voters), whereas the French Communist Party, for instance, failed to make any real inroads among the 68-generation.[28] The SAP admittedly was not able to win over the entire youth anti-war vote, but VPK and/or Maoists would almost certainly have made far greater gains within this demographic category if not for the Social Democrats' aggressive Vietnam posture. In evaluating the relative success of this policy, one additionally has to consider what the alternative would have been had the SAP instead opted for a more timid course of action. Judging by what occurred in Denmark and Norway, one might deduce that this would have gone rather badly for the party.

It is clear that the war caused considerable problems for all West European Social Democratic parties.[29] Generally speaking, they had difficulty responding to the youth revolt, and the same can be said for most Communist parties as well. This was largely because the "Old Left" was not very well equipped to deal with concerns raised by the baby boom generation, and it failed to grasp the connection between "the personal and the political." Nor did the traditional Socialist and Communist parties have much patience for the younger generation's libertarian streak. This antagonism was of course mutual, and more often than not there was considerable hostility between the New Left and the Old Left, and in almost all cases this also prevented the former from overtaking the latter. Nevertheless, the emergence of the New Left often had a destabilizing impact on the Communist and Social Democratic parties of Western Europe – at least initially.[30]

In view of this general situation, the SAP faired reasonably well, particularly for a ruling party. Part of the party's political strength had historically been its ability to accurately decipher the mood of the Swedish electorate, and its adjustment to the radicalization of the political climate in the 1960s was no exception. In contrast to many of its foreign counterparts, the SAP was able to successfully absorb new radical influences, but not to the point of becoming overwhelmed by them as occurred in the Netherlands where the entire Social Democratic party apparatus was captured by the New Left.[31] In the end, the SAP's standoff with its Marxist competitors resulted in a draw – the Social Democratic administration's political profile was radical enough to hold on to its own left wing, but not militant enough to appeal to the most extreme elements of the baby boom generation.

In Sweden, a disproportionate number of radicals from this age bracket eventually ended up in VPK rather than in the SAP.[32] This was more or less the norm in Western Europe, where in most instances the New Left in time found a home in the reformulated, de-Stalinized Euro-Communist parties.[33] That a majority of this group finally landed in the VPK obviously was not a result of a deliberate Social Democratic strategy; still, this worked out rather nicely for the Swedish Social Democrats. This development insured that VPK received enough votes to surpass the 4 per cent mark needed to be represented in parliament, and in light of the reality that the Social Democrats after 1970 would be dependent on Communist parliamentary support, it was also very much in the SAP's interest that the VPK was able to reach this electoral threshold. From a Social Democratic point of view, this scenario was really the best of both worlds because the Communists' gains among the 68-generation guaranteed VPK's political survival, and the SAP was simultaneously spared much of the unrest that this group created within VPK for many years to come.[34]

Finally, it should be underscored that to the extent that the Social Democrats lost this generation, this was not a consequence of the party's Vietnam stance. While the cabinet's inept handling of the DRV aid package undoubtedly cost the party some radical sympathizers, the permanent estrangement of scores of young radicals from the SAP was chiefly caused by disclosures about the government's surveillance and illegal harassment of the far left, not its Vietnam policy. Once these activities became public knowledge in late 1973, a sizeable segment of the 68-generation would never again politically identify with the Social Democrats.[35]

Alienated or not, this section of the electorate at least remained within the parliamentary system, which after all had been one of the SAP leadership's main concerns. By going on the offensive against the revolutionary faction of the anti-war movement in early 1968, the Social Democrats ostensibly prevented the youth from being drawn outside of the parliamentary fold. This turn of events was averted, and the Social Democratic establishment likewise deserves some credit for the relatively peaceful nature of the student protests in Sweden.[36]

While Swedish political culture admittedly did not provide fertile soil for the type of left wing terrorism that emerged in other parts of the West during these years, the potential nonetheless existed.[37] The fact that terrorism never took root was in large part due to the fact that the Swedish far left renounced such tactics,[38] but it can also partially be attributed to the Social Democratic administration's willingness to pander to domestic radicalism, first in conjunction with the Vietnamese conflict, and then later in relation to the Palestine question.

The validity of this assessment is seemingly confirmed by a comparative examination of the SAP and SPD's respective approaches to the far left. By initially refusing to make any effort to meet the youth revolt halfway, the West German Social Democrats inadvertently opened the door to left wing extremism, and indirectly also to terrorism.[39] Owing to vastly different national historical experiences, one cannot draw an exact parallel between the SAP and the SPD's handling of this issue, but even so, the Swedish Social Democrats' decision to accommodate popular anti-war agitation in hopes of preserving the democratic status quo was not without merit.

In the long run, the German SPD was actually far more successful in bringing the extraparliamentary left back into the Social Democratic camp than the SAP was – this despite the SPD's consistent refusal to compromise on the Vietnam question.[40] After 1969, the West German Social Democrats made a concerted effort to encourage the far left to (re)join the party, which much of it did (though at the price of heightened internal turmoil within the SPD).[41] It should be noted, however, that this process was made much easier by the West German Communist Party's utter irrelevance, which, in turn, gave the SPD far more leeway vis-à-vis the extreme left than the SAP ever had. Still, one might question whether the Swedish Social Democrats were too eager to court militant anti-war opinion because, in the end, the advent of the New Left did not cause lasting political damage to most of Europe's traditional Socialist and Social Democratic parties.[42]

Leaving the long-term consequences of the SAP's radicalization aside for a moment, it is evident that the Social Democratic leadership at the time regarded the party's leftward shift as a tactical asset in its pursuit of younger voters.[43] This was quite discernable in the case of the party's Vietnam stance, which, as we have seen, the SAP hierarchy accredited with having energized the cadre prior to the 1968 and 1973 elections.

By the early 1970s, the Social Democratic establishment realized that it could no longer afford to fall behind on international issues that engaged the public, as it had originally done on Indochina. Therefore, when Chile's Socialist government was overthrown in September 1973, the SAP leadership instantly sought to seize the initiative before its Marxist rivals could exploit this question. Closely mimicking its previous Vietnam strategy, the party at once organized collection drives and mass protests against the Pinochet-led coup. Hereafter, the Social Democrats and the far left alike increasingly turned their attention away from South East Asia and toward Central America, Africa, and the Middle East.

This new proactive approach to events outside of Europe would subsequently become the *leitmotiv* of Social Democrats' international identity for the next decade and a half until Olof Palme's death. In the post-Vietnam era, Sweden's so-called "activist" foreign policy came to be principally associated with the Social Democrats' outspoken critique of South African Apartheid and US policy in Latin America.[44] Typically the party sought to occupy the moral high ground on international matters that had little direct bearing on Sweden, but which still had some domestic appeal. This book's argument concerning the primacy of domestic politics could just as easily be applied to the SAP's energetic promotion of developmental aid, its vocal opposition to the Regime of the Colonels in Greece, or its policy toward southern Africa in this period. In all instances, the SAP's profile was informed by the need to placate internal agitation, while at the same time avoiding being outflanked by the either the Maoists or the Communists, and in select cases even by the Liberal and Center Parties.[45] Most of the above mentioned policies were presumably also partially directed at Third World audiences, and toward the USSR as well.

Again, this is not to suggest that the Social Democrats' positions on these various questions completely lacked sincerity, but only that there was always also a heavy dose of party tactical calculations involved in the formulation of these policies. In the beginning, the government's newfound profile in international matters was very popular at home, not least among the Social Democratic faithful. To the Social Democratic establishment, then, the main value of this "activist" posture was its ability to mobilize the party cadre, whereas its electoral significance was ordinarily deemed to be of less importance. This new course in world affairs had the added advantage that it allowed the party to retain control over Swedish foreign policy[46] to the point that the Social Democrats' initiatives in this area were largely followed (albeit in a more low-key manner) by the two non-socialist coalition governments that succeeded the Palme administration after 1976.[47]

Another indirect benefit of this policy was that it diverted the focus away from more potentially divisive issues, such as a prospective Swedish membership in the European Economic Community (EEC). At the end of the 1960s, leading members of the Social Democratic establishment (including Palme) were open to joining the EEC when Britain once again decided to submit a membership application. The problem was that there existed considerable internal resistance to such a move within the SAP and the Swedish left overall. In the end, this opposition appears to have been a decisive factor in the government's decision not to seek full entry into the EEC.[48] Thus, by concentrating on the more activist Third World-oriented aspects of Swedish foreign policy instead, the SAP leadership was likewise able to sidestep the internal havoc that the EEC question had wreaked among the Norwegian and Danish Social Democrats.[49]

The SAP hierarchy, conversely, had championed the Vietnam issue precisely because of its highly valued ability to unite the party around a common cause. This question was also useful in that it could be employed to channel radical internal energies away from more politically sensitive domestic issues. In this sense, the Vietnam War acted as a safety valve for the Swedish Social Democrats because this was an area in which concessions could be made to the party's left wing without undue political risks. Giving in to the radicals' domestic demands, such as their calls for the nationalization of banks or the abolition of the monarchy, was, in comparison, bound to harm the party's standing among moderate swing voters, and therefore the SAP hierarchy consistently sought to avoid taking such rash actions on the domestic front.[50] Palme at one point purportedly conceded as much to John Guthrie, the American *chargé d'affairs* in Stockholm,[51] and this admission only acted to reinforce long-standing US suspicions that the Social Democratic administration was using this question to redirect radical political sentiments into harmless byways.[52] (The Communist government in East Germany incidentally utilized the situation in South East Asia pretty much in the exact same fashion, seizing upon it as a safe outlet for popular passions.)[53]

The party's aggressive posture on the Vietnam War – and the government's "activist" foreign policy more generally – had originally permitted the SAP to hold the line against leftist extremism in the domestic sphere, but eventually this ceased to function as a stopgap measure against radical initiatives directly affecting "bread and butter" issues at home. Looking back, the danger in this strategy was that Social Democratic leaders over time lost control of this radicalization process, and it soon came to shape the party's domestic profile as well. As this radicalization gained additional momentum in the 1970s, Social Democratic trade unionists and party activists began to move much further leftward than was desirable from an electoral point of view.[54]

While the SAP hierarchy had at first encouraged this development, it quickly became evident that this radicalization was starting to spiral out of control. Not only did this create expectations that the party and government could not live up to, but it also served to unify the non-socialist opposition. As a consequence, after the 1970 elections, Social Democratic leaders actively tried to moderate the party's outward image.[55]

The leadership's attempt to reign in this radical impulse came too late, however, and by the mid-1970s the party had effectively become a hostage to internal left wing lobbying, which contributed to its defeat in the 1976 election. At no time was this as manifest as during the 1978 SAP Congress, when the party – against the leadership's wishes – embraced the demand for the introduction of the so-called "wage earner funds" that would have compelled large-scale private enterprises to share a portion of their profits directly with their employees. The party's endorsement of this scheme was a political disaster, alienating moderate swing voters and thereby ensuring that the non-socialist bloc stayed in office for a second term.[56] One would have to go back to the late 1920s to find the last occasion that the SAP had suffered two consecutive election defeats, and even when the party finally returned to power in 1983 it never regained its earlier electoral dominance.

With this in mind, the Social Democratic establishment's decision to accommodate itself to the radical *zeitgeist* of the Vietnam era was probably not in the party's best long-term interest. While the SAP was ousted from office in 1976 as the political winds began to swing back toward the right, the German Social Democrats conversely held on to power into the late 1980s. The Germans did so by adopting a distinctly more moderate political profile, and an identical observation can, for instance, also be made about the Austrian Social Democrats.[57]

The SAP's leftward shift in the 1960s was, therefore, of dubious electoral value in the long run, and the same reservations can likewise be raised about the party's pursuit of an "activist" foreign policy. Judging by the international reaction to its Vietnam stance, the government's new international profile probably did not cause any permanent harm to the country's reputation, but, on the other hand, it does not appear to have produced any real durable benefits either.

Although there can be little doubt that the Social Democratic administration's new course in global affairs was well received in the Eastern bloc, as well as in some, but not all, parts of the developing world,[58] its apologists nevertheless tend to underestimate the amount of ill will that this policy generated in Western Europe and the United States.[59] This was especially obvious in relation to the United States, where many conservatives continued to nurse resentments toward Sweden over the course of the next two decades, and it is no coincidence that Olof Palme was never granted a personal presidential audience in Washington.[60] One would be hard pressed to come up with another example of a Western European head of state who was in office as long as he was without receiving such an invitation from the White House. Thus, while Social Democratic Vietnam policy undeniably had some international admirers, it also created unprecedented hostility and suspicion toward Sweden. This raises the question, then, whether the country's improved relations with the developing world came at the expense of its ties to the rest of the First World.[61]

The long-term economic and political upside (or the lack thereof) of this "activist" phase in Swedish diplomacy still needs to be examined. To begin with, much of Sweden's developmental assistance to Communist regimes was squandered by its recipients, creating few positive results beyond propping up a series of one-party dictatorships. Secondly, from the point of view of pure national self-interest, the Social Democratic administration's courtship of the developing world (or alternatively, its opening towards the Eastern bloc) never produced anything near the profits that Sweden accrued from its trade with the West, and it is not evident that this policy brought any tangible economic benefits to Sweden at all.[62] One might furthermore ask whether this preoccupation with the Third World inadvertently harmed the country by postponing its move toward closer economic integration with the rest of Western Europe.

Though there is little argument that the Social Democrats' "activist" foreign policy raised the country's international visibility, its detractors doubt that this really translated into an increased Swedish say in world affairs.[63] While this topic certainly deserves more study, there is little concrete evidence to support the contention that Sweden's international influence was actually enhanced by this policy, and especially not in the rest of the Western world where it really would have mattered. If we look at the Vietnam issue specifically, it is hard to make a credible claim about the country's international leadership when no other Western governments, with the partial exceptions of Norway and Denmark, followed the Swedes' lead. (For example, it is striking that not even France decided to diplomatically recognize the DRV until the war was over.)

Swedish skeptics of this "activist" policy ultimately propose that, if anything, its principal accomplishment was that it gave the Swedes an inflated sense of self-importance and that the Swedish public was misled into believing that the government's outspokenness on these various international matters had a major impact abroad.[64] Domestic opponents of this policy have also repeatedly questioned the appropriateness of Sweden casting itself in the role of the world's conscience.[65] They contend that this overly sanctimonious approach to world affairs left the Swedes with a false sense of moral superiority and an exaggerated national hubris.[66] Swedish scholars who have studied this topic essentially agree with this conclusion. [67]

Palme's critics further point out that many of his international activities after Vietnam, whether within the confines of the Socialist International or in the United Nations did not really resonate far beyond Sweden. Nor can the majority of his global endeavors be said to have produced any substantial results, as was highlighted by the utter irrelevance of the so-called "Palme Commission" on nuclear disarmament.[68]

This being the case, why did the myth of Sweden's international significance survive as long as it did? Ann-Marie Ekengren suggests that the answer can largely be found in internal Social Democratic political calculations. She maintains that without the persistence of this fiction it would have been difficult for the SAP leadership to justify its continued pursuit of an "activist" foreign policy, which, in turn, was very desirable for purely party tactical reasons.[69] This is because the success of this policy at the domestic level did not necessarily require concrete outcomes, but only needed continued international visibility. Consequently, one might deduce that Sweden's "activist" policy toward the Third World mostly reflected its lack of influence in Europe.

A foreign policy that was verbalized in more idealistic terms, such as solidarity with other small states like Vietnam, was, moreover, promoted exactly because it enhanced the government's international status in the eyes of the Swedish public. Ostensibly, this approach was touted for the simple reason that as a small state Sweden's significance in global affairs would inevitably be diminished if it were instead examined through the lens of basic power politics. From a *Realpolitik* perspective, small states are usually attributed little agency, and their fates are subject to the whims of the Great Powers. A more idealistically articulated foreign policy, in contrast, allows small states like Sweden to indulge in the illusion that they are the masters of their own destiny. For all practical purposes, this fiction had little bearing on the actual formulation of Swedish state policy, but it did satisfy popular nationalism.

In other words, this myth's staying power was very much attributable to the Swedish public's own self-delusional willingness to believe in it. In relation to the Vietnam issue, in particular, Sweden's alleged effect on world opinion was not just praised by Social Democratic spokesmen,[70] but by the entire anti-war movement.[71] As already discussed, the SAP hierarchy carefully nurtured this fallacy, insisting that Sweden made a decisive contribution to the growth of international opposition to the war.[72] However, the political utility of this illusion would prove to be short lived.

Once the last American troops withdrew from Vietnam in March 1973, the Swedish public's preoccupation with Indochina rapidly died out. By extension, this reduced this question's domestic significance, and the entire left (including the SAP hierarchy) soon lost interest in it.[73] Following the Vietnamese invasion of Cambodia in 1979, this indifference turned into outright hostility as most former Swedish sympathizers of the Hanoi regime now turned against it.[74]

Not only did most of the left cease to pay attention to the situation in South East Asia, but the Swedish public started to care less and less about international matters in general. For this reason, an "activist" foreign policy ceased to engage the voters, and its domestic political usefulness began to decline in the late 1970s.[75] By this point, the domestic political mood in Sweden (like elsewhere in the West) had swung back toward the right, which also acted as a detriment against any further radical departures in Swedish diplomacy. These changes additionally ensured that the SAP's left wing lost much of its earlier influence over both the party's and the government's handling of international matters.

This does not mean that the Swedish Social Democrats instantly modified their international image, but the "activist phase" in Swedish foreign relations had indisputably peaked by 1976, and the country's posture in world affairs grew more muted thereafter, especially in the wake of Palme's assassination in 1986. This was mainly a reflection of the reality that this policy no longer struck a chord at home, though it was also because the global balance of power had undergone a major transformation with the end of the détente. All in all, the emergence of the Second Cold War gradually had a sobering effect on Swedish diplomacy because it greatly reduced the country's freedom of maneuver internationally.[76]

This overall change was likewise attributable to the less confrontational personal temperament of Ingvar Carlsson, Palme's successor.[77] That said, an "activist" foreign policy in a more moderate form was still pursued until Göran Persson took over the helm of the SAP in 1996. Only then was this policy, in effect, repudiated. During his tenure, Persson rarely ever mentioned Palme by name, and he definitely did not seek to emulate the latter's high-profile diplomacy. Under Persson, the Social Democratic government adhered to a pragmatic and mostly European-centered and US-friendly course in world affairs (a tact that was also subsequently adopted by its non-socialist successors). This shift was additionally reinforced by Sweden's entry into the European Union in 1995 – a development that by extension placed greater constraints on the country's ability to formulate an independent foreign policy.[78]

Nostalgia and the Failure of Critical Review

Sweden's new and more judicious approach to world affairs was perhaps best exemplified by the Persson administration's muted response to the American-led Iraq War. This new, more cautious, course in Swedish foreign relations was not welcomed by everybody within the party and led some of Palme's former Social Democratic colleagues to reminisce warmly about both the dynamic style and content of his international initiatives.[79]

Nor have such sentiments been solely restricted to Social Democrats,[80] and nowhere has this nostalgia been as discernable as in relation to Palme's earlier Vietnam criticism. This policy has continued to have plenty of apologists[81] who typically like to call attention to Walter Mondale's 1977 comment that "we [the US] were wrong [about the war], and you [Sweden] were right," which they cite as proof of the righteousness of the Swedish position."[82] Mondale's "admission," however, is a far cry from the kind of vindication that the defenders of Palme's Vietnam stance purport it to be. In truth, remarks to this effect from a Democrat who himself had been an outspoken critic of Nixon's Vietnam policy mean practically nothing, and especially not from a politician who needed to appease a large ethnically Swedish constituency in Minnesota.

Another weakness of this kind of retroactive defense of Palme and the government's Vietnam policy is that it completely overlooks the latter's support for a Communist dictatorship, which quickly revealed itself to be quite brutal. Even as this policy was being implemented, the senior members of the SAP leadership privately harbored few illusions about the true nature of Communist rule in Vietnam,[83] but this did not prevent the cabinet from continuing to provide substantial political and economic assistance to the NFL/DRV. After the fact, Social Democratic leaders from this period have had a hard time facing up to all of the ramifications of this policy,[84] and for this reason this subject has normally been glossed over.[85]

These leaders are hardly unique in this respect, for in Sweden as a whole there has existed precious little willingness to squarely confront this particular subject. This is not terribly surprising given that during these years the government's backing of the Vietnamese Communists enjoyed near universal support, not least among many people who would later constitute the country's political establishment. A critical inspection of this topic would not only cast the entire Swedish left in a bad light, but the non-socialist opposition would not fare much better, and consequently there is no real incentive for anyone to revisit this topic. A similar reluctance has also been discernable among the country's intellectual, media, and cultural elites,[86] and this is partially because many members of these same elites had themselves previously been affiliated with the revolutionary branch of the Swedish anti-war movement.[87]

This has also shaped the historiographical debate on this topic. Scholars of this generation have characteristically defended the Social Democratic government's former backing of Communist movements in Vietnam (and in other parts of the developing world) on the grounds that this was part and parcel of Sweden's efforts to serve as a bridge-builder between the global North and South. Swedish assistance to these various Marxist groups and regimes is further interpreted as an act of solidarity with the Third World and is normally justified in terms of the developing world's right to national self-determination.[88]

The problem with this line of argumentation in relation to Vietnam is that it exclusively focuses on the intent, rather than on the consequences, of Swedish policy. In other words, even if the Swedish Social Democrats were correct to oppose the American war effort (and also to reject the Saigon regime), this does not automatically mean that Sweden ended up on the "right side of history." To this day, the Swedish narrative about the war continues to be overly simplified, and it avoids lots of tough questions about the Vietnamese Communists' actions both during and after the war and what implications this should have had for Swedish policy. (By "actions" I am referring to the summary execution of political opponents, the establishment of political reeducation camps, and so forth.)[89]

Beyond this selective (and effectively sanitized) memory of the Vietnamese conflict, there are a series of underlying contradictions in the government's approach to the war that have yet to be satisfactorily resolved. For starters, one might ask why the Swedes helped to sustain a dictatorial system of government in Vietnam that they never would have accepted for themselves. Implicitly, this points to the existence of a disquieting double standard in which vastly different political expectations were applied to Europeans and non-Europeans. One might additionally object that the Social Democratic administration's assistance to assorted Communist regimes in the developing world was profoundly hypocritical given its simultaneous practice of spying on the Swedish sympathizers of these same states. Last but not least, Sweden's harsh criticism of the American war effort was not easily reconciled with the country's covert military ties to the United States, and some scholars who have otherwise defended the government's record on Vietnam have also recognized a number of these discrepancies.[90]

If anything, it could be argued that the government's Vietnam policy was partially of value exactly because it served to cloak this other clandestine side to the Swedish–American relationship. Conversely, this policy can concomitantly be criticized for indirectly contributing to the growth of American isolationism during these years. In this respect, this policy seems rather short-sighted considering that this latter development could potentially have paralyzed US foreign policy at a future point in time when Sweden might have been in desperate need of American military intervention. At the present, none of these stark incongruities in Swedish Vietnam policy have been adequately sorted out. This is because they only make sense when understood within the context of the Social Democratic establishment's dogged pursuit of its own party tactical objectives, and in regard to Vietnam the "primacy of domestic politics" formula simply did not add up to a coherent set of policies at the international and security level.

Although the baby boomers no longer dominate Swedish political and cultural life to the extent that they once did, their generally positive picture of Swedish Vietnam policy has nonetheless survived intact. This was, for instance, quite manifest in the popularly acclaimed 2012 documentary about Olof Palme, which celebrated his opposition to the war as one of his most vital and enduring legacies.[91] This evident sympathy for Palme's stance on the war is likewise on display in both Kjell Östberg and Henrik Berggren's biographies of Palme – even though neither author is blind to the party tactical dimensions behind this policy.[92] That these basically favorable interpretations of Palme's stance on the war continue to go more or less unopposed speaks to the fact there still does not exist any genuine appetite to collectively tackle many of the more problematic dimensions of this policy.

This disinclination to fundamentally reconsider Swedish Vietnam policy, however, is not just a byproduct of political expediency or of narrow self-interest, but it appears to be born out of a more broadly diffused sense of sentimentality about the 1960s. At least in the eyes of the graying 68-generation, this was a period when Sweden basked in the international limelight as a result of Palme's high-profile diplomacy and the foreign acclaim that then surrounded the Swedish welfare state. In many ways, this is remembered as a more innocent time when Sweden was still genuinely committed to fighting social and political injustices both at home and abroad.

To most Swedes, this era came to an abrupt end with Palme's murder in 1986, and the Swedish national self-image has never been quite the same since then. Indeed, in the years that immediately followed Palme's assassination a handful of different events combined to profoundly shake the country's self-confidence.[93] Doubts about the continued sustainability of the Swedish model first emerged in the 1970s when the country's economic postwar boom finally ground to a halt. Once this occurred, it did not take long before the welfare state began to show deep fissures. As the country's financial situation continued to hit new lows the late 1980s and early 1990s, this led to increased political and socio-economic tensions, including a startling outburst of popular xenophobia. Confronted by sweeping structural changes in the international economy, Sweden was not only compelled to reverse course and join the European Union, but also to make sharp cuts in social expenditures.[94]

All of these developments caused the Swedish model to (temporarily) lose much of its international appeal,[95] though late in the first decade of the 2000s the country's stock was once again on the rise. The difference this time was that this occurred under a Conservative-led coalition government that distinguished itself by its readiness to cut taxes and to privatize vast segments of the public sector. The coalition government's management of the economy won it many new foreign admirers. This was because it was able to keep Swedish exports competitive and inflation well contained during a period when many other European countries found themselves mired in a deep recession.[96]

The downside was that these same policies also resulted in heightened unemployment and rapidly escalating income disparities. Furthermore, the Conservative-led government's emphasis on fiscal retrenchment, in effect, hastened the continued dismantling of the Swedish welfare state. All of these experiences have, in turn, united and mobilized the Swedish left in opposition against the coalition government's intensified deregulation of the economy. In this political environment, Palme's historical legacy has suddenly taken on renewed importance because it was under his tenure that the Swedish welfare state had reached its absolute apex. Heading in to the 2014 elections to the European Parliament, the Social Democrats notably used Palme's voice in an advertisement calling for enhanced socio-economic justice in the workplace.[97] Nor is such nostalgia about the welfare state exclusively limited to Palme's former party colleagues, and as Sweden entered the second decade of the twenty-first century such nostalgia could be found across the entire Swedish left[98] and was even referenced in contemporary pop culture.[99]

∗ ∗ ∗

Occasionally, a likeminded sentimentality still surrounds the memory of Palme's earlier international endeavors (particularly among Social Democrats),[100] although no one in Sweden is currently calling for a return to an "activist" foreign policy. Presumably this is chiefly the result of a more levelheaded appreciation of what Sweden as a small country can realistically accomplish independently on the world stage,[101] but it is also attributable to the reality that since Palme's death both the ethics and sincerity of some his foreign dealings have increasingly been called into question. While this has not necessarily translated into a collective commitment to critically inspect all aspects of the country's previous "activist" foreign policy, the consensus nevertheless seems to be that this approach to global affairs no longer offers a suitable blueprint for action. All of these insights have contributed to a more nuanced view of Palme's international legacy that in hindsight has proven to be far more complex and morally ambiguous than it initially appeared to be. This conclusion certainly applies to Swedish Vietnam policy under Palme, which this book has shown was not always as unwavering, principled, or as earnest as its apologists have insisted.

Chapter 7: Notes

[1] Eugenie Blang, *To Urge Common Sense on the Americans* (Dissertation. College of William and Mary. 2000) 15–31; Frank Costigliola, "The Vietnam War and the Challenges to American Power in Europe" in Lloyd Gardner and Ted Gittinger (eds.), *International Perspectives on Vietnam* (College Station: Texas A & M University Press, 2000) 145–153.

[2] Thomas Schlesinger, *The United States and the European Neutrals* (Vienna: Braumüller, 1991) 89; Alastair Parker, "International Aspects of the Vietnam War" in Peter Lowe (ed.), *The Vietnam War* (New York: St Martin's Press, 1998) 211–212.

[3] Carl-Gustaf Scott, "Swedish Vietnam Criticism Reconsidered" *Cold War History* 2009 9(2): 243–266.

[4] For example, in the wake of his condemnation of the Christmas bombings, Palme received close to 200 letters of support from individual anti-war activists and peace groups from all over the world. Statsministerns korrespondens. "Brev med anledning av Vietnamuttalandet." Vol. 110–111, 114–119. Statsrådsberedningens Arkiv. E1 1972–1973.

[5] Adam Roberts, "Det icke helt trovärdiga Sverige" *Internationella Studier* 1976 (1): 34–36; Parker, "International Aspects of the Vietnam War," 211–212. For a specific illustration, see the Leader of the British Liberal Party, Jeremy Thorpe, as cited in *Svenska Dagbladet* 30 Dec. 1972.

[6] B. Vivekanandan, *International Concerns of European Social Democrats* (New York: St Martin's Press, 1997) 11; Donald Sassoon, *One Hundred Years of Socialism* (London: IB Touris Publishers, 1996) 320; 327–328. The best example of this probably came in the aftermath of Palme's condemnation of the Christmas bombings, when Willy Brandt privately admonished Palme that in the future Sweden needed to be far more careful about how it says things, and further stressed the importance of both Bonn *and* Stockholm remaining in Washington's good graces. 23 March 1973. Brandt letter to Palme. Olof Palme. Brevsamling. Vol 89.

[7] Kaj Björk, *Vägen till Indokina* (Stockholm: Atlas, 2003) 164–165, 170, 206–207; Yngve Möller, *Sverige och Vietnamkriget* (Stockholm: Tiden, 1992) 292–294, 306; 336, 369.

[8] See, for instance, Nils Elvander, *Skandinavisk arbetarrörelse* (Stockholm: Liber, 1980) 206. and Sassoon, *One Hundred Years of Socialism*, 321.

[9] Harto Harkovirta, *East–West Conflict and European Neutrality* (Oxford: Claredon Press, 1988) 174, 200–201; Schlesinger, *The United States and the European Neutrals*, 39–52.

[10] Efraim Karsh, *Neutrality and Small States* (New York: Routledge, 1988) 137–138, 155, 164–168.

[11] Kjell Östberg, *1968* (Stockholm: Prisma, 2002) 151–153; Salomon, *Rebeller i takt med tiden*, 310–312. See also Åke Kilander, *Vietnam var nära* (Stockholm: Leopard, 2007) 354–358.

[12] Richard Barnet, *The Alliance* (New York: Simon and Schuster, 1983) 275–276.

[13] Swedish scholars have interpreted this development either as expression of guilt for the Swedes' own prosperity, or alternatively as a form of psychological overcompensation for the country's earlier policy of accommodation towards Nazi Germany. This time the Swedes wanted to be on the "right side" of history. Alf W. Johansson, "Vill du se monument, se dig omkring" in Kurt Almqvist and Kaj Glans (eds.), *Den stora framgångssagan* (Stockholm: Fisher & Co, 2001) 201–202; Ann-Sofie Nilsson, *Den moraliska stormakten* (Stockholm: Timbro, 1991) 71.

[14] Per Ohlsson, *Svensk politik* (Lund: Historiska Media, 2014) 403–404; Östberg, *1968*, 152–156.

[15] Jussi Hanhimäki, *Scandinavia and the United States* (New York: Twayne Publishers, 1997) 135. See also Olav Riste, *Norway's Foreign Relations* (Oslo: Universitetsförlaget, 2001) 260.

[16] Jean-Christophe Öberg, *Varför Vietnam?* (Stockholm: Rabén & Sjögren, 1985) 184–187; Richard Hichens-Bergström, "Norge och Vietnamdramat" *Svensk Tidskrift* 1981 (1): 61–62.

[17] Möller, *Sverige och Vietnamkriget*, 293. See also Sten Andersson, *I de lugnaste vatten...* (Stockholm: Tiden, 1993) 265.

[18] For specific examples, see Torsten Nilsson as cited in "Vår Utrikespolitik" in SAP, *Nu gäller det 70-talet* (Stockholm: SAP, 1969) 35. and Krister Wickman as cited in *Aftonbladet* 6 Jan. 1973.

[19] Möller, *Sverige och Vietnamkriget*, 365. Möller was a former Social Democratic newspaper editor, and he was also the Ambassador designate to the US at the time of the Christmas bombings.

[20] Fredrik Logevall, "America Isolated" in Andreas Daum, *et al* (eds.), *America, the Vietnam War and the World* (Cambridge: Cambridge University Press, 2003) 195–196.

[21] Elvander, *Skandinavisk arbetarrörelse*, 113–115, 123–125, 193–218, 327–328.

[22] *Ibid.*, 314–316, 326–333. The combined effect of de-proletarization, expansion of the middle class, and the decline of an older distinct working class culture had the same negative consequences for almost all Western European Socialist/Social Democratic parties in this period. Geoff Eley, *Forging Democracy* (New York: Oxford University Press, 2002) 406–408.

[23] Stephen Padget and William Patterson, *A History of Social Democracy in Postwar Europe* (New York: Longman, 1991) 91.

[24] Lars Olof Lampers, *Det grå brödraskapet* (SOU 2002: 92) 507–508. See also Enn Kokk, *Vitbok* (Stockholm: Hjalmarson & Högberg, 2001).

[25] Lars Bengtsson, *et al.*, *Svenska partiapparater* (Stockholm: Bonnier, 1972) 52–53; Eley, *Forging Democracy*, 417.

[26] Elvander, *Skandinavisk arbetarrörelse*, 185–189; Bengtsson, et al., *Svenska partiapparater*, 235.

[27] Sven-Arne Stahre, *Arbetarrörelsen* (Stockholm: Forum, 1978) 138–139; Elvander, *Skandinavisk arbetarrörelse*, 206.

[28] Sassoon, *One Hundred Years of Socialism*, 398–401; Eley, *Forging Democracy*, 346–350.

[29] See, for instance, Leopoldo Nuti, "The Center Left Government in Italy and the Escalation of the Vietnam War" in *America, the Vietnam War and the World*, 267, 278. and Marianna Sullivan, *France's Vietnam Policy* (London: Greenwood Press, 1978) 78.

[30] Eley, *Forging Democracy*, 352–354; Sassoon, *One Hundred Years of Socialism*, 303–304, 384, 392, 396–397.

[31] Padgett and Patterson, *A History of Social Democracy in Postwar Europe*, 39, 82–83.

[32] Mikael Gilljam and Sören Holmberg, *Väljare och val i Sverige* (Stockholm: Bonnier, 1987) 313.

[33] Sassoon, *One Hundred Years of Socialism*, 346, 401–403; Eley, *Forging Democracy*, 415–416.

[34] Sven Olsson, "VPK 1968–1978" in Jan Engberg, et al (eds.), *Utanför Systemet* (Stockholm: Rabén & Sjögren, 1978) 188–197.

[35] Östberg, *1968*, 75–76, 157. See also Gunder Andersson and Gunnar Fredriksson, *Socialdemokratin och de intellektuella* (Stockholm: Författarförlaget, 1976) 9–11.

[36] Henry Bäck, *Den utrikespolitiska dagsordningen* (Stockholm: Gotab, 1979) 60–61.

[37] Lars-Åke Augustsson and Stig Hansén, *De svenska maoisterna* (Göteborg: Lindelöws, 2001) 63, 68. See also *Aftonbladet* 20 Dec. 1998.

[38] For a specific illustration, see KFML, *Studera, praktisera socialism* (Stockholm: Oktobers Förlag, 1972) 179–181.

[39] Michael Belfour, *West Germany* (New York: St. Martins Press, 1983) 225–227, 252–254.

[40] Yet the SPD's success on this front should perhaps not be exaggerated, given that it would later lose droves of supporters to the Green Party. Philip Gorski and Andrei Markovits, *The German Left* (New York: Oxford University Press, 1993) 79–81.

[41] Padget and Patterson, *A History of Social Democracy in Postwar Europe*, 38–40, 52–53, 78–83.

[42] Sassoon, *One Hundred Years of Socialism*, 390, 405.

[43] Olof Palme as cited in *SAP PS-protokoll* 30 Sept. 1970. See also *Tiden* # 8 1968, 449–452.

[44] Ulf Bjereld, *Kritiker eller medlare?* (Stockholm: Nerenius & Santérus, 1992) 52–53, 64, 70–72.

[45] Nils Andrén and Yngve Möller, *Från Undén till Palme* (Stockholm: Norstedt, 1990) 119–120, 141–142. See also Ove Nordenmark, *Aktiv Utrikespolitik* (Stockholm: Almqvist & Wiksell, 1991) and Tor Sellström, *Sweden and National Liberation in Southern Africa Vol II* (Uppsala: Nordiska Afrikainstitutet, 2002).

[46] Bjereld, *Kritiker eller medlare?*, 169; Andrén and Möller, *Från Undén till Palme*, 72–76, 82–86.

[47] Ulf Bjereld and Marie Demker, *Utrikespolitken som slagfält* (Stockholm: Nerenius & Santérus, 1995) 187; Nilsson, *Den moraliska stormakten*, 74–77, 165–167.

[48] Olof Petersson, *Väljarna och världspolitiken* (Stockholm: Norstedt, 1982) 69–73; Sven O. Andersson, "Den rastlöse reformisten" in Bo Huldt and Klaus Misgeld (eds.), *Socialdemokratin och svensk utrikespolitik* (Göteborg: M H Publishing, 1990) 117–118.

[49] Elvander, *Skandinavisk arbetarrörelse*, 193, 197–207.

[50] Olof Ruin, *I välfärdsstatens tjänst* (Stockholm: Tiden, 1986) 250–253; Jon Pierre, *Partikongresser och regeringens politik* (Lund: Kommunal Fakta, 1986) 246–247.

[51] 12 Dec. 1972. John Guthrie. Telegram to State. Re: Private conversation with Olof Palme during yesterday's Nobel Prize festivities. Subject Numeric Files 1970–1973. Political and Defense. Sweden. RG 59.

[52] 17 Sept. 1965. First Secretary US Embassy Stockholm. George Andrews. Telegram to State. US Subject Numeric Files 1964–66. Political and Defense. Sweden. RG 59; 25 Oct. 1968. *Chargé d'affairs* US Embassy Stockholm. Cameron Turner Jr. Telegram to State. Central Foreign Policy File 1967–69. Political and Defense. Sweden. RG 59; 30 April 1970. US Ambassador to Sweden 1970–1972. Jerome Holland. Telegram to State. Subject Numeric Files 1970–73. Political and Defense. Sweden. RG 59.

[53] Günther Wernicke, "World Peace Council and the anti-war movement" in *America, the Vietnam War and the World*, 315–318.

[54] Pierre, *Partikongresser och regeringens politik*, 246–253, 280–281; Elvander, *Skandinavisk arbetarrörelse*, 176–180, 212–213.

[55] Östberg, *1968*, 124–125, 157–158; Elvander, *Skandinavisk arbetarrörelse*, 329.

[56] Pierre, *Partikongresser och regeringens politik*, 252–253, 266, 280–281; Elvander, *Skandinavisk arbetarrörelse*, 176, 212–213.

[57] In this context, it is of some interest that the Danish Social Democrats were likewise punished electorally for having moved too far to the left during the early 1970s. Elvander, *Skandinavisk arbetarrörelse*, 200–204; 218, 252.

[58] Magnus Jerneck, "Olof Palme – en internationell propagandist" in Huldt and Misgeld (eds.), *Socialdemokratin och svensk utrikespolitik*, 135.

[59] For specific illustrations, see Sverker Åström, *Ögonblick* (Stockholm: Bonnier Alba, 1992) 128–133 and Pierre Schori, "Tydilighet, tradition, och trovärdighet" in Hans Haste, *Boken om Olof Palme* (Stockholm: Tiden, 1986) 162–171.

[60] Andrén and Möller, *Från Undén till Palme*, 94. In October 1970 Palme did, however, briefly visit the White House as part of a larger UN delegation.

[61] Jerneck, "Olof Palme – en internationell propagandist," 135.

[62] Björk, *Vägen till Indokina*, 215.

[63] See, for instance, Bertil Östergren, *Vem är Olof Palme?* (Stockholm: Timbro, 1984) 311–312.

[64] Nilsson, *Den moraliska stormakten*, 12. See also Ulf Nilson, *Sverige. Sluten anstalt* (Stockholm: Komintern Instant Media, 1998) 206–213.

[65] For specific illustrations, see Gösta Bohman, *Så var det* (Stockholm: Bonnier, 1983) 188–191 and Jonas Gummesson, *Olof Palmes ungdomsår* (Stockholm: Ekerlids, 2001) 168–169. For earlier examples, see Erik von Heland, *Välfärdssamhällets förfall* (Stockholm: Lindqvists, 1970) 105–106. and Bo Siegbahn, *Den svenska säkerheten* (Stockholm: Bonnier, 1971) 16–25.

[66] See, for instance, Per Ahlmark, *Vänstern och tyranniet* (Stockholm: Timbro, 1994) 147. and Olof Rydbeck, *I maktens närhet* (Stockholm: Bonnier, 1990) 273–276.

[67] Bo Peterson, "Den svenska neutraliten" in Kurt Almqvist och and Kristian Gerner (eds.), *Kalla Kriget* (Stockholm: Axel och Margaret Ax:son Johnsons stiftelse, 2012) 115; Johansson, "Vill du se monument," 202–203.

[68] Nilson, *Sverige. Sluten anstalt*, 206–213; Östergren, *Vem är Olof Palme?*, 302–304; Nilsson, *Den moraliska stormakten*, 7–17, 114–119. Some of Palme's apologists also concede this point. See, for instance, Sven O. Andersson, "Den rastlöse reformisten" in Huldt and Misgeld (eds.), *Socialdemokratin och svensk utrikespolitik*, 115–116.

[69] Ann-Marie Ekengren, *Av hänsyn till folkrätten?* (Stockholm: Nerenius & Santérus, 1999) 312.

[70] See, for instance, Krister Wickman as cited in *Aftonbladet* 6 Jan. 1973. See also Schori, "Tydilighet, tradition, och trovärdighet," 164–165.

[71] For a specific example, see Jan Myrdal as cited in Tommy Hammarström, FNL i Sverige (Stockholm: AB Solidaritet, 1975) 176. See also Kilander, *Vietnam var nära*, 357–358.

[72] See, for instance, Olof Palme as cited in *Riksdagsprotokollet* # 48, 21 March 1973, 59–60.

[73] According to Lennart Klackenberg, Palme completely lost interest in Vietnam as soon the war was over. (Klackenberg, interview with the author, 8 May 2003.) Bjereld and Demker further point out that the Social Democratic administration's relations to the Hanoi regime became much more problematic once the Americans withdrew. During the conflict, the government's backing of the DRV could be justified in terms of supporting a small country's right to national self-determination, but afterwards Sweden was at pains to establish a working relationship with a Marxist regime that it did not otherwise share much in common with. Bjereld and Demker, *Utrikespolitiken som slagfält*, 300–302.

[74] Erik Svanfeldt, "Svenska kommittén för Vietnam" (University of Uppsala, 1990) 33; Östberg, *1968*, 177. According to Carl Erad Lindahl, who in 1979 was the Swedish Ambassador to Vietnam, Palme was personally furious at the Vietnamese after the invasion, and Swedish–Vietnamese relations considerably cooled thereafter. Lindahl, interview with the author 4 May 2003. Sten Andersson stated that following the invasion most Social Democrats became disillusioned with the Vietnamese cause. Andersson interview with the author 27 May 2004.

[75] Peter Esaiasson and Sören Holmberg, *De folkvalda* (Stockholm: Bonnier, 1988) 208.

[76] Ulf Bjereld, Alf W. Johansson and Karl Molin, *Sveriges säkerhet och världens fred* (Stockholm: Santérus, 2008) 312–313.

[77] Nils Andrén, "Istället för syntes" in Huldt and Misgeld (eds.), *Socialdemokratin och svensk utrikespolitik*, 222.

[78] Ulf Bjereld, "Svensk utrikespolitik i ett historiskt perspektiv" in Douglas Brommesson and Ann-Marie Ekengren (eds.), *Sverige i världen* (Malmö: Gleerup, 2007) 45–46; Bjereld, Johansson and Molin, *Sveriges säkerhet och världens fred*, 315–329.

[79] See, for instance, Björn Kumm, "Om global makt och vanmakt" in Enn Kokk (ed.), *Var blev ni av ljuva drömmar?* (Stockholm: Ordfront, 2002) 160–173. See also Sten Andersson, Lena Hjelm-Wallén and Peter Weiderud's op-ed in *Svenska Dagbladet* 27 Feb. 2006.

[80] For specific illustrations, see Sara Lidman's op-ed in *Svenska Dagbladet* 28 Oct. 1999 and Anders Melbourn's op-ed in *Svenska Dagbladet* 28 March 2004.

[81] See, for instance, Anders Ferm, *Caleb J. Andersson* (Stockholm: Bokförlaget DN, 1997) 18, 64–65, 78–80, 103–107, 120–121. and Gunnar Fredriksson, *Farvatten* (Stockholm: Norstedt, 1989) 250–251.

[82] For specific illustrations, see Thage G. Peterson, *Olof Palme som jag minns honom* (Stockholm: Bonnier, 2002) 395. and Jan Eliasson, "Olof Palme och utrikespolitiken" in Erik Åsard (ed.), *Politikern Olof Palme* (Stockholm: Hjalmarson & Högberg, 2002) 172.

[83] See, for instance, Torsten Nilsson as cited in *SAP Riksdagsgruppens protokoll* 12 March 1968. and Sten Andersson as cited in *SAP PS-protokoll* 17 March 1970.

[84] For two important exceptions, see Yngve Möller, *Mina tre liv* (Stockholm: Tiden, 1983) 311. and Björk, *Vägen till Indokina*, 94, 103, 108–111, 120, 126–127, 145–146, 161, 165–166, 172–174, 184. A few Social Democrats that have, in hindsight, also questioned Palme's (and the party's) support for Communist movements elsewhere in the developing world. For a specific illustration, see Gun-Britt Andersson, "Drömmar om en rättvisare värld" in *Var blev ni av ljuva drömmar?*, 146–159.

[85] For specific illustrations, see Torsten Nilsson, *Utanför protokollet* (Stockholm: Tiden, 1986) 383 and Birgitta Dahl, "Solidaritetsarbetet för Vietnam" in *Var blev ni av ljuva drömmar?*, 198–201.

[86] Svante Lundberg, *Sextioåttor* (Stockholm: Symposium AB, 1993) 180–190, 200–202. See also Göran Skytte, *Självbekännelser och andra texter* (Stockholm: Sellin & Partner, 1997) 13–15, 128–130. and Göran Rosenberg and Mikael Wiehe as cited in Micke Leijnegard, *Var blev ni av ljuva drömmar. 68:orna* (Stockholm: Norstedt, 2013) 129–139, 233–248. Skytte, Rosenberg and Weihe are, however, notable exceptions to this rule.

[87] Augustsson and Hansén, *De svenska maoisterna*, 170–190; Östberg, *1968*, 78–80. See, for instance, Anders Berggren's op-ed in *Göteborgs-Posten* 17 June 1996.

[88] Kjell Östberg, *När vinden vände* (Stockholm: Leopard, 2009) 108–147, 411; 417; Alf W. Johansson and Torbjörn Norman, "Sweden's Security and World Peace" in Klaus Misgeld, *et al* (eds.), *Creating Social Democracy* (University Park, PA: The Pennsylvania State University Press, 1988) 365–369; Bjereld, Johansson and Molin, *Sveriges säkerhet och världens fred*, 224–275.

[89] For an overview, see Jean-Louis Margolin, "Vietnam and Laos: The Impasse of War Communism" in Stéphane Courtois, *et al.* (eds.) *The Black Book of Communism* (Cambridge: Harvard University Press, 1999) 565–576.

[90] See, for instance, Östberg, *När vinden vände*, 147.

[91] "Palme." (2012) Directed by Kristina Lindström and Maud Nycander. www.imdb.com/title/tt2070768/ accessed 01/02/2013.

[92] Henrik Berggren, *Underbara dagar framför oss* (Stockholm: Norstedt, 2010) 354–357, 390, 464–467, 510–511; Östberg, *När vinden vände*, 14, 108–147.

[93] Karl Molin, "Historical Orientation" in Klaus Misgeld, *et al* (eds.), *Creating Social Democracy* (University Park: The Pennsylvania State University Press, 1988) xxix; Johansson, "Vill du se monument, se dig omkring," 204–205.

[94] Ohlsson, *Svensk politik*, 447–450, 513–536; Anders Ivarsson Westerberg, *et al.*, "En ny tid" in Anders Ivarsson Westerberg, *et al* (eds.), *Det långa 1990-talet. En bok om när Sverige förändrades* (Umeå: Borea 2014) 9–31.

[95] Sassoon, *One Hundred Years of Socialism*, 476; Padgett and Patterson, *A History of Social Democracy in Postwar Europe*, 260.

[96] Lars Trägårdh, "Pippi och Sveriges särart" www.axess.se/magasin/default.aspx?article=895#.U3xvoC-W_8B accessed 04/04/2014.

[97] "Rättvisa villkor – Socialdemokraternas EU-valfilm 2014" 9 May 2014 www.youtube.com/watch?v=0UfcHZ78HUI#t=29 accessed 05/24/2014.

[98] For specific illustrations, see "Välfärd istället för vinster" [undated 2014] www.vansterpartiet.se/politik/ accessed 04/28/2014 and "Ta tillbaka välfärden!" [5 May 2010-present] www.facebook.com/Tatillbakavalfarden?fref=nf accessed 05/01/2014.

[99] For a specific example, see Timbuktu, "Den Svenska Skammen (Lyric Video)" [uploaded 11 April 2014] www.youtube.com/watch?v=DqqKpEbqvvQ#t=18 accessed 05/05/2014.

[100] See, for instance, "Olof Palme" 27 Oct. 2010 http://www.socialdemokraterna.se/Webben-for-alla/Partidistrikt/Jonkopingslan/Var-politik-ny/Var-historia/Olof-Palme/ accessed 04/04/2014 and Pierre Schori as cited in Leijnegard, *Var blev ni av ljuva drömmar. 68:orna*, 151–168.

[101] Douglas Brommesson and Ann-Marie Ekengren, "Sverige i världen – idag och imorgon" in Brommesson and Ekengren (eds.), *Sverige i världen*, 204.

Bibliography

Primary Sources

Interviews with the Author

Sten Andersson. SAP Party Secretary 1963–1982. 27 May 2004. (phone)

Birgitta Dahl. Social Democratic parliamentary representative, cabinet minster, etc. Chairman of the Swedish Committee for Vietnam 1971–1977. 27 May 2004. (phone)

Gunnar Fredriksson. Chief Editor of *Stockholms-Tidningen* 1965–1966. Chief Editor of *Aftonbladet* 1966–1980. 27 April 2003. (phone)

Carl Erad Lindahl. Swedish Foreign Ministry. 1963–1984. Swedish Ambassador to Vietnam 1985–1989. 4 May 2003. (phone)

Lennart Klackenberg. Specialist on Developmental Aid Issues. Swedish Ministry of Finance, 1970–1976. 8 May 2003.

Ingemar Källberg. Lawyer. Ministry of Immigration 1969–1976. Prior to this, Källberg had worked with immigration issues within the Ministry of the Interior. 20 July 1999. (phone)

Walt W. Rostow. Special Assistant to the President for National Security Affairs, 1966–1969. 29 May 2002.

Gunnar Sommarin. Former Member of the State Alien Board, Press Secretary for the State Alien Board. 2 July 1999.

Anders Thunborg. Former SAP International Secretary and Undersecretary of Defense, 1974–1979. 4 May 2003. (phone)

Jim Walch. Former Counselor and Deserter Advocate. 2 July 1999.

Sverker Åström. Swedish Undersecretary of State 1972–1977. 20 July 1999, 6 May 2003.

Written Correspondence with the Author

Robert Argento. Former Peer Counselor and Deserter Advocate. 10 Sept. 2002. (email)

Desmond Charragher. Former Peer Counselor and Deserter Advocate. 18 Dec. 1999. (email)

Sven Erlander. Tage Erlander's Son. 4 Oct. 1999. (mail)

Eric Holmqvist. The former Minister of the Interior. 15 Oct. 1999. (mail)

Michael Lindner. One of the Intrepid Four. 15 Jan. 2000. (mail)

Bengt Ranland. Former Bureau Chief Ministry of Immigration. Sept. 1999. (email)

Swedish Foreign Ministry Archives

Kungl. Utrikesdepartementet:

Avd HP. Grupp 1. Mål Ua. Politik Allmänt. Förenta Staterna. 1965–1974. # 208–285.

Avd HP. Grupp 1. Mål Er. Politik Allmänt. Sovjetunionen. # 306, 309.

Avd HP. Grupp 1. Mål Xv. Politik Allmänt. Vietnam. 1965–1974. # 1188–1211.

Avd HP. Grupp 1. Mål O. Opinionsyttringar. Vietnam. 1964–1979. # 110–113.

Avd HP. Grupp 12. Mål Xv. Erkännande av stater och regeringar. Vietnam. 1957–1973. # 61–63.

Avd R. Grupp 191. Mål K. Svensk visitering. Förrymda krigsfångar, militärarbetare, desertörer, m.m. May 1967–Nov. 1986. # 6–11.

Kungl. Utrikesdepartementet. Printed Materials:

Utrikesfrågor (1965–1974)

Sverige och Vietnamfrågan (1968)

Sverige i utländsk press (1965–1974)

Swedish Government Documents (Published Materials)

Försvarsdepartementet. *Folkrätt i krig* (Stockholm: SOU, 1984)

Försvarets underrättelsenämnd. Redovisning av vissa uppgifter om den militära underrättelse- och säkerhetstjänsten. 26 Nov. 1998.

Statens offentliga utredningar. Om kriget kommit. Förberedelser för mottagande av militärt bistånd 1949–1969 (Stockholm: SOU 1994: 11)

Statens offentliga utredningar. *Fred och säkerhet. Svensk säkerhetspolitik, 1969–1989* (Stockholm: SOU 2002: 108)

Statistiska Centralbyrån. *Data om invandrare* (Stockholm: SCB, 1981)

Statistiska Centralbyrån. Statistisk Årsbok för Sverige 1965–1975.

Sveriges Riksdag. Riksdagsprotokollet 1965–1973.

Sveriges Riksdag. Motioner 1965–1973.

Sveriges Riksdag. Utrikesnämndens utlåtande 1965–1973.

Labour Movement Archives and Library, Sweden (Arbetarrörelsens arkiv och bibliotek)

Hans Göran Franck:

Handlingar rörande amerikanska Vietnam-desertörer/-veteraner. Vol 1–2 (28/4/3/7).

LO:

LO Kongressprotokoll. 17:e Kongressen 3–9 Sept. 1966.

Olof Palme:

Appendix: Utrikespolitik: Vietnam. Vol 1–18 (676/10/13).

Brevsamling. Vol 51, 58, 89 (676/3/2).

Brevsamling. Brev angående Vietnamtalet 1968. Vol 31–33 (676/3/2).

Handlingar ordnade efter ämne: Vietnamfrågan 1965–1968. Vol 31 (676/4/2).

Intervjuer 1969–1970. Vol 6–7 (676/2/6).

Tal. Vol 18 (676/2/4).

SAP:

Handlingar rörande andra länder. Vietnam. 1972–1976 (1889/F/2/D).

Kongressprotokoll. Extrakongressen. 1967.

Kongressprotokoll. Extrakongressen. Motioner 1967.

Kongressprotokoll. 23:e Kongressen. 1968.

Kongressprotokoll. 23:e Kongressen. Motioner 1968.

Kongressprotokoll. 24:e Kongressen. 1969.

Kongressprotokoll. Motioner 24:e Kongressen. 1969.

Kongressprotokoll. 25:e Kongressen. 1972.

Kongressprotokoll. Motioner 25:e Kongressen. 1972.

Partistyrelsens (PS) protokoll 1965–1974.

Riksdagsgruppens protokoll 1965–1973.

Verkställande utskottets (VU) protokoll 1965–1974.

SKSF:

Årsberättelser. Program. Motioner. 1965–1970, 1972, 1974.

Årsberättelser. 1968–1972.

SSKF:

Kongressprotokoll. 12:e Kongressen. 5–8 May 1968.

SSSF:

Handlingsprogram med förslag och uttalanden. 1964–1967. Vol 2–5.

Representantskapsprotokoll med bilagor. 1964–1969. Vol 3.

Stockholms arbetarekommun:

Stockholms arbetarekommun. Verksamhetsberättelser 1965–1973.

Stockholms arbetarekommun. Årsmötesprotokoll, 1966–1970.

Svenska kommittén för Vietnam, Laos och Kambodia:

Handlingar rörande Indokina. Vol 1967–1973 (1568/F/1/9).

Korrespondens. Vol 1967–1968 (1568/E/1/2).

Korrespondens. Vol 1969 (1568/E/1/2).

Utgående handlingar. Vol 1967–1989 (1568/B/1/1).

National Archives, Sweden
(Riksarkivet)

DFFG:

Blandade protokoll m.m. 1967–1973. # 1.

Handlingar rörande SAP-FNL 1973–1974. # 1.

Ö:A. Vietnambulletinen 1965–1974. # 1–3.

Inrikes/Arbetsdepartmentet:

Inrikesdepartementet. Konseljakter avseende utlänningsärenden. E:VII. 1970. Vol 1–2.

Statsrådsberedningen:

E:1. Statsministerns korrespondens. Brev med anledning av USA-resan. # 37–38.

Brev med anledning av Vietnamuttalandet. # 110–111, 114–119.

Svenska Vietnamkommittén. # 203.

Statens Utlänningsnämnd:

Föredragningspromemorior. F:2 A. April 1967–March 1973. # 37–48.

Protokoll. A:1. April 1967–March 1973. # 9–17.

Statens Utlänningskommission:

2:a Byrån. E:1 A. Korrespondens med UD. 1962–1969. # 3.

2:a Byrån. E:3. Byråchefens Korrespondens. 1953–1968. # 2.

Hemliga Arkivet. E:8. 1953–1969. # 1.

SÄPO Archive:
"ADC/Deserters folder 1968–1970."

Swedish TV and Radio Archive

TV 1. "Aktuellt."

TV 2. "Hell no! We won't go!" (24 April 1997)

TV 2. "Jimmy." (16 May 1971)

TV 2. "Rapport."

Radio. P1. "Dagens Eko."

Radio. P1. "Lunchekot."

Radio. P1. "Kvällsekot."

US Government Documents

National Archives II:

Nixon Project. White House Special Files. 1969–1974. Country File: Sweden. Box 9.

Nixon Project. NSC. Country File. "Palme Visit – June 1970." Box 938.

US Dept. of State. Subject Numeric Files 1964–1966. Political and Defense. Sweden. RG 59.

US Dept. of State. Central Foreign Policy File 1967–1969. Political and Defense. Sweden. RG 59.

US Dept. of State. Subject Numeric Files 1970–1973. Political and Defense. Sweden. RG 59.

US Dept. of State. Bureau of European Affairs. Office of Northern Affairs. Records relating to Sweden 1957–1975. RG 59.

USIA. Office of Research. Special Reports. 1964–1982. Box 8. S # 50.

Lyndon B. Johnson *Presidential* Library:

WHCF. Country File. Sweden. Box 68.

Memos to the President. Walt W. Rostow. Box 30–31, 44.

The President's Daily Diary. Box 4.

The President's Evening Reading. NSF. Agency File. Box 50.

Office Files of Frederick Panzer. Box 218.

Office Files of Marvin Watson. Box 32.

William W. Heath. US Ambassador to Sweden 1967–1969. Oral History Interview. 20 May 1970 and 25 May 1970. (Interviewer Joe B. Franz.)

Georgetown University. Special Collections:

Oral History Collection. John Owens. Desk Officer for Finland and Sweden 1972–1974. European Section. Dept of State.

Freedom of Information Act:

Central Intelligence Agency. March 2002.

Dept. of the Army. January 2002, April 2002.

Dept. of the Navy. April 2002.

Dept. of State. March 2002.

Federal Bureau of Investigation. December 2001.

US Government Documents (Published Materials)

Foreign Relations of the United States. 1964–1968. Vietnam. Vol I–IV.

Foreign Relations of the United States. 1964–1968. Western Europe. Vol XIII.

Congressional Record 1965–1975.

US House of Representatives. Committee on the Armed Services. Report of the Special Subcommittee on National Defense Posture. "Review of the Vietnam Conflict and Its Impact on US Military Commitments Abroad." 90th Congr., 2nd Sess., 24 Aug. 1968.

US House of Representatives. House Committee on Foreign Affairs. "American Deserters in Sweden. Report of a Staff Study by the House Subcommittee on Europe." 92nd Congr., 1st Sess., Sept. 1971.

US Senate. Committee on the Armed Services. Report to the Subcommittee on Treatment of Military Deserters. "Treatment of Deserters from Military Service." 91st Congr., 1st Sess., 6 March 1969.

Newspapers

Aftonbladet

Arbeiterbladet (NOR)

Arbetaren

Arbetet

Arbetarbladet

Austin American

Baltimore Sun

Bangkok Post

Barometern

Beirut Daily Star

Blekinge Läns Tidning

Bohuslänningen

Borås Tidning

Chicago Tribune

Dagbladet (NOR)

Dagbladet Nya Samhället Sundsvall

Dagens Nyheter

Daily Telegraph

Dala-Demokraten

Eskilstuna-Kuriren

Expressen

Falu-Kuriren

Folkbladet Östgöten

Folket

Frankfurter Allegemeine Zeitung

Frankfurter Rundschau

Gefle Dagblad

Gotlands Allehanda

Gotlands Folkblad

Gotlänningen

Göteborgs handels- och sjöfartstidning

Göteborgs-Posten

Göteborgs-Tidningen

Hallands Nyheter

Helsingborgs Dagblad

Helsingin Sanomat (FIN)

Hindustan Times

Houston Chronicle

Houston Post

Hudiksvalls Tidning

Information (DEN)

International Herald Tribune

Jönköpings-Posten

Katrineholms-Kuriren

Kronobergaren

Kvällsposten

Le Monde

Lincoln Star

London Daily Telegraph

London Times

Los Angeles Times

Länstidningen Östersund

Minneapolis Tribune

Nerikes Allehanda

New York Times

Norrköpings Tidningar

Norrländska Socialdemokraten

Norrskensflamman

Ny Dag

Nya Norrland

Nya Wermlands-Tidningen

Ontario Star (CAN)

Oregonian

Orlando Sentinel

Philadelphia Inquirer

Piteå-Tidningen

Politiken (DEN)

Päivän Sanomat (FIN)

Skånska Dagbladet

Skövde Nyheter

Smålands Allehanda

Smålands Folkblad

Smålandsposten

Stockholms-Tidningen

Stuttgarter Zeitung

Sundsvalls Tidning

Svenska Dagbladet

Sydsvenska Dagbladet

Sydöstra Sveriges Dagblad

Söderhamns-Hälsingekuriren

Uusi Soumi (FIN)

Uppsala Nya Tidning
Vestmanlands Läns Tidning
Vimmerby Tidning
Värmlands Folkblad
Västgöta-Demokraten
Västerbottens Folkblad
Västerbottens-Kuriren
Västernorrlands Allehanda
Västerviks-Tidningen
Wall Street Journal
Washington Evening Star
Washington Post
Örebro-Kuriren
Örnsköldsviks Allehanda
Östgöta Correspondenten
Östra Småland

Newsletters and Magazines:

ADC Second Front Review
Aktuellt (Aktuellt i politik och samhälle)
American Exile Newsletter
American Deserter Committee Newsletter
Chaplin 88
Clarté
Fackföreningsrörelsen
Frihet
FIB/Kulturfront
Gaudeamus
Liberal Debatt
Libertas
Metallarbetaren
Mullvaden
Newsweek
The New Yorker
Se

Soldattidningen

Svensk Export

Tiden

Tidsignal

Time Magazine

U.S. News & World Report

Veckojournalen

Vi

Vietnambulletinen

Vietnam nu

Vår Kyrka

Electronic Resources

"Olof Palme" 27 Oct. 2010 http://www.socialdemokraterna.se/Webben-for-alla/
Partidistrikt/Jonkopingslan/Var-politik-ny/Var-historia/Olof-Palme/ accessed 04/04/2014.

"Palme." (2012) Directed by Kristina Lindström and Maud Nycander. www.imdb.com/title/tt2070768/ accessed 01/02/2013.

"Rättvisa villkor – Socialdemokraternas EU-valfilm 2014" 9 May 2014 www.youtube.com/watch?v=0UfcHZ78HUI#t=29 accessed 05/24/2014.

Timbuktu, "Den Svenska Skammen (Lyric Video)" uploaded 11 April 2014 www.youtube.com/watch?v=DqqKpEbqvvQ#t=18 accessed 05/05/2014.

"Ta tillbaka välfärden!" [5 May 2010–present] www.facebook.com/Tatillbaka valfarden?fref=nf accessed 05/01/2014.

"Välfärd istället för vinster" [undated 2014] www.vansterpartiet.se/politik/ accessed 04/28/2014.

Memoirs, Autobiographies, Debate Books

Ahlmark, Per. Vänstern och tyranniet. Det galna kvartsseklet (Stockholm: Timbro, 1994)

Alsterdahl, Alvar. Samtal med Tage Erlander mellan två val (Stockholm: Tiden, 1967)

Andersson, Sten. I det lugnaste vatten... (Stockholm: Tiden, 1993)

Arnberg, Teddy, et al. Vietnam i dokument (Stockholm: Prisma, 1968)

Aspling, Sven. Med Erlander och Palme. Sven Aspling berättar för Arvid Lagercrantz (Stockholm: Hjalmarson & Högberg, 1999)

Boheman, Erik. *Tankar i en talmansstol* (Stockholm: Norstedt, 1970)

Bohman, Gösta. *Inrikes utrikespolitik. Det handlar om Vietnam* (Stockholm: Geber, 1970)

Bohman, Gösta. *Så var det. Gösta Bohman berättar* (Stockholm: Bonnier, 1983)

Brandt, Willy. *My Life in Politics* (London: Penguin, 1992)

Cassel, Leif. *Så vitt jag minns. Memoarer* (Stockholm: Askild & Kärnekull, 1973)

Dahlberg, Leif. *Över folkets huvud. Om svensk utrikespolitik* (Stockholm: Bonnier, 1967)

Enochsson, Jorma. *Den unga Centern. Ett politiskt reportage och debattinlägg* (Stockholm: Norstedt, 1969)

Erlander, Tage. *Sjuttiotal* (Stockholm: Tiden, 1979)

Erlander, Tage. *1960-talet. Samtal med Arvid Lagercrantz* (Stockholm: Tiden, 1982)

Fredriksson, Gunnar. *Farvatten* (Stockholm: Norstedt, 1989)

Hammar, Bo. *Ett långt farväl till kommunismen* (Stockholm: Bromberg, 1992)

Hermansson, Carl-Henrik. *För Socialismen* (Stockholm: Arbetarkultur, 1974)

Hermansson, Carl-Henrik. *CH Minnen* (Stockholm: Arena, 1993)

Hichens-Bergström, Richard. *Spillror från en sällskapsresa* (Stockholm: Norstedt, 1989)

Jarring, Gunnar. *Utan glasnost och perestrojka. Memoarer 1964–1973* (Stockholm: Bonnier, 1989)

Johnson, Alexis U. *The Right Hand of Power* (Englewood Cliffs, NJ: Prentice-Hall, 1984)

Johnson, Claes G. *Ny Giv – Samtal med Yngve Holmberg* (Stockholm: Almqvist & Wiksell, 1969)

Johnson, Lyndon Baines. *The Vantage Point: Perspectives of the Presidency 1963–1969* (New York: Holt, Rinehart & Winston, 1971)

Kissinger, Henry. *The White House Years* (Boston: Little Brown, 1979)

Lagercrantz, Olof. *Ett år på sextiotalet* (Stockholm: Wahlström & Widstrand, 1990)

Lappalainen, Armas. *Om socialismen* (Stockholm: Prisma, 1969)

Leijon, Anna-Greta. *Alla rosor ska inte tuktas!* (Stockholm: Tiden, 1991)

Lindström, Ulla. *Och regeringen satt kvar. Ur min politiska dagbok 1960–1967* (Stockholm: Bonnier, 1970)

Malmström, Åke. *Tjugofem år med riksdagen* (Stockholm: Tiden, 1975)

Moberg, Vilhelm. *Den okända släkten* (Stockholm: PAN/Norstedt, 1968)

Mårtensson, Jan. *Att kyssa ett träd. Memoarer* (Stockholm: Wahlström & Widstrand, 2000)

Möller, Yngve. *Mina tre liv. Publicist, politiker och diplomat* (Stockholm: Tiden, 1983)

Nilson, Ulf. *Sverige. Sluten anstalt* (Stockholm: Komintern Instant Media, 1998)

Nilsson, Torsten. *Åter Vietnam. Memoarer och reportage* (Stockholm: Tiden, 1981)

Nilsson, Torsten. *Utanför protokollet* (Stockholm: Tiden, 1986)

Nixon, Richard. RN: *The Memoirs of Richard Nixon. The Richard Nixon Library Edition* (New York: Simon & Schulster, 1990)

Palme, Olof. *Politik är att vilja* (Stockholm: Prisma, 1968)

Palme, Olof. *Att vilja gå vidare* (Stockholm: Tiden, 1974)

Palme, Olof. Olof Palme. *Med egna ord. Samtal med Serge Richard och Nordal Åkerman* (Uppsala: Bromberg, 1977)

Peterson, Thage G. *Resan mot mars. Anteckningar och minnen* (Stockholm: Bonnier, 1999)

Peterson, Thage G. *Olof Palme. Som jag minns honom* (Stockholm: Bonnier, 2002)

Petri, Lennart. *Sverige i stora världen* (Stockholm: Atlantis, 1996)

Ramel, Stig. *Pojken i dörren* (Stockholm: Atlantis, 1994)

Rostow, Walt W. *The Diffusion of Power. An Essay in Recent History* (New York: MacMillan, 1972)

Rydbeck, Olof. *I maktens närhet. Diplomat. Radiochef. FN-ämbetsman* (Stockholm: Bonnier, 1990)

Samuelsson, Eivor. *Nordvietnam en beskrivning av ett u-land* (Stockholm: Utbildningsförlaget, 1972)

Schori, Pierre. *Dokument inifrån* (Stockholm: Tiden, 1992)

Schori, Pierre. "Tydlighet, tradition, trovärdighet. Olof Palmes utrikespolitik bidrag till att rädda människoliv" in Hans Haste, *Boken om Olof Palme. Hans liv, hans gärning, hans död* (Stockholm: Tiden, 1986) 162–171.

Siegbahn, Bo. *Den svenska säkerheten. Tankar om utrikespolitik, svenska världsförbättrare och Marx* (Stockholm: Bonnier, 1971)

Sjöström, Hans. *Klassens ljus* (Stockholm: Norstedt, 1987)

Skytte, Göran. *Självbekännelser och andra texter* (Stockholm: Sellin & Partner Bok och Idé AB, 1997)

Säfve, Torbjörn. *Rebellerna i Sverige. Dokumentation, kritik, vision* (Stockholm: Författarförlaget, 1971)

Takman, John. *Vietnam – ockupanterna och folket* (Malmö: Bo Cavefors, 1965)

Thorsson, Inga. *Att internationalisera Sverige* (Stockholm: Tiden, 1971)

von Heland, Erik. *Välfärdssamhällets förfall* (Stockholm: Lindqvists, 1970)

Wachtmeister, Wihelm. *Som jag såg det. Händelser och människor på världsscenen* (Stockholm: Norstedt, 1996)

Åström, Sverker. *Ögonblick. Från ett halvsekel i UD-tjänst* (Stockholm: Bonnier Alba, 1992)

Öberg, Jean-Christophe. *Varför Vietnam? Ett kapitel i svensk utrikespolitik 1965–1970* (Stockholm: Rabén & Sjögren, 1985)

Other Printed Primary Sources
(Published Speeches, Political Pamphlets, Platforms and Manifestos, etc.)

Arfwedson, Anders, Anders Björk, and Hans Sandebring. *Moderat samhällssyn. Analys och perspektiv* (Stockholm: Almqvist & Wiksell, 1970)

Axelsson, Kaj. *Ungdom i en föränderlig värld. Glimtar från efterkrigstidens SSU* (Stockholm: SAP, 1967)

Carlshamre, Nils. *Vad gäller valet? De stora stridsfrågorna inför 1968 års andrakammarsval belysta av representanter för (h) (c) (fp) (s) (vpk)* (Stockholm: Prisma, 1968)

Demokratisk Ungdom. "Dagens Ungdom – politisk ungdomsrevy" # 3 1965 (Stockholm: SKP, 1965)

DFFG. Solidaritet Sverige–Vietnam. Vietnamarbetet i Sverige januari–februari 1973. DFFG:s skriftserie # 15 (Stockholm: AB Solidaritet, 1973)

Kokk, Enn. *VPK och SKP. De grälande tvillingpartierna* (Stockholm: Tiden, 1974)

KFML. *Vad vill KFML. Kommunistiska Förbundet Marxist-Leninisterna* (Uppsala: Marxistiskt Forum, 1970)

KFML. *Studera, praktisera socialism. Marxist-Leninistisk grundkurs* (Stockholm: Oktobers Förlag, 1972)

Nilsson, Torsten. "Vår utrikespolitik" in *Nu gäller det 70-talet. Sju tal från partikongress - 69* (Stockholm: SAP, 1969) 29–41.

Petersson, Åke. "Centeridéer i utrikespolitiken" in *Samarbete och skiljelinjer. En skrift till bondeförbundets/centerpartiets 60-års jubileum* (Stockholm: LT:s Förlag, 1970) 157–168.

Ringholm, Bosse. *Efter 1970 års val...* (Stockholm: Frihets Förlag, 1970)

Rouge, André. *Sådan är oppositionen* (Stockholm: SAP, 1970)

SAP. *Valboken 66. SAP teknisk valhandledning, politiska fakta och argument* (Stockholm: SAP, 1966)

SAP. "Vietnamdebatten" (Stockholm: Partistyrelsens informationstjänst, 1969)

SAP. "Fakta och argument i valrörelsen" # 17 (Stockholm: SAP, 1970)

SKfV. "Röster för Vietnam" (Stockholm: SKfV, 1968)

SKfV. *Vietnam-69* (Stockholm: Rabén & Sjögren, 1969)

Socialistiska Förbundet. *Program för socialism. Socialistiska Förbundets programförslag* (Stockholm: Bonnier, 1967)

SSU. *Ungdomsinsamlingen* (Stockholm: SAP, 1966)

SSU. *SSU. Ung Mening* (Stockholm: SAP, 1964)

SSU. "Utblick # 8. USA-Kriget i Vietnam" (Stockholm: Frihets Förlag, 1968)

Verdandi. *Verdandi debatt. Vietnam i svensk pressdebatt sommaren 1965* (Stockholm: Prisma: 1965)

VPK. *Samling vänster i svensk politik. Material från Vänsterpartiet Kommunisternas 21:a kongress 13–16 maj 1967* (Göteborg: VPK, 1967)

Wirmark, David. "Solidaritet för en mänskligare värld" in *För ett mänskligare samhälle. Liberal politik inför 70-talet* (Stockholm: Folk och samhälle, 1970) 207–221.

Secondary Sources

af Malmborg, Mikael. *Neutrality and State Building in Sweden* (New York: Palgrave, 2001)

Agrell, Wilhelm. *Fred och fruktan. Sveriges säkerhetspolitiska historia 1918–2000* (Lund: Historiska Media, 2000)

Alandh, Tom and Birgitta Zachrisson. *Berättelser om Palme. I samtal med Tom Alandh and Birgitta Zachrisson* (Stockholm: Norstedt, 1999)

Andersson, Gun-Britt. "Drömmar om en rättvisare värld" in Enn Kokk (ed.), *Var blev ni av, ljuva drömmar?* (Stockholm: Ordfront, 2002) 146-159.

Andersson, Gunder and Gunnar Fredriksson. *Socialdemokratin och de intellektuella. Tryckt och otryckt i Aftonbladsdebatten* (Stockholm: Författarförlaget, 1976)

Andersson, Leif. *Beslut(s)fattarna. Socialdemokratiska riksdagsgruppen 100 år* (Stockholm: PM Bäckström, 1996)

Andersson, Sven O. "Den rastlöse reformisten. En uppsats om Olof Palme och världen" in Bo Huldt and Klaus Misgeld (eds.), *Socialdemokratin och svensk utrikespolitik. Från Branting till Palme* (Göteborg: M H Publishing, 1990) 91–120.

Andrén, Nils. "I stället för syntes" in Bo Huldt and Klaus Misgeld (eds.), *Socialdemokratin och svensk utrikespolitik. Från Branting till Palme* (Göteborg: M H Publishing, 1990) 213–223.

Andrén, Nils. *Den totala säkerhetspolitiken* (Stockholm: Rabén & Sjögren, 1972)

Andrén, Nils and Yngve Möller. *Från Undén till Palme. Svensk utrikespolitik efter andra världskriget* (Stockholm: Norstedt, 1990)

Anners, Erik. *Den socialdemokratiska maktapparaten* (Stockholm: Askild & Kärnekull, 1976)

Antman, Peter and Pierre Schori. *Olof Palme. Den gränslöse reformisten* (Stockholm: Tiden, 1996)

Augustsson, Lars Åke and Stig Hansén. *De svenska maoisterna* (Göteborg: Lindelöws, 2001)

Barnet, Richard. *The Alliance: America, Europe, Japan: Makers of the Postwar World* (New York: Simon & Schuster, 1983)

Baskir, Lawrence and William Strauss. *Chance and Circumstance: The Draft, the War and the Vietnam Generation* (New York: Vintage Books, 1978)

Belfour, Michael. *West Germany: A contemporary history* (New York: St. Martins Press, 1983)

Bengtsson, Lars. *Svenska partiapparater. De politiska partiernas organisatoriska uppbyggnad* (Stockholm: Bonnier, 1972)

Berggren, Henrik. *Underbara dagar framför oss. En biografi över Olof Palme* (Stockholm: Norstedt, 2010)

Birgersson, Bengt Owe, et al. *Socialdemokratin i Stockholms län 1907–1982* (Stockholm: SAP, 1982)

Bjereld, Ulf, Alf W. Johansson and Karl Molin, *Sveriges säkerhet och världens fred. Svensk utrikespolitik under kalla kriget* (Stockholm: Santérus, 2008)

Bjereld, Ulf. "Svensk utrikespolitik i ett historiskt perspektiv" in Douglas Brommesson and Ann-Marie Ekengren (eds.), *Sverige i världen* (Malmö: Gleerup, 2007) 34–48.

Bjereld, Ulf. *Kritiker eller Medlare? En studie av Sveriges utrikespolitiska roller 1945–1990* (Stockholm: Nerenius & Santérus, 1992)

Bjereld, Ulf and Marie Demker. *Utrikespolitiken som slagfält. De svenska partierna och utrikesfrågorna* (Stockholm: Nerenius & Santérus Förlag, 1995)

Bjurström, Jan and Christer Isaksson. "Vietnamkonfliktens behandling i sju svenska morgontidningar under perioden 12 Februari–10 Mars" (University of Göteborg, 1969)

Björk, Kaj. *Vägen till Indokina* (Stockholm: Atlas, 2003)

Blang, Eugenie M. *To Urge Common Sense on the Americans: US relations with France, Great Britain and the Federal Republic in the context of the Vietnam War, 1961–1968* (Dissertation. College of William and Mary, 2000)

Block, Eva. *Amerikabilden i svensk dagspress 1964–1968* (Lund: Gleerup, 1976)

Brands, H.W. *The Wages of Globalism. Lyndon Johnson and the Limits of American Power* (Oxford: Oxford University Press, 1995)

Brigham, Robert K. *Guerilla Diplomacy: The NLF's Foreign Relations and the Vietnam War* (Ithaca: Cornell University Press, 1999)

Brommesson, Douglas and Ann-Marie Ekengren. "Sverige i världen – idag och imorgon" in Douglas Brommesson and Ann-Marie Ekengren (eds.), *Sverige i världen* (Malmö: Gleerup, 2007) 200–206.

Brown-Fleming, Suzanne. "Ambassador George Crows McGhee and the Vietnam Crisis" in *SHAFR Newsletter* 26 1995 (4): 19–34.

Bäck, Henry. *Den utrikespolitiska dagsordningen. Makt, protest och internationella frågor i svensk politik 1965–1973* (Stockholm: Gotab, 1979)

Costigliola, Frank. "The Vietnam War and the Challenges to American Power in Europe" in Lloyd C. Gardner and Ted Gittinger (eds.), *International Perspectives on Vietnam* (College Station, TX: Texas A&M University Press, 2000) 143–153.

Costigliola, Frank. "L.B.J., Germany and the End of the Cold War" in Warren Cohen and Nancy Bernkopf Tucker (eds.), *Lyndon Johnson Confronts the*

World: American Foreign Policy, 1963–1968 (Cambridge: Cambridge University Press, 1994) 173–210.

Cramér, Per. *Neutralitetsbegreppet. Den permanenta neutralitetens utveckling* (Stockholm: Norstedt, 1989)

Cromwell, William C. *The United States and the European Pillar* (New York: St. Martins Press, 1992)

Dahl, Birgitta. "Solidaritetsarbetet för Vietnam" in Enn Kokk (ed.), *Var blev ni av, ljuva drömmar?* (Stockholm: Ordfront, 2002) 174–204.

Dalsjö, Robert. *Life-Line Lost: The Rise and Fall of "Neutral" Sweden's Secret Reserve Options of Wartime Help from the West* (Stockholm: Santérus Academic Press, 2006)

Davidsson, Ulla, *et al.* "Amerikanska desertörer i Sverige" (University of Stockholm, 1970)

Duffet, John (ed.) *Against the Crime of Silence: Proceedings of the Russell International War Crimes Tribunal* (New York: O'Hare Books, 1968)

Ekengren, Ann-Marie. *Olof Palme och utrikespolitiken* (Umeå: Boréa Förlag, 2005)

Ekengren, Ann-Marie. *Av hänsyn till folkrätten? Svensk erkännandepolitik 1945–1995* (Stockholm: Nerenius & Santérus, 1999)

Eley, Geoff. *Forging Democracy: The History of the Left in Europe, 1850–2000* (New York: Oxford University Press, 2002)

Elgström, Ole. *Aktiv utrikespolitik. En jämförelse mellan svensk och dansk parlamentarisk utrikesdebatt 1962–1978* (Lund: Studentlitteratur, 1982)

Eliasson, Jan. "Olof Palme och utrikespolitiken" in Erik Åsgard (ed.), *Politikern Olof Palme* (Stockholm: Hjalmarson & Högberg, 2002) 172–176.

Elmbrant, Björn. *Palme* (Stockholm: Författarförlaget, 1989)

Elmbrant, Björn and Erik Eriksson. *Det bidde en tumme. Historien om den svenska vietnamhjälpen* (Stockholm: Prisma, 1970)

Elvander, Nils. *Skandinavisk arbetarrörelse* (Stockholm: Liber, 1980)

Engberg, Jan. "RMF/KAF: Visionen om den obefläckade fanan" in Jan Engberg, *et al* (eds.), *Utanför systemet. Vänstern i Sverige 1968–1978* (Stockholm: Rabén & Sjögren, 1978) 121–154.

Esaiasson, Peter. *Svenska valkampanjer 1866–1988* (Stockholm: Allmäna Förlaget, 1990)

Esaiasson, Peter and Sören Holmberg. *De folkvalda. En bok om riksdagsledamöterna och den representiva demokratin i Sverige* (Stockholm: Bonnier, 1988)

Faurby, Ib. "Danish Alliance Policy 1967–1993: From Quiet Adaptation via Loud Disagreement to Cautious Involvement" in Carsten Due Nielson and Nikolay Petersen (eds.), *Adaptation and Activism: The Foreign Policy of Demark 1967–1993* (Copenhagen: Dansk Udenrigspolitik Institut, 1995) 55–91.

Ferm, Anders. *Caleb J. Andersson. Palmes okände rådgivare* (Stockholm: Bokförlaget DN, 1997)

Fink, Carole, *et al.* "Introduction" in Carole Fink, Phillip Gossart and Detlef Junker (eds.), *1968: The World Transformed* (New York: Cambridge University Press, 1998) 1–27.

Fischer, Fritz. *Germany's War Aims in the First World War* (London, W.W. Norton & Co, 1967)

Gilljam, Mikael and Sören Holmberg. *Väljare och val i Sverige* (Stockholm: Bonnier, 1987)

Gorski, Philip and Andrei Markovits. *The German Left: Red, Green and Beyond* (New York: Oxford University Press, 1993)

Gummesson, Jonas. *Olof Palmes ungdomsår. Bland nazister och spioner* (Stockholm: Ekerlids, 2001)

Gustafsson-McFarland, Sofia. "Americans, Once in Exile, Now at Home in Sweden" (New York University, 1990)

Hagan, John. *Northern Passage. American War Resisters in Canada* (Cambridge: Harvard University Press, 2001)

Hadenius, Stig, Björn Molin and Hans Wieslander. *Sverige efter 1900. En modern politisk historia* (Stockholm: Bonnier, 1993)

Hadenius, Stig. *Svensk politik under 1900-talet. Konflikt och samförstånd* (Stockholm: Tiden Athena, 1996)

Hammarström, Tommy. *FNL i Sverige. Reportage om en folkrörelse under tio år* (Stockholm: AB Solidaritet, 1975)

Hanhimäki, Jussi M. *Scandinavia and the United States: An Insecure Friendship* (New York: Twayne Publishers, 1997)

Harkovirta, Harto. *East–West Conflict and European Neutrality* (Oxford: Claredon Press, 1988)

Haskel, Barbara. "Det moraliserande Sverige" *Internationella Studier* 1976 (1): 30–32.

Haste, Hans. *Boken om Olof Palme. Hans liv, hans gärning, hans död* (Stockholm: Tiden, 1986)

Hayes, Thomas. *American Deserters in Sweden: The Men and their Challenge* (New York: Association Press, 1971)

Herring, George C. (ed.) *The Secret Diplomacy of the Vietnam War: The Negotiating volumes of the Pentagon Papers* (Austin: University of Texas Press, 1983)

Hichens-Bergström, Richard. "Norge och Vietnamdramat" *Svensk Tidskrift* 1981 (1): 61–62.

Hirdman, Yvonne. *Vi bygger landet. Den svenska arbetarrörelsens historia från Per Götrek till Olof Palme* (Stockholm: Tiden, 1988)

Hjort, Magnus. *Den farliga fredsrörelsen. Säkerhetstjänsternas övervakning av freds-organisationer, värnpliktsvägare och FNL-grupper 1945–1990* (SOU 2002: 90)

Holmberg, Susan. "Welfare Abroad. Swedish Developmental Assistance" in Bengt Sundelius (ed.), *The Committed Neutral: Sweden's Foreign Policy* (Boulder: West-view Press, 1989) 123–166.

Holmberg, Sören and Olof Petersson. *Inom felmarginalen. En bok om politiska opinionsundersökningar* (Stockholm: Liber, 1980)

Holmström, Mikael. *Den dolda alliansen – Sveriges hemliga Nato-förbindelser* (Stockholm: Atlantis, 2011)

Huldt, Bo. *Sweden, the United Nations, and Decolonization* (Lund: Esselte Stadium, 1974)

Isaksson, Christer. *Palme privat. I skuggan av Erlander* (Stockholm: Ekerlids, 1995)

Isberg, Magnus, et al. *Partierna inför väljarna. Svensk valpropaganda 1960–1966* (Stockholm: Allmäna Förlaget, 1974)

Ivarsson Westerberg, Anders,. et al. "En ny tid" in Anders Ivarsson Westerberg, *et al* (eds.), *Det långa 1990-talet. En bok om när Sverige förändrades* (Umeå: Borea 2014) 9–31.

Jerneck, Magnus. "Olof Palme – en internationell propagandist" in Bo Huldt and Klaus Misgeld (eds.), *Socialdemokratin och svensk utrikespolitik. Från Branting till Palme* (Göteborg: M H Publishing, 1990) 121–142.

Jerneck, Magnus. *Kritik som utrikespolitiskt medel. En studie av de amerikanska reaktionerna på den svenska Vietnamkritiken* (Lund: Dialogus, 1983)

Johansson, Alf. W. "Vill du se monument, se dig omkring! Några reflektioner kring nationell identitet och kollektivt minne i Sverige efter andra världskriget" in Kurt Almqvist and Kaj Glans (eds.), *Den svenska framgångssagan?* (Stockholm: Fisher & Co, 2001) 197–210.

Johansson, Alf. W. and Torbjörn Norman. "Sweden's Security and World Peace: Social Democracy and Foreign Policy" in Klaus Misgeld, *et al* (eds.), *Creating Social Democracy: A Century of the Social Democratic Labor Party in Sweden* (University Park, PA: The Pennsylvania State University Press, 1988) 339–373.

Josefsson, Sven-Olof. *Året var 1968. Universitetskris och studentrevolt i Stockholm och Lund* (Dissertation. University of Göteborg, 1996)

Kaplan, Lawrence S. *NATO and the United States: The Enduring Alliance* (New York: Twayne Publishers, 1994)

Karlsson, Jan. "Vietnamkonfliktens behandling i TT:s utgående material under perioden 11.2–9.3 1968" (University of Göteborg, 1968)

Karsh, Efraim. *Neutrality and Small States* (New York: Routledge, 1988)

Kasinsky, Reneé. *Refugees from Militarism: Draft Age Americans in Canada* (New Brunswick, NJ: Transaction Books, 1976)

Kassman, Charles. *Arne Geijer och hans tid 1957–1979* (Stockholm: Tiden, 1991)

Kaufman, Burton. "Foreign Aid and the Balance-of-Payments Problem: Vietnam and Johnson's Foreign Economic Policy" in Robert Devine (ed.), *The Johnson Years. Vol. II. Vietnam, the Environment and Science* (Lawrence: University of Kansas Press, 1987) 79–112.

Kilander, Åke. *Vietnam var nära: En berättelse om FNL-rörelsen och solidaritetsarbetet i Sverige 1965–1975* (Stockholm: Leopard, 2007)

Kleberg, Olof. "De stora och de små: Olof Palmes syn på supermakter och småstater" in Bertil Dunér (ed.), *Är svensk neutralitet möjlig? Nio bidrag till en svensk fredspolitik* (Stockholm: Liber, 1977) 61–87.

Kokk, Enn. "Vart tog den där elden vägen" in Enn Kokk (ed.), *Var blev ni av, ljuva drömmar?* (Stockholm: Ordfront, 2002) 9–59.

Kokk, Enn. *Vitbok. Militärens hemliga nätverk i arbetarrörelsen* (Stockholm: Hjalmarson & Högberg, 2001)

Kokk, Enn. "Laboremus 1902–1987" in Tuula Eriksson, *et al* (eds.), *Framtidens utmaningar. Socialdemokratin inför 90-talet* (Uppsala: Laboremus, 1987)

Kumm, Björn. "Om global makt och vanmakt" in Enn Kokk (ed.), *Var blev ni av, ljuva drömmar?* (Stockholm: Ordfront, 2002) 160–173.

Lampers, Lars Olof. *Det grå brödraskapet. En berättelse om IB. Forskarrapport till säkerhetskommissionen* (SOU 2002: 92)

Leifland, Leif. *Frostens år, om USA:s diplomatiska utfrysning av Sverige* (Stockholm: Nerenius & Santérus, 1997)

Leijnegard, Micke. *Var blev ni av ljuva drömmar. 68:orna* (Stockholm: Norstedt, 2013)

Lewin, Leif, *et al. The Swedish Electorate 1887–1968* (Stockholm: Almqvist & Wiksell, 1972)

Lidman, Kent. "Vietnamdebatten i Sverige. En studie i riksdagsprotokoll, riksdagsdokument och övriga offentliga uttalanden" (University of Umeå, 1973)

Liljenroth, Bengt. "Vietnamrörelsen i Sverige" in Lars Torbiörnsson (ed.), *Tålamodets triumf. Tradition, befrielsekamp och samhällsutveckling i Vietnam* (Stockholm: Prisma, 1973) 231–248.

Lindholm, Stig. *U-landsbilden. En undersökning av den allmänna opinionen* (Stockholm: Almqvist & Wiksell, 1970)

Lindkvist, Kent. *Program och parti. Principprogram och partiideologi inom den kommunistiska rörelsen i Sverige 1917–1972* (Lund: Studentlitteratur, 1982)

Link, Ruth. "Ambassador Holland and the Swedes" *Crisis* 1971 78 (2): 43–48.

Lithner, Klaus. "De amerikanska desertörerna" *Svensk Tidskrift* 1968 (55): 86–90.

Logevall, Fredrik. "America Isolated. The Western Powers and the Escalation of the War" in Andreas Daum, Lloyd Gardner and Wilfred Mausbach (eds.), *America, Vietnam and the World: Comparative and international perspectives* (Cambridge: Cambridge University Press, 2003) 175–196.

Logevall, Fredrik. *Choosing War: The Last Chance for Peace and the Escalation of the Vietnam War* (Berkeley: University of California Press, 1999)

Logevall, Fredrik. "The Swedish–American Conflict over Vietnam" *Diplomatic History* 1993 17 (3): 421–445.

Lundberg, Bengt. *Jämlikhet? Socialdemokratin och jämlighetsbegreppet* (Lund: Dialog, 1979)

Lundberg, Harald. *Broderskap(s) rörelsen i svensk politik och kristenhet 1930–1980* (Stockholm: Broderskapets Förlag, 2004)

Lundberg, Svante. *Sextioåttor. Studie av en politisk generation* (Stockholm: Symposium AB, 1993)

Lödén, Hans. *För säkerhetens skull. Ideologi och säkerhet i svensk aktiv utrikespolitik 1950–1975* (Stockholm: Nerenius & Santérus, 1999)

Manning, Robert and Michael Janeway (eds.) *Who We Are: An Atlantic Chronicle of the U.S. and Vietnam* (Boston: Little Brown, 1969)

Margolin, Jean-Louis. "Vietnam and Laos: The Impasse of War Communism" in Stéphane Courtois, *et al* (eds.), *The Black Book of Communism* (Cambridge: Harvard University Press, 1999) 565–576.

Molin, Karl. "Historical Orientation" in Klaus Misgeld, *et al* (eds.), *Creating Social Democracy: A Century of the Social Democratic Labor Party in Sweden* (University Park, PA: The Pennsylvania State University Press, 1988) xvii–xxix.

Möller, Yngve. *Sverige och Vietnamkriget, ett unikt kapitel i svensk utrikespolitik* (Stockholm: Tiden, 1992)

Nilsson, Ann-Sofie. *Den moraliska stormakten. En studie av socialdemokratins internationella aktivism* (Stockholm: Timbro, 1991)

Nordenmark, Ove. *Aktiv utrikespolitik. Sverige – södra Afrika 1969–1987* (Stockholm: Almqvist & Wiksell, 1991)

Nordin, Rune. *Fackföreningsrörelsen i Sverige. I uppkomst och utveckling* (Stockholm: Prisma, 1981)

Nuti, Leopoldo. "The Center-Left Government in Italy and the Escalation of the Vietnam War" in Andreas Daum, Lloyd Gardner and Wilfred Mausbach (eds.), *America, Vietnam and the World: Comparative and international perspectives* (Cambridge: Cambridge University Press, 2003) 259–278.

Ohlsson, Per. *Svensk politik* (Lund: Historiska Media, 2014)

Olivencrona, Gustaf. *Hur väljarna vanns. Ett politiskt reportage* (Stockholm: Wahlström & Widstrand, 1968)

Olsson, Sven. "VPK 1968–1978. Mellan Socialdemokratin och vänstern" in Jan Engberg, *et al* (eds.), *Utanför systemet. Vänstern i Sverige 1968–1978* (Stockholm: Rabén & Sjögren, 1978) 181–219.

Oredsson, Sveker. *Svensk oro. Offentlig fruktan i Sverige under 1900-talets senare hälft* (Lund: Nordic Academic Press, 2003)

Ortmark, Åke. *Maktspelet i Sverige – ett samhällsreportage* (Stockholm: Wahlström & Widstrand, 1968)

Ortmark, Åke. *De okända makthavarna. De kungliga – Militärerna – Journalisterna* (Stockholm: Wahlström & Widstrand, 1969)

Ottosson, Sten. *Sverige mellan öst och väst. Svensk självbild under kalla kriget* (Stockholm: Utrikespolitiska Institutet, 2003)

Padget, Stephen and William Patterson. *A History of Social Democracy in Postwar Europe* (New York: Longman, 1991)

Page, Caroline. *U.S. Official Propaganda during the Vietnam War: The limits of persuasion* (London: Leicester University Press, 1996)

Palm, Thede. "Vietnamkriget i historien" *Svensk Tidskrift* 1981 (3): 173–178.

Parker, Alastair. "International Aspects of the Vietnam War" in Peter Lowe (ed.), *The Vietnam War* (New York: St. Martin Press, 1998) 196–218.

Peterson, Bo. "Den svenska neutraliten – reflektioner king politisk myt och nationell identitet" in Kurt Almqvist and Kristian Gerner (eds.), *Kalla Kriget. Sverige en stormakt utan vapen?* (Stockholm: Axel och Margaret Ax:son Johnsons stiftelse, 2012) 109–117.

Petersson, Carl-Gunnar. *Ungdom och politik. En studie av Sveriges socialdemokratiska ungdomsförbund* (Stockholm: Frihets Förlag, 1975)

Petersson, Lasse. "KFML(r): På jakt efter en proletär identitet" in Jan Engberg, *et al* (eds.), *Utanför systemet. Vänstern i Sverige 1968–1978* (Stockholm: Rabén & Sjögren, 1978) 83–120.

Petersson, Olof. *Väljarna och världspolitiken* (Stockholm: Norstedt, 1982)

Petersson, Olof and Bo Särlvik. *Valet 1973. Del 3* (Stockholm: SCB, 1974)

Pierre, Jan. *Partikongresser och regeringens politik. En studie av den socialdemokratiska partikongressens beslutsfattande och inflytande 1948–1978* (Lund: Kommunfakta Förlag, 1986)

Prasad, Devi. *They love it, but leave it. American Deserters* (London: War Resisters International, 1971)

Queckfeldt, Eva. *"Vietnam." Tre tidningars syn på vietnamfrågan 1963–1968* (Lund: Gleerup, 1981)

Quester, George. "Det anti-amerikanska Sverige" *Internationella Studier* 1976 (1): 32–34.

Rasmusson, Ludvig. *Fyrtiotalisterna* (Stockholm: Norstedt, 1985)

Rehnberg, Gun. "Efter Gävle och Sergels torg. En studie i svensk pressdebatt" in Lars Svedgård. *Palme. En Presentation* (Stockholm: Raben & Sjögren, 1970) 131–169.

Richard, Michael. "American Deserters in Stockholm" *Interplay* 1970 (12): 28–37.

Riste, Olav. *Norway's Foreign Relations – A history* (Oslo: Universitetsförlaget, 2001)

Roberts, Adam. "Det icke helt trovärdiga Sverige" *Internationella Studier* 1976 (1): 36–38.

Romin, Johan. *Desertören och Vietnamkriget* (Stockholm: Prisma, 2008)

Ruin, Olof. *I välfärdsstatens tjänst. Tage Erlander 1946–1969* (Stockholm: Tiden, 1986)

Ryen, Dag. "Misted Mirrors: The Vietnam Experience as Reflected in Major European Newspapers" (University of Kentucky, 1992)

Salomon, Kim. *Rebeller i takt med tiden. FNL-rörelsen och 60-talets politiska ritualer* (Stockholm: Rabén Prisma, 1996)

Sassoon, Donald. *One Hundred Years of Socialism: The West European Left in the 20th Century* (London: IB Touris Publishers, 1996)

Schiff, Martin. "The United States and Sweden: A troubled relationship" *American Scandinavian Review* 1973 61 (4): 359–372.

Schwartz, Thomas. *Lyndon Johnson and Europe. In the Shadow of Vietnam* (Cambridge: Harvard University Press, 2003)

Schwartz, Thomas. "Lyndon Johnson and Europe. Alliance Politics, Political Economy and Growing Out of the Cold War" in H.W. Brands (ed.), *The Foreign Policies of Lyndon Johnson. Beyond Vietnam* (College Station, TX: Texas A& M University Press, 1999) 37–60.

Schlesinger, Thomas O. *The United States and the European Neutrals* (Vienna: Braumüller, 1991)

Schurman, Franz. *The Foreign Policies of Richard Nixon. The Grand Design* (Berkeley: University of California Press, 1987)

Scott, Carl-Gustaf. "'Sweden might be a haven, but it's not heaven': American War Resisters in Sweden during the Vietnam War" *Immigrants & Minorities* 33 2015

Scott, Carl-Gustaf. "Swedish Vietnam Criticism Reconsidered: Social Democratic Vietnam policy a Manifestation of Swedish *Ostpolitik?*" *Cold War History* 2009 9 (2): 243–266.

Scott, Carl-Gustaf. "Olof Palme, the Swedish Far Left, and the Vietnam War" *Arbetarhistoria* 2005 115 (3): 49–54.

Sellström, Tor. *Sweden and National Liberation in Southern Africa Vol. II: Solidarity and Assistance* (Uppsala: Nordiska Afrikainstitutet, 2002)

Sjölin, Åke. "Vietnamdramat i Skandinavien" *Svensk Tidskrift* 1981 (10): 510–514.

Sjölin, Åke. "Torsten Nilsson om Vietnam" *Svensk Tidskrift* 1985 (1): 41–46.

Sjöström, Hans. "Han rör ju på sig" in Enn Kokk (ed.), *Var blev ni av, ljuva drömmar?* (Stockholm: Ordfront, 2002) 205–219.

Sparring, Åke. "The Communist Party of Sweden" in A. F. Upton (ed.), *The Communist Parties of Scandinavia and Finland* (London: Weidenfeld & Nicholson, 1973) 61–101.

Stahre, Sven-Arne. *Arbetarrörelsen. En uppslagsbok* (Stockholm: Forum, 1978)

Stene, Birgitta. "The Swedish Image of America" in Paul Houe and Sven Hakon Russel (eds.), *Images of America in Scandinavia* (Atlanta: Rodopi, 1998) 145–191.

Stenelo, Lars-Göran. *The International Critic* (Lund: Studentlitteratur, 1984)

Ström, Margareta. "Norska reaktioner på Sveriges erkännande av Nordvietnam" (University of Stockholm, 1969)

Sullivan, Marianna. *France's Vietnam Policy: A study in French–American Relations* (London: Greenwood Press, 1978)

Sundgren, Christofer. "Splittrad Solidaritet. Om förhållandet mellan De förenade FNL-grupperna och Svenska kommittén för Vietnam" in Maj-Lis Erikson, *et al* (eds.), *Med eller mot strömmen? En antologi om svenska folkrörelserna* (Stockholm: Sober, 1980) 135–161.

Svanfeldt, Erik. "Svenska kommittén för Vietnam. Regeringens megafon eller folklig kravmaskin?" (University of Uppsala, 1990)

Svedgård, Lars. *Palme. En Presentation* (Stockholm: Rabén & Sjögren, 1970)

Svensson, Sven. *I maktens labyrinter* (Stockholm: Bonnier, 1968)

Särlvik. Bo. *Riskdagsmannavalen 1965–1968. Del 2* (Stockholm: SCB, 1970)

Särlvik. Bo. *Allmäna valen 1970. Del 3* (Stockholm: SCB, 1973)

Thorsell, Staffan. *Sverige i Vita Huset* (Stockholm: Bonnier Fakta, 2004)

Trägårdh, Lars. "Pippi och Sveriges särart" www.axess.se/magasin/default.aspx? article=895#.U3xvoC-W_8B accessed 04/04/2014.

Tängerstad, Erik. "Att organisera ett engagemang. Om tillkomsten av den svenska FNL-rörelsen" (University of Stockholm, 1988)

Törnqvist, Kurt. *Svenskarna och omvärlden. En opinionsundersökning om svenska folkets attityder till några internationella problem* (Stockholm: Beredskapsnämnden för psykologiskt försvar, 1969)

Ulfner, Bengt. "Inställningen till Vietnamkriget i AB, DN och Svd" (University of Uppsala, 1969)

Vivekanandan, B. *International Concerns of European Social Democrats* (New York: St. Martins Press, 1997)

Wahlbäck, Krister. "Från medlare till kritiker" *Internationella Studier* 1973 (3): 93–96.

Waite, James. "Sweden and the Vietnam Criticism" *Southeast Asia* 1973 2 (4): 455–473.

Waite, James L. *Contemporary Swedish Foreign Policy: A Systemic Analysis*, (Dissertation. Southern Illinois University, 1971)

Wallensteen, Peter. "Aktiv utrikespolitik. Finns ett borgerligt alternativ" in Bertil Dunér (ed.), *Är svensk neutralitet möjlig? Nio bidrag till en svensk fredspolitik* (Stockholm: Liber, 1977) 88–103.

Westerståhl, Jörgen. "Vietnam i Sveriges Radio. En studie av opartiskhet och saklighet i nyhetsförmedlingen. Utförd på uppdrag av Radionämnden" (University of Göteborg, 1968)

Wernicke, Günter. "The World Peace Council and the Antiwar Movement in East Germany" in Andreas Daum, Lloyd Gardner and Wilfred Mausbach (eds.), *America, Vietnam and the World: Comparative and international perspectives* (Cambridge: Cambridge University Press, 2003) 299–320.

Wibbe, Sören. "Från pacifism till marxism-leninism" in Jan Engberg, *et al* (eds.), *Utanför systemet. Vänstern i Sverige 1968–1978* (Stockholm: Rabén & Sjögren, 1978) 11–45.

Young, Marilyn B. *The Vietnam Wars, 1945–1990* (New York: Harper Collins, 1991)

Zetterberg, Kent. "Det strategiska spelet" in Lars Wedin and Gunnar Åselius (eds.), *Mellan byråkrati och stridskonst. Svenska stategier för det kalla kriget* (Stockholm: Försvarshögskolan, 1999) 14–62.

Åkerman, Nordal. *Apparaten Sverige. Samtal med beslutsfattare i politik, ämbetsverk, företag* (Stockholm: Wahlström & Widstrand, 1970)

Östberg, Kjell. *När vinden vände. Olof Palme 1969–1986* (Stockholm: Leopard, 2009)

Östberg, Kjell. *1968. När allting var i rörelse* (Stockholm: Prisma, 2002)

Östberg, Kjell. "Inledning" in *Olof Palme i sin tid* (Stockholm: Södertörns Högskola, 2001) 7–29.

Östergren, Bertil. *Vem är Olof Palme. Ett politiskt porträtt* (Stockholm: Timbro, 1984)

Södertörn Academic Studies

1. Helmut Müssener & Frank-Michael Kirsch (eds.), *Nachbarn im Ostseeraum unter sich. Vorurteile, Klischees und Stereotypen in Texten*, 2000.

2. Jan Ekecrantz & Kerstin Olofsson (eds.), *Russian Reports: Studies in Post-Communist Transformation of Media and Journalism*, 2000.

3. Kekke Stadin (ed.), *Society, Towns and Masculinity: Aspects on Early Modern Society in the Baltic Area*, 2000.

4. Bernd Henningsen et al. (eds.), *Die Inszenierte Stadt. Zur Praxis und Theorie kultureller Konstruktionen*, 2001.

5. Michal Bron (ed.), *Jews and Christians in Dialogue*, ii: *Identity, Tolerance, Understanding*, 2001

6. Frank-Michael Kirsch et al. (eds.), *Nachbarn im Ostseeraum übwer einander. Wandel der Bilder, Vorurteile und Stereotypen?*, 2001.

7. Birgitta Almgren, *Illusion und Wirklichkeit. Individuelle und kollektive Denkmusterin nationalsozialistischer Kulturpolitik und Germanistik in Schweden 1928–1945*, 2001.

8. Denny Vågerö (ed.), *The Unknown Sorokin: His Life in Russia and the Essay on Suicide*, 2002.

9. Kerstin W. Shands (ed.), *Collusion and Resistance: Women Writing in English*, 2002.

10. Elfar Loftsson & Yonhyok Choe (eds.), *Political Representation and Participation in Transitional Democracies: Estonia, Latvia and Lithuania*, 2003.

11. Birgitta Almgren (eds.), *Bilder des Nordens in der Germanistik 1929–1945: Wissenschaftliche Integrität oder politische Anpassung?*, 2002.

12. Christine Frisch, *Von Powerfrauen und Superweibern: Frauenpopulär-literatur der 90er Jahre in Deutschland und Schweden*, 2003.

13. Hans Ruin & Nicholas Smith (eds.), *Hermeneutik och tradition. Gadamer och den grekiska filosofin*, 2003.

14. Mikael Lönnborg et al. (eds.), *Money and Finance in Transition: Research in Contemporary and Historical Finance*, 2003.

15. Kerstin Shands et al. (eds.), *Notions of America: Swedish Perspectives*, 2004.

16. Karl-Olov Arnstberg & Thomas Borén (eds.), *Everyday Economy in Russia, Poland and Latvia*, 2003.

17. Johan Rönnby (ed.), *By the Water. Archeological Perspectives on Human Strategies around the Baltic Sea*, 2003.

18. Baiba Metuzale-Kangere (ed.), *The Ethnic Dimension in Politics and Culture in the Baltic Countries 1920–1945*, 2004.

19. Ulla Birgegård & Irina Sandomirskaja (eds.), *In Search of an Order: Mutual Representations in Sweden and Russia during the Early Age of Reason*, 2004.

20. Ebba Witt-Brattström (ed.), *The New Woman and the Aesthetic Opening:Unlocking Gender in Twentieth-Century Texts*, 2004.

21. Michael Karlsson, *Transnational Relations in the Baltic Sea Region*, 2004.

22. Ali Hajighasemi, *The Transformation of the Swedish Welfare System: Fact or Fiction? Globalisation, Institutions and Welfare State Change in a Social Democratic Regime*, 2004.

23. Erik A. Borg (ed.), *Globalization, Nations and Markets: Challenging Issues in Current Research on Globalization*, 2005.

24. Stina Bengtsson & Lars Lundgren, *The Don Quixote of Youth Culture: Media Use and Cultural Preferences Among Students in Estonia and Sweden*, 2005.

25. Hans Ruin, *Kommentar till Heideggers Varat och tiden*, 2005.

26. Ludmila Ferm, *Variativnoe bespredložnoe glagol'noe upravlenie v russkom jazyke XVIII veka* [Variation in non-prepositional verbal government in eighteenth-century Russian], 2005.

27. Christine Frisch, *Modernes Aschenputtel und Anti-James-Bond: Gender-Konzepte in deutschsprachigen Rezeptionstexten zu Liza Marklund und Henning Mankell*, 2005.

28. Ursula Naeve-Bucher, *Die Neue Frau tanzt: Die Rolle der tanzenden Frau in deutschen und schwedischen literarischen Texten aus der ersten Hälfte des 20. Jahrhunderts*, 2005.

29. Göran Bolin et al. (eds.), *The Challenge of the Baltic Sea Region: Culture, Ecosystems, Democracy*, 2005.

30. Marcia Sá Cavalcante Schuback & Hans Ruin (eds.), *The Past's Presence: Essays on the Historicity of Philosophical Thought*, 2006.

31. María Borgström & Katrin Goldstein-Kyaga (ed.), *Gränsöverskridande identiteter i globaliseringens tid: Ungdomar, migration och kampen för fred*, 2006.

32. Janusz Korek (ed.), *From Sovietology to Postcoloniality: Poland and Ukraine from a Postcolonial Perspective*, 2007.

33. Jonna Bornemark (ed.), *Det främmande i det egna: filosofiska essäer om bildning och person*, 2007.

34. Sofia Johansson, *Reading Tabloids: Tabloid Newspapers and Their Readers*, 2007.

35. Patrik Åker, *Symboliska platser i kunskapssamhället: Internet, högre lärosäten och den gynnade geografin*, 2008.

36. Kerstin W. Shands (ed.), *Neither East Nor West: Postcolonial Essays on Literature, Culture and Religion*, 2008.

37. Rebecka Lettevall & My Klockar Linder (eds.), *The Idea of Kosmopolis: History, philosophy and politics of world citizenship*, 2008.

38. Karl Gratzer & Dieter Stiefel (eds.), *History of Insolvency and Bankruptcy from an International Perspective*, 2008.

39. Katrin Goldstein-Kyaga & María Borgström, *Den tredje identiteten: Ungdomar och deras familjer i det mångkulturella, globala rummet*, 2009.

40. Christine Farhan, *Frühling für Mütter in der Literatur?: Mutterschafts-konzepte in deutschsprachiger und schwedischer Gegenwartsliteratur*, 2009.

41. Marcia Sá Cavalcante Schuback (ed.), *Att tänka smärtan*, 2009.

42. Heiko Droste (ed.), *Connecting the Baltic Area: The Swedish Postal System in the Seventeenth Century*, 2011.

43. Aleksandr Nemtsov, *A Contemporary History of Alcohol in Russia*, 2011.

44. Cecilia von Feilitzen & Peter Petrov (eds.), *Use and Views of Media in Russia and Sweden: A Comparative Study of Media in St. Petersburg and Stockholm*, 2011.

45. Sven Lilja (ed.), *Fiske, jordbruk och klimat i Östersjöregionen under förmodern tid*, 2012.

46. Leif Dahlberg & Hans Ruin (eds.), *Fenomenologi, teknik och medialitet*, 2012.

47. Samuel Edquist, *I Ruriks fotspår: Om forntida svenska österledsfärder i modern historieskrivning*, 2012.

48. Jonna Bornemark (ed.), *Phenomenology of Eros*, 2012.

49. Jonna Bornemark & Hans Ruin (eds.), *Ambiguity of the Sacred: Pheno-menology, Politics, Aesthetics*, 2012.

50. Håkan Nilsson, *Placing Art in the Public Realm*, 2012.

51. Per Bolin, *Between National and Academic Agendas: Ethnic Policies and 'National Disciplines' at Latvia's University, 1919–1940*, 2012.

52. Lars Kleberg & Aleksei Semenenko (eds.), *Aksenov and the Environs/Aksenov iokrestnosti*, 2012.

53. Sven-Olov Wallenstein & Brian Manning Delaney (eds.), *Translating Hegel: The Phenomenology of Spirit and Modern Philosophy*, 2012.

54. Sven-Olov Wallenstein and Jakob Nilsson (eds.), *Foucault, Biopolitics, and Governmentality*, 2013.

55. Jan Patočka, *Inledning till fenomenologisk filosofi*, 2013.

56. Jonathan Adams & Johan Rönnby (eds.), *Interpreting Shipwrecks: Maritime Archaeological Approaches*, 2013.

57. Charlotte Bydler, *Mondiality/Regionality: Perspectives on Art, Aesthetics and Globalization*, 2014.

58. Andrej Kotljarchuk, *In the Forge of Stalin: Swedish Colonists of Ukraine in Totalitarian Experiments of the Twentieth Century*, 2014.

59. Samuel Edquist & Janne Holmén, *Islands of Identity: History-writing and identity formation in five island regions in the Baltic Sea*, 2014.

60. Norbert Götz (ed.), *The Sea of Identities: A Century of Baltic and East European Experiences with Nationality, Class, and Gender*, 2015.

61. Klaus Misgeld, Karl Molin & Pawel Jaworski, *Solidaritet och diplomati: Svenskt fackligt och diplomatiskt stöd till Polens demokratisering under 1980-talet*, 2015.

62. Jonna Bornemark & Sven-Olov Wallenstein (eds.), *Madness, Religion, and the Limits of Reason*, 2015.

63. Mirja Arnshav & Anna McWilliams, *Stalins ubåtar: En arkeologisk undersökning av vraken efter S7 och SC-305*, 2015.

64. Carl-Gustaf Scott, *Swedish Social Democracy and the Vietnam War*, 2017.

www.ingramcontent.com/pod-product-compliance
Lightning Source LLC
Chambersburg PA
CBHW031424270326
41930CB00007B/566